Aphra Behn was England's first professional woman writer, but her status as a major author has only recently become clear. Between the seventeenth and nineteenth centuries Behn was denigrated for her 'unwomanly' subject matter and intellectual immodesty. In the twentieth century she has been increasingly viewed as an important dramatist and poet of the Restoration and a founder of the English novel.

This book sets Behn firmly in an historical context of political factions, theatre developments and colonial encounters. Her work is remarkably diverse. There are chapters on each of the genres in which she wrote: drama, fiction, poetry and translation, and on other aspects of her life, from her publishing struggles to her involvement in American slavery.

The authors adopt different approaches to Behn's work and biography. Most provide an historical appreciation of Behn as a writer in a specific moment of English culture; others examine her in the light of current interests in gender, race and class, and in the manipulation of linguistic signs and codes.

Nowadays Aphra Behn is widely read. This book is an important resource for those studying seventeenth-century English literature and drama, and for those interested in the development of women's writing.

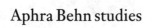

Aphra Behn studies

Aphra Behn studies

EDITED BY JANET TODD

Professor of English Literature, University of East Anglia

CAMBRIDGE
UNIVERSITY PRESS

1996

Published by the Press Syndicate of the University of Cambridge
The Pitt Building, Trumpington Street, Cambridge CB2 1RP
40 West 20th Street, New York, NY 10011–4211, USA
10 Stamford Road, Melbourne 3166, Australia

First published 1996

Printed in Great Britain at the University Press, Cambridge

A catalogue record for this book is available from the British Library

Library of Congress cataloguing in publication data

Aphra Behn studies / edited by Janet Todd.
     p.   cm.
  ISBN 0 521 47169 9 (hardback)
    1. Behn, Aphra, 1640–1689 – Criticism and interpretation.   2. Women
and literature – England – History – 17th century.   I. Todd, Janet M.,
1942– .
PR3317.Z5A64   1996
822'.4 – dc20   95–18356   CIP

ISBN 0 521 47169 9 hardback

SE

Contents

Introduction

JANET TODD

Aphra Behn has been constructed and quickly reconstructed, read and reread in a far shorter space of time than any other major writer – for Behn *is* a major writer, although her status has only recently become clear. That clarity has partly been due to the cultural movements of the present, just as the eclipse of her reputation depended on cultural shifts. Race has become the most topical issue in literary studies and it has necessarily brought into focus one of the few texts that deals, if trickily, with the subject of race: *Oroonoko or the Royal Slave*.

But if Behn was not much acknowledged before present preoccupations, she was none the less a considerable writer in her time. In the 1670s and 1680s she was second only to Dryden in dramatic output and she was courted as a political poet of some stature. In addition she had claim to writing the earliest, or one of the earliest, novels: *Love-Letters between a Nobleman and his Sister*. Her works are topical and political, as fitted with the times in which she wrote, but they also allow the present age to apply to them criticism of great subtlety and complexity, for they are open to ironies and ambiguities now demanded of canonized literature.

Her extraordinary breadth and diversity could hardly be disputed. And yet between the Restoration and the twentieth century Aphra Behn was almost invariably denigrated: the concept of gendered literature held sway, and, with her conventional immodesty, she fell foul of the new taste. Where she had hobnobbed with Dryden, Rochester and Otway and been patronized by James II and the Duke of Norfolk, she was now vilified as unwomanly by Richardson, Fielding and Pope. The combination in her work of much condemned Restoration excess and femaleness ensured that she became a bye-word for lewdness and dissipation.

As Behn lacked sexual modesty she also sinned against the standard of feminine intellectual modesty. A woman writer of the eighteenth century did not go before the public without proper apology and submission. Behn, with her ringing declaration that she was not writing only for a third night and that she wanted fame, just like the men, was hardly a suitable mother for an increasingly respectable tradition of women's writing. Later when Restoration naughtiness could no longer shock the sophisticated reader, another style of thinking was in fashion, demanding that literature transcend its moment and not grub in the dirt of state and gender politics. Curiously enough her male colleagues escaped censure on this score, and Rochester and Dryden were valued anew with no mention of the political setting of Dryden's *Essay of Dramatic Poesy*, for example, or the fact that he was a man.

The seeds of censure on account of her sex had of course been sewn in her time. It seemed not to matter when choosing and staging a play what sex the author displayed. But she herself was very much aware of it and made something of it when, like most other playwrights, she sold herself in prefaces and prologues as an interesting new or, later, an interesting experienced *woman* writer. But she had less control over how others commented on her sex. The Earl of Rochester, so much admired by Behn, could still write, 'That whore is scarce a more reproachful name / Then poetesse', and the satirist Robert Gould, thinking particularly of Behn, could declare that '*Punk* and *Poetesse* agree so pat. / You cannot well be *This* and not be *That*.' Wycherley could compare her getting of plays to the begetting of bastards, while after her death Pope in his *Epistle to Augustus* imagined, 'The stage how loosely does Astrea tread, / Who fairly puts all characters to bed!' Surely worse could have been said of Wycherley but he was always 'manly' Wycherley. Samuel Johnson, too, chose to attack Behn's style of eulogy in her dedication to Nell Gwyn, implying that it was worse even than that of the similarly eulogistic but by now canonized John Dryden.

These overtly sexist comments were all in many ways comic enough and she herself had a nasty line in abuse of her fellow poets and critics, as *To Poet Bavius*, the still disputed 'On Mr Dryden, Renegate', and the preface to *The Dutch Lover* testify. But the mixture of denunciation and defamation that began with Richard Steele in the eighteenth century and was fanned by the poems and prose printed by Tom Brown in *The Muses Mercury* in 1707 and *Familiar Letters* in 1718, accompanied by dark hints that the verses had been 'reduc'd to bring them within the Rules of Decency', was more devastating. Not all female opinion followed this critical line: if the *Tatler* disapproved, the contemporary *Female Tatler*, written by the fictional Mrs Crackenthorpe (possibly in some part a creation of Delarivier Manley), did not and it classed Aphra Behn with the much admired and respectable Katherine Philips, 'the Matchless Orinda' and the translator and learned lady, Anne Dacier. But the overall cultural tendency to sully her reputation was clear.

Following the growing apprehension of woman as all feeling and authenticity, subject matter could not easily be separated from female experience, and the widow Behn, about whose sex life we know almost nothing for sure, was condemned as hopelessly sexy. The emphasis on the gendered pen made certain kinds of expression not only improper but almost impossible for a woman – the woman who *had* so expressed herself had forfeited her claim to membership of the 'Fair Sex' while she could not associate herself with the other. By the nineteenth century the attacks had intensified and there was no voice of man or woman that could easily be used to defend a woman who was now seen, not as a combination of manly strength and feminine grace as her contemporary eulogists described her, but as unfeminine and monstrous. The result was that apology prefaced the few presentations of her work. Only *Oroonoko*, rewritten, emptied of political comment and filled with humanitarian sentiment and sentimentality, existed in a special space – as some might argue it does today.

Why has the interest been so late? Partly no doubt because of Behn's resistances and later aesthetic practices. Feminist criticism took time to embrace the concept of multiple voices, of playful positions and subversive rhetoric. Now it perhaps faces a danger in finding Behn too much to its taste. For Aphra Behn responds to the concept of the subject dispersed and plays with a masculinizing desire so well that she may seem to become too pliant to our theories. She may display too adroitly the fragmentary ideological conditions of her production and be too neat an exponent of the discursive crisis of construction of state, sex and nature. It is to this danger that several of the essays in this volume respond by foregrounding the very specific and raw historical texture of her writings and by refusing patterns that appear too orderly and too indulgent to contemporary taste and desire. The late seventeenth century was as complex as any other time and more so than we from the present can ever imagine.

The essays in the volume have been positioned according to the genre or subject they mainly concern, with the biographical ones coming at the end. There are many other divisions that could have been followed, one based on primary method of criticism for example, and, arguably, the 'life' essays could form part of the fiction section since Behn's life may be her biggest fiction. There is an apprehension that biographical studies of Behn have predominated until now. In fact the interest has again been primarily in *Oroonoko* and its putative relationship with its author's life. Archival historical studies of the kind Jane Jones and Mary Ann O'Donnell follow are in fact rather rare within Behn studies.

Aphra Behn is suitably commemorated in a collection or miscellany of essays. She herself was collaborative, especially in her plays and poetry, and a large portion of her output was arrangement and modification of other people's work. Her poems often give the appearance of being written within literary competitions or dashed off in the midst of conversation and dispute. According to the theatre critic Gerard Langbaine and some other of her contemporaries, her plays were plagiarized, but a kinder age sees them as adaptations and rewritings, and many were no doubt further modified by actors and managers in rehearsals. Behn is never a lone writer and even *Oroonoko* was, so it was alleged, written in a room full of talking people after many rehearsals as oral narrative.

Although modern Behn criticism has no long life, it has been long enough for various myths to grow up with the help of those who decontextualize one or two texts such as *Oroonoko* and *The Rover*. One of these myths according to Susan J. Owen in 'Sexual politics and party politics in Behn's drama, 1678–83' is that Behn was a Tory because she was a feminist and that Toryism offered a liberating space to women which was closed with the departure of the last Stuart king, James II. Owen shows the specific party political nature of Behn's plays during the Exclusion Crisis and the Popish Plot and reveals how they change in their feminist components according to political needs as Behn's tone and slant respond to precise political pressure. *The Revenge* and *The Feign'd Curtizans*, staged early in the Crisis, have a large component of royalist satire of Whigs and their manic fear of popery; in them the satire coexists with Behn's brand of feminism which tends to destabilize male assumptions and stereotypes of women. In *The Young King*, however, where Behn is more engaged in the political subject of Exclusion, she appears to imply a rare criticism of the royal brothers, Charles and James, and of their stunted education in exile. Here feminism must give way to political aim, and sexuality and gender stereotypes be used to convey a clear and single message: that exclusion is inappropriate. Similar contrasts occur in *The Second Part of The Rover* placed beside *The Roundheads*, and *The City-Heiress*. All three plays appear to oppose exciting royalist rakes to hypocritical Puritans; none the less the first, probably staged at a moment of Whig ascendance, allows a feminist questioning of the cavalier and courtly libertine ethos where the other two, more useful as strict Tory drama, either associate royalism firmly with virtue, as in *The Roundheads*, or with sympathetically depicted sexual freedom, as in *The City-Heiress*.

In the same mode as Owen, Alison Shell in 'Popish Plots: *The Feign'd Curtizans* in context' discusses religion, noting Behn's pro-Catholic stance in these years of turmoil and the difficulty of defining 'Catholic' in the seventeenth century since it covers so wide a range of options: from formal Roman Catholicism to crypto-Catholicism. The plots of Behn's plays and novels problematize representation and misrepresentation and they may comment on the nature of the state plot, the Popish Plot. Theatrical plots and state plots come together in the 'plotting Age' as Catholic women stage plots in *The Feign'd Curtizans* where Behn appears to champion Roman Catholicism which, unlike in many other loyalist plays of the time, she does not correct with Anglicanism. The Catholic women's plotting is analogous to the Popish Plot in which, in Behn's view, Catholics are as innocent as her heroines. The play trivializes the great state Plot by this analogy and at the same time highlights the horror of the deaths it caused. The implication for Behn may be that she had Catholic leanings or that, as a freethinker, she flirted with Catholicism as something outlawed and scandalous.

Following on from Shell's discussion, Ros Ballaster's 'Fiction feigning femininity: false counts and pageant kings in Aphra Behn's Popish Plot writings' takes 'The Court of the King of Bantam' and *The False Count* as examples of Behn's later response to the Popish Plot and its sham conspiracies. In both these works there are plots, and in both the central male character aspires to greatness and is fooled by other men while he involves himself with women. Ballaster describes the widespread association of plot with female sexuality, a connection made again in the case of the Meal Tub Plot involving the Roman Catholic midwife, Elizabeth Cellier, depicted as a Catholic seducer. Where Behn's dramatic plots remain comic, however, the Popish Plot, pushed too far – as her plots are not – is certainly tragedy.

If some criticism of Behn has suffered from lack of specific historical reference, even more so has her drama suffered from wholesale ignorance of the theatre for which she wrote. In her essay 'More for seeing than hearing: Behn and the use of theatre', Dawn Lewcock argues for the professionalism of Behn as a playwright who well understood the potential of the scenic stage, introduced into the public theatre at the Restoration. She was always a visual playwright, Lewcock asserts, but she does not in her earliest plays have her later consummate comprehension of all the possibilities of the scenic stage. More than any other dramatist of the time, Behn appreciates the visual effects of performance and uses them to affect the perceptions of the audience and, when necessary, change their understanding of her themes and plots. An important new Restoration device was the discovery or disclosure scene which Behn used in play after play, whether comedy or tragedy, to emphasize her overriding themes of political and sexual deception and dissimulation. The device allows her to make the audience misunderstand in anticipation of a later enlightenment. Like Owen, Shell and Ballaster, Lewcock stresses the analogy between the Popish Plot, in which Behn along with many at court did not believe, and the multiple plots of *The Feign'd Curtizans* including its ridiculous fake plots.

Jane Spencer in '*The Rover* and the eighteenth century' follows the fate of Behn's most successful play through succeeding decades. Through the history of its adaptations and reception she reveals how Behn's work continued to entertain audiences at a time when the author's actual reputation had tumbled from what it had been in the Restoration and for some years after her death. The early eighteenth-century changes to *The Rover* reveal a worry over bawdy elements, especially in the treatment of the sexual threat of Blunt and in the bold speeches of the heroine Hellena. In later revisions Willmore becomes less of the mocked libertine and more of the heroic and reformed rake.

Paul Salzman's 'Aphra Behn: poetry and masquerade' opens the section mainly concerning Behn's poetry. He takes her foray into intelligence in the 1660s as a starting point for a study of her staging of her poetry, which he considers exists in a context of male work and misogynist forms. Using current theory on femininity and masquerade, he finds Behn unsettling the conventions of the Restoration lyric by writing counter poems designed wittily to overturn the misogynist attitudes of her fellow poets. Her unsettling culminates in her poems of female passion and unfixed sexual categories in which she negotiates an economy of desire by offering the image of woman as commodity back to the male negotiator. By excessive production of gendered positions, especially in such a poem as 'To the Fair Clarinda', she counteracts some of the force of the masculine economy.

In his essay Salzman notes the lack of discussion of Behn's political poetry. Virginia Crompton makes this body of work her main concern in her essay, '"For when the act is done and finish't cleane, / what should the poet doe, but shift the scene?": propaganda, professionalism and Aphra Behn'. In it she surveys Behn's use of political propaganda and then concentrates on two late poems which explore the nature of this genre: those to the most famous and opposing propagandists, Sir Roger L'Estrange and Gilbert Burnet. With L'Estrange Behn shared a theoretical and political perspective and his propaganda became true, where Burnet's remained pleasing and corrupting. But Burnet's propaganda recreates power, and in the poem to him Behn inevitably considers her own future as a professional writer and propagandist and holds open the possibility and perhaps necessity of compromise.

In 'Aphra Behn: the politics of translation', Elizabeth Spearing discusses the translations, a body of work that has, except for 'The Disappointment', been as little studied as the political poetry. Spearing begins by looking at the translations in the context of the translation controversies of the seventeenth century, and then goes on to argue that Behn politicizes and eroticizes her sources, adding both satire and sensuality to her French translations. Concentrating on *The Voyage to the Island of Love* and *Lycidus*, she shows how frequently Behn makes the sexual into the political and how often she combines national politics and religion with the personal and the sexual. For example, advice to the presumptuous lover, found in her source, becomes also advice to the presumptuous politician, probably the Duke of Monmouth, so strong a presence in her propagandist writings. Beyond expressing her political position, Behn in her translations manages to convey to the reader her identity as a woman: she panders to the notion of the female writer in being consciously indecorous and, when writing as a man, gives the effect of being an actress in a breeches role.

In different mode from the essays on the drama, those on the fiction and poetry often tend less towards providing precise historical and political contexts than to revealing the subtleties of representation, along with the excitement of modern criticism. Since Behn's poetry and prose have become of such interest in recent years, critics can have the confidence to concern themselves solely with one or two of her works. In this tradition, Jessica Munns in '" But to the touch were soft": sex, property and the politics of the penis' sees Behn's two poems 'The Disappointment' and 'The Golden Age' as significant contributions to the Restoration discourse of masculinity. The concern over impotence, so famously presented in 'The Disappointment', was a manifestation of a general crisis over the representation of masculinity, as well as anxiety over the phallic order. One of many poems of 'imperfect enjoyment', 'The Disappointment' shifts the emphasis from the man, his penis, his fear of displaying sexual inadequacy, his sense of heterosexual desire and sexual intercourse itself as emasculating, to the failure of response and of any exchange of pleasure for pleasure. 'The Golden Age' offers a visionary solution to the nightmare, in which the soft penis does not represent anxiety and fear of failure but becomes an object of beauty: a female paradise is created as an alternative to the capitalist and phallic world of 'The Disappointment'.

My own essay, 'Who is Silvia? What is she? Feminine identity in Aphra Behn's *Love-Letters between a Nobleman and his Sister*', concerns Behn's single long novel and treats the creation of the identity of the heroine Silvia, based loosely on the historical figure of Lady Henrietta Berkeley. This creation is an achievement both of the novel and of the character herself. I argue that the instability of genre of a work that slides between epistolary and third-person narrative parallels the instability of personality; both the text and the various images of Silvia can always be interrogated. Through the three parts of the novel the heroine moves from being the virgin daughter through transgressing royalist to becoming an image of the capitalist entrepreneur who can even market herself; it is an image much denigrated by Behn when it is combined with Whiggism, but more ambiguous when associated with Tory marketing and acquisitiveness. Silvia is educated into the masquerade of femininity and finds her main identity in the theatre in which women act for money. Identity is destabilized in a moving world in which letters become metonyms for circulating selves. The greatest instability is enacted in relation to the text and the reader who comes, against the expressed ethics of the narrator, to appreciate flexible selves and gain sympathy for energy.

The issue of race so much on the agenda of modern criticism concerns the next three critics, Jacqueline Pearson, writing primarily on Behn's drama but also inevitably touching on her most famous work *Oroonoko*, and Catherine Gallagher and Joanna Lipking, both of whom treat only *Oroonoko*. In 'Slave princes and lady monsters: gender and ethnic difference in the work of Aphra Behn', Pearson investigates Behn's use of race and racial imagery, arguing that, although she sometimes seems close to using 'black' and 'white' as conventional racial opposites, she mostly destabilizes the terms. This is certainly so in *Oroonoko* where the prevailing effect is not of binary opposites of any sort but of multiple differences. Even in *Abdelazer*, apparently a vehicle for the display of Moorish wickedness, Behn manages to avoid complete polarization by eschewing the use of the term 'white' eulogistically, as happens in her source play, *Lusts Dominion*. In the short story, 'The Unfortunate Bride:

or, The Blind Lady a Beauty' the horror of the black Moorea is subtly undercut by the similarity of this character to the author herself, since both in different ways are trying to control male texts.

Catherine Gallagher's essay, '*Oroonoko*'s blackness', provides a richly speculative reading of *Oroonoko*, the starting point of which is the detail of Oroonoko's extreme blackness. This Gallagher connects with a print culture and the notion of the transcendental text celebrated by Behn as she moved from staging plays to publishing fiction and, singularly in *Oroonoko*, inserts herself as author into her own work. Gallagher then finds the blackness both of print and of the African Oroonoko as metonyms for commodification: the printed text and the black man are both heroic and both can be exchanged and sold. The commodification ratifies kingship, so salient a part of Oroonoko's depiction, since in absolutist thinking the king alone allows exchange because all property – as well as all proprietors – is held by royal gift.

A very different and equally illuminating approach to *Oroonoko* is taken by Joanna Lipking in her historical study, 'Confusing matters: searching the backgrounds of *Oroonoko*'. She argues persuasively that *Oroonoko* resists penetrating readings and notes that there seems no clear guides for the construction of a tale which appears sometimes arbitrary and formula-ridden. Instead of providing a totalizing reading, she tries to illuminate the text by contemporary writings, the 'commonplaces' of which are no doubt closer to Behn's than our own can possibly be. So she places *Oroonoko* by the heroic romances of La Calprenède, the accounts of slavery in the works of French and English travellers and traders to the West Indies, descriptions of the old customs of the Fantis in the Gold Coast, and also records of how slaves were viewed and managed in the colonies. Thereby she sees a richer tale than was seen before, a curious narrative that confronts slavery in a variety of complex and perplexing ways.

The final section consists of biographical and bibliographical essays by Mary O'Donnell and Jane Jones, each dependent on archival work and each revealing the shakiness of the basis of so much criticism that assumes an identity of the author, Aphra Behn. In 'Private jottings, public utterances: Aphra Behn's published writings and her commonplace book', Mary Ann O'Donnell has taken up the questions of biography through an analysis of a manuscript miscellany of satirical poetry entitled 'Astrea's Booke for Songs and Satyr's' and including poems which O'Donnell believes to have been copied out in Behn's own hand, supposedly between the years 1685 and 1689. For the committed Tory royalist we assume Behn to be, they are a surprising collection of satirical and scurrilous works often attacking the very men and women Behn was supposed to revere such as L'Estrange and Dryden. The manuscript also includes 'On the Ladies of Honor', a vicious attack on court women such as Nell Gwyn and Hortense Mancini, Duchess of Mazarine, to both of whom Behn dedicated works. The main coincidence between Behn's presumed political views and the poems occurs in the marginal comments on a poem elsewhere entitled 'A Heroic Scene'; these fit with her public position in their support of L'Estrange against the charges of treachery made against him, while suggesting a knowledge of his secret Catholicism.

The final, reprinted, article by Jane Jones discusses Behn's birth and background. Building on the pioneering work by Maureen Duffy on the parentage of Aphra Behn, Jones finds further evidence for Bartholomew Johnson as her father when she discovers that this man was not an inn keeper as had been supposed but a barber who had once lived in the village of Wye. This identification fits happily with the assertion both of Thomas Culpepper that her mother was his wet-nurse and of Anne Finch, Countess of Winchilsea, who wrote of Behn in the margin of a poem, 'Though the account of her life before her works pretends otherwise', she was in fact 'Daughter to a Barber, who liv'd formerly at Wye a little market town (now much decay'd) in Kent.' Jones also throws some light on the elusive Mr Behn and his possible connection with shipping.

Apart from generic resemblances, some of the essays in this volume echo and illuminate each other and some are clearly in dispute. The new historical discussion of Behn's plays and fiction by Jacqueline Pearson, regarding Behn in the light of late twentieth-century interests in race, could be placed with Susan J. Owen's historical essay which sets Behn's plays firmly in the political history of the Popish Plot and the Exclusion Crisis. Where Pearson sees the changes from the source play *The Dutch Courtesan* to Behn's *The Revenge* as allowing ethnic difference rather than opposition –

the absurd Dutch courtesan is made English and sympathetic – Owen sees it as a manoeuvre to allow the full force of hostility to fall on the Whig citizens, those responsible in Behn's view for the Exclusion Crisis. It is they who become the Other of the play. In a different but equally interesting way, Lewcock's close analysis of Restoration staging connects with Jane Spencer's equally close investigation of the later stage history of a single play, *The Rover*, while Catherine Gallagher's new historical reading of Behn's *Oroonoko* in terms of blackness, monarchical function and print culture, complements the more historical reading of Joanna Lipking who situates the text in the discussions of Africa and slavery in the late seventeenth century. Despite the scurrilous poems in 'Astrea's Booke', O'Donnell constructs Behn as a sincere supporter of the Stuarts whose 'dedication to the Stuart kings and the Tory cause has never been questioned', where Virginia Crompton notes the opportunism in Behn's final poems and concludes that at her death her politics were moving with the times.

Behn needs all methods, opinions and speculations. The revelation in her work of modern interests initially attracts a reader to her multifaceted oeuvre, while the historical placings make the reading informed. But in the end anything said about Behn's work and life has to be a little tentative. No critical method can fix so slippery an author.

PART I • PLAYS

1 Sexual politics and party politics in Behn's drama, 1678–83

SUSAN J. OWEN

Behn was the first woman professional dramatist in England. She was also a Tory. I want to clarify the relationship between Toryism and feminism in Behn's work by focusing on her plays of the Exclusion Crisis, 1678–83: this was the time when party politics began in England and when Behn became a Tory. An exploration of the relationship between party politics and sexual politics in these plays will help us to understand Behn's ideas. Taking these ideas out of context has led to much confusion. I want to delineate the context in which Behn was writing very precisely, and to suggest that some of the apparent complexities and contradictions in her thought might be accounted for by reference to the precise historical moments in which the particular plays are located. This will also have wider implications for understanding the relationship between drama-tists and their society, and the way in which drama engages with politics in moments of struggle and crisis.

I also hope to shed some light on the wider relationship between pol-itics and sexual politics in the Restoration. In particular, I want to examine the relationship between Toryism and feminism, and to dispel rosy-tinted views of a symbiosis between the two. The idea that late Stuart ideology created a liberating space for women is as false as the school child's notion of the jolly cavalier, but it persists in part because studies of Behn's sexual politics have placed her in relation to other women writers rather than thoroughly examining her relationship to her own society. Moreover, we do Behn as a woman dramatist a great disservice by not considering her as a Tory dramatist whose political commitment was equal to that of Dryden and others.

Feminist scholars have demonstrated that the sexual is political. In

15

the Restoration, the political is often expressed through the sexual. The political battle was often conducted in the language of sexual politics.[1] For example, both sides used rape as a trope of monstrosity, associated by Tories with rebellion, and by Whigs with tyranny and popery.[2] The monstrous woman was used by the Whig Settle to demonize popery and arbitrary power in *The Female Prelate* and by the ultra-royalist Whitaker to demonize rebellion and usurpation in *The Conspiracy*. The use of sexual themes in political discourse means that questions of sexual politics acquire an extra political resonance in addition to that which they might have in their own right. In order to explore the complexities of the sexual politics of Behn's drama, I want first to examine three plays which appear to belong to the early part of the Crisis, 1678/80: *The Feign'd Curtizans*, *The Revenge*[3] and *The Young King*. Then I shall examine the dichotomy in outlook between two 1681 plays, *The Second Part of the Rover* and *The Roundheads*, before concluding with a discussion of the Tory Reaction piece, *The City-Heiress* (1682).[4]

The Feign'd Curtizans and *The Revenge* have witty heroines like those in earlier plays such as *The Rover*. There is a powerful resonance, particularly in *The Feign'd Curtizans*, in the spectacle of these women evading an oppressive destiny of arranged marriage and enforced celibacy, plotting to take control of their lives, civilizing rakes and winning marriage choice and freedom of sexual manoeuvre. When necessary these heroines dress as men and fight alongside men. The feminist force of this[5] was increased by the fact that actresses now played the parts. In both plays Behn criticizes sexual double standards. She also extends qualified sympathy to prostitutes, victimized by double standards. This is particularly true of *The Revenge*. Behn's source is Marston's *The Dutch Courtesan*; but Marston's whore, Franceschina, is a laughing-stock, set apart by a ridiculous way of speaking, and gleefully humiliated. In Behn's play the prostitute Corina is made a native rather than a foreigner, and the ending is altered to permit her to repent and find a husband.

This enables the full force of hostility to be directed to the citizen, Dashit. The citizens of London provided the social base of the Whig Opposition, and Behn gives topical force to the humiliation of Dashit at the hands of a dispossessed young aristocrat, Trickwell. Dashit is made

credulously and ridiculously anti-popish, which accords with the Tory
view that the Popish Plot scare was a fabrication.[6] Dashit demonstrates
the 'busy' nosiness and credulity for which London's citizens are often
criticized in Tory prologues and epilogues. He laps up a tale told by
Trickwell, disguised as a barber, of monstrous whales coming ashore,
turning into elephants, then cockatrices, then into 'Giants in Scarlet, with
Triple Crowns on their heads, and forked Tongues that hiss so loud, the
noise is heard to the Royal Exchange; which has put the Citizens into such
a Consternation, that 'tis thought the world's at an end' (ii.iii.p. 23).[7] For
Dashit 'this must portend right-down Poperie, that's certain' (p. 24).
Later, the worst revenge Dashit can think of for his tormentor is, 'I'll hire
a Priest to make a Papist of him before Execution; and when he's dead, I'll
piss on's Grave' (iv.iv.p. 45). Unjustly hounded into Newgate himself, he
exclaims, 'To Newgate, amongst the prophane Jesuits too? oh, oh!'
(iv.iv.p. 48). Dashit's puritan hypocrisy is satirized, in line with Tory
attacks on dissenters who supported the Whigs. The fear of French
influence and imports which fuelled Whiggery becomes mere boorish-
ness and stupidity, as Dashit is mocked for preoccupation with English
Protestant drinks, as opposed to 'Popish' French wines (ii.iii.p. 22; iii.ii.p.
30; v.iv.p. 67).

Similarly in *The Feign'd Curtizans* Behn satirizes 'cits', parvenues
and puritans. The Englishman, Sir Signall Buffoon boorishly apes Italian
manners and language, though his father sent him into Italy with a puritan
chaplain as a safeguard against 'the eminent danger that young Travellers
are in of being perverted to Popery' (i.i.p. 5). This puritan father is 'a fool
and knave' who 'had the attendant blessing of getting an Estate of some
eight thousand a year' (i.i.p. 5), so presumably he is an upstart, sequestrat-
ing puritan of the type satirized in Howard's *The Committee* (1662) and
Behn's own *The Roundheads*. The tutor, Tickletext, is tasteless and mercenary, making his pupil trade in gloves, stockings and pins on the Grand
Tour. He is also crudely anti-papist and foolishly proud of being English.
In the Exclusion Crisis, patriotism and hostility to the influence of Popish
countries were weapons in the Whig arsenal.

Tickletext is hypocritically glad to exploit Roman custom to get a
whore. He is a philistine, condemning Roman church architecture for

reasons of religious bigotry. He believes 'harmless Pictures are Idolatrous' (I.ii.p. 12). He himself aspires to a literary style which combines puritan plainness, bathos and credulity about portents: 'April the Twentieth, arose a very great storm of Wind, Thunder, Lightening, and Rain – which was a shrewd sign of foul weather' (III.i.p. 31). Behn thus associates anti-Popery and patriotism with hypocrisy, folly and pretension, as well as philistinism and low-class money-grubbing. Tickletext's faults are generic: 'we have a thousand of these in *England* that go loose about the streets, and pass with us for as sober discreet religious persons' (IV.i.p. 45). Satire of him is satire of the Protestant, mercantile middle class which was the Opposition's chief base of political support. It is also satire of the prevailing mentality in 1679, as seen by royalists.

Thus in *The Feign'd Curtizans* and *The Revenge* royalist satire of Whiggish citizens and puritans coexists quite comfortably with feminism. Women scheme for greater freedom and control within the framework of upper-class solidarity and shared values. In *The Feign'd Curtizans* Behn emphasizes that, whilst middle-class patriots are to be derided, upper-class good taste is international. She seems in her prologue to be making a political point of the conventional Italian setting: '*To what a wretched pass will poor Plays come, / This must be damn'd, the Plot is laid in Rome*' (sig.A4r). The play opens with hospitable exchanges between the Italian Julio and the English Fillamour. Later, English gentlemen court Italian ladies. Wit and good taste cross national boundaries, and hostility to Catholic countries is misconceived.

However, in *The Young King*, Behn switches from comedy to tragicomedy and offers a much more profound engagement with the Exclusion Crisis. The use of gender and sexuality as political discourse leads to a radical departure from feminism. The full title of the play is *The Young King; or, The Mistake*. The mistake is the Queen's exiling of the heir to the throne, her son, Orsames, and her training of her daughter, Cleomena, to rule in his stead. Just as the contemporary Whig Opposition wanted to exclude James from the throne due to fear of popery, and of his temperamental intransigence and 'arbitrariness', the play's Queen exiles her son, Orsames, because she believes an oracle which has foretold his tyranny. At the end of the play she repents of this 'superstitious errour' (v.iv.p. 62).

Female cross-dressing is used to emphasize the unnaturalness of the Queen's actions. Cleomena has no problem with dressing and fighting as an 'Amazon' until she falls in love, whereupon her true womanly nature asserts itself. Therefore the spectacle of a woman dressing and fighting as a man is a temporary reversal of roles which are not fundamentally questioned in this play. The effects of enforced and unnatural passivity on Orsames are harder to undo. Even though his restoration to the throne comes about as a natural process, there are some residual doubts about his suitability to rule. His early tyrannical posturings do not survive the mellowing influence of the love of his family and future wife. However, because he has been excluded from Court life, he is characterized by a lack of political sagacity. He announces his intention of relying for political advice upon his country's erstwhile enemy, the King of Scythia (v.iv.p. 63). His exile has engendered a lack of human sympathy, political judgement or political propriety, and an associated absence of sexual decorum. In Act II he tries to grab a woman's breasts, and his last action at the end of the play is to bestow a maiden upon a soldier with naive high-handedness, without consulting the wishes of either party. Behn's point might well be that the much criticized faults of the Stuart brothers – Charles's licentiousness and perceived passivity, James's arbitrariness – are attributable to their respective exiles at the hands of an ungrateful and misguided nation. Behn's depiction of the disastrous results of political exclusion on the royal personality reflects fears expressed by Parliamentary opponents of the Exclusion Bills that excluding James from the succession might make him desperate and lead to civil war. Behn associates sexual inversion and unnatural motherhood with political exclusion; Tories argued that Charles would be unnatural if he consented to the Exclusion of his own brother. The play thus mobilizes traditional gender values and family values in the interests of political conformity.

Now I want to contrast Behn's feminist interrogation of the libertine ethos prevalent in Court circles in *The Second Part of the Rover* with the sexual conservatism of *The Roundheads*. At first sight these plays appear similar. Both are set in the interregnum and both appear to counterpose the jolly rakishness of royalists to the hypocrisy of parliamentary puritans. *The Second Part of the Rover* was published with a Dedication to James,

Duke of York, in which Behn identifies James with her hero, Willmore. Royalist politics and cavalier sexual mores are contrasted to the hypocrisy, '*ingratitude*' and '*Arbitrary Tyranny*' of the '*seeming sanctifi'd Faction*' in the Civil War and their Whig descendants in the Exclusion Crisis (sig. A3v–A4r). In the play the verb 'Cavaliering' is used to convey both adherence to the royalist cause and sexual adventurism: cheated out of sexual fulfilment and otherwise discomfited, the character Fetherfool resolves: 'If this be the end of travelling, I'le e'ne to old *England* again, take the Covenant, get a Sequestrators place, grow rich, and defie all Cavaliering' (v.p. 84). James was himself a rake, so he is likely to have found the glorification of cavalier behaviour congenial.

The connection between politics and sexual politics in *The Second Part of the Rover* is spelt out by the play's royalist hero, Willmore. In Act II he contrasts his own libertinism with the sexual habits which typify a parlimentarian. He expects free sex, both in the sense that he wants to be open about it, and because he wants it without monetary or social cost: 'Let the sly States-man, who Jilts the Commonwealth with his grave Politiques, pay for the sin that he may doat in secret' (p. 18). In Act III he says of his pursuit of a large woman, 'better to be Master of a Monster / than Slave to a damn'd Commonwealth' (p. 43). In other words, the royalist rake has a control in the sexual sphere which is denied to him in the political sphere. The plays ends with rakishness triumphant, there being no reformation of the rake, as in *The Rover*.

Yet I would argue that this play contains as profound a questioning of libertinism as is to be found in any other Restoration comedy. Despite her avowed intention of celebrating cavaliers, Behn comes close to the excoriation of libertinism which in the Exclusion Crisis was receiving explicitly Whiggish coloration in the plays of Shadwell. Firstly, the callousness of the rake is stressed. He speaks of his wife's death 'With a Sham sadness' (i.p. 5) and seems to be as much concerned with the loss of her fortune as with the loss of her. This mercenary motivation competes with sex for priority in his mind, for 'money speaks sense in a Language all Nations understand, 'tis Beauty, Wit, Courage, Honour, and undisputable Reason' (III.p. 43). Desire for wealth (as opposed to mere bewailing of poverty) is usually associated with grasping cits like Dashit in *The Revenge* or, in Exclusion Crisis tragedies, with villains who thirst for reward, so it is disconcerting to find the royalist hero so mercenary.

Secondly, it is emphasized that libertinism not only renders woman an object, but renders the identity of the object secondary: several characters, including Willmore, pursue two rich jewesses, one of whom is a dwarf and the other a giantess. The function of 'these Lady Monsters' (1.p. 8) is to show the monstrousness of libertinism itself: its object is so irrelevant that it can even be a freak (in Restoration terms), so long as there is the spice of novelty. In Act v the poor giant is pushed and pulled to and fro by the various men as if she were literally an object. In the dark in iv.ii Willmore sees the maiden Ariadne and the courtesan La Nuche just as two women, and remarks, 'no matter which, so I am sure of one' (p. 51). In iv.iv he issues instructions to another man's servants to serenade whatever lady is to be pursued, for he neither knows nor cares who it will be. The object of Willmore's pursuit changes constantly. His aim is simple: 'I must dispose of this mad fire about me' (iv.ii.p. 58). The lack of closure at the end reinforces our sense of unregenerate cavalier predatoriness. Willmore disguises himself as a mountebank to further his love plots and the guise is symbolically appropriate.

Thirdly, we are distanced from the action in a way which encourages us to reflect upon the various sex plots, rather than to engage with the characters. Thus in Act i we watch Ariadne and Lucia watching Willmore watching La Nuche watching her bawd, Petronella, gull Fetherfool. Similarly in Act ii Ariadne and Lucia follow Willmore and Blunt who follow Fetherfool and La Nuche's 'bravo'. This leads to my fourth point: there is much dizzying farcical by-play and endless confusion of identity as men carry off the wrong woman and climb into bed with other men by mistake and women dress as men and (for various devious reasons) pursue each other as well as men. The effect is to engender mockery rather than royalist sympathies. Fifthly, and most disturbingly, the misogyny beneath the surface of libertinism is explicitly revealed. Willmore hates the women he desires for their beauty and wealth and for their power over himself: 'by Heaven, I will possess this gay Insensible, to make me hate her – most extremely curse her' (1.p. 13). The wit which is generically supposed to excuse all often wears rather thin.

Since Behn has explicitly coupled royalism and cavalier sexual mores, it is disturbing from a Tory point of view that rakishness is seen to be so obnoxious in *The Second Part of the Rover*. The tone of *The Roundheads* is very different. It works much better as Tory drama because, as in *The Young King*, Behn chooses to abandon feminist anatomization of libertinism in favour of a more conventional Tory association of royalism with virtue, and rebellion with sexual monstrosity. She sharpens the satire of interregnum Parliamentarians and puritans in her source, Tatham's *The Rump*, and makes it more topical. She adds cavalier heroes, Loveless and Freeman, who attempt to cuckold the Parliamentarian leaders, Lambert and Desboro'. Yet, Lady Desboro', though a royalist at heart, and happy to mock her husband, refuses to be unfaithful to him: 'No, I'm true to my / Allegiance still, true to my King and Honour. Suspect my loyalty when I / lose my virtue' (iv.i.p. 33). Behn thus specifically associates royalism and 'virtue'. This bizarre yoking of cavalier mores and the virtue of chastity somehow succeeds, so thoroughly does Behn link lust and secret sex with canting, hypocritical puritans.

In Lady Lambert and Lady Cromwell, Behn makes conservative use of the figures of the shrew and the upstart woman aping the great Lady. Lady Lambert beats up and bosses her husband, and interferes in political meetings. Lady Cromwell is jealous of her dignity and indignant when other women encroach on what she calls 'our Royal Family' (v.ii.p. 49). The gender transgression reinforces the social presumption, typifying a world upside-down. Lady Lambert's capacity for love – and the superior sexiness of the cavaliers – eventually restores her to the 'sanity' of political and sexual submissiveness. Behn also inserts the comic interlude of a Council of Ladies, infiltrated, and satirized 'aside', by the heroes in drag. Here Behn constructs a paradigm of presumptuous folly and impropriety which both reflects and typifies the rebel world; she also focuses on a peculiarly female propensity for pettiness. She shows women in power behaving in a way which anti-suffragists were to depict two centuries later, elevating private grievances, bitchy, competitive and silly. Thus Behn's habitual – and liberating – depiction of women who are wiser and wittier than their husbands coexists with and is overdetermined by a conventional Tory rhetoric of gender difference and female subordination.

In *The City-Heiress* Behn offers an even more sympathetic view of the rake than in *The Roundheads*: the association between royalism and virtue is abandoned, and the libertine allowed his sexual triumphs. Moreover, rather than being obliged to undergo reformation before marriage, the chief rake, Tom Wilding, is allowed to complain that his former mistresses have betrayed his love by marrying other men. It is no accident that these exculpated rakes are labelled by the Whig, Sir Timothy, 'Tarmagent Tories' (i.p. 2). The phrase 'Tory-rory' (i.p. 6) applied to the Tory knight, Sir Anthony, denotes a certain rollicking and roistering mentality.[8] Behn seems concerned to suggest that Tory libertinism is something jolly, wild and cavalier, and preferable to whey-faced Whiggery and puritan sexual hypocrisy.

It seems significant that Shadwell's savage attack on Court libertinism, *The Libertine*, was revived around this time as *The Libertine Destroy'd*.[9] Shadwell was now a committed Whig, and criticism of court libertinism and attacks on the royal mistresses were weapons in the Whig arsenal. Behn's vindication of the rake in *The City-Heiress* might thus have its motivation in part in the fact that she reverses Shadwellian tropes.[10] Disgust at the promiscuity and venereal disease which lurks beneath the facade of nobility permeates *The Libertine*. Behn satirizes it in Mrs. Clacket, 'A City-Bawd & Puritan' (Actors' Names), and a 'true Protestant' (ii.i.pp. 12–13). In *The Libertine*, rape is a serious threat and women resist it, by suicide if necessary. In *The City-Heiress*, Lady Galliard is a willing participant in her own seduction, putting up the expected token resistance, but willingly won over by libertine arguments. In *The Libertine*, libertine arguments are ruthlessly exposed. For example, the argument that the rake acts in self-defence against the woman's beauty which is a form of cruelty is satirized when Don John kills the governor of Seville: 'The jealous Coxcomb deserv'd death, he kept his Sister from me; her eyes would have kill'd me if I had not enjoy'd her, which I could not do without killing him.'[11] The libertine's claim to be 'following the Dictates of Nature, who can do otherwise?' (iii.p. 55; cf iv.iii.p. 82), is ridiculed by the depiction of real pastoral virtues in the countryside in iv.ii: 'Nature is here not yet debauch'd by Art.' Libertine irreligion is a serious sin, punished by death and damnation. In Behn's play, Tories are cheerfully irreligious.

Behn predictably levels the charge of sexual hypocrisy at the godly, whereas in Shadwell's Act III, the libertine's attempt to label a virtuous man of being a hypocrite and a godly whoremaster is simply monstrous. Behn has venial and ridiculous servants; Shadwell has a serious critique of corruption in great men ramifying downwards: ''Tis true, my Master's a very *Tarquin*; but I ne'r attempted to ravish before' (Jacomo, IV.ii.p. 78).

Other Shadwellian themes are reversed: Shadwell's *The Woman Captain* begins with a satirical depiction of a young aristocrat who is preparing to waste the inheritance from his decent, puritan father, and to associate with rakes and wastrels. *The City-Heiress* opens with a satirical depiction of the Oliverian, Sir Timothy, foolishly objecting to his nephew and heir, Tom Wilding, being corrupted by fun-loving Tory rakes. Shadwell's Sir Humphrey is reproached by the old-fashioned steward who acts as the ignored voice of his master's conscience: 'I would have you cleanly, and serve God as my old Mr. did' (I.p. 2). Behn's Sir Timothy laments: 'Before he fell to Toryism, he was a Sober civil Youth, and had some Religion in him' (I.p. 2). This is given further point by a regret for the passing of 'the days of old *Oliver*' (p. 3). Then comes the familiar taint of puritan sexual hypocrisy: 'he [Cromwell] by a wholsome Act, made it death to boast; so that then a man might whore his heart out, and no body the wiser' (ibid).[12] Behn's treatment of libertinism in the Tory Reaction period seems to have shifted to outright indulgence, in the face of Whig disapproval.

How may we account for these shifts in Behn's treatment of sex and gender issues? It seems to me that it is no accident that the shifts parallel changes in the political situation.[13] *The Feign'd Curtizans* was performed early in the Exclusion Crisis period, at a time when few dramatists had taken sides. This is not to say that political concerns are not apparent in the drama. Concerns about popery predated the Popish Plot scare. James's marriage to the Catholic Mary of Modena had led to parliamentary protest in 1673. Marvell's 'An Account of the Growth of Popery and Arbitrary Government in England' had been published in 1677. Dryden responded to the situation in the 1678/9 theatrical season by demonizing political rebellion in *Oedipus*, and by suggesting in *Troilus and Cressida* that the government might have to use machiavellian means if necessary to secure order and deal with trouble-makers. In *Oedipus*, as in *The Feign'd Curtizans*, class is a stable referent: the Thracian Prince Adrastus is Oedipus' worthy enemy and then his ally, the populist Creon and the people themselves are to be mistrusted and kept down. Yet *Oedipus* is coloured by a sense of darkness and of the difficulty of right action, as are other plays in this season with a royalist colouration, such as Crowne's *The Ambitious Statesman*. In *Oedipus*, *The Ambitious Statesman* and *Troilus and Cressida* royal lust is problematized alongside rebellion. It is no surprise then that Behn's royalism emerges in the form of satire of fairly safe targets, upstarts and puritans, and in celebration of upper-class good nature and good taste across national boundaries.

The Young King was a response to a new situation of deepening polarization and of vigorous royalist response to the Opposition's successful exploitation of the Popish Plot scare. In the autumn of 1679 the Government really began to go on the offensive against the Opposition. It is in this season that William Whitaker produced *The Conspiracy*, one of the most fervent and idealistically royalist plays of the Crisis, if not of all time, and Elkanah Settle produced a scathing satire of the Catholic Church in *The Female Prelate: being the History of the Life and Death of Pope Joan*. Whitaker and Settle use female monstrosity to demonize rebellion and popery respectively. In this climate Behn is inspired to produce (or exhume, or rework) a piece which can offer a more thoroughgoing and explicitly topical critique of contemporary Exclusionists. She turns from comedy to tragi-comedy in order to do this, and in the process (temporarily) abandons feminism in favour of a much more reactionary use of sexual inversion to invoke moral and political horror.

Not all plays produced at this time are political or partisan. D'Urfey's *The Virtuous Wife*, also premièred in this season, seems to be offered as a humorous distraction in difficult times, though some extraneous political allusions are thrown in for good measure. Behn's own *The Revenge* is a less politically 'engaged' piece than *The Young King*, despite the satire of anti-papist 'cits' referred to above. It is also a slighter piece, bearing signs of hasty composition: *The Young King* is a more substantial reworking of Calderon and of Fletcher's *Love's Cure; or, The Martial Maid* than *The Revenge* is of *The Dutch Courtesan*. Perhaps *The Revenge* was published anonymously for reasons of literary insouciance rather than political strategy.

In *The Second Part of the Rover* Behn is 'back on form' with a profound commitment of dramatic energy to the anatomization of libertinism. This coexists oddly with her expressed commitment to cavalier politics in the Dedication. However, the Dedication was supplied upon publication.[14] The play itself was produced earlier in 1681: references in the epilogue suggest that it was performed before the dissolution of Parliament in January. This means that it was performed in the period before the Oxford Parliament in March 1681, during a period of apparent Whig ascendancy. At this time many dramatists made concessions to Opposition sentiment. Perhaps they were motivated in part by a desire to cater to a more Whiggish audience, as the second Exclusion Parliament was sitting at this time. Lee offers a critique of royal effeminacy and irresponsibility in *Theodosius* and a politically emotive dramatization of the expulsion of the Tarquins in *Lucius Junius Brutus*. Shadwell, in *The Lancashire Witches*, gives a sweeping indictment of the decay of old-fashioned, Protestant, parliamentarian, gentry values. He satirizes not only popery, but collusion with popery and misplaced lust within the Church of England. Perhaps more surprising are the shifts made by Dryden in *The Spanish Fryar* and Crowne in *Henry the Sixth, the First Part*. Dryden said in later life that he offered *The Spanish Fryar* 'to the people'.[15] The play has anti-Catholic satire in the 'low' plot and a main plot which offers a message of moderation, and of reconciliation of royalists and parliamentarians around the values of 1660.[16] Crowne makes an astounding shift in this season from the triumphant and successful Toryism of *The Misery of Civil War* in the previous season to an attack primarily directed at corrupt, effeminate and popish courts in *Henry VI: The First Part*.[17] There is a striking shift in the tone of prologues and epilogues in this season: the sneering at Whiggery, anti-popery and newsmongering which predominated in the previous season is almost entirely absent, replaced by jocular misogyny or mock-deference to the ladies, or by apolitical complaints of the hardship suffered by poets, and of the philistinism and folly of the age.

Such shifts were not necessarily opportunistic: it was unfashionable to be a zealot after 1660. It may have seemed both logical and rational for dramatists to foreground those aspects of their vision of society most in accordance with the spirit of the times. Possibly the shift in the political situation empowered the dramatists to be more explicit in criticizing royal lust and impropriety, and court corruption, than they might otherwise have been. Dryden and Crowne make their political shifts explicit in their Dedications to Whiggish patrons, whereas Behn boldly dedicates *The Second Part of the Rover* to James. Yet it might well be the case that Behn has space in this season to offer a critique of libertinism which would have been misplaced or misapplied a little earlier or a little later in the Exclusion Crisis.

Although *The Roundheads* was produced later in the same year as *The Second Part of the Rover*, the situation was very different indeed. In the autumn of 1681, it had become clear that the Oxford Parliament had been a victory for the King. In the theatres, as in society, the 'Tory Reaction' set in with a vengeance. The dramatists atoned for their apostasy by writing fervently royalists plays, vigorously declaring their allegiance in Dedications and Prefaces, and writing Tory prologues and epilogues which were published as broadsides in the pamphlet war. The Whigs were satirized in plays like *Sir Barnaby Whigg* and *Mr Turbulent*, and Whig plays were no longer being performed in the theatres.[18] Of course this is not to say that tensions, anxieties and contradictions did not persist in the drama. However, what seems clear is that there was a specific context and a substantial motivation for Behn to make a vigorous effort at this time to subordinate her capacity for feminist insight to the sexually conservative tropes of Toryism in order to demonize the Whigs' attempt to 'turn the world upside-down'. This is even more true in 1682 when the backlash against Whiggery was underway. Behn's technique of reversing Shadwellian themes and tropes in *The City Heiress* parallels D'Urfey's method in *Sir Barnaby Whigg*, where a similar reversal is undertaken of themes and tropes in Shadwell's *The Lancashire Witches*.

My argument, then, is twofold: Behn, like her fellow dramatists, responds to the needs of the particular historical moment, and the moments at which it becomes most urgent to give ideological affirmation to Toryism produce the plays in which there is least space for feminism. Feminist anatomization and critique of the libertinism associated with the

Court must give way to the invoking of conventional gender values to justify the established order.

NOTES

1 See my ' "Partial tyrants" and "Freeborn people" in *Lucius Junius Brutus*' *Studies in English Literature*, 31 (1991), 463–82; also Paul Hammond, 'The king's two bodies: representations of Charles II', in *Culture, Politics and Society in Britain, 1660–1800*, ed. Jeremy Black and Jeremy Gregory (Manchester, 1991) pp. 13–48.

2 See my ' "He that should guard my virtue has betrayed it": the dramatization of rape in the Exclusion Crisis,' *Restoration and Eighteenth-Century Theatre Research* 9 (1994), 59–68.

3 *The Revenge* was published anonymously. For attribution to Behn see my ' "Suspect my loyalty when I lose my virtue": sexual politics and party in Aphra Behn's plays of the Exclusion Crisis, 1678–83', *Restoration* 18 (1994), 37–47, p. 45, n.4.

4 Probable première dates are: *The Feign'd Curtizans*, early 1679; *The Young King*, autumn 1679; *The Revenge*, early 1680; *The Second Part of the Rover*, January 1681; *The Roundheads* autumn 1681; *The City Heiress*, late April or early May 1682. See *The London Stage, 1660–1800* ed. W. Van Lennep et. al. (Carbondale, 1965), Judith Milhous and Robert D. Hume, 'Dating play premières from publication data, 1660–1700', *Harvard Library Bulletin* 22 (1974), 374–405, Pierre Danchin, *The Prologues and Epilogues of the Restoration, 1660–1700* (Nancy, 1981–8), and my own Ph. D. thesis, 'Drama and politics in the Exclusion Crisis: 1678–83' (Leeds, 1992) and forthcoming book, *Restoration Theatre and Crisis* (Oxford). Behn states in her Dedication to *The Young King* that this play was her first: it may have been staged (and reworked?) at this time because of its topicality. The statement might be intended as a rhetorical denial of topicality, as was common.

5 On the feminist effect of cross-dressing in Behn's plays see Jacqueline Pearson, *The Prostituted Muse: Images of Women and Women Dramatists, 1642–1737* (New York, 1988) pp. 154–9.

6 The tide of anti-popery began to ebb in autumn 1679: J.P. Kenyon, *The Popish Plot* (Harmondsworth, 1974), chapter 2. However, there was scepticism about the Popish Plot in Court circles from the earliest stages: ibid., p. 86.

7 All quotations from plays are from the first editions, unless otherwise stated.

8 This phrase had been used by Dryden in *The Kind Keeper* (1678) without political overtones. The *OED* makes no mention of this, citing only the origins of 'Tory' in Irish Gaelic as a term for an outlaw which became extended to papists and royalists.

9 *London Stage*, p. 309. A topical reference in the prologue suggests that *The City-Heiress* premièred in late April or early May 1682. Shadwell's play was revived on 18 May.

10 My argument stands if Behn's play went on first: the intention to revive Shadwell's play was not likely to have been secret.

11 *The Works of Thomas Shadwell*, ed. Montague Summers, 5 vols. (London, 1927), III, I, p. 27.

12 Shadwell's 'slant' in *The Woman Captain* seems itself a product of the Exclusion Crisis. Just as Behn's position on libertinism shifts under the pressure of Toryism, so Shadwell, under the pressure of Whiggery, emphasizes anti-court aspects of his social satire. He still mocks foolish cits in *The Woman Captain*, but there is a shift of emphasis from *The Virtuoso* where he mocks an 'old fashion'd Fellow' (*Works*, ed. Summers, III, p. 115) who hankers after the morals and fashions of the 1640s, whilst hypocritically keeping a whore.

13 See my 'Interpreting the politics of Restoration drama', *Seventeenth-Century* 8 (1993), 67–97.

14 The play was entered in the *Term Catalogues* under June 1681, so was probably published by then.

15 Preface to *De Arte Graphica*, *The Works of John Dryden*, ed. H. T. Swedenberg et al., 20 vols. (Berkeley, 1956 onwards), xx, 76, line 16.

16 See my 'The politics of John Dryden's *The Spanish Fryar; or, the Double Discovery*', *English* 43 (1994), 97–113.

17 See my *Restoration Theatre and Crisis*, chapter 3.

18 The Dedication to the Whig leader Shaftesbury of *Rome's Follies; or, The Amorous Fryars* (1681) states that the play had to be performed at a private house because 'the Subject being not a little Satyrical against the Romanists, would very much hinder its taking, and [it] would be . . . difficult to get play'd' (sig. A3r).

2 Popish Plots: *The Feign'd Curtizans* in context

ALISON SHELL

Nay, even the Women now pretend to reign;
Defend us from a Poet Joan again!
That Congregation's in a hopeful way
To Heaven, where the Lay-Sisters teach and pray.

In this, a quatrain from the prologue to *Sir Patient Fancy* (1678) Aphra Behn's glancing sarcasm touches on three of her favourite themes: anti-Puritanism, feminism and Catholicism.[1] These are themes which are to recur, with a vengeance, in her next play *The Feign'd Curtizans* (1679), the subject of this article: anti-Puritanism because the play is tied to the political moment of the Popish Plot, feminism because of its mockery of the stereotypes of whoredom, and Catholicism because, as I shall maintain, Behn's literary sympathies during this period and subsequently can be demonstrated to be not only pro-Tory but pro-Catholic. Affirming kinship with Pope Joan, the fictional ninth-century prelate whose life was as transgressive as her own, Behn's 'Poet Joan' may be a wry epithet for herself.[2]

It is difficult at the best of times to define what is meant by a Catholic in seventeenth-century England. The term can be used – in the orthodox manner – of those who have been born or formally received into the Catholic church, who divide into church-Papists and recusants, of people who deliberately absented themselves for short or long periods from the Anglican communion, often as a prelude to the profession of formal Catholicism, and of the crypto-Catholic, especially to be found in courtly circles, whose sympathy with Catholicism was an open secret.[3] The last category, in which I would place Behn, is for good contemporary reasons a fugitive one to define; while penal laws and recusancy fines still existed to incapacitate Catholics, there was an advantage to allowing one's allegiances to remain ambiguous.

Any difficulties are multiplied in the case of Behn, a playwright whose life has been peculiarly subject to critical myth-making. There is still very little that is definitely known about her life, and, consequently, almost nothing about her religious affiliations before she started writing; she remarks in passing in the opening passages of *The History of the Nun: Or, The Fair Vow-Breaker* (1668) that she was 'design'd for a Nun', thus engendering intense critical debate as to whether these were the words of the biographical Behn, or of a persona that Behn created for herself, or simply a comment of the fictional narrator.[4] Nevertheless, there are a certain number of other indications that she may at some stage in her life have been a Catholic. The most striking of these is a stop-press cancellation in the first edition of *Oroonoko* (1688), deleting her praise of the dedicatee, the 4th Earl of Lauderdale, for being 'so great a Champion for the Catholic Church'.[5] Mary Ann O'Donnell, in the introduction to her bibliography of Behn, remarks on Behn's detailed knowledge of continental Catholicism, the high proportion of Catholics among her dedicatees, and what can be read as an explicit avowal of Catholicism in her comments upon Viscount Stafford's death in *A Poem to Sir Roger L'Estrange*:[6]

> Here noble Stafford fell, on Death's great Stage,
> A Victim to the Lawless Peoples Rage.
> Calm as a Dove, receiv'd a Shameful Death,
> To Undeceive the World, resign'd his Breath;
> And like a God, dy'd to redeem Our Faith. (40–4)[7]

Nothing as explicit is to be found in her plays; yet some of her plays enshrine a tantalizing ideological flirtation with Catholicism under the guise of Toryism, rendered all the more convincingly because her Toryism was genuine.[8] Like other writers with Catholic sympathies – most strikingly Matthew Medburne, as discussed below – Behn also uses the automatic equation of Catholics with sin to put opponents off the scent, and to engage in a wry discourse with sympathizers.

The Popish Plot began in the autumn of 1678, when Titus Oates and Israel Tonge's story of a Catholic plot to kill the King, fire the City and enthrone the Duke of York received accidental or deliberate corroboration from the murder of the official to whom they had made their disclosures, Sir Edmund Bury Godfrey. The scandal was fanned by the first Whigs, in whose interests it was to prevent the Duke of York succeeding to the throne, and it prompted an unprecedented flow of vicious pamphlet propaganda from both Whig and Tory after the lapse of the Licensing Act in 1679. Throughout the 1660s and 1670s , there had been some degree of practical toleration for Catholics in London; but London was the Plot's centre, and for Catholics in the capital the situation rapidly became uncomfortable. A series of proclamations and orders in Council issued by Charles II from November 1678 required that laws against Catholics should be enforced, and that certain categories of Catholics should depart from within ten miles of London. In the early months of 1679, it seemed possible that governmental proposals on registering recusants, obliging them to take oaths, banishing all Catholics from London and excluding them from all trades connected with printing would reach the statute-book. Numbers convicted of recusancy in London were certainly lower than they should have been, but a writer identified as a recusant would have risked a number of possible fates, from enforced oath-taking to censorship and imprisonment.[9]

The Feign'd Curtizans was the first play that Behn wrote after the advent of the Popish Plot. It was performed in March 1679, at a time when the Popish Plot had had two effects on the theatre: firstly, of injecting a high degree of political content into most plays, and secondly, of making audiences stay away.[10] But it would be a mistake to assume that because plays were poorly attended, they were not attended to. One can postulate that the reverse was the case, and that attendance at a play when the political convictions of the author were known was a declaration of allegiance in itself; Crowne's epilogue to *The Ambitious Statesman*, written at this time, complains that 'Now no divertisement does pleasure bring, / The Pope has set his foot in everything.'[11] Dryden's adaptation of Shakespeare's *Troilus and Cressida*, entered in the Stationers' Company registers on 14 April 1679, had the original title restored at the last minute, with Dryden's own title, *Truth Found Too Late*, being relegated to the subtitle: a move which – his editors suggest – was intended to nullify any political overtones it might have had, in a year of forced confessions and recantations. The playbook itself shows an unexceptionable desire to be identified with the majority, with the Earl of Sunderland being praised as a moderate in the dedication.[12] Nevertheless, Dryden adds to Shakespeare some specifically anti-Catholic anticlericalism in his rewriting of the 'fugitive Rogue Priest' Calchas, which the epilogue reinforces:

> I could rayl on, but 'twere a task as vain
> As Preaching Truth at Rome, or Wit in Spain: . . .
> If guilty, yet I'm sure o'th' Churches blessing,
> By suffering for the Plot, without confessing.
>
> (XIII.pp. 354–5, lines 23–4, 27–8)

Dryden went on to greater polemical heights, writing the virulently anti-papistical *Spanish Friar* in 1680; his own conversion to Catholicism was still many years away.

Whatever the circumstances, *The Feign'd Curtizans* is a triumph of delicate misdirection. Its dedication to Nell Gwyn – a personal friend of Behn's who was Protestant, but avowedly apolitical – has been described by Maureen Duffy as a proclamation of Behn's Protestantism.[13] But the important and suggestive point about this dedication is that, at a time when to emphasize whatever Protestantism one possessed was politically expedient, Behn creates a rhetorical artifact that directs the reader completely away from banal comparisons of religious allegiance. The only deity in it is Nell Gwyn herself:

> MADAM 'Tis no wonder that hitherto I followed not the good example of the believing Poets, since less faith and zeal than you alone can inspire, had wanted power to have reduc't me to the true worship. . . . I make this Sacrifice with infinite fear and trembling, well knowing that so Excellent and perfect a Creature as your self differs only from the divine powers in this; the Offerings made to you ought to be worthy of you, whilst they accept the will alone . . .[14]

Its windy baroque apotheosis, criticized by Dr Johnson,[15] diverts the reader from noticing that a commonplace of Restoration dedication, which Behn usually exploited as far as she could, is absent: the praise of the ideological views of the dedicatee insofar as they coincide with the author's. This is a long way from the indiscretion so nearly committed in the dedication to *Oroonoko*.

The first few pages of a playbook typically juxtapose three fictions: the dedication, the prologue and the play itself. In the case of *The Feign'd Curtizans* there is an obvious but retrospective irony about this juxtaposition, which pivots on the prologue. The character of a prostitute that the actress Betty Currer assumes here does not tally, as is usual, either with the anonymity of a theatrical commentator or with her role in the play as Marcella, one of the *feigned* courtesans; and the progress from a dedication to Nell Gwyn, the Protestant whore, through a prologue spoken by an actress in the character of a prostitute whose religion self-confessedly varies according to her client's, to that actress's character within the play of a Catholic virgin pretending to be a whore, is either unusually serendipitous or not accidental at all.[16]

This insight, of course, is available only to the reader; in the theatre a prologue is not so much pivotal as prescriptive. Invoking the topos of comparing real-life and theatrical plots, Behn begins it in a mood of deceptively artless bathos:

> The Devil take this cursed plotting Age,
> 'T has ruined all our Plots upon the Stage. . .   (II.p. 307, lines 1–2)[17]

Part of the anti-Catholic stereotype, owing a good deal to debased Machiavellianism, was that all adherents to the Romish religion were compulsive, tortuous and casuistical plotters. Given some impetus from the Gunpowder Plot, and still more from the persistent myth throughout the century that the hand of popery could be discerned behind everything from the Fire of London to Anabaptism, the English public was ready to believe the tales of Oates and Tonge precisely because they fell into an easily recognizable pattern.[18] The stereotype was prominent on the stage, where it provided dramatists with an imaginatively convincing rationale for complexity of plot, justifying the switchbacks and conflicts on which both comedy and tragedy are dependent. From the earlier seventeenth century a play like *The Duchess of Malfi* (1614) depended for its plot and characterization on the notion that Catholics gained a perverse pleasure from supererogatory plotting. Comedy is perhaps the more typical manifestation of the later seventeenth century, as in Thomas Shadwell's *The Lancashire Witches* of 1681; this play, also engendered by the Popish Plot but from the opposite camp to *The Feign'd Curtizans*, displays the villainous Irish priest Tegue O'Dively creating imbroglio around him. It could be argued, indeed, that the comedy of intrigue in which Behn specialized could be seen as allowing Catholics, for once, to triumph in the traditionally Catholic pursuit of plotting.

Continuing after the equation of theatrical plots with real, and suggesting by implication that the Popish Plot is equally illusory, the prologue laments the fact that fools now 'turn Politician'; politics – as never elsewhere in Behn, the most political of writers – is set in antithesis to wit. Wit itself, in contrast, is coupled with the subtlety of 'Plots upon the stage', and, briefly, with jesuitry itself:

> But Wit, as if 'twere Jesuitical,
> Is an Abomination to ye all.   (lines 13–14)[19]

Wit and jesuitry alike suffer the opprobrium of the interlocutor, one of Behn's comic Dissenters – like Tickletext in the play – whose speech is dotted with abominations; and jesuitry is upgraded by the association. The next couplet is both disarming and titillating in its frank recognition that 'This must be damn'd, the Plot is laid in Rome' (line 16). The caesura implies interchangeable cause and effect. Both the plot of the play and the Popish Plot are being referred to, and the audience is disingenuously asked to sympathize with the play's unlucky timing.

In the second half of the prologue, Betty Currer proclaims her own scepticism in the face of Dissent:

> Not one amongst ye all I'll undertake,
> E'er thought that we should suffer for Religion's sake:
> Who wou'd have thought that wou'd have been th'occasion
> Of any contest in our hopeful Nation? . . .

> Who says this Age a Reformist wants,
> When Betty Currer's Lovers all turn Saints?
>
> (pp. 307–8, lines 18–21, 28–9)

The positive vocabulary – 'hopeful', 'Saints' – has, as often in Behn, a tincture of whiggery and cant about it; and, as Betty Currer ends the prologue by elegizing her unwanted charms, she adds to it implications of the sexual hypocrisy so common in anti-Puritan satire. Her ex-lovers 'piously pretend these are not days, / For keeping Mistresses, and seeing Plays' (lines 26–7). Even though Currer proclaims herself to be 'of the Religion of [her] Cully' (line 23) she still goes on to say of cullies that 'till these dangerous times they'd none to fix on, / But now are something in mere Contradiction' (lines 24–5); the satirical complaint that Protestants only defined themselves in relation to what they disagreed with was a common one among those of high-church and Catholic sympathies.[20] Moreover, the sexual abstinence of Puritan gallants means unemployment for actresses of easy virtue, and thus for the players; again employing double-entendre, Betty Currer complains that her erstwhile Puritan lovers will 'scarce do any thing for Charity now' (line 31). And as the prologue ends as it began, with bathos, an increase in hypocrisy is seen as the Popish Plot's only important effect:

> Who wou'd have thought such hellish Times to have seen,
> When I shou'd be neglected at Eighteen?
> That Youth and Beauty shou'd be quite undone,
> A Pox upon the Whore of Babylon.
>
> (41–4)

The Popish threat is definitely trivialized into the object of a prostitute's professional jealousy, and mild curse.

This prologue accomplishes three things: anti-Whig criticism and diminution of the Popish Plot, both characteristics of literary Toryism, and something far less common, debunking the Catholic threat altogether. There are a number of respects in which it differs from the classic Tory Anglican position.[21] Plays adhering to the Tory party line – Thomas Southerne's *The Loyal Brother*, Crowne's *City Politiques* – tend to occur later than *The Feign'd Curtizans* in the course of the Popish Plot: between

1680 and 1683, when it was becoming increasingly clear that the Plot was a fiction. Moreover, such plays usually stress that the fact that the Popish Plot is a fiction does nothing to legitimize popery. *The Coronation of Queen Elizabeth, with the Restauration of the Protestant Religion: or the Downfall of the Pope* (1680), for instance, treats the Whiggish lower orders and the Catholic church with an equal degree of jocular disdain.[22]

A number of Behn's other prologues and epilogues specifically criticize Puritan and Whiggish anti-Catholicism, notably in *The Rover II* (1681).[23] Here her criticism focuses particularly on the pope-burning processions organized by the Whig Green Ribbon Club from 1679.[24] The prologue promises 'We've Monsters too, / Which far exceed your City Pope for Shew' (i.p. 115, lines 24–5), the play's parade of freaks reinforces the topical reference, and the epilogue implies that the Whig members of the audience, in enjoying the spectacle of Catholic monstrosity, are missing a double-edged jibe at themselves:

> Giants, fat Cardinals, Pope Joans and Fryers,
> To entertain Right Worshipfuls and Squires
> Who laugh and cry Ads Nigs, 'tis woundy[25] good,
> When the fuger's all the Jest that's understood.   (i.p. 212, lines 18–21.)

The word 'fuger' – on which the Oxford English Dictionary is enigmatic – seems to be a variant of 'figure': in this context, the outward form of a satirical enigma that turns the tables on Whiggery. A systematic analysis of the numerous religious references in Behn's drama, which this article makes no pretence to be, is an essential future project to determine whether her codified pro-Catholic bias informs other plays than *The Feign'd Curtizans*.

But, to give one further example, Behn's epilogue to her Tory propagandist history play *The Roundheads* (1681) makes almost explicit the hinted connection between players and papists. Both groups have polemical connotations of theatricality, but Lady Desbro' takes the offensive in equating puritans with affectation, speaking part of the epilogue in a puritan 'preaching Tone'. The sermon complains that 'those cursed Tories . . . exclude the Saints; yet open Th'Door / To introduce the Babylonian Whore.' (i.p. 425, lines 25–8). This is disingenuous, being exactly what Behn proceeds to do. Having linked Tories with Catholics through the reported speech of her *advocatus diaboli*, every subsequent pro-Tory sentiment can also be read as pro-Catholic. Tories 'rail'd foolishly for Loyalty and Laws' throughout the Civil Wars, and the Puritans 'left them Loyalty, and took their Land' (lines 36, 38). The sermonizer's climax, 'Yea, and the pious work of Reformation / Rewarded was with Plunder, Sequestration' (lines 39–40) introduces a pejorative use of the term 'Reformation' which can be interpreted either as anti-Puritan or anti-Protestant.[26] The four lines which follow end in a manner unusually enigmatic for Behn:

> Thus cant the Faithful: nay, they're so uncivil,
> To pray us harmless Players to the Devil.
> When this is all th'Exception they can make,
> They damn us for Our Glorious Master's sake. (41–4)

Assuming that the players' profession is the exception or objection which the Puritans have against them, it remains to ascertain the identity of the 'Glorious Master': the King, perhaps, to crown the Puritans' disloyalty, or the Devil, or God. The epithet is many-voiced, and the couplets allow all these interpretations, but the resolution comes immediately in the concluding quatrain:

> But why 'gainst us do you unjustly arm?
> Our small religion sure can do no harm;
> Or if it do, since that's the only thing,
> We will reform when you are true to th'King. (45–8)

Players, because of the stage's traditional associations with immorality and falsehood, could be stigmatized as unreformed; the word and concept of reformation has been mocked to death earlier in the epilogue, in a manner both pro-Tory and implicitly pro-Catholic; and Behn, by championing the religion of the players, is proselytizing for a faith hinted at only through the mouths of the enemy. If this were not the case, the word 'religion' would be distracting: players had no distinctive faith, and other words would serve to convey the idea of a tight beleaguered community. But the conclusion – not, perhaps, to be read as entirely flippant – is entirely characteristic of Behn in subordinating sectarian religious spirit, Puritan or Catholic, to Tory monarchical loyalty. Again, the interpretative luxury afforded by the printed page must not be forgotten. Spoken, the offending couplets pass quickly, leaving behind nothing but a mild stimulant or irritant; but when read, they demand solution.

Another difference of emphasis between *The Feign'd Curtizans* and comparable plays written during the Popish Plot is almost as much to do with Behn's sex as her religious allegiance: the variations improvised upon the theme and stereotype of whoredom. In Protestant England the scarlet woman sitting upon the seven-headed beast in the Book of Revelation was synonymous with the Catholic Church, whose idolatry of images and of the Host during the Mass was seen as spiritual whoredom, and whose coruscating outward show of worldly power and ritual splendour concealed disease, vanity and emptiness. Behn's transcendence of gender stereotype, as a woman who wrote, combines with her sympathy to Catholicism to bring about a realization that neither print nor popery need imply a loss of female chastity:[27] it is striking, indeed, that women from Henrietta Maria to Elizabeth Cary, Lady Falkland, from the English Benedictine nuns on the Continent to the Jacobite Jane Barker, figure so prominently in English recusant literature and theatrical history.

The permutations of women, religion and whoredom in the dedication and the prologue are the preludes to the plot of the play: popish but chaste, it forces the conclusion that courtesans can be more innocent than they seem. A brief summary of the plot may be helpful. Two virtuous young women, Marcella and Cornelia, run away to Rome when their uncle threatens to marry Marcella off to a husband she does not love. In Rome they pose as courtesans under assumed names; two young English travellers fall in love with them, the high-principled Sir Harry Fillamour and his more worldly companion Frank Galliard. The dénouement is postponed by the scruples of Fillamour and by Marcella's uncle Count Morosini pursuing the fugitives. A farcical subplot is provided by the antics of two other English travellers, Sir Signal Buffoon and his guardian Mr Tickletext, a Dissenting preacher. Tickletext makes abortive attempts at an assignation with the supposed courtesans but is duped through the machinations of the girls' wily servant Pedro, who may be seen as an anti-pimp.

Tickletext is Behn's main vehicle for satire. His conception is explicitly anti-Dissent, following in a long line of lustful Puritans in stage and pamphlet which stretches from Zeal-of-the-Land Busy in Jonson's *Bartholomew Fair* (1614), through the farcical Royalist pamphlets written during the Civil War, to the heirs of these pamphlets in Tory polemic; but as these need not be, he is implicitly anti-Protestant.[28] Tickletext has been appointed Sir Signal Buffoon's guardian to ward off the 'eminent danger that young Travellers are in of being perverted to Popery' (i.i.p. 316), and his position as the Englishman abroad suggests that he is to be seen as a contemporary national type. His nationalism is stressed: when Sir Signal Buffoon calls his man Jack by the Italianization Giovanni, Tickletext retorts: 'Sir, by your favour, his English Protestant name is John Pepper, and I'll call him by ne'er a Popish name in Christendom' (i.ii.p. 321). Tickletext's type-name is carefully chosen, coupling the standard bawdy pun on 'conventicle' with a hint that, as indeed proves to be the case, he combines foreplay with improving scriptural reflections. When Pedro refers to him as 'my amorous Ananias' (iii.i.p. 362) he anticipates the name of Behn's other debauched Dissenting divine, Ananias Goggle in *The Roundheads* (1681).

When Sir Signal Buffoon at the beginning of the play flippantly suggests a visit to an Italian 'Bonaroba', Tickletext shows outrage and Sir Signal retreats, muttering 'Now my Tutor's up . . . and ever is when one names a Whore; be pacify'd, Man, be pacify'd, I know thou hat'st 'em worse than beads or Holy-water.' (i.ii.p. 320); and the referential conjunction of prostitution with Catholic paraphernalia is enough to suggest the Whore of Babylon. But in the same scene Tickletext attempts to arrange an amorous assignation, using the specious reasoning that sin is excusable in a notoriously sinful city.[29] The Scapinesque Petro, wily apologist for the Catholics, is trimming Tickletext's hair fashionably to help him ape Roman *mores*:

> T Why, Barberacho, I do not conceive any great matter of Sin only in visiting a Lady that loves a man, hah.

P Sin, Sir! 'tis a frequent thing now-a-days in Persons of your Complexion.[30]

T Especially here at Rome too, where 'tis no scandal.

P Ah, Signor, where the Ladies are privileged and Fornication licensed.

T Right! and when 'tis licens'd, 'tis lawful; and when 'tis lawful, it can be no Sin: besides, Barberacho, I may chance to turn[31] her, who knows?

P Turn her, Signor, alas, any way, which way you please.

T He, he, he! There thou wert knavish, I doubt – but I mean convert her – nothing else, I profess, Barberacho.

P True, Signior, true, she's a Lady of an easy nature, and an indifferent Argument well handled will do't.   (I.ii.pp. 3 1 7–1 8)

III.ii contains an episode, characteristic of Behn's exploitation of the satir-ical potential of stage properties, in which Tickletext is rallied by Fillamour on the enormous book he is carrying: 'But what Folio have you gotten there, Sir, *Knox*, or *Cartwright?*' Pedro is also at the scene, dis-guised as an antiquary, and his reaction is suggestive; suddenly retracting to Catholic orthodoxy, he says in an aside that if this is so, the whole thing has suddenly got beyond a joke: 'Nay, if he be got into that heap of Nonsense, I'll steal off and undress.' (p. 3 5 2).

When Sir Signal Buffoon catches Tickletext pursuing Cornelia in IV.i, he regurgitates the cant to which Tickletext has previously subjected him:

> For you, I say, to be taken at this unrighteous time of the Night, in a flaunting Cavaliero Dress, an unlawful Weapon by your side, going the high way to Satan, to a Curtezan; and to a Romish Curtezan! Oh Abomination! *O scandalum infinitum*!

Tickletext's instinctive reaction is to mutter 'Paid in my own Coin.' (p. 369). He then remembers his cover-story – that he is trying to convert Roman courtesans to Protestantism – and starts preaching at Cornelia, who naturally thinks he is mad; Sir Signal reassures her in classic anti-Puritan terms:

> Why we have a thousand of these in England that go loose about the streets, and pass with us for as sober discreet religious Persons, as a man shall wish to talk nonsense withal . . . nay, I confess . . . my Governour has a Fit that takes him now, and then, a kind of frensy, – a figary – a whimsy – a maggot, that bites always at the naming of Popery.   (p. 372)

With the diminishing of Sir Signal's epithets anti-Catholic prejudice becomes something that has to be explained away embarrassedly; in the middle of the Popish Plot, this speech is taking up an unequivocal party line.

Tickletext could not, perhaps, stand up to a point-by-point correspondence with Titus Oates, but he is an Oates-like figure. On the continent Oates travelled from one English Catholic seminary to another, while Tickletext travels Europe in the tireless quest to search out and condemn popery; both prove by their machinations popery's essential innocence of the charges laid against it.[32] Perhaps the most suggestive point in Tickletext's character is that he is pitifully superstitious; when he and Sir Signal find themselves in an unfamiliar house in v.iv, he believes Sir Signal's preposterous fantasy that it belongs to a rapacious giant, as something that is bound to happen in a 'Romish Heathenish Country' (p. 404). The suggestion that anti-Catholic myth springs from Dissenters' superstition and fear could hardly be more overt; and no Anglican corrective is presented. It is this dimension that makes Behn's anti-Dissent satire not only pro-Tory but pro-Catholic.

At least one other Catholic playwright had previously introduced onto the London stage Catholic sentiment half-concealed under criticism of Dissent. In 1670 Molière's *Tartuffe* had been performed in London, translated by the writer, comedian and Catholic Matthew Medburne.[33] Medburne comments in the dedication that 'what considerable Additionals I have made thereto, in order to its more plausible Appearance in the English Theatre, I leave to be observ'd by those who shall give themselves the trouble of comparing the several Editions of this Comedy' (A3). Medburne certainly tilts his translation at English puritans, but it is the epilogue which gives the most unmistakable direction as to how the play should be read. Spoken by Medburne himself, it contained a justification of Catholicism at once defiant and multi-layered in its irony:

> We Godly phrase [lust] Gospel-Propagation;
> Just as Rebellion was called Reformation.[34]
> Though Zeal stand Centry at the Gate of Sin,
> Yet all who have the Word pass freely in;
> Silent and in the Dark for fear of Spies
> We march, and take damnation by surprise:

There's not a Raving Blade about the Town
Can go so far towards Hell for Half a Crown
As I for Six-pence;[35] 'cause I know the way;
For want of Guides men are too apt to stray.   (p. 66)

On one level, this is conventional satire attacking the puritans for hypocrisy, sexual immorality and sedition. Their night-time business is left unclear; the 'Gate of Sin' may lead either to a conventicle or a bawdy-house, and the 'fear of Spies' can be read as wariness of sexual scandal or of government informers. This lack of definition also allows Medburne to incorporate a further layer of reference, not merely anti-Puritan but anti-Protestant. The 'Rebellion . . . called Reformation' suggests both the godly risings of the 1640s and the Protestant Reformation as a whole; and the line 'For want of Guides men are too apt to stray' is not merely Tartuffe's claim to urbanity but Medburne's comment on the displacement of papal authority by private judgement. Tartuffe speaks more wisely than he is aware; and Medburne is utilizing the extremely common polemical device of condemning an opponent out of his own mouth.[36]

Moreover, it must not be forgotten that Medburne is speaking Tartuffe's lines. As with Betty Currer in her role as feigned courtesan, the interplay between character and actor must be attended to as part of the irony. The dangerous word 'Reformation' would have called to attention those members of the audience who knew of Medburne's Catholicism, and from then onwards, the passage is susceptible to ironic inversion. Puritan Zeal positively encourages Catholics, 'all who have the Word', to pass through the gate of that which puritanism defines as sin; and Medburne admits that he is better able to head towards hell than most, because he knows 'the way' and is unlikely to confuse hell with heaven. The underground force of Catholics, 'Silent and in the Dark for fear of Spies', is then shown to have had the virtuous aim of surprising and confounding damnation head-on.

When suspicion and accusation threatened on one side, and Laodiceanism or apostasy on the other, Catholic and pro-Catholic wits like Medburne and Behn had to be practised at the various ironies necessary to deflect and redirect accusations that they were damned. Irony, the casuistry of the comic, was a tool necessary for physical and spiritual survival. But it could not save Medburne, who was to become one of the minor martyrs of the Popish Plot: a one-time friend and associate of Oates, he was exposed by Oates and died in prison in the spring of 1679, the season that *The Feign'd Curtizans* was performed.[37]

Behn was less overt and less passionate than Medburne, and survived. Nothing in *The Feign'd Curtizans* is as overtly provocative as Medburne's epilogue to *Tartuffe*, but the gaps demand to be read. Only Catholicism is demonstrated as filling the moral vacuum that Behn's mockery of Dissent leaves behind it. The English hero Fillamour, as well as the Italian characters in the play, seems to subscribe to this prevailing moral climate: when Tickletext complains in Act 1 Scene ii that the religious pictures he sees all around him are 'Superstition, idolatrous, and flat Popery', he replies 'I'll convince you of that Error, that persuades you that harmless Pictures are idolatrous' (p. 325). That there is a moral vacuum to fill is remarkable, and suggests that Behn must have been unusually concerned with portraying Catholicism in a respectable light in this play, and at this time. Fillamour is unusually moral for a Behn hero, and his testimony carries weight; more usually, her anti-heroic banished cavaliers lend street credibility but not moral force to doing as the Romans do. It is a characteristic of Behn's that she both undercuts and exploits notions of Catholic naughtiness; a novel like *The History of the Nun* would be inconceivable outside a tradition of lascivious convent anecdote.[38] Not even *The Feign'd Curtizans* is without vestigial traces of this: a minor character, Laura Lucretia, confesses at the start of the play when accused of flirting with a stranger in St Peter's that she has not gone to church this morning 'with any other Devotion, but that which warms my Heart for my young English Cavalier' (1.i.p. 310), a remark which sounds indignantly respectable at first, then quite irreligious. But this needs to be assessed against the background of Behn's entire comic corpus; it is very underplayed compared to a play like *The Rover II* (1681), set in Catholic Madrid, which, like most of her comedies, conforms to the Restoration model of amorality and intrigue.

Given that *The Rover II* was performed in the same year as the cautious apologetics of *The Roundheads*, it is tempting to accuse Behn of inconsistency. There is some truth in this, but it affords a way of understanding both Behn's mentality and that of her age. Like Restoration atheism, Catholicism could be avowed as a writerly technique of shocking: but shocking within an arena where discussion of the subject was common. Restoration London was not a society where the subject was placed under referential interdiction and its practitioners obliged to foregather in complete secrecy. Though officially proscribed, it was visible – especially at court – and the wit of Behn and others, which postulates an audience, may imply that in some circles it was winked at in practice. But more visible still were anti-Catholic laws and pamphlets; like practising homosexuals in societies illiberal towards their activities, Catholics could make their preferences more or less evident, yet could never be certain of toleration. A rueful acknowledgement of forced marginalization, shot with complicated ironies, may lie behind what seems Behn's blatantly amoral adoption of stereotype; but at times, irony seems very like advocacy. Behn, the ex-spy with libertine leanings, can perhaps be said to have formulated and enjoyed a kind of Catholic camp: a combination of elaborate secrecy, wit, implied revelrous misbehaviour and cautious proselytization.[39] The equation of Catholicism with sin, which both Behn and Medburne employ to put Protestants off the scent, seems also to have had a more straightforward and more impious use; Behn may have been attracted to Catholicism not in spite of its status as an officially outlawed faith, but because of it.

The comparison with freethinking does not end there. If one is to describe Behn as a Catholic, or even simply as pro-Catholic, one must immediately afterwards stress some very important provisos. Her habit of mind is characteristically eclectic, even sceptical; she flirts with the commonplaces of religion to an extent which, in the seventeenth century, earned the epithet of atheist.[40] Deep spiritual needs cannot be demonstrated from her writing. She seems to have valued Catholicism for a number of non-religious reasons: for its visual beauty – the description of Octavio being received into the Bernardines in *Love-Letters between a Nobleman and his Sister* (1694) is a masterpiece of baroque [41] – for its cloak-and-dagger aspects so well demonstrated by the comedy of intrigue she wrote, and for the opportunities it gave her for Tory mischief. In these respects she conforms to the baldest of anti-Catholic stereotypes: how deliberately it is hard to say, but Behn was adept at self-fashioning. *The Feign'd Curtizans* is unique in Behn's oeuvre in downplaying Catholic wickedness reconceived as Catholic naughtiness; but in so doing, in the charged times in which it was written, it demonstrates her characteristic combination of acute political sensitivity and provocativeness.

NOTES

1 *The Works of Aphra Behn*, ed. Montague Summers (London, 1915), IV, p. 8, lines 15–18. All quotations are taken from this edition in cases where the relevant volume of Janet Todd's edition (see below) has not yet been published.
2 Pope Joan was often regarded as historical in the seventeenth century: see C.A. Patrides, *Premises and Motifs in Renaissance Thought and Literature* (Princeton, New Jersey, 1982), ch. 10. A hostile dramatic account of her appeared during the Popish Plot: Elkanah Settle's *The Female Prelate* (1680).
3 Two standard accounts are John Bossy, *The English Catholic Community 1570–1850* (London, 1975); Edward Norman, *Roman Catholicism in England* (Oxford, 1975).
4 See the general introduction (esp. pp. xiii–xiv) in vol. 1 of *The works of Aphra Behn*, ed. Janet Todd (London, 1992). Both Maureen Duffy, *The Passionate Shepherdess* (London, 1976), pp. 92–3, and Angeline Goreau, *Reconstructing Aphra* (Oxford, 1980), p. 13, suggest that there may have been a Catholic influence in her upbringing, but the most recent study of Behn's early life suggests a Protestant family: see Jane Jones, 'New light on the background and early life of Aphra Behn', reprinted in this volume.
5 Gerald Duchovnay, 'Aphra Behn's religion', *Notes and Queries* 221 (1976), 235–7.
6 *Aphra Behn: An Annotated Bibliography of Primary and Secondary Sources* (New York, 1986), pp. 2–3.
7 Behn, *Works*, ed. Todd, 1, p. 292.
8 The word 'flirt' was used by Patrick Lyons in 'From Astraea to Aesop: Aphra Behn's versions of pastoral' (unpublished lecture delivered at the University of London Department of Extra-Mural Studies' conference on Behn, January 1988). For a succinct discussion of the effect of Behn's Toryism on her drama, see George Guffey, 'Aphra Behn's *Oroonoko*: occasion and accomplishment', in *Two English Novelists: Aphra Behn and Anthony Trollope* (Los Angeles, 1975), pp. 9–15.

9 See John Kenyon, *The Popish Plot* (London, 1972), esp. pp. 161–8 for the
   penalties that a declared recusant would have suffered; John Miller, *Popery
   and Politics in England, 1660–1688* (Cambridge, 1973), esp. pp. 163–9. In
   'Pretences of state: Aphra Behn and the female plot', in *Rereading Aphra
   Behn: history, theory, and criticism*, ed. Heidi Huttner (Charlottesville, 1993)
   Ros Ballaster points to the discussions in Behn's novels of oath-taking
   during the Popish Plot, and the possibility of Catholic perjury: see also
   Susan Staves, *Players' Sceptres: Fictions of Authority in the Restoration*
   (Lincoln, 1979), p. 193.

10 See Allardyce Nicoll, 'Political plays of the Restoration', *MLR*, 16 (1921),
   pp. 224–42; George Whiting, 'Political satire in London stage plays,
   1680–1683', *MP*, 28 (1930), pp. 29–43; Robert Hume, *The Development of
   English Drama in the Late Seventeenth Century* (Oxford, 1976), esp. ch. 8.
   The epilogue to *The Feign'd Curtizans* laments the plight of the
   playhouses: see Behn, *Works*, ed. Summers, II, pp. 411–12.

11 *The Dramatic Works of John Crowne*, ed. James Maidment and W.H. Logan
   (Edinburgh, 1873–4), III, p. 240.

12 See *The Works of John Dryden*, ed. Alan Roper et al., 19 vols. (Berkeley,
   1984), XIII, pp. 219–24 (dedication), 498, 516, 522, 354–5.

13 Duffy (1976), p. 170.

14 Behn, *Works*, ed. Summers, II, p. 305.

15 As 'unequalled in hyperbolical adulation': *Lives of the English Poets*, ed.
   George Birkbeck Hill (Oxford, 1905), I, p. 399.

16 It will become clear that I take a more suspicious attitude to the play than
   Jane Spencer does in her recent essay, '"Deceit, dissembling, all that's
   woman": comic plot and female action in *The Feign'd Curtizans*' (Huttner
   (ed.) (1993), pp. 86–101), where she asserts that it has 'no prominent
   political message' (p. 92).

17 cf. Dryden's dedication to *The Kind Keeper, or Mr Limberham*: 'The Great
   Plot of the Nation, like one of Pharaoh's lean Kine, has devour'd its
   younger Brethren of the Stage . . .' (Dryden, *Works*, ed. Roper et al., XIV,
   p. 3).

18 See W.C. Abbott, 'The origin of Titus Oates's story', *English Historical
   Review*, 25, pp. 126–9; Caroline Hibbard, *Charles I and the Popish Plot*
   (Chapel Hill, 1983), esp. the appendix on the Plot tradition and Catholic
   historiography.

19 cf. Behn's prologue to *The False Count* (1681): 'For Wit's profane, and
   Jesuitical, / And Plotting's Popery, and the Devil and all'. (III, p. 100,
   lines 42–3.)

20 'Cully' probably means 'client' in this context (*OED*).

21 There is only one sympathetic Anglican character in Behn's plays, Merriwill in *The City-Heiress* (1682).

22 *pace* Tim Harris, *London crowds in the reign of Charles II: propaganda and politics from the Restoration to the Exclusion Crisis* (Cambridge, 1987), p. 103. A broadsheet political verse of 1685, attributed to Behn, incorporates a mischievous pro-Catholic reference to expelling 'Shamploting Sin' and other evils by 'an holy Water': see Janet Todd, '*Rebellions Antidote*: a new attribution to Aphra Behn', *Notes and Queries* 236 (1991), pp. 175–7.

23 cf. also in the epilogue to *The Rover* (i, p. 105, lines 1–5); prologue to *The Roundheads* (i.p. 341, lines 1–7); prologue to *The Young King* (ii.p. 106, lines 25–6); prologue to *The False Count* (iii, p. 100, lines 29–42).

24 See David Cressy, *Bonfires and Bells* (London, 1989), for the fullest recent account of this and other political celebrations on Queen Elizabeth's 'crownation' day.

25 Woundy = very (*OED*).

26 Arnold Hunt suggests that the reference to 'Plunder, Sequestration' is intended to refer more directly to the Henrician dissolution of monasteries than to events during the Civil War.

27 See Catherine Gallagher, 'Who was that masked woman? the prostitute and the playwright in the comedies of Aphra Behn', in Huttner (ed.) (1993), pp. 65–85.

28 Examples are *The Puritaine, or the Widow of Watling-streete* (1607), *Sphinx Lugduno-Genevensis* (1683). See also Lois Potter, *Secret rites and secret writing: Royalist literature 1641–1660* (Cambridge, 1989).

29 Behn has earlier played upon Rome's reputation by giving Galliard the lines 'Innocent Passion at Rome! Oh, 'tis not to be nam'd but in some Northern Climate: to be an Anchoret here, is to be an Epicure in Greenland . . .' (i.i.p. 312).

30 Given the contemporary pronunciation of 'persons', an anticlerical gibe may be intended.

31 For this use of 'turn' cf. iv.i, p. 369.

32 Behn alludes to Oates mockingly throughout the prologue of *The City-Heiress* (1682): (ii, pp. 201–2, and note at p. 433.)

33 *Tartuffe* is usually interpreted as a critique of Jansenism, and the cartoon characteristics which puritans and Jansenists shared are those which interested Medburne. However, it has also been argued that *Tartuffe* is anti-Jesuits; see Andrew Calder, 'Dramaturgie et polemique dans *Le Tartuffe de Molière*', in *Les Jesuites parmi les hommes, aux XVIe et XVIIe siècles* (Faculté des Lettres et Sciences Humaines de L'Université de Clermont-Ferrand ii, 1987), pp. 235–43.

34 See Behn's use of 'Reformation' in the epilogue to *The Roundheads*, discussed above. Its subsidiary bawdy implication is also apparent here: cf. the title of Joseph Arrowsmith's *The Reformation* (1673) in which a new moral order is planned that will allow sexual licence to women.

35 Sixpence may have been the stock comic sum for a miserly client to pay to a whore: see 'The penurious Quaker' in T. D'Urfey's *Pills to purge melancholy* (1719–20), in which the Quaker tells the whore '. . . thou wilt make me pay, / So here is Six pence for thee.' (Quoted by David Blamires, 'Quakers observed in verse and prose', in Blamires et al. (eds) *A Quaker Miscellany for Edward H. Milligan* (Manchester, 1985), p. 19.)

36 This technique was particularly associated with Catholic controversialists, not just as a rhetorical device but as a means of expressing their own enforced silence. See Peter Milward, *Religious controversies of the Jacobean age* (London, 1978), p. 151.

37 Kenyon (1972), pp. 47, 63, 82. See also William Smith, *Intrigues of the Popish Plot Laid Open* (1685).

38 See Jacqueline Pearson, 'The history of *The History of the Nun*', in Huttner (ed.) (1993), pp. 234–52.

39 For Behn's career in espionage, see Alan Marshall, *Intelligence and espionage in the reign of Charles II, 1660–1685* (Cambridge, 1994), pp. 136–7.

40 See Behn, *Works*, ed. Todd, I, pp. xiii, xxxi (note 11).

41 Behn, *Works*, ed. Todd, II, pp. 379–83. See also Maureen Duffy's comments in the introduction to her edition, p. xiv.

3 Fiction feigning femininity: false counts and pageant kings in Aphra Behn's Popish Plot writings

ROS BALLASTER

Aphra Behn's writing of the late 1670s and early 1680s explores the potential of artifice as a form of political agency, a preoccupation which seems to have been crystallized for her in the greatest political 'fraud' of the century, that of the Popish Plot. The startling twists and turns of the plot disclosures functioned for many writers in this period, many of them Behn's close associates, as a form of political theatre to be watched and interpreted. Entering the war of words around the Popish Plot was a risky business for the professional writer however, as Behn's arrest, along with the actress who delivered it (Lady Slingsby), for an incendiary epilogue to an anonymous play called *The Tragedy of Romulus* in August 1682 demonstrates.[1] The literary analogy of 'plotting' with the political controversy of a supposed Catholic plot to assassinate the king, seems to have been so powerful that no author could evade the association. Even a disclaimer functioned as an indicator of satire. An epilogue to a now lost play by Behn of 1682, *Like Father, Like Son*, announces 'Nor *Whigg*, nor *Tory* here can take offence, / It libels neither Patriot, Peer nor Prince.'[2] The epilogue goes on to claim:

> Tho' here are Fools of every Fashion,
> Except State Fools, the Fools of Reformation.
> And these Originals decline so fast,
> We shall have none to Copy by at last. (*Poetry*, p. 21)

Behn here highlights the peculiar reversal whereby literary representation in this period felt itself to be subordinate to the proliferating fictions

50

acted out in political life. The 'real' world has become a vast fiction which provides the source for the 'fictional' worlds attempt to filter out the reality behind the plots. As the political plot moves towards its conclusion, the fictional plot is running short of 'copy'.

It is this period toward the close of the Popish Plot controversy that forms the focus for this article. Turning from Alison Shell's discussion of *The Feign'd Curtizans*, written and produced at the height of the Popish Plot in 1679, I will focus on two works: first, a later comedy, *The False Count*, written and produced when the crisis appeared to be averted in November 1681 and second, a short comical fiction, 'Memoirs of The Court of the King of Bantam', not published until 1698 in *All the Histories and Novels Written by the Late Ingenious Mrs Behn*, but set at Christmas 1682 and composed before February 1685.[3]

The narrative that provided the analogical source for these two works can be summarized as follows. In August 1678, a country parson, Israel Tonge and a gentleman who held a minor appointment in the royal laboratory, Christopher Kirkby, brought to the attention of Charles II a supposed plot led by English Catholics to murder him in order to secure the succession of his Catholic brother, James, Duke of York. Charles appears to have been sceptical, but handed the matter over to Danby, the Lord Treasurer, to receive information from their informant, Titus Oates, an Anglican clergyman who had converted to Catholicism in March 1677. Oates claimed to have acted as courier for letters between the Jesuit seminary of St Omers in Northern France and the English Jesuits. Charles's scepticism increased when James showed him five forged letters to Thomas Bedingfield, James's Jesuit confessor, which appear to have originated with Oates. The entire matter might have been contained to the king and his brother, Danby and the Privy Council, and been quietly dropped, if the Justice of the Peace who had heard Oates swear to the truth of his information on 6 September and 28 September, Sir Edmund Bury Godfrey, had not been found dead on the evening of 17 October in a ditch at the foot of Primrose Hill. He appeared to have been strangled and subsequently run through with his own sword some days before the discovery of the body. On 23 October, Oates was called to give evidence at the bar of the House of Commons.

The forty-three articles which Tonge had originally presented from Oates to Danby were swollen to eighty-one in his sixty-eight page deposition, listing some ninety-nine conspirators ranging from Catholic peers to James's secretary, Edward Coleman, to the Queen's physician, Sir George Wakeman, to four Irish ruffians supposedly hired to dispatch the King at Windsor. On 27 October, Oates's lone voice was strengthened by a letter from a con-man in Bristol named William Bedloe who claimed to have evidence on Godfrey's death. On 26 November the first execution in connection with the Popish Plot was carried out – that of one William Staley, a Catholic banker from Covent Garden who had been overheard calling the king a heretic and expressing his willingness to kill him. On 3 December, Coleman was executed at Tyburn. In December 1678 two more witnesses added yet more 'credibility' to the evidence – Miles Prance, a Catholic silversmith in Covent Garden who appears to have turned evidence in exchange for a pardon and Stephen Dugdale, land steward to the Catholic Lord Aston in Staffordshire.

Entering into print without the protection of anonymity could incur serious penalties in this period. Elizabeth Cellier, a Catholic midwife and the wife of a French merchant, was cleared in June 1680 of treason in the famous 'Meal-Tub-Plot' trial; she had been accused of manufacturing evidence of a republican Protestant plot to cast suspicion on Catholics. But in September she was tried and convicted of publishing a libel (*Malice Defeated*), her sentence a thousand pound fine and three hour-long pillories at the Strand, Charing Cross and Covent Garden with her books burned before her. Cellier was allowed to carry a wooden shield at the pillory to fend off the violence of her attackers.

Writing lay at the centre of the Popish Plot from Titus Oates's published depositions to Elizabeth Cellier's vindications. Writing was a means for literate observers of and protagonists in political culture to 'make public' their views on subjects as varied as international relations, sovereign power, religious controversy, recent history, politicians, peers and royalty. Yet, the attempt to 'make sense' of this profound public crisis was often expressed through an analogue with the private world, that of sexual relations between men and women or familial relations between parents and children. Analogy, according to Holman and Hannon's *Handbook to English Literature* can be understood as 'A comparison of two things, alike in certain aspects; particularly a method used in EXPOSITION and DESCRIPTION by which something unfamiliar is explained or described by comparing it to something more familiar.'[4] In the publications surrounding the Popish Plot, one 'plot' (a political one) is insistently 'explained' by another (a sexual one). However, this ideological attempt to 'secure' a crisis (a threat to the monarch by his rebellious subjects) by interpreting it through another narrative of conflict and resolution (the rebellion of women and/or children contained by the arbitrary power of a patriarch), has a curiously destabilizing effect in that it leaves uncertain which narrative is the 'fiction', that of political difference or sexual difference.

At first sight, the Popish Plot appears to have been a controversy in which women have no place; men were the primary actors in this drama from the king and his brother, to Commons' members of Parliament and the members of the House of Lords, to the bishops, judges, witnesses, and writers whose versions of events appeared in the flood of printed matter associated with the plot. Yet, one of the most publicized trials involved a woman, the Catholic midwife, Elizabeth Cellier. Protestant satirists presented Cellier in familiar anti-Papist terms as Babylonian whore, exploiting her professional association with the management of childbirth and succession.

A poem entitled 'The Loyal Protestants New Litany' that appeared on 24 November 1680, some three months after Collier's conviction for libel for her pamphlet, *Malice Defeated*, neatly demonstrates this slippage from biblical metaphor to concrete instance:

> From the Romish Whore with her Tripple Crown,
> From the Plots she hath hatch'd, and her Babes now disown,
> Though they dy'd with a Lie in their mouth is well known.
> > *Libera nos Domine.*

> From such as presume to speak ill of Queen *Bess*.
> From a Popish Midwife in a Sanctifyed Dress,
> Adorn'd with a wood Ruff for a Crest   *Libera nos Domine.*[5]

A number of ideological prompts are given simultaneously in these two opening stanzas. The Catholic church is a foreign whore who foists her 'children' (the plots against the English King's life) on an England whose virtue is secured by the image of Queen Elizabeth, protector of the Church of England and virgin Queen. Her 'babes', whom she then 'disowns' (claims are not her own) are the plotters who were executed insisting on their innocence. The fact that so many convicted plotters refused to confess and declared their innocence on the scaffold was a constant source of anxiety to those who insisted on the truth of the plot, but was frequently explained by recourse to representations of the Catholic practice of absolution as a means of exonerating Catholics of sin if they were acting on behalf of the Church.

The image of Elizabeth Cellier at the pillory defending herself with a wooden shield is presented as a mockery of familiar images of Queen Elizabeth in her ruff and royal regalia. Where the Queen's virgin body prevented foreign pollution from entering the country, Elizabeth Cellier's trade of midwifery aids the foisting of illegitimate children upon virtuous Protestant families. The language of contamination and corruption by foreign powers through the medium of the female body was extended in pamphlet writing of the period to the Crown itself, and in particular to Charles II's perchant for Catholic foreign women, extending from the Queen, Catherine of Braganza (whom Titus Oates accused of conspiring with her physician, George Wakeman, to poison her husband) to his mistress Louise de Kéroualle, Duchess of Portsmouth, who had come to England with Charles's sister, the Duchess of Orleans, in 1670 when the Treaty of Dover was being negotiated, a Treaty which had resulted in increasing leniency toward English Catholics. An indictment of 1679, 'Articles of High Treason, and other high Crimes and Misdemeanours against the Duchess of Portsmouth', took as its first article the claim that the Duchess had 'foul, nauseous, and contagious distempers . . . to the manifest danger and hazard of the King's person'. A satirical poem of the same year, probably written by Charles Sackville, Earl of Dorset, entitled 'Colin' adopted the conceit of representing the Duchess as an important Minister of State who, under public pressure, is obliged to 'sell' her place to a successor. A number of English court ladies compete for the honour. This poem too represents Louise de Kéroualle as a danger to the King's person – her sexual activities drain him of financial potency:

> Each night with her dear was as sessions
> O'th'House, and fuller of petitions,
> Which drain'd him till he was not able
> To keep his Council or a table.[6]

The association of Catholicism with female sexual licence and rebellion becomes conventional in representations of the Popish plot. Narcissus Luttrell in the entry for April 1679 of his *A Brief Historical Relation of State Affairs* records that:

> Severall maid servants are committed to prison on suspition of fireing their masters &c. houses; and particularly the servant of one Mr Bird, an atturney in Fetter lane: which fire was happily discovered by the watch, and quenched in time. She has since confest she did it at the instigation of a popish preist.[7]

A pamphlet of the same year, 'The Present Great Interest both of King and People' argued that papists had particular success 'among a sort of religious women, who, when they had thrown off all sense of modesty and honesty, sheltered themselves under the priests shroud of confession and absolution'. Thus, women figured as both seducers and seduced in the analogical drama of the Popish Plot. They were understood to be particularly vulnerable to the seductive strategies of the Catholic Church, which allowed them to conceal and continue sexually unorthodox behaviour and they in turn employed their seductive powers in the bedchamber to drain English Protestant men of their loyalty, financial power and political authority. The response to women's involvement in the plot then clearly indicates a connection between femininity and fraud, the dissemination of scandal and the birth of illegitimate rumour with female reproductive capacity.

Elizabeth Cellier's narrative of her imprisonment and trial for treason is remarkably astute in its recognition of this process whereby women are excluded from a 'masculine' romance of politics and simultaneously subjected to accusations of inventing their own fraudulent versions of events. At a number of points in *Malice Defeated*, literary analogies of narratives of sexual intrigue are employed to present Cellier as distressed victim of masculine plotting. Her questioner, Sir Robert Waller, who visited her in Newgate, she firmly rebuffs with the words:

> *I am not such a* Distressed Damosel *to use your Service. For as the Devil can do harm, but not good; so, though you have put me in, yet it is not in your power to fetch me out of* this inchanted Castle, *but I shall come out e'er long to a Glorious Death, or an Honourable Life, both which are indifferent to me, blessed be God.*[8]

When she is questioned before the Privy Council, Cellier turns to analogues from the drama:

A LORD Your Tryal will come soon enough, you will be put to death.
CELLIER *Blessed be God, then I hope the Play is near an end, for Tragedies whether real or fictious, seldom end before the Women die.*
A LORD You talk very peremptorily.
CELLIER *My Lord, I thank God Death is no Terror to me, and she that fears not to die, cannot fear to speak Truth.*   (p. 30)

Finally, Cellier turns to her own 'romance making' as a counter to the chief witness against her, Thomas Dangerfield, who, having gained the trust of Cellier and her confederates, had turned evidence against them. Dangerfield produced a picaresque narrative of his own life and times under the title, *Don Tomazo, or the Juvenile Rambles of Thomas Dangerfield* in 1680, which Cellier swiftly countered with *The Matchless Rogue; or, a Brief Account of the Life and Many Exploits of Don Thomazo*. Cellier's version turns out to be an 'anti-romance' in which she deflects the accusations of fabricating plots back onto its source, describing Thomazo and his partner in crime, Don Roderigo, as 'both right *Romantick Heroes*', who 'have added much to the small adventures of others, and related many imaginary ones of me, which never entered into my thoughts, I having from my Childhood abominated such Practices' (p. 1). Whether the 'practices' are to do with the creation of romances or sexual slurs cast upon

Cellier in the course of Dangerfield's narrative and her trial remains deliberately ambiguous, and it is precisely this slippage between fictionalizing and female sexuality that Behn exploits so effectively in her Popish Plot writings.

Since most Popish Plots writings were published anonymously, it cannot be stated with confidence that Behn and Cellier were the only women to enter the controversy in print.[9] However, they are remarkable in their consistent advertisement of the relevance of their female authorship to the position they take on the 'truth' of the plot and the sexual dynamics of its representations. Aphra Behn, like Cellier, was a Catholic sympathizer writing and publishing at the same time as the Popish Plot controversy came to a head. Like Cellier, Behn uses gendered analogies culled from the tropes and conventions of contemporary literary culture to dramatize the Popish Plot and the metaphorical and material roles of women in its representation. Like Cellier, too, her defence of a pro-Catholic Toryism hinges on the issue of the fictional nature of the Protestant Exclusionists' accusations.

As the trials, debates and publications on the Popish Plot continued to proliferate and the conviction of the 'truth' of the plot became increasingly hard to maintain, it became common for commentators to acknowledge the 'fictional' nature of politics in general. The political order itself came to be understood as a kind of necessary 'fiction', maintained through the balancing of different narrative versions of 'events', the truth of which were ultimately irretrievable. Roger North's anecdote concerning Anthony Ashley Cooper, Earl of Shaftesbury, prime mover in the Exclusion Bill and the subsequent Protestant Rye House Plot to establish Charles II's illegitimate son, James Scott, Duke of Monmouth as his successor, neatly demonstrates this process:

> A certain Lord of his Confidence in Parliament, once asked him what he intended to do with the Plot, which was so full of Nonsense, as would scarce go down with *tantum-non* Ideots; what then could he propose by pressing the Belief of it upon men of Common Sense, and especially in Parliament? It's no Matter, said he, the more Nonsensical the better; if we cannot bring them to swallow worse Nonsense than that, we shall never do any Good with them.[10]

The Popish Plot seems to have become a form of popular entertainment in its own right. As Jonathan Scott puts it, trials were 'acts of political theatre, to express, and to that extent assuage, a general public concern'.[11] The Prologue to Behn's *The Feign'd Curtizans: or, a Night's Intrigue* of 1679 had the actress, Mrs Currer, complain 'The Devil take this cursed plotting Age, / 'T has ruin'd all our Plots upon the Stage'. In an important way, of course, the scandal surrounding the Popish Plot did nothing of the kind, rather it gave artists and writers a peculiar power, which they readily exploited, as themselves 'plotters' of a different, yet analogical, kind. Claiming to 'plot' in a preface, prologue, epilogue was to point to the analogical status of the literary production, to invite the reader or spectator to interpret the text in the light of contemporary events. Behn took a particular and gender-specific advantage of this new linking of artistic with political activity.

'The Court of the King of Bantam' and *The False Count: or, a New Way to Play an Old Game* are both concerned with 'pageant kings' and a counterplot of trickery in which women are the prime movers. In the former Mr Would-Be, a commoner convinced by a prophecy in his youth that he will be a king is tricked by a group of impoverished aristocrats into sleeping with a prostitute convinced she is an heiress and providing a dowry for a woman so that she can marry the man she really loves.[12] In the latter, a wealthy commoner, jealous of his beautiful wife, is convinced that he has been captured by Turks and persuaded in fear of his life to prostitute his wife to her lover, while his daughter, obsessed with marrying into the nobility, is tricked into marriage with a chimney sweep passing himself off as an aristocrat.[13] These aspiring aristocrats neatly satirize a number of Whig figures, in particular Shaftesbury who in 1675 aspired to rival John Sobieski for the elective monarchy of Poland, and James Scott, Duke of Monmouth who, along with Shaftesbury, was reputed to place considerable weight on augurs, prophecy and astrology and was of course a 'would-be king'. The figure of the 'would-be king' might also apply to Titus Oates who sought to buy himself a peerage and was famous for his false claims. However, both the novella and play are also comedies of intrigue in which women co-operate in a 'plot' engineered by their lovers to free them from oppression in marriage 'passing themselves off' as something other than they are, 'prostitutes' and 'virtuous wives', two sides of the same coin. Like Behn's 'feigned courtesans', Marcella and Cornelia, these heroines have to learn to gain control of the mechanics of fiction. 'Truth', in these re-versions of the Popish Plot, provides no effective counterweight to hypocrisy and lies.

Behn, in other works, does invoke truth as an important, if ineffec-tive, political tool. 'A Poem to Sir Roger L'Estrange', first published in a broadside in 1688, praised the Tory journalist and official press 'Licenser' for his 1687 *Brief History of the Times* in which he argued that Sir Edmund Berry Godfrey's death was a suicide rather than, as Protestant agitators claimed, a murder by Catholics seeking to prevent disclosure of the plot. L'Estrange's unpopular and vocal views resulted in his retreat abroad in the winter of 1680–1 and the burning of his effigy in London. Behn opens her poem by describing L'Estrange as one who 'like a pitying God, does *Truth* advance, / Rescuing the *World* from stupid Ignorance'.[14] The poem, like Behn's 'The Golden Age', is coloured by a pastoral nostalgia for a prelapsarian world in which truth formed souls:

> 'Till Man by *Vice* and *Villany* betray'd,
> By *Perjury* and false *Ambition* sway'd,
> Banisht the Noble *Vertue* from its Seat,
> As *Useless* in the Politick, and Great. (p. 291)

As in 'The Golden Age' and the utopian rendering of the Surinam Indian culture in her novella *Oroonoko*, however, the invocation of a 'state of nature' seems to perform an ambiguous function, since truth emerges as a virtuous but entirely ineffective form of political behaviour. L'Estrange's truth is, the poem acknowledges, not necessarily 'heard': ''Tis plain! and he denies the Noon-day light, / Who questions the vast Reason which you write' (p. 293). That there are those who 'deny the Noon-day light' is equally plain.

Behn's writings in the early 1680s suggest a more complex form of response than the truth claims of l'Estrange: a form of 'counter-plotting' or fictionalizing which exploits rather than simply decrying the paranoia of the Whig advocates of Popish plotting. In *The False Count*, Francisco, the English shoemaker turned wealthy merchant recently married to a young Spanish bride, is revealed to be a creature of superstition and misogyny; his wife's lover, Carlos, the Governor of Cadiz, develops a complex trick to win Julia back and trap Francisco into providing a dowry for his daughter's marriage to a chimney-sweep, built on those prejudices. Francisco is persuaded that the ship on which Guiliom, the chimney-sweep passing himself off as an aristocrat, is entertaining his future father-in-law and his entourage, has been seized by Turks. Don Carlos' estate is transformed into a Turkish court and Carlos himself is presented as the Sultan who will castrate Francisco unless he persuades his wife to sleep with his captor. This revenge, presented explicitly in the play as a 'Plot', works because it realizes Francisco's paranoid fantasies of cuckoldry. Chiding his wife for her desire to accept the Governor's invitation for her and her sister, Clara, to visit him, Francisco rants: 'what pity 'twas I carried you not in my hand, presented you to him my self, and beg'd him to favour me so much to do my office a little for me, or the like' (Act I, Scene ii, *Five Plays*, p. 314).

Francisco's particular venom is reserved for his wife's woman, Jacinta, whom he 'reads' on the model of Luttrell's account of incendiary serving-maids, admitting unholy influences into honourable families. He walks in on a conference between his wife, her sister, and Jacinta exclaiming:

FRANCISCO So, together consulting and contriving.
 JACINTA What, are you jealous of the Petticoat?
FRANCISCO Petticoat! Come, come, Mistress *Pert*, I have known as much
  danger hid under a Petticoat, as a pair of Breeches. I have heard of two
  Women that married each other – oh abominable, as if there were so
  prodigious a scarcity of Christian Mans Flesh.
 JACINTA No, the Market's well enough stored, thanks be praised, might
  very Woman be afforded a reasonable Allowance.
FRANCISCO Peace, I say, thou Imp of Lucifer; wou'd thou hadst thy Bellyful,
  that I might be fairly rid of thee. . . (Act II, Scene i, p. 321)

Francisco locates sexual conspiracy in the all-female community he has created by locking his wife away from the social environment which he fears will give her access to her lover. His paranoia about his wife's accessibility to other lovers extends to her maid-servant and the imagined possibility of lesbianism. His fears are not of course baseless – his wife *is* seeking opportunities to meet with her lover and Jacinta *is* the prime mediator in their affair. However, he is, like the Protestant conspiracy-theorists of the Popish Plots, looking in the wrong place. While he has his eyes firmly fixed on his wife, the 'conspirators' (Carlos and his friend Antonio who is in love with Julia's sister) are setting up Guiliom the chimney-sweep to court his daughter Isabella and engineer the abduction of Francisco and family to the 'mock' seraglio. Behn approaches here the more explicit analogy between the Civil War years and those of the Popish Plot that she makes in her 1681 comedy *The Roundheads* in which the Popish Plot is presented as a creation of Whig Protestants in order to discredit James, Duke of York and lay the ground for a repetition of the Civil War overthrowal of the Stuart monarchy. Focussing on a supposed Catholic threat deflects attention from and enables the resurgence of republican revolution.

Francisco's misogyny is compounded by his ignorance about religious and racial difference which enables the trick that Carlos' country estate is located in Turkey to be convincing (he is persuaded Turkey is off the coast of Cadiz and that castration is a common form of punishment for captives). Here too, Behn appears to be highlighting the ways in which the 'fiction' of the Popish Plot mobilized ignorant religious prejudices around Catholicism. Most importantly, however, Francisco understands women as the dangerous sexual source of conspiracy and denial of patriarchal power so that he is not suspicious of the 'false count', Guiliom. We might extend the analogical reading of Behn's play to the argument that it neatly demonstrates the ways in which what she, as a Tory and Catholic sympathizer, took to be transparent sham could be passed off on an unsuspecting public because of the ideological management of shared cultural prejudices (about female sexual licence and Catholic conspiracy) which averted attention from those who served to profit most from the disclosure, male Parliamentarians.

In similar vein, the 'Memoirs of the Court of the King of Bantam' is a story in which women are offered as bait to a wealthy commoner with aspirations to the aristocracy who is so mesmerized by their sexual charms that he fails to see the plotting on the part of the men who introduce him to them. Mr Would-be King is persuaded by Sir Philip Friendly that he can cuckold Valentine Goodland with the woman he loves, Philibella, and also gratify his equal passion for her supposed elder 'sister', Lucy (in fact Sir Philip's 'quondam mistress') by conferring a three-thousand pound 'dowry' on Philibella. Both women will accede to his sexual demands in return for the money. While he indulges himself with Lucy, Valentine Goodland is privately married to Philibella, whom his father had debarred him from marrying due to her lack of a fortune. Mr Would-be is persuaded to support Lucy and her child by Sir Philip, leaving both the conspirators, Valentine and Sir Philip, free of financial obligations and happy with the women of their choice. Mr Would-be is drawn into the plot by playing on his foolish belief in a prophesy he was 'told, when he was yet a stripling, either by one of his nurses, or by his own grand-mother, or by some other gipsy, that he should infallibly be what his sirname imply'd, a king, by providence or chance, e'er he dy'd, or never' (*Oroonoko and Other Stories*, p. 209). He is crowned King at a twelfth-night party to Lucy's Queen as a result of locating a pea and a bean in the Christmas cake. Their 'child', we are told at the end of the story, is comically named 'Hayoumorecake Bantam'. Would-be equates financial power with monarchical power and with sexual power. His courtship of Lucy consists of 'throwing . . . naked guinea's into her lap' which she at first disdains but then 'began by degrees to mollify, and let the gold lie quietly in her lap' (p. 225). Like Francisco, Would-be understands money to provide him with absolute and arbitrary power over those around him. He asserts his 'divine right' over his subjects by showering money and gifts upon them, where Francisco attempts to lock his wealth (signified in his wife) away. In the light of popular perceptions of Charles II's sexual and financial promiscuity, Behn, like her monarchist contemporary, Dryden in his 1680 poem *Absalom and Achitophel*, seems to have considered it necessary to acknowledge at some level that Charles's extravagance contributed to a willingness to support the strengthening of Parliamentary power over the monarchy on the part of people and politicians.

However, the key factor in the satirical presentation of Would-be is his belief in the possibility of his own potential to be a monarch and the ludicrous image of a world peopled by sovereigns with no subjects that his ambition conjures, which makes him vulnerable to exploitation and conspiracy on the part of impoverished aristocrats. This displaces the charges laid at Charles's door onto his rivals, an action Behn also performs in the third volume of her longer scandal fiction, *Love-Letters between a Nobleman and his Sister* (1687). Here Hermione (Lady Henrietta Wentworth, Monmouth's mistress) introduces her lover, Caesario (Monmouth) to the necromancer, Fergusano (the Presbyterian minister, Robert Ferguson). Fergusano offers Cesario ambiguous visions of prospective kingship similar to those extended to another famous 'false king' in fictionalized history, Macbeth.[15] Those who claim to secure the throne from the dangers of undue foreign influence, financial and sexual vulnerability, in fact simply 'mirror' the same weaknesses, a satirical attack which gains particularly ideological persuasiveness in that Monmouth was known to mirror the physical and temperamental tendencies of his father.

In this complex web of plotting and counterplotting in both *The False Count* and 'The Court of the King of Bantam' what Behn stresses is the comic potential of sexual intrigue, which reminds us of the discrepancy rather than similarity between the literary and the political fiction. On two occasions Guiliom, the false count, is reminded not to press the sham too far. Antonio, on their first introduction, warns him: 'know our Design is only comical, though if you manage not Matters well, it may prove tragical to you' (Act ii, Scene ii, p. 323). Later, when Francisco and his party have been brought to Carlos' country estate, Carlos warns his servant, Guzman: 'Whatever you do, have a care you do not overfright the Coxcomb, and make a Tragedy of our Comedy' (iv. iv. p. 353). *The Court of the King of Bantam* is presented as a complex and light-hearted seasonal joke in which a fool is exposed but not bankrupted. Sir Philip Friendly obtains from Mr Would-be King only what is required to provide Philibella with a suitable fortune to marry Valentine and support Sir Philip's cast-off mistress, Lucy, and his illegitimate child by her. The narrator presents the story as nothing more than a clever prank in which she invites the reader to share a joke which enables the woman she terms 'my dear Philibella' (p. 208) to escape ruin.

Behn, then, exploits the epistemological confusion raised by the Popish plot to point to the fictionality of both gender identity and political identity. In so doing, she also dramatizes the need to recognize the analogical dialectic between the two as a rhetorical effect, 'a new way to play an old game' as the sub-title to *The False Count* puts it, rather than an expression of a true and fixed relation. While sexual relations and political relations are understood through the analogy to share the status of 'fiction', however, Behn's retrospective 're-writings' of the Popish Plot as a complex game of bluff and double bluff also remind us that when fiction becomes the primary motor of politics proper it can result in tragedy rather than comedy. Even in recognizing the dangerous effects of fictionality in the realm of politics, however, Behn highlights the necessity of continuing to play the game rather than attempting to speak the truth. The only 'truth' that can be revealed in this nexus of representation is the representational status of the nexus itself. Behn's stories of sexual intrigue analogically draw our attention to the fictional status of women themselves – they are constructions of male desire or pawns in power games between men. As female and fiction-maker, Behn neatly turns the tables by offering a 'new way to play an old game' where it is *she* who exploits that fictional power.

Behn succeeds in turning a misogynistic practice of deploying images of female transgression as a metaphor for political crisis, a practice which effectively excludes women from agency in the public sphere of politics, into an asset for the woman writer. The case of Elizabeth Cellier may have served as a monitory model here. Cellier succeeded, unlike a number of other Popish Plot defendants, in escaping the charge of high treason not by proving her innocence but by proving the unreliability of the witness against her, Thomas Dangerfield. She was then charged with and found guilty of libel when she sought to give her account of her imprisonment and trial in *Malice Defeated*. To speak 'safely' on the Popish Plot, then, was not to claim to tell the truth about it, but rather to expose all discourse on it as a fiction. For women to find a mode of expression in the maelstrom of words generated in the 1680s around a public political crisis it seems to have been necessary, as Behn recognized, to exploit the analogical association between fiction, fraud and femininity rather than deny it.

NOTES

1 The arrest was recorded in the *True Protestant Mercury* (Saturday, 12 August – Wednesday, 16 August 1682). It is not known what action was taken as a result. The epilogue criticized James Scott, Duke of Monmouth, Charles II's illegitimate son by Lucy Walter for aligning himself with the Exclusionists in open rebellion to his father.

2 Janet Todd ed., *The Works of Aphra Behn*, vol. 1, *Poetry* (London, 1992), Poem 8, p. 21. Hereinafter cited as *Poetry*.

3 See Maureen Duffy, *The Passionate Shepherdess: Aphra Behn 1640–80* (London, 1989), p. 233.

4 C. Hugh Holman and William Hannon, *A Handbook to Literature*, 6th edn (New York, 1992).

5 'The Loyal Protestants New Litany' (London, 1680).

6 'Colin', in *Poems on Affairs of State: Augustan Satirical Verse, 1660–1714*, ed. Elias F. Mengel (New Haven and London, 1965), vol. 2 of *Poems on Affairs of State*, general ed. George de F. Lord, p. 168.

7 Narcissus Luttrell, *A Brief Historical Relation of State Affairs from September 1678 to April 1714* (Oxford, 1957), vol. 1, p. 9.

8 Elizabeth Cellier, *Malice Defeated: Or a Brief Relation of the Accusation and Deliverance of Elizabeth Cellier* (London, 1680), p. 27. Rpt. with *The Matchless Rogue* in Augustan Reprint Society nos. 249–50 (1988).

9 The Anglo-Catholic writer and printer, Elinor James, attacked Titus Oates in her broadsides and in person as an Anabaptist and, like Behn and Cellier, supported James II in the Glorious Revolution. My thanks to Paula McDowell, University of Maryland, for information on James.

10 Roger North, *Examen* (London, 1740), p. 95.

11 Jonathan Scott, 'England's Troubles: Exhuming the Popish Plot', in *The Politics of Religion in Restoration England*, eds. Tim Harris, Paul Seaward and Mark Goldie (Oxford, 1990), pp. 107–31, p. 120.

12 Aphra Behn, 'Memoirs of The Court of the King of Bantam', in *Oroonoko and Other Stories*, ed. Maureen Duffy (London, 1986), pp. 208–28.

13 Aphra Behn, *The False Count*, in *Aphra Behn: Five Plays* (London, 1990), pp. 297–378.

14 Aphra Behn, *A Poem to Sir Roger L'Estrange, on his Third Part of the History of the Times. Relating to the Death of Sir Edmund Bury-Godfrey*, Poem 82, in *Poetry*, p. 291.

15 Janet Todd ed., *The Works of Aphra Behn*, vol. II (1993), pp. 404–9.

4 More for seeing than hearing: Behn and the use of theatre

DAWN LEWCOCK

Almost all Behn's early writing was for the theatre. How and why she chose this route to attempt to support herself is merely another teasing question mark in the many that surround that enigmatic woman. The king's edict that actresses should be used instead of the boys for women characters would have already set a climate that could accept a female writer, and Lady Davenant had, at least nominally, taken over the Duke's Company on her husband's death in 1668, which may have helped the presentation of Behn's first play by that company. Nevertheless it was remarkable at a time when virtually all the accepted dramatists were men, and men from a very narrow social class most of whom wrote for pleasure and not for profit. But what is really surprising is the sheer professionalism Behn's plays show, particularly in the ways in which she understands and uses the potential of the scenic stage to enhance and enlarge her plots. Literary analysis of her work shows her use of a narrator's voice to comment on her stories, sometimes as the dispassionately passionate observer in *Oroonoko*, sometimes in an ironic aside with the implicit assumption of a common understanding with her readers, as in her shorter novels and longer poems. Such analysis of her plays finds her use of satire and irony displaying and undercutting the absurdities of 'ridiculous mankind'. But dramaturgical analysis, which takes into account the effects of the theatrical elements on an audience, shows how she interweaves the staging with the dialogue to provide a visual commentary to the audience. This is done by several of her fellow dramatists. What is unique to Behn is not only her appreciation of the visual effects of a performance but also the way that she uses this to affect the perceptions of the audience and change their conception and comprehension of her plots and/or her underlying theme as she wishes by integrating the theatrical possibilities into her dramatic structure.

The Amorous Prince, at Lincoln's Inn Fields in 1671, makes surprisingly little use of the scenic stage but shows a remarkable grasp of the visual possibilities of theatre as such. The plot revolves around honour and the honourable treatment of women by men and shows the duty due to a prince by his subjects must be reciprocated by scrupulous conduct towards them. However the theme is about deception and dissimulation, the deliberate use of deceit and disguise in order to attain some particular purpose. Mistaken identities and disguise of one sort or another feature largely in mid-seventeenth-century plays, both in tragic and comic plots. Behn gives full details of the visual details of the costume or disguise different characters are to wear and how they are to appear to each other and to the audience. For the plot depends on mistaken identities as well as mistaken intentions and mistaken loyalties.

There is no ambiguity in the opening scene, when Cloris enters 'drest in her night attire, with Frederick dressing himself', reinforcing the view Behn wants the audience to have of Cloris' true innocence and her belief in the Prince's promises of marriage. They need to know that Frederick has taken full advantage of Cloris' unsophisticated naivety. When they then hear Frederick's cynical account of his debauch of Cloris to Curtius they can judge their characters accordingly. They discover, at the end of the scene, that Curtius is her brother and are ready to anticipate conflicts of honour and revenge, with complications from the implication that Curtius is hindered in his own honourable courtship of Laura. They then hear Lorenzo arguing with Isabella over the cost of his attempts to make Isabella's mistress Clarina his mistress and they understand that the play is to be about the differing attitudes and relationships between men and virtuous women. The audience see and hear all the complicated deceptions, know much more than the characters about what is going on, and can enjoy their confusion. Having set out all the strands of the plot Behn reintroduces Cloris in Act iii, Scene iii, now in the disguise of 'a Country-Boy, followed by Guilliam a Clown'. The audience see her reactions to watching Frederick fight Curtius and see Frederick accept her as a youth rather than herself. They see the clown taken up by Lorenzo and can make the contrast between the straightforward, simple countryman who retains his honesty with his hat, and remains himself under any change of clothes, and the devious courtier. They see Curtius return, disguised 'in a black Peruke and beard, with Pietro disguis'd also' (Act IV, Scene ii) to try and succeed in avenging Cloris and Laura. He encounters Guilliam, who in keeping Cloris' secret, has to decide to lie and say that she is dead. They see Frederick attracted to the disguised Cloris/Philibert in a scene reminiscent of Orsino with Viola, and see the possible homosexual connotations which Lorenzo makes explicit in his advice to Cloris/Philibert. They watch her pain as Frederick decides to visit the supposed 'beauties from Greece' for whom Curtius is pretending to pander in order to entrap Frederick (Act IV, Scene iii).

The culmination of the disguises and confused identities comes in the final scene where Frederick is confounded and shamed into reformation. Behn's directions are very specific and detailed in the action she requires from the actors to represent the attitudes between all the various couples and their relationships. While not using any more of the theatrical facilities than would have been available to her before the introduction of the scenic stage this play shows that Behn had an unusually acute feel for the visual opportunities the stage offered to enhance story-telling; that she understood how the relationship between stage and audience could be used to augment her plot and, more importantly, to communicate the moral dilemma underlying it. For what the audience also absorb from *The Amorous Prince* is the implicit questioning of the morality of deceit. If it is wrong for Frederick to deceive Cloris is it not also wrong for her to disguise herself to deceive him that she is a boy and then risk homosexual advances? If it is wrong for Lorenzo to try to entrap Clarina through deception, is it right for the sisters to deceive their men in order to chasten them and is it not wrong for Curtius to entrap Frederick through acting the part of a whoremaster? Behn is asking if the ends always justify the means. Since she has Frederick reform and a happy ending all round she seems to think it must be so, but then perhaps it was not apposite for her to suggest otherwise in the light of contemporary politics. But deceit is a theme that she returns to again and again, and from now on she uses the scenery and the staging to show the resulting discoveries and disclosures visually.

By the time her plays appeared the use of scenery was well established. It is not known how she obtained her theatrical knowledge: at the least she must have seen the early experiments with the scenery that were initiated in the ten years from 1661 to 1671 particularly by Sir William Davenant and the Duke's Company at Lincoln's Inn Fields, one of the two theatres licensed by Charles II when he returned. The other theatre was that run by Thomas Killigrew and the King's Company at Bridges Street. Both theatres were small and intimate by modern standards without, for example, the barrier of an orchestra pit and with a main curtain that was not closed during the performance. Little is known about the stages and the way that they were fitted out to manage the scenery and scene changing but a great deal has been deduced from the plays written for the theatres, playgoers' comments in letters and diaries and the facilities John Webb provided in the Hall Theatre at Whitehall.[1] Some of the conclusions may be debatable but it is generally accepted that all the theatres had a forestage which projected beyond the proscenium arch far enough to have two entrance doors either side; that within the proscenium there were sets of side shutters or wings and a set of shutters centre stage across the stage, all of which were painted to give an impression of a location, usually in perspective; that the shutters could be slid on and off at the side of the stage and apart at the centre of the stage to change the entire painted picture; that action took place not only on the forestage but also in and around the scenery; that the back shutters could be parted to show action behind them. As, for example, Wycherley does by using shutters to open in perhaps the best-known play of the time, *The Country Wife* to show Margery Pinchwife deceiving her husband by writing to Horner immediately after the audience has seen Horner plotting to deceive her. All without the need for explanatory dialogue.

This staging derived from the court masque stage devised by Inigo Jones for James I and Charles I. The masque stage had used the sliding shutters, the machina ductilis, or the turning platform on a spindle, the machina versatilis, to show spectacle and embellish the visual effects. Jones had shown how this rear stage area could provide successive transformations of all kinds with actors and or furnishings placed all ready in situ but the general public theatres had not had this facility before and few outside the pre-interregnum court circle would have seen it or have had working experience of it. The masque ideas were utilized in the set-pieces and spectacular effects in the new 'operas' and some of the heroic tragedies by Dryden and Settle amongst others. But what certain drama-tists also realized was that they could now imply a change in location, a change in time or a change in both together. They could suggest simulta-neous or sequential action to increase the pace of a play, increasing the tension in tragedy or the laughter in comedy. Behn seems to have had an instinctive grasp of the possibilities for she uses the understood stage con-ventions that were evolving from those in being on the earlier platform stage, adapts them as she uses them and becomes more adept at using them than some of her colleagues. She was one of the earliest to realize that the greatest possibility for change was in the discovery spaces provided by the sliding shutters on which the scenery was painted; discovery places which it is believed were not available except in very rudimentary form behind hangings or similar on the platform stages. It had only been possible to surprise an audience visually on the platform stage by a character popping up through a trap, or by drawing aside hangings. The former method was obviously only suitable for certain plays while drawn hangings implied that something or someone was to be disclosed and raised the audience's anticipation. Once sliding shutters were in use for plays as well as masques it was possible literally to show the audience what was happening 'behind the scenes'; what was closed could be opened (disclosed) to show what was happening at the same time elsewhere, what had been covered or hidden could be uncovered (discovered) either to a character and the audience or solely to the audience.

Behn's use of disclosure scenes has been derided by critics of her dramatic style yet this misunderstands how closely the theatrical ele-ments are interwoven with the dialogue, not only in her plays but also in others of this period, and disregards the visual element of the total the-atrical experience. It also disregards the environment at the time when dissimulation permeated the social life, emanating from the king. George Savile's remarks on the dissimulation of Charles II in his dealings with his cronies as well as in his formal relationships with his advisers seems very apposite in suggesting the ambience in which the plays were written.[2] Most of the drama has the theme of deceit or deception in one form or another leading to death and disaster in the tragedies or to a comic dénouement in the comedies. In Behn's plays the disclosures are not used solely to startle or surprise. They usually serve a specific purpose beneath their obvious part in her plots, giving signals to the audience to guide the ways in which Behn wants them to perceive and receive the play, even at times deliberately deceiving the audience into misunderstanding the events on stage.

Dramaturgical analysis of *The Forc'd Marriage* shown at Lincoln's Inn Fields in 1670 demonstrates very clearly her use of the discovery scenes not only to direct the audience's attention but also to deceive and misdirect them. Ostensibly the disclosures are used to heighten the anticipation of the audience in the events to come and are carefully set in the structure of the whole play. Each instance has a slightly different purpose in the scheme of the play yet each works on the audience's anticipated responses to particular situations.

The first is Act II, Scene vi.

> Draws off discovers Philander and Alcander with
> Musick at the Chamber-door of Erminia; to them
> Pisaro, who listens whilst the song is sung.

This is not a surprise to the audience, they have already heard Philander arrange with Alcander that they shall go and serenade Erminia as she is supposedly being bedded by her new husband Alcippus, Act II, Scene iv. The audience anticipate a fight when Alcippus discovers that Philander is outside Erminia's bedchamber and can wonder if Pisaro will let friendship outweigh his own jealousy, Act II, Scene vi. As they know, while Philander does not, that Erminia is not in the bedchamber they can also anticipate further misunderstandings before all is cleared up. The drawing aside of the shutters here then, heightens the audience's anticipation of events in a way not possible on a platform stage.

The second discovery scene is Act IV, Scene vi:

> Draws off discovers Erminia in a dishabit, sitting; to her Philander who
> falls at her feet, on his knees.

Again the audience are not surprised by the discovery of Philander with Erminia for they have heard the pressures brought to bear on Erminia to give in to him, Act III, Scene iii. It is their anticipation of what will happen when Alcippus arrives and discovers Erminia and Philander together that is heightened by actually seeing their meeting. This anticipation is kept up by the ambiguity of Erminia's invitation to Philander to retire into the inner room, and the direction that, Act IV, Scene iv:

> They go into the Scene which draws over.

The audience still cannot be positive that Erminia has succumbed to temptation. They see Alcippus return immediately, fight off Alcander outside the bedroom door and go off as the shutters draw apart to Act IV, Scene vi.

> A Bedchamber. Discovers Erminia, Philander sitting on the bed, to them Isillia. A sword and hat on the table.

The following directions explain the whole scene without the need for the dialogue which separates them.

> He hides himself behind the bed and in haste leaves his sword and hat on the table; Alcippus comes in . . . Isillia goes to take the hat and sword and slide into her lap which he sees and calls to her . . . He gives him his sword; Philander goes out, Alcippus locks the door after him . . . He strangles her with a garter which he snatches from his leg, or he smothers her with a pillow . . . Throws her on a bed, and sits down on a chair . . . One knocks; he rises after a little pause and opens the door; enter Page . . . Pisaro draws him out, the scene closes.

So far as the audience are concerned they have seen Erminia murdered (the choice of method probably means that Behn waited to see which would be most effective for the actors on stage), although they are pretty sure from her protestations that she was actually innocent. Their understanding of the sequence of events in this act has been aided by the rapid changes of scene from fore-stage to the first discovery, back to the fore-stage and the second discovery, culminating in the murder. The immediate transitions made possible by the use of discovery scenes has emphasized the emotional content of the play in a way not so possible on the platform stage where each scene would have had the tiny hesitation given by a cleared stage before and after it. Although one scene could follow rapidly on another even so, the infinitesimal breaks between would slow down the headlong fall to disaster and make the overall impression more measured.

Having accustomed the audience to anticipating events Behn is able to use the next discovery scene to much greater effect. The murder of Erminia is confirmed in their hearing by the reports of it to the king, the demands for vengeance from her father Orgulius and the pleas for Alcippus' life from the Princess Galatea, Act iv, Scene iv. The audience wait to see whether or not he is to die, or whether Galatea will be allowed to prevail, but find the king's decision depends on whether or not Philander can survive the distress of Erminia's murder. They share the shock when Falatius and Fabree faint at the sight of Erminia's ghost only to hear the 'ghost' tell them, Act iv, Scene viii:

> This was a happy mistake, now I may pass with safety.

Suddenly the play has reversed direction, the ending they have been anticipating will not happen. Erminia is alive yet dressed so as to be mistaken for a ghost 'veil'd in thin tiffany' and the audience are no longer sure what to expect. The act ends with Erminia revealing herself to Philander and Galatea and the audience left wondering what is to happen to Alcippus, her 'murderer'.

The last act opens with Pisaro telling Galatea of Alcippus' despair and then the shutters disclose Alcippus to the audience and they see and hear his remorseful repentance before Pisaro brings in Erminia, Act v, Scene ii. The audience, knowing Erminia is not the ghost Alcippus takes her for, are able to judge the effect on him of her exhortations, as Galatea and others pass by him dressed as symbolic figures. They show the future that could be his if only he will forego his mourning of a wife who could never have been truly his and accept Galatea. The audience have not been able to anticipate events here. They have not been told what to expect, they have to listen to the arguments Erminia puts forward and watch the symbolic gestures.

> All the Disguis'd enter again and dance, with Love in the midst, to whom
> they dance, they in order make an offer of what they carry, which must be
> something to represent them by; which Love refuses with Nods still
> pointing to Alcippus: the Dance done, they lay them at his feet, or seem
> to do so, and go out.

This is no conventional resolution of the plot but one which would keep
the audience involved and interested to see how it comes out. They hear
the king agree to allow Philander to 'carry on your innocent design, / And
when you've done, the last act shall be mine', and will still wonder what
punishment Alcippus will receive, Act v, Scene iii. The final scene of the
play opens a second tableau, of a hearse and mourners: a tableau reminiscent of the finale of Henry Killigrew's *Pallantus and Eudora*, Act v, Scene v.
However, where Killigrew is simply concerned to demonstrate the over-
throw of the tyrant and the successful outcome with a visual display Behn
uses the visual effect to emphasize to the audience, as well as ostensibly to
Alcippus, the tragedy that would have resulted if he had been successful in
murdering Erminia in his jealous frustration. The moral is made clear, he
has allowed his ambition to overcome his judgement in aspiring to marry
someone who already belongs to the Prince to whom he owes allegiance.
The result would have been death and unhappiness for many others
besides himself. It is not a moral that appeals to modern thought but it
would have been perfectly clear to an audience who had lived through the
Civil Wars, and to whom the panoplies of death were more commonplace.
The ironies inherent in the dialogue would be visually complemented by
the black draped hearse and the mourners who, as Alcippus challenges
Philander,

> run all away crying . . . leaving some of their veils behind them,
> some half off, some half on.

Showing the grief normally decently veiled is a similar technique to the
disclosure of one scene by the withdrawal of the one in front. The fact of
Erminia's survival is not disclosed to Alcippus until he has humbly
acknowledged his faults and been granted pardon by the king and
Philander. Then the audience see and hear him beg her pardon for all the

wrongs he has done her. The happy ending they have anticipated from the moment they found out that Erminia had not died has been achieved but not in a manner they expected. Behn has used their anticipation and their anticipated reactions not only to enhance their reception of her plot but also to enlarge their perception of her theme. Underlying their under-standing too would be their knowledge that the Duke of York had married a commoner, Anne Hyde; that her father had recently been exiled. What is also implicit is the sense of irony throughout. For example, the Prince is called Philander yet wins Erminia because of his status.[3] More than this however, is the ironic use of the shutters in disclosing what the audience already commonly understand and then twisting the audience's anticipa-tion against themselves. Behn's manipulations of the audience response in this way continued in her later plays and implicitly comments on contem-porary attitudes, opinions or behaviour.

Analysis of *Sir Patient Fancy*, seen at Dorset Gardens in 1678, shows one visual discovery behind another as well as other uses of disclosure that further the theme of the play. This was Behn's first overtly political play. She makes Molière's hypochondriac a rich, non-conformist, London Alderman, a typical city figure and someone to be scorned by the audi-ence, open to deception by false foreign doctors, and then gives him a totally amoral and unfaithful wife in love with a penniless Cavalier. The audience immediately find their sympathies divided. It has been argued that the play is also a metaphor for the imaginary sickness of the Whigs deceived by false doctrines but curable like Sir Patient if they would admit to true, Tory, beliefs.[4] This may be so but the theatrical emphasis is in the comedy of the deceptions which are played on various characters and in the unexpected ways they react to each one. Three discoveries find Lady Fancy in compromising situations which keeps the attention of the audience focussed on her peccadillos and displays that she has no scruples about deceiving and being unfaithful to her husband with whomever she finds in her bed. But each discovery has a particular function in the per-ception of the plot, visually reinforcing what is found in the dialogue. The first time Lady Fancy awaits her lover but receives Lodwick by mistake, the audience anticipate outrage and distress when she discovers her mistake in Act III, Scene iv. The second discovery shows clearly that this was far from the case: both have enjoyed the encounter but are now likely to be found out by both Sir Patient and Isabella (Act III, Scene vii). However, once again the plot twists, Lady Fancy avoids retribution while another discovery acts as a quick scene change and keeps up the tension as in a cut from one scene to another on film (Act III, Scene viii). One moment the audience see Lady Fancy fooling Sir Patient into believing Lodwick has been visiting Isabella, the next they see Lodwick and Wittmore come to blows in the garden because of her mischief making, giving an immediacy to the situation with a taut visual emphasis only possible in the theatre.

Scene settings called for in *Sir Patient Fancy*

ACT I A room

ACT II A garden

Scene changes to a chamber

ACT III Act draws off and discovers Lady Knowell, Isabella, Lucretia,
Lodwick, Leander, Wittmore, Sir Credulous, other men and
women, as going to a dance

Lady Knowell's chamber

A garden

Draws off and discovers Lady Fancy in a chamber as by dark

Changes again to a garden

Draws off to Lady Fancy's anti-chamber

Changes to Lady Fancy's bed-chamber discovers her as before. . .

Scene draws over Sir Patient and Lady

Draws again and discovers The Garden, Wittmore, Fanny
and Isabella.

Scene changes to the Long Street, a Pageant of an Elephant
coming from the farther end with Sir Credulous on it and
several others playing on strange confused instruments.

ACT IV Lady Knowell's house

A table and chairs

A hall

The Lady Fancy's bed chamber; she's discover'd with Wittmore in
disorder. A table, sword and hat.

ACT V A table and six chairs

Sir Patient is a character who never communicates directly with the audience, whereas Lady Fancy takes them into her confidence and tells them she is only waiting for him to settle money on her before she leaves him. By building such relationships through direct asides or comments to the audience by some characters and not by others Behn is able to sway the audience's sympathies to or from any particular character in a way that is again only possible in the theatre. Many echoes of earlier action in this complex play add to the ambivalent impressions the audience receive. The various asides, discoveries and disclosures serve both to direct the audience's perception where Behn wants it at any particular moment and to keep up the pace of the comic action.

There are subtle, often ironic, patternings in all her plays, particularly in the ways in which certain scenes are echoed, paired or doubled in a particular play. The asides, discoveries and disclosures are carefully placed in relation to each other in order to point the plot for the audience and thus affect the response from the audience. It is very easy to find extracts to support one view or another in dramaturgical analysis but the examples of pairing found in Behn's plays are too many for coincidence. Moreover, they are not formulaic. That is, one cannot find any strict formula in the structuring of her plays. There is no common pattern, no predetermined point in every play for a disclosure scene for instance, in the ways shes uses the staging. She fits the staging to the plot rather than the reverse so that each play is constructed according to the climaxes in its own story-line. Most disguisings and mistaken identities are not hidden from the audience. They are told or shown what is going on and it is this knowledge that Behn relies on in her plays when she leads them to believe they know what is happening until she chooses to enlighten them and disclose the true state of affairs. No audience could predict with certainty how any play would develop and what the outcome might be, which would keep them interested and alert to follow her 'design'.

In *The Feign'd Curtizans* 1679 Behn manipulates this relationship with the audience by *not* misleading them. She uses the theme of deceit to demonstrate the harm done by allowing oneself to be deluded by a clever trickster and by being 'in the dark' about people and events. But she does this theatrically in a particularly unusual way by using disguise and disclosure subtly combined with several scenes supposedly in darkness. She must have been writing it when the Popish Plot was at its height and it seems to reflect contemporary behaviour: the Prologue makes clear that plotting was in her mind and there are implications in the play that seem to show that she meant it for an analogy. The overt interest for the audience is in the plan of the girls to disguise themselves as courtezans and to see how and when the men will discover who they really are. The audience's attention is kept by structuring the play around the more public locations of the gardens and the street, so that they anticipate the more intimate moments to come in the interiors when it seems the girls must be discovered. But gradually they find out that there is more than this fairly innocent deception taking place. The audience discover that Petro is pimping for Galliard as well as managing Sir Signal Buffoon, and then see him disguise himself to play various different roles in order to trick the others. They hear that Sir Signal is a fool, abroad with his father's chaplain Mr Tickletext for his education, that Tickletext is hypocritically venal. Some of Behn's most detailed directions for movement which illustrate the underlying motivations are in this play, as in the one visual discovery scene when the shutters draw apart on Act i, Scene ii to show Petro in his first role as barber to Tickletext. Behn's directions for the behaviour of both gives gestures which highlight the insolent dominance of Petro and the blinding vanity of Tickletext.

> Draws off and discovers Mr Tickletext a trimming, his Hair under a Cap. a Cloth before him: Petro snaps his fingers, takes away the Bason, and goes to wiping his Face . . . Tick. sets himself and smirks in the Glass, Pet. standing behind him, making Horns and Grimaces, which Tick sees in the Glass, gravely rises turns towards Petro.

A short encounter in the second act set supposedly in the Gardens of the Medices (sic) Villa tells the audience that Morosini and Octavio have come to Rome looking for Marcella and Cornelia before the girls themselves enter dressed as courtezans. They discuss half seriously whether to become courtezans in earnest before being directed to 'walk down the Garden' as Galliard, Fillamour and Julio enter. The actors continue to move up and down the scene the intention giving the clear impression of people strolling around a public place. Similar scenes occur in earlier plays, for instance, *The Country Wife* in 1673 and *The Man of Mode* in 1676. But Behn considerably extends the scene, when, having established this atmosphere of casual encounters, she makes the action more specific and the audience see the men being deceived by the girls.

> Mar. retires, and leans against a Tree, Cor. walks about reading . . . Gal. goes bowing by the side of Cornelia. Fil. walks about in the Scene.

Philippa and 'attendance' make up the stage picture as Galliard and Cornelia flirt and Fillamour eyes Marcella until Octavio enters with his following. A fight starts and the audience see the cowardice of Sir Signal and Tickletext as they hide in the painted bushes and then the dishonesty of Petro as he teaches Sir Signal and Mr Tickletext how to take snuff, and then picks their pockets as he explains how to tell a story without words.

In the third act is the unusual, if not unique, example of acting directions and dialogue which present together a lapse of time during the action of the scene. Behn has characters gradually finding themselves more and more 'in the dark' and thus behaving foolishly by mistaking friends for enemies in full sight of the audience. The act opens in daylight with an exterior scene, which again uses the depth of the stage in directions for 'Going down the scene' and 'coming up the scene'. Again Behn establishes a public place where Laura can be seen overhearing the encounters of the others and later Crapine can see the girls when they appear in a balcony. It could be the Corso, as Summers assumes, but the first edition does not specify. The first mention of time passing is by Galliard,

> . . . for now the hour of the Berjere approaches, Night that was made for Lovers . . . I have given order for Musick, Dark Lanthorns and Pistols.

When Marcella and Cornelia appear above Marcella says

> I've only time to tell you Night approaches, and then I will expect you.

Cornelia adds

Well, Signor, 'tis coming on, and then I'll try what courage the Darkness
will inspire me with – till then – farewell.

The act continues without a break. Galliard tells Fillamour

Besides, thou'st an hour or two good, between this and the time requir'd
to meet Marcella.

They stop to watch Petro, in his role as an Antiquary, fooling Sir Signal
and Tickletext and Galliard overhears Sir Signal mention that

I am this night to visit, Sirrah, – the finest, the most delicious young
Harlot,. . .

Galliard forces Sir Signal to renounce his engagement with Silvianetta
and then adds as he exits with Fillamour

Come, 'tis dark, and time for our Design, – your Servant, Signors.

Sir Signal and Tickletext discover they have been robbed by Petro, in his
role as the Civillity Master, while they both plot with him as the Barber to
get them to their whores. Crapine and Octavio plot to catch Octavio's
rival. Meanwhile the audience understand that all these things are to take
place at the same time and place and can anticipate the confusion that is
about to happen when Marcella enters, dressed as a man, with Philippa
carrying a lantern. The audience know that night has now fallen and the
rest of the action must be assumed to be taking place in the dark. This is
confirmed when a moment later

Enter Tickletext with a Periwig and Crevat of Sir Signal's: A Sword by
his side, and a dark lanthorn; she opens hers, looks on him, and goes out
. . . Enter Galliard with a dark Lanthorn

After an encounter with Galliard

Tickletext retiring hastily runs against Octavio, who is just entering,
almost beats him down; Oct. strikes him a good blow, beats him back and
draws: Tick. gets up in a corner of the Stage; Oct. gropes for him, as Gal.
does, and both meet and fight with each other . . . Enter Sir Signal . . .

Advancing softly, and groping with his hands, meets the point of Oct.
Sword as he is groping for Gal . . . Hops to the door: and feeling for his
way with his out-stretched Arms, runs his Lanthorn into Julio's face, who
is just entring; finds he's oppos'd with a good push backward, and slips
into a corner over against Tickletext; Julio meets Octavio, and fights him;
Oct. falls, Julio opens his Lanthorn, and sees his mistake.

This has now become a scene in the dark where the audience can see the
actors and the actors can see each other but where both accept that the
characters cannot see each other in the story. It is another facet of the ways
in which mistaken identities are used in comedies to add to the confusion
and to the humour. Implicit in these dark scenes is the comfortable superiority of the audience over the characters and also over the actors playing
those characters. They are not only watching actors pretend they are in
the dark they are also aware of the misunderstandings of the actors as the
characters in the plays are building and entangling. This makes for an odd
ambivalence in their response, there is the direct response to the humour
of the situation of the characters in the play, but there is also the sight of
the actors as known individuals making fools of themselves in pretending
it is too dark to see each other when anyone can see them playing the fool.
They accept the fiction as well as the reality of what they are seeing. Pepys
makes this ambivalence clear when he remarks to his neighbour on the
incongruity of Beeston having to read his part when the scene was supposed to be in the dark on 2 February 1669. But Behn has added another
dimension in the implicit assumption that the audience will see all this
against contemporary events by continuing to set more of the action 'as in
the dark'. Sir Signal and Tickletext try to frighten each other as Devils and
fight with a wooden sword before Tickletext finishes with a Base Viol
round his neck. The comedy is obvious but all the time the audience are
aware of the growing misunderstandings because the two fools have not
seen the truth.

    The last scene of the play starts in the dark and then finds Tickletext
and Sir Signal sharing a curtain as they hide and peep from either side of it
before lights are brought in and all is resolved. A buffoon and a venal cleric
have mistaken each other for enemies because they allowed themselves to
be fooled by a trickster who assumed many disguises and kept them in

'darkness'. Behn must have meant this as a theatrical metaphor, a comic allegory of what had been happening in real life where during the hysteria surrounding the Popish Plot many people from the king downwards had been 'in the dark' about who was plotting what with whom; had been tricked by Oates and his confederates in their assumption of a moral stance; and had mistaken friends for enemies and denounced them.

Behn shows a rare sense of spatial relationships and the ability to translate such relationships into texts which incorporate visual as well as aural effects, signals and signs for both actors and audience. What appears to govern her staging is not the subject matter nor the style of the play so much as the relationship she wants for any particular piece of action or business with the audience, or how she wishes the audience to perceive the happenings on the stage. She structured her plays to take into account not only the dialogue but also the action bound up with it and thus all the potentialities of the stage of her time. This was not to add verisimilitude to the plots but rather to make the sequential action of the stories more coherent, more exciting, more funny; to add the element of surprise to comedy; to suggest simultaneously action in two or more locations; to indicate a lapse of time; to manipulate the relationship between audience and actor by deliberately aiding or restricting intimacy; but particularly to give a visual dimension to the themes of deceit and deception.

This structuring was a conscious integration of the visual with the aural, both as a stage picture and as a complicated pattern of sound and movement. The integration is such that in most of Behn's plays the play is not fully comprehensible without taking into account the visual effects she requires; the indications of location; the scene changes; the positioning and movement patterns of the actors, and the ways in which all are made to relate to the audience. Although others also used many of the same techniques none show such a mastery of the technical problems involved. She well deserves distinction as an unrivalled theatrical craftswoman.

NOTES

1 Discussion of the theatres can be found in: Peter Holland, *The Ornament of Action* (Cambridge, 1979); Eleanor Boswell, *The Restoration Court Stage 1660–1702* (London, 1966); Elkanah Settle, *The Empress of Morocco: a Tragedy with Sculptures* (London, 1673); prints [by Dolle] of scene settings, used by Langhans, 'The Dorset Gardens Theatre in Pictures' in *Theatre Survey* 6 (1965), 134–46; and E. Langhans, 'A Conjectural Reconstruction of the Dorset Gardens Theatre' in *Theatre Survey* 13 (1972), 74–93. Langhan's reconstruction based on his interpretation of the Wren section drawing challenged by J. R. Spring, 'Platforms and Picture Frames: a Conjectural reconstruction of the Dorset Gardens Theatre' in *Theatre Notebook* 31 (1977), 6–19, and in J. R. Spring, 'The Dorset Gardens Theatre: Playhouse or Opera House?' in *Theatre Notebook* 34 (1980), 60–9. This is partially defended by Robert D. Hume in 'The Dorset Gardens Theatre: a Review of Facts and Problems' in *Theatre Notebook* 33 (1979), 4–17 and 'The Nature of Dorset Gardens Theatre' in *Theatre Notebook* 36 (1982), 99–109.

   Discussion of the staging can be found in Holland and in Richard Southern *Changeable Scenery* (London, 1952); Marjorie Dawn Lewcock, 'Aphra Behn on the Restoration Stage' (unpublished doctoral dissertation, Cambridge, 1987); Dawn Lewcock, 'Computer Analysis of Restoration Staging, I: 1661–1672' in *Theatre Notebook* 47 (1993), 20–9; Dawn Lewcock 'Computer Analysis of Restoration Staging, II: 1671–1682 in *Theatre Notebook* 47 (1993), 141–56; Dawn Lewcock 'Computer Analysis of Restoration Staging 1682–1694' in *Theatre Notebook* 48 (1994), 103–15. Documentary theatrical history and other references in David Thomas, *Restoration and Georgian England, 1660–1788* (Cambridge, 1989).

2 George Savile, Marquis of Halifax, 'His dissimulation' in *Lord Halifax's Character of King Charles the Second* (London, 1750; Peter Davies limited edition 1927) 22–7.

3 Philander, the Dutch knight who flirted with Gabrina in Ludovico Ariosto's *Orlando Furioso* (1532), see Brewer, *The Dictionary of Phrase and Fable* (Leicester, 1990).

4 See Maureen Duffy, *The Passionate Shepherdess* (London, 1977), pp. 157–65.

5 *The Rover* and the eighteenth century

JANE SPENCER

It is now a commonplace of feminist literary history that Aphra Behn's reputation suffered a sharp decline in the eighteenth century.[1] For about fifteen years after her death, she had a degree of the honourable fame she had craved. There were posthumous productions, posthumous publications, memoirs, and collected editions of her novels and later of her plays. Her fiction was adapted for the stage by Thomas Southerne in *Oroonoko* (1696) and Catharine Trotter in *Agnes de Castro* (1696). During the 1690s, despite attacks on her reputation, she was explicitly taken as a model to be followed by women writing for the theatre. Early in the 1700s, commentary on Behn took a sharp turn to the unfavourable. Praise of her became far less common and hostile comments increased. Many of the major figures in eighteenth-century letters contributed: Richard Steele, Alexander Pope, Henry Fielding and Samuel Richardson all recorded their disparagement of her and her work.

Two factors combined to make attacks on Behn frequent and sharp: the general reaction against the licentiousness of Restoration comedy, and objections to a woman's success in a world so inimical to emergent ideals of feminine delicacy. The movement for stage reform animated many criticisms. Steele, exaggerating wildly, complained that the hero of *The Rover* had sex 'above once every act', and objected to the scene where the country squire, Blunt, was seen to 'strip to his Holland drawers'.[2] Pope famously joked that 'Astraea' 'fairly puts all Characters to bed'.[3] The wish for poetic fame to remain a male preserve is evident in the essay 'The Apotheosis of Milton' in the *Gentleman's Magazine* in 1738, which figuratively exhumes Behn from her Westminster Abbey resting place. The writer falls asleep and is taken to a hall sacred to the spirits of bards buried

84

in the Abbey. The occasion is Milton's acceptance into the company of bards; among this company Behn appears, only to be ejected. In this vision Behn, 'dressed in the loose *Robe de Chambre* with her neck and Breasts bare', with 'fire in her Eye' and 'Assurance in her Features', has the demeanour of a Restoration tragedy-queen, uniting the sexual confidence and self-assurance so discouraged in eighteenth-century women. She is firmly told by no less an authority than Chaucer '*that none of her Sex has any Right to a Seat*' with the great poets.[4]

Contemplating such attacks, it is easy to forget how strongly they testify to the opposite of what their writers desire. They are reactions to Behn's continuing popularity and influence; and eighteenth-century theatre records make it quite clear that actors and audience did not share the disdain for Aphra Behn which journalists and men of letters have made so deceptively available to us. Behn's apparent loss of reputation in the early eighteenth century needs to be reassessed in the light of her continued success on the stage. This essay, through an examination of the stage history of her most popular play, *The Rover*, together with an analysis of the way it was played and adapted, shows how it was that Behn's work continued to entertain audiences at a time when her reputation and that of Restoration comedy was supposedly low. It also suggests that, in order to adapt Behn to eighteenth-century conditions, some of her bolder and more original effects were diluted.

The Rover was one of Behn's two great successes on the eighteenth-century stage, the other being her farce *The Emperor of the Moon*. It was revived at Drury Lane in 1703, and became a regular feature on the London stage for the next forty years.[5] After 1743 it was performed less frequently. There was a revival at Covent Garden in 1748, and another, also at Covent Garden, in 1757, which remained on the boards till 1760. After that the play was dropped until 1790, when a revised version, *Love in Many Masks*, had some success at Drury Lane. After this Behn seems to have been dropped from the repertoire altogether until the 1970s.

The first half of the eighteenth century, then, was the heyday of *The Rover*'s career. The *London Stage* records would suggest that the 1720s was her most popular decade, with fifty-one performances recorded (as against twenty in 1700–9, twenty-three in 1710–19, thirty-eight in

1730–9, and ten in 1740–9). These records must be treated with caution: early eighteenth-century performances may be under-represented in the figures.[6] We can conclude, though, that the play was very popular in the first three decades of the century, with some decline after 1730.

Another index of the play's popularity is the number of different theatres presenting it during the same season. Early in the century Drury Lane regularly put on *The Rover* with Robert Wilks as Willmore. In 1704 the Drury Lane production was joined by one at Lincoln's Inn Fields. From 1705–10 *The Rover* was performed both at the Queen's Theatre and at Drury Lane every year, though this does not necessarily indicate rival productions: sometimes it is the same cast moving between theatres. In 1710 a new theatre was opened at Greenwich, and a new set of actors played *The Rover*, with Ned Blunt, played by 'the famous true comedian, Mr Cave Underhill' as the star attraction. After 1710 the Drury Lane *Rover* was the only one for some years. Then, in 1725, the play was put on at Lincoln's Inn Fields with Lacy Ryan as Willmore. Ryan was to play the character at intervals over the next twenty-three years, almost equalling Robert Wilks's record of thirty years as the rover. In 1730 the play was put on at the new theatre in Goodman's Fields. There were now three rival *Rovers* on the stage: in April 1730 a theatregoer could have seen the play in three different productions, at Goodman's Fields, Drury Lane and Lincoln's Inn Fields. Throughout the early 1730s there were two, sometimes three, *Rovers* on in London, but after 1737 this play, like many others, was affected by the narrowing of theatrical opportunities brought about by the Licensing Act, and only the Covent Garden production survived.

In outline, *The Rover*'s stage history follows the course we would expect for a Restoration comedy: popularity early in the century followed by steep decline in the second half. Leo Hughes has traced a similar trajectory for Etherege's *The Man of Mode*, which continued to be performed for nearly fifty years after Steele attacked it in *The Spectator*, but gradually lost favour with audiences, and was dropped after being badly received in 1755.[7] *The Rover*'s progress closely follows that mapped out for Restoration drama in general by James Lynch: he notes that Restoration drama made up a large part of the London repertory during the first third

of the eighteenth century, but was less important thereafter, and he dates
'a considerable moral reformation of the theatre' from around 1760 on, a
date that coincides with the last performance of *The Rover* under its own
name.[8] Given the well-known moralization and sentimentalization of the
late-eighteenth-century theatre, it is not surprising that Behn, with her
reputation for bawdy, was rarely performed from the 1760s onwards. But
this tells us little about what, exactly, was found objectionable in her work.
Detailed attention to alterations made can show what moralization and
sentimentalization mean in terms of stage practice.

One of the ways Restoration comedy was sanitized for eighteenth-
century audiences was through the creation of revised versions. The
'vogue of revision and revival that struck the theatres in the mid-sixties'
meant that many plays were presented not just relieved of their smuttier
passages but deprived of their main points. Wycherley's *The Country Wife*
appeared in Garrick's version, *The Country Girl*, in 1776, without its hero,
the infamous Horner.[9] Hannah Cowley, adapting Behn's *The Luckey
Chance* as *A School for Greybeards* in 1786, got rid of the adulterous plot-
line. *The Rover*, too, was revived in an altered form: J. P. Kemble's *Love in
Many Masks* (1790), discussed below. Kemble, however, did not need to
alter his chosen play so drastically as Garrick and Cowley did theirs: his
alterations preserve the main characters and plot. In fact, despite Behn's
continued reputation among theatre historians for an unusual degree of
indecency, *The Rover* was much more suited to eighteenth-century tastes
than many other Restoration comedies.

Lynch and Hughes, in their studies of eighteenth-century audience
tastes, offer a picture in which Restoration comedies survive unaltered,
though heavily criticized, up to the middle of the century, and are replaced
by bowdlerized versions in the later years. Close study of *The Rover*'s
changing fortunes suggests a picture of more gradual change. On the one
hand, *Love in Many Masks* sticks relatively close to its original; on the
other, there is evidence to suggest that Behn's play was being appreciably
altered for performance fairly early in the century. The continuing popularity of Restoration comedies up to the 1750s, during decades when new
plays had to adhere to much stricter moral codes, has been explained in
terms of the audience's double standard: in older plays, lax morals could

be enjoyed. While there is probably truth in this, *The Rover* will not do as one of 'the most notorious examples of the public's willingness to accept licentious drama undiluted from its original Restoration form'.[10] For one thing, Behn's plays are no more bawdy than those of contemporaries like Wycherley, who was also popular on the eighteenth-century stage. For another, *The Rover* as played in the eighteenth century was not always in its original Restoration form. It may have been 'diluted' quite early in its stage career.

Some of the reasons for *The Rover*'s continued popularity can easily be named. Unlike Behn's political comedies such as *The City-Heiress*, it did not depend on topical reference: its cavalier theme could easily be (and was) de-emphasized in favour of a generalized carnival setting. The sex was less offensive than that in many Restoration comedies: although some of her characters, as Pope complained, are put to bed, they are not committing adultery. In comparison, Wycherley's *The Country Wife* is about cuckolding, and Behn's own *The Luckey Chance* (which was not revived in original form after 1718) treats adulterous lovers sympathetically. In addition to these largely negative reasons, *The Rover* had the positive advantage of being easily adaptable to – and, in some cases, anticipating – eighteenth-century tastes. It is this positive advantage I am examining. My question is: *how* was *The Rover* played during the eighteenth century? What alterations made it enjoyable for successive generations of playgoers? Though bawdy has caused the most fuss, it is not the only element to need investigation. Important changes were also made to the balance among the major roles in the play. I am therefore concentrating on two aspects: the various elements that were found objectionable under the name of 'bawdy', and the way the relationship between the roles of Willmore, Angellica and Hellena was interpreted.

The question of alteration and adaptation of *The Rover* needs to be viewed in the light of the play's own genesis as an adaptation of an earlier play: Thomas Killigrew's two-part, ten-act closet drama *Thomaso, or the Wanderer*, written in the Interregnum and published in 1663.[11] There is not space here for a full comparison between the two plays, but I will draw comparisons with *Thomaso* where this helps illuminate the history of either the bawdy or the main roles.

Behn uses a number of incidents from *Thomaso*, and many of her lines closely echo Killigrew's. She bases her rakish hero on Thomaso, and takes from Killigrew the idea of portraying the rejected mistress, Angellica Bianca, with sympathy and a serious consideration of her social position as a courtesan. She also extensively reshapes the play, not only tightening the organization and speeding up the action, but also rethinking the main male and female roles. Killigrew's play centres on the adventures of a rake-hero, who dominates the action. His satellites include a strongly drawn, sympathetic courtesan and a less interesting heroine who functions as his prize. Behn has focussed on and remodelled this triangle, creating a delicate balance among three strong roles: the lively, thoughtless Willmore, an object of affectionate mockery, the near-tragic Angellica and the witty comic heroine Hellena. In my examination of eighteenth-century treatment of *The Rover* I have found that this careful balance, created by Behn, was altered in performance for various reasons.

There is a variety of material to answer questions about *The Rover*'s eighteenth-century history. I have three kinds of evidence. The first is contemporary comment, gleaned from newspapers or stage histories, related to particular performances. I have found some of this, but not a great deal. The second is easier to find but more difficult to use: evidence about the casting of performances. Where an actor or actress's general reputation and style of performance are known, it may be possible to make some inferences about how *The Rover* was played. While I will bring both these kinds of evidence into play where appropriate, my argument is in the main based on the third kind of evidence – textual. I am going to discuss three altered texts of the play.

The first is a prompt copy of the first edition of *The Rover*, now in the University of London library. Edward Langhans has described it in detail, and in his more recent work suggests that it was prepared for a Covent Garden production of the play in 1740. He adds that the prompter may have worked from an earlier prompt copy, possibly from the 1720s.[12] The alterations are mainly cuts, and demonstrate that *The Rover* was toned down for performance by 1740, and possibly earlier.

The second is the 1757 edition of the play, printed 'With the

Alterations, As it is now reviv'd and Acting at the Theatre-Royal in Covent-Garden.'[13] While there were probably alterations not recorded in the printed version – which may well print in full some scenes that were cut in performance – this edition does give us plenty of evidence of change. Someone has taken a good deal of trouble to make a large number of mainly minor verbal changes in the text, often to the detriment of Behn's rhythmic prose. The intention seems to be to modernize the language use, clearing up possible obscurities and making the diction more 'correct'. The changes are more numerous at the beginning of the play, suggesting that the adapter lost steam as the work went on.

The third text is *Love in Many Masks*, altered from *The Rover* by John Philip Kemble for the 1790 production at Drury Lane.[14] This is the most thoroughly altered version. Kemble cuts a good deal and adds about thirty lines of his own. The result is not only to extend the bowdlerization of the text begun earlier in the century, but to change the whole emphasis of the play. I will offer some remarks on *Love in Many Masks* separately, after looking at all the altered versions together.

The play was updated in various ways, and several changes were clearly made in order to get rid of outdated topical references. The largest group of changes, however, is concerned with bawdy. For eighteenth-century audiences, the term seems to have encompassed a number of things, including sexual and scatological references in speech (especially criticized when given to female speakers), representations of sexual activity or sexual violence, and undressing or displaying the body. *The Rover* does not feature the displays of women 'in a provocative state of semi-nudity' that were common in Restoration comedy.[15] (It does make use of the breeches part, which displayed women's legs, but was not defined as bawdy.) The play does feature male undressing, in Blunt's role, and this, as we will see, was the focus of much hostile comment. The point seems to have been not so much the display of the body – Blunt keeps his drawers on – as the suggestion of imminent sexual activity made by the undressing. In my analysis of changes I have concentrated on bawdy, but the examination of this also entails investigation of the way the main characters' roles changed. I have selected some aspects of each of four characters – Blunt, Hellena, Angellica, and Willmore – that seem to have been especially

subject to change, and compared treatment of them across four versions –
1677, the prompt copy, 1757, and 1790.

The incidents and speeches I compare across the four versions are
grouped as follows: (1) Ned Blunt. I look at his Act III scenes in Lucetta's
bedroom and afterwards crawling out of the sewer, and his threats to rape
Florinda in Act IV. (2) Hellena. I look especially at her outspokenness in
the first scene. (3) Angellica. I look at the way her retreat into the bedroom
with Willmore is handled, and at what happens to her soliloquy in Act IV
lamenting Willmore's infidelity. (4) Willmore. I look at his attack on
Florinda in Act II. Other aspects of his role are considered in the discussion of *Love in Many Masks*.

Of all the characters in the play, Ned Blunt seems to have given most
offence to eighteenth-century audiences, particularly because of his scene
in Lucetta's chamber. Stage directions in the 1677 text indicate that he
undresses on stage – down to his shirt and drawers – before moving
towards her bed, and falling through a trapdoor. The following scene has
him '*creeping out of a Common-Shoar, his face, &c. all dirty*', and cursing
Lucetta for her trick and himself for his gullibility (1677: III.iv.p. 40). The
scene of him crawling out of the sewer is ruled around in the promptbook,
indicating that it was omitted. It is printed in the 1757 edition, so may have
been performed in the 1757 production. It is omitted from the 1790
version. Economy as well as decency may be a motive for cutting this
scene: the omission saves one scene change in a crowded act. It is worth
noting, too, that this scene is the one in which the fool is most graphically
humiliated by the whore. It is one of Behn's own touches (in *Thomaso*
Blunt's counterpart, Edwardo, is tricked, but not tipped in the sewer, and
he has his revenge by getting his bravoes to cut Lucetta's face) and one that
very soon offended eighteenth-century audiences.

Blunt's undressing caused the most comment. The relevant stage
directions are left intact in both the promptbook and the 1757 edition. It is
only in the 1790 version that they are altered: here, Blunt no longer takes
any of his clothes off but merely lays '*his sword, hat, watch, purse etc. on the
table*' (1790: III.iii.p. 35). His undressing was a contentious issue much
earlier, though. Steele, as we have seen, objected to it in 1711. From two
letters placed in *The London Daily Post, and General Advertiser* in 1741, it is

clear that the Covent Garden revival of March of that year was carefully changed to avoid offending the audience. Blunt still appeared in his shirt and drawers, but he went offstage to undress. This change may have been directed, and was certainly advertised, by Lacy Ryan, the actor who was playing Willmore.[16] In the 1757 production, Blunt's indecent undressing was restored to the stage, as we know from the offence it caused to the critic in the *London Chronicle*.[17]

Another offensive scene involving Blunt is at the end of Act IV, when Florinda arrives at his house just as he has been vowing revenge on womankind for the humiliation visited on him by Lucetta. He threatens to rape and beat Florinda, and Frederick, who arrives in the middle of the scene, is initially quite willing to join in, only changing his mind once he suspects that her social status is too high for her to be raped with impunity. The scene – based on a similar incident in *Thomaso* – is a chilling one, revealing the ugliness of the power relations behind the facade of gentlemen's gallantry, and depriving sexual violence of the rakish glamour sometimes invested in it in Restoration comedy. It was considerably toned down in some eighteenth-century performances. In the promptbook a number of cuts were made to Blunt's threats. In the examples cited below, words deleted in the promptbook are placed in square brackets. When Blunt insults Florinda and 'pulls her rudely', she cries, 'Dare you be so cruel?' He replies:

> Cruel, adsheartlikins as a Galley-slave, or a *Spanish*-Whore. [Cruel, yes, I will kiss and beat thee all over; kiss, and see thee all over; thou shalt lye with me too, not that I care for the injoyment, but to let thee see I have ta'en deliberated Malice to thee, and will be reveng'd on one Whore for the sins of another;] I will smile and deceive thee, flatter thee, and beat thee, kiss and swear, and lye to thee, imbrace thee and rob thee, as she did me, fawn on thee, and strip thee stark naked, then hang thee out at my window by the heels, with a Paper of scurvy Verses fasten'd to thy breast, in praise of damnable women – Come, come along.
>
> (1677: IV.v.p. 65)

In the promptbook, Frederick's initial reaction to Florinda's plight is still to mock her – 'What's this, a Person of Quality too, who is upon the ramble to supply the defects of some grave impotent Husband?' – but his nastiest comment is cut:

BLUNT No, no, Gentlewoman, come along, adsheartlikins we must be better
   acquainted – [we'l both lye with her, and then let me alone to bang her.
  FRED I'm ready to serve you in matters of Revenge that has a double
   pleasure in't.
BLUNT Well said. You hear, little one, how you are condemn'd by public Vote
   to the Bed within,] there's no resisting your Destiny, sweat heart.

(IV.v.p. 66)

The 1757 production seems again to have stuck closer to the original than
the one served by the promptbook. Blunt's threats to Florinda are almost
untouched in the 1757 edition, and this does not seem to be a case of printing unaltered a scene that was cut in performance, because there are
enough minor verbal changes to suggest that the text is taking account of
alterations made for performance.

In 1790, however, great changes were made to this scene for *Love in
Many Masks*. The alterations go far beyond those in the promptbook. The
scene (now placed in Act v) is considerably shortened. Blunt's threats to
Florinda are carefully unspecified. When she asks, 'Can you be so cruel as
to –' he replies, 'Cruel! Adsheartlikins as a galley-slave – Come along – or I
shall –' The remainder of the two passages quoted above is omitted.
Frederick's participation in the scene is given an altogether new colouring. He immediately ranges himself with Florinda against Blunt, telling
her, 'Fear nothing, madam' (1790: v.iv.p. 57). This is one of many indications of sentimentalization of all the young lovers' roles. Blunt is a comic
butt and as such can be allowed to retain his threats, though their expression has to be obscured; but Frederick is to marry Valeria, Florinda's
cousin, and by 1790 it is quite inappropriate for him to threaten a lady.

When we turn to Hellena's part, we find a similar pattern of alteration: some toning down in the promptbook, hardly any in 1757, and
much more in 1790. Hellena is a bold heroine who, determined to avoid
being sent to a nunnery, dresses as a gipsy to find a man during the carnival,
and disguises herself as a boy during her pursuit of Willmore. Special
emphasis was probably laid on her boy-disguise in the middle and later
years of the century, when she was frequently played by actresses famous
for breeches parts – Margaret Woffington in 1741, 1748 and again in 1757,
and Dorothy Jordan in 1790.[18] At the same time, however, the cheeky

speech which goes with her boldness is being toned down (though not consistently). My examples are taken from the first scene, where Hellena's insistence on exceeding the proper bounds of a young girl's behaviour is the main theme. On the subject of Florinda's projected marriage with old Don Vincentio she is aggressive and bawdy. In the citation below, the phrases deleted in the promptbook are enclosed in square brackets.

HELLENA That Honour being past, the Gyant stretches itself; yawns and sighs [a Belch or two, loud as a Musket, throws himself into Bed, and expects you in his foul sheets], and e're you can get your self undrest, call's you with a Snore or two – and are not these fine Blessings to a young Lady?
PEDRO Have you done yet?
HELLENA And this Man you must kiss, nay you must kiss none but him too – and nuzel through his Beard to find his Lips. – And this you must submit to for Threescore years, and all for a Joynture.
PEDRO For all your Character of *Don Vincentio*, she is as like to Marry him, as she was before.
HELLENA [Marry *Don Vincentio*! hang me such a Wedlock would be worse than Adultery with another Man.]   (1677: I.i.p. 4)

It might be argued that whoever prepared this promptbook was only continuing a process of bowdlerization begun by Behn herself. The remarks about the disgusting husband in *Thomaso* read: 'the Gyant stretches himself, yawns and sighs a belch or two, stales in your pot, farts as loud as a Musket' (Part II, Act II, Scene ii, p. 400). In *Thomaso*, though, these lines are not spoken by Hellena's counterpart but by Harrigo, one of the hero's male friends, to Serulina. Similarly, Hellena's audacious remark about adultery is taken from another Killigrew character, Calis – a female servant. *The Rover*'s boldness is not simply a matter of what is said but who says it; Behn is giving lines designed for rakish men and serving-women to her high-born heroine.

The 1757 text, here as in other instances, preserves Behn's boldness. Hellena's speeches here are uncut, and even at one point embellished: Vincentio now calls his bride 'with a Snore or two *but nothing else*' (I.i.p. 6; my italics). This is in keeping with the general endeavour of the 1757 text to make meanings explicit. In 1790, on the other hand, Hellena's bawdy speech is carefully excised.

Angellica's part also receives some alterations in the eighteenth-century versions. The issue here is how much and what kind of attention is paid to her situation as a courtesan. In Act II, Scene ii, abandoning her trade, she offers Willmore her love, and they retire to her bedroom. The stage is left to Angellica's bawd, Moretta, who concludes the act with a bitter comment on the courtesan's folly.

ANGELLICA   The pay, I mean, is but thy Love for mine. – Can you give that?
WILLMORE   Intirely – come, let's withdraw! where I'll renew my Vows – and
   breath 'em with such Ardour thou shalt not doubt my zeal.
ANGELLICA   Thou hast a Pow'r too strong to be resisted.
                    Ex. Will. and Angellica.
  MORETTA   Now my Curse go with you – is all our Project fallen to this? to
   love the only Enemy to our Trade? nay, to love such a Shameroone, a
   very Beggar, nay a Pyrate Beggar, whose business is to rifle, and be gone,
   a no Purchase, no Pay Taterdemalion, and *English* Piccaroon. A Rogue
   that fights for daily drink, and takes a Pride in being Loyally Lousie – Oh
   I cou'd curse now, if I durst. – This is the Fate of most Whores.
   Trophies, which from believing Fops we win,
   Are spoils to those who couzen us agen.   (1677: II. ii. pp. 28–9)

In the promptbook this passage receives a couple of alterations. Angellica's 'Thou hast a Pow'r too strong to be resisted' is cut, and in Moretta's speech the euphemism 'of our Proffession' is substituted for the word 'Whores'. In 1757 this passage is left untouched. In 1790 it is completely altered. Moretta's speech is omitted, and Angellica closes the act with a new speech.

ANGELLICA   The pay I mean, is but thy love for mine. – Can you give that?
WILLMORE   Intirely.
ANGELLICA   Then I receive you as my future servant.
WILLMORE   Madam –
ANGELLICA   But mark me, Sir – my birth, my breeding and pride raise me far
   above the coarse interchange of mere convenient pleasures – I offer my
   heart for your's: Yet how depend on men for constancy!
WILLMORE   Depend! – may I depend on your's?
ANGELLICA   Ah! this is one of the virtues you always blame the want of in us,
   though you never practise it yourselves.

Virgins or wives, for us our tyrants claim
A strict performance of the task of fame;
Yet to themselves indulgently allow
The breach of honour and the marriage vow.
No more let man our weaker sex condemn
For faults, originally taught by them;
Since, if from Virtue's holy path we stray,
We only follow where you point the way.   (1790: II.ii, pp. 25–6)

Here, Angellica is presented as a victim of seduction, and her plight is taken as representative of all women's. Her final speech attacks the sexual double standard and excuses her own (and other women's) sexual behaviour by blaming men for all lapses from 'virtue'.

In stressing Angellica as victim, Kemble's 1790 text echoes some of the concerns of Killigrew's *Thomaso*. Behn's scene is based on *Thomaso*, Part I, Act II, Scene iv; but a major concern for Killigrew's Angellica, unlike Behn's, is that she is not pure enough for the hero. She wishes

> that such a stream [of her tears] could make me as pure a Virgin as I am now a perfect Lover; then I would beg to be thy wife; but that must not be; for love bids me not ask that which honour forbids thee to grant; yet you may be my friend.   (*Thomaso*, Part I, Act II, Scene iv, p. 341)

Killigrew's and Kemble's texts make the fact of Angellica's being a courtesan the focus for their sympathetic treatment of her. Behn's text is distinctive in its attempt to see Angellica positively, as a sexually experienced woman who offers free love. The problem is not her profession, but Willmore's inability to appreciate the importance of her offer to renounce it.

Though Kemble gave Angellica extra lines and extra pathos at certain points, on the whole he reduced her part in favour of the hero's; and in this he was developing a trend begun in earlier eighteenth-century performances. In Act IV, Scene ii, a scene not based on any counterpart in Killigrew, Willmore is comically pursued by both Angellica and Hellena. The scene ends with Angellica left alone on stage:

WILLMORE Yes, you can spare me now, – farewel, till you're in better
    Humour – [*aside*] I'm glad of this release – Now for my Gipsie:
    For tho' to worse we change, yet still we find
    New Joys, new Charms, in a new Miss that's kind.
                      Ex. Willmore
ANGELLICA He's gone, and in this Ague of my Soul
    The Shivering fit returns;
    Oh with what willing haste, he took his leave,
    As if the long'd-for Minute, were arriv'd
    Of some blest assignation.
    In vain I have Consulted all my Charms,
    In vain this Beauty priz'd, in vain believ'd,
    My Eyes cou'd kindle any lasting fires;
    I had forgot my Name, my Infamie,
    And the reproach that Honour lays on those
    That dare pretend a sober passion here.
    Nice reputation, tho' it leave behind
    More vertues than inhabit where that dwells;
    Yet that once gone, those Vertues shine no more.
    – Then since I am not fit to be belov'd,
    I am resolv'd to think on a revenge
    On him that sooth'd me thus to my undoing.   (1677: IV.ii.p. 60)

This passage is considerably altered in the promptbook. Angellica leaves the stage after dismissing Willmore. Her soliloquy disappears and Willmore closes the scene with his couplet. This cut perhaps indicates a tendency in some eighteenth-century productions to simplify the emotional effect of the comedy. Up till this point the scene has been exploiting the comic potential of Willmore's infidelity, which makes him temporarily embarrassed by the simultaneous attentions of both women. The shift of tone involved in Angellica's final speech may have jarred in performance. The 1757 text, however, preserves the soliloquy. The 1790 text once again has the biggest alteration. As in the promptbook, Angellica leaves the stage before Willmore and loses her soliloquy. He ends the scene – and, in this text, the act – with his couplet and his resolve to find his gipsy. The couplet, though, has been changed from a breezy declaration in favour of new mistresses to a confession that Hellena has conquered his heart:

For though I wildly roam from fair to fair,
I feel she holds unrivall'd empire here. (iv.ii.p. 53)

This brings us to the changes made to Willmore, the rover himself. In general, his part is not much altered before 1790. One scene which is modified in the promptbook is the scene in Act III where he makes a drunken attempt to seduce Florinda. (This scene is in itself an indication of Behn's willingness to laugh at her hero: a similar episode in her source play is given to the fool, Edwardo.) Willmore's libertine arguments in favour of sex without vows are expunged. Square brackets enclose the promptbook's cuts in the passage cited:

FLORINDA Heavens! what a filthy Beast is this?
WILLMORE I am so, and thou ought'st the sooner to lye with me for that reason – [for look you Child, there will be so sin in't, because 'twas neither design'd nor premeditated. 'Tis pure Accident on both sides – that's a certain thing now – indeed shou'd I make Love to you, and you vow fidelity – and swear and lye till you believ'd and yielded – that were to make it wilful Fornication – the crying Sin of the Nation – thou art therefore (as thou art a good Christian) oblig'd in Conscience to deny me nothing. Now – come be kind without any more idle prating.
FLORINDA Oh I am ruin'd – Wicked Man unhand me.
WILLMORE Wicked! – Egad Child a Judge were he young and vigorous, and saw those Eyes of thine, wou'd know 'twas they gave the first blow – the first provocation – come prithee let's lose no time, I say – this is a fine convenient place.] (1677: III.v.p. 42)

1757 omits only 'that were to make it wilful Fornication – the crying Sin of the Nation'; and in this the text is following cuts made in an earlier edition rather than representing an alteration made for the 1757 performance. The 1790 text cuts out the whole passage after Florinda's first speech, and also omits from the scene Willmore's offer of money to Florinda. While the promptbook alterations mainly reflect a concern to cut out Willmore's irreligious expressions, the 1790 revisions also ensure that he does not treat Florinda as a whore.

It is in the treatment of Willmore that the 1790 version most clearly differs from the earlier texts. Kemble alters his whole behaviour, and in doing so changes the nature of his relationships with Hellena and

Angellica. *Love in Many Masks* becomes a different kind of play from *The Rover*, and it needs some separate consideration.

From his first appearance, the Willmore of *Love in Many Masks* is less of a rover than Behn's original character. His lewd remarks to the courtesan in Act I, Scene ii are omitted. He no longer says there is only one way for a woman to oblige him, or longs to have his arms full of 'soft, white, kind – Woman!' (1677: II.i.p. 16). He does go to bed with Angellica, but all references to his taking money from her are taken out. His love for Hellena is cleared of its mercenary taint. Hellena's fortune is still mentioned, but Willmore is shown to be more interested in her gentility than her money. His love for Hellena is clearly his real love, and his desire for Angellica just a temporary aberration. He still makes a speech to Angellica about virtue being an infirmity in woman, but it's clear he doesn't mean it. The ending of the play shows a thoroughly reformed and sententious hero. The original Willmore teases Hellena about their imminent marriage: 'Have you no trembling at the near approach?' She replies 'No more than you have in an Engagement or a Tempest', and his rejoinder closes the play:

WILLMORE   Egad thou'rt a brave Girle, and I admire thy Love and Courage.
    Lead on, no other Dangers they can dread,
    Who venture in the Storms o'th'Marriage Bed.   (1677: v.i.p. 83)

In *Love in Many Masks*, this final exchange is converted from a contemplation of marriage as a battle to a discussion of a rake's reform – that favourite subject of late eighteenth-century sentimental drama. Willmore closes the play with a new set of couplets:

WILLMORE   Thou'rt a brave girl! – I admire thy love and courage, and will give
    thee as little cause as I can to repent 'em.
    Henceforth no other pleasures can I know,
    Than those of fond fidelity to you;
    Your pow'r my captive heart in chains shall bind,
    Sweet as the graces of your heart and mind:-
    Blest in my friends, and doubly blest in love,
    My joy's complete indeed – if you approve.   (1790: v.iv.p. 70)

Willmore, then, seems to be tamed – the heroine's captive. The need to chasten both his role and Angellica's makes it difficult to present a coherent version of their relationship. On the one hand Angellica is detached as far as possible from her life as a courtesan, and made a representative female victim of male seduction. On the other hand her seducer is also absolved as far as possible from blame: he didn't really mean it, and he gives up roving as soon as he can for the love of a good woman. Hellena emerges as the winner, in the name of virtuous woman; but in the process she has lost the sauciness that made her a heroine fit to match her rover. Her encounters with Willmore are marked less by witty repartee than by her maidenly retreats; she runs away from him twice, which she had not done in previous versions.

Both female parts lose out in this version, while Willmore gains in dignity what he loses in libertine speech. Behn's original hero is often made to look foolish where money is concerned. His fine speeches scorning Angellica's trade are undercut when he takes her money and leaves her for a rich woman. All this is absent from the 1790 version, and so, too, are the hints that Willmore's own sense of manhood is threatened by his lack of money. In 1677, when Willmore hears of Angellica's prohibitive price, he cries, 'The very thought of it quenches all manner of fire in me' (I.ii.p. 15); in 1790 it is simply desire Willmore feels: 'The very thought of her makes me mad' (I.ii.p. 14). Kemble's Willmore is more conventionally heroic in the fighting scenes, and shows more humanitarian feeling. He is transformed from a Restoration libertine to an eighteenth-century reformed rake.

From comparing the four texts, then, we can conclude that *The Rover* was bowdlerized for performance in the eighteenth century, and that this was happening by 1740 at the latest. There was no smooth progression towards greater decency as the century went on, though; rather, different productions had different emphases. The Covent Garden production of 1757–60 stands out as something of an anomaly, restoring many of the controversial elements that earlier productions had omitted. Kemble's 1790 adaptation went much further than previous productions, and altered the character of the play so that it corresponded to late-eighteenth-century notions of humanity, benevolence, and reform.[19]

More was at stake in the alterations than bowdlerization. The conception of the roles of Hellena, Angellica, and Willmore changed during the century. The case of Kemble's version is clearest. In *Love in Many Masks*, the balance of roles between Willmore, Hellena and Angellica is changed. In a return to the dynamics of Behn's original source, *Thomaso* (in other respects so very different from Kemble's sentimental work), the hero dominates the stage. Angellica is given some additional pathos, but her part as a whole is reduced in importance. Hellena has no real rival in Willmore's affections, and her part is the undisputed female lead: however, much of its original spice has disappeared.

These changes can be traced in the text itself and are supported by what we know of the cast. Kemble himself played Willmore, having adapted the role as a vehicle for his acting. His opposite was Hellena, played by famous comic actress Dorothy Jordan. Angellica was played by Sarah Ward, a reasonably successful but much lesser-known actress.[20] This contrasts with what we know of casting practice in the early years of the century, when Angellica as well as Hellena was strongly cast. This partly reflects a general change in stage practice over the period: in the Restoration and early eighteenth century most parts in a play, even the minor ones, would be given to well-known actors, whereas later in the century a 'star' system developed, and famous actors tended only to play important parts.[21] Even taking this into account, Angellica seems to have been given more attention early in the century. The part seems to have been passed on, with other roles, among actresses whose main fame was in tragedy. Elizabeth Barry played Angellica, and later Mary Porter took the role, playing it over forty times between 1715 and 1730.[22] Productions in which two leading actresses – Anne Bracegirdle and Elizabeth Barry, on one occasion – played Hellena and Angellica must have been very different from the one of 1790, when Hellena was played by Dorothy Jordan, and Angellica by Sarah Ward. Angellica passed from being a part suitable for a major tragedienne to being a supporting role.

If Angellica's importance declined, Willmore's increased, and by 1790 his role had become more simply heroic. I have been suggesting here that Behn's play gently mocks its rake-hero in several places; and mockery of heroes can be seen as a distinctive feature of the 'covert' feminism of early women playwrights.[23] This contrasts with the attitude to the hero found in male-authored versions, where there may have been some identification for the male writer or adapter between himself and the hero. The original play, *Thomaso*, gave power and dignity to its hero, who can be seen as an idealized version of his author, Sir Thomas Killigrew. Kemble adapted the play with his own starring role in mind, and his senti-mentalized version of Willmore, though very different from Killigrew's in terms of behaviour, is similar in terms of male centrality and importance. In the context of these versions, Behn's Willmore stands out more clearly as a woman's affectionate but telling undercutting of male pretension.

This mockery may not have been fully transmitted in eighteenth-century performances, even when Behn's text remained unaltered. It is worth reflecting on the importance of this attractive leading role to the survival and adaptation of Behn's most popular comedy. It is likely that one reason for the frequency of performance was the play's popularity with leading actors. Wilks was a dominant figure – a leading actor, and from 1710, one of the managers – at Drury Lane. He carried on playing Willmore till he died at the age of sixty-seven. Meanwhile a younger rival, Lacy Ryan, took up the part, and as we have seen, he took pains to see that the play was made acceptable to audiences. How these actors interpreted Willmore it is hard to know. A hero with something of the fool in him could be seen as an attractive opportunity for the comic actor; on the other hand, the roles of more conventional comedy heroes may have exerted a pull on interpretations of Willmore. There is some evidence that the hero's part was being softened quite early on. William Mountfort, playing Willmore in 1690, was known for his representations of 'the fine Gentleman', and 'his Spirit shone the brighter for being polished with Decency'. Cibber reported that Queen Mary, despite her disapproval of the play, enjoyed Mountfort's Willmore, because 'even in that dissolute Character of the *Rover* he seem'd to wash off the guilt from Vice, and give it Charms and Merit'.[24] Robert Wilks had made his name as Sir Harry Wildair in Farquhar's *The Constant Couple*, a role in which he is said to have captivated the women in the audience.[25] He was known for being graceful, spirited and gentlemanly in his comic roles, and was called 'the genteelest Actor of his time'.[26] His long-running Willmore is likely to have been more of a charming gentleman than a rake in danger of losing his dignity.

The Rover survived so long because it anticipated, or was readily adaptable to, eighteenth-century tastes. If one important factor was the appeal of Willmore's role to the leading men who tended to choose plays, another was its treatment of female roles. In the treatment of Angellica, both Killigrew and Behn were anticipating the concerns of female-centred pathetic tragedy in the 1690s and later; and part of *The Rover's* popularity in the early decades of the eighteenth century are probably attributable to this. These are the years when Angellica was commonly played by leading tragediennes, though it is important to bear in mind that the cutting of her role may have begun in these early years. Hellena, in contrast, was given more prominence in the middle and later years of the century, when actresses famous for breeches roles took her part: but she was also toned down.

The challenge of a woman entering the male preserve of sex-comedy was evident in *The Rover* in Behn's mocking treatment of male characters and her unusually strong treatment of female ones. During the eighteenth century, as one point or another of her love-triangle was sharpened or flattened, it was pulled out of its original equilateral shape. Both of the main female parts were lessened in the process. Making *The Rover* acceptable on the eighteenth-century stage was not just a matter of getting rid of bawdy, but reducing the challenge posed by its female characters. One area, though, needs further research. If we knew more about the way Elizabeth Barry, for example, played Angellica in 1709, or how Margaret Woffington played Hellena in 1748, we might find that strong performances from actresses did something to counter the movement which I have been describing here, an eighteenth-century movement towards the dilution of Aphra Behn's work.

NOTES

1 This decline is fully discussed in Jeslyn Medoff, 'The daughters of Behn and the problem of reputation', in Isobel Grundy and Susan Wiseman, eds, *Women, Writing, History 1640–1740* (London, 1992), pp. 33–54. Medoff places Behn's loss of reputation early, emphasizing attacks on her

during her lifetime and soon after. Though I agree that these attacks were significant, they need to be read in the context of a general tendency for her contemporaries to treat her as an important writer, to be praised or vilified according to poetic occasion. It is in the period after 1700 that attitudes to Behn become more dismissive.

2 *The Spectator* 51, 28 April 1711. In *The Spectator*, ed. D. F. Bond (Oxford, 1965), vol. I, p. 218.

3 Alexander Pope, *The first Epistle of the Second Book of Horace Imitated* (1737), 291. In *The Poems of Alexander Pope*, ed. John Butt (London, 1939), vol. IV, *Imitations of Horace*, p. 221.

4 *The Gentleman's Magazine and Historical Chronicle* 8 (1738), 469.

5 Unless otherwise indicated, information about performance dates and cast-list is taken from *The London Stage 1660–1800*, Part 2, ed. Emmet L. Avery, Part 3, ed. Arthur H. Scouten, Part 4, ed. G. W. Stone, and Part 5, ed. C. B. Hogan (Carbondale, 1960–8).

6 See *The London Stage*, Part 2, 1700–29. Discussion of sources is placed at the introduction of each season's calendar. In the early years of the century records are often noted to be incomplete (see for example p. 3, p. 15); later, *The Daily Courant* is mentioned as a regular, though not necessarily complete source. During the 1730s newspaper advertising expanded further, and fuller records of performances were preserved: see *The London Stage*, Part 3, 1729–47, pp. cii–ciii.

7 Leo Hughes, *The Drama's Patrons: A Study of the Eighteenth-Century London Audience* (Austin and London, 1971), p. 123.

8 James J. Lynch, *Box Pit and Gallery: Stage and Society in Johnson's London* (New York, 1953, reiss. 1971), p. 270.

9 Hughes, *The Drama's Patrons*, p. 124 and p. 125.

10 Lynch, *Box Pit and Gallery*, p. 270.

11 Thomas Killigrew, *Thomaso, or the Wanderer: A Comedy. The Scene Madrid. Written in Madrid by Thomas Killigrew. In Two Parts* (London, 1663).

12 A full description of the copy is in Edward A. Langhans, 'Three early eighteenth-century promptbooks', *Theatre Notebook* 20 (1966), 142–50. Here it is conjectured that the promptbook was used for a Drury Lane performance in the 1720s. Langhans reconsiders this promptbook in *Eighteenth Century British and Irish Promptbooks: A Descriptive Bibliography* (New York and London: Greenwood Press, 1987), and suggests that the notes were made by Richard Cross at Covent Garden between 1739 and 1741, perhaps for the 12 May 1740 performance (p. 9). If this is the case the same promptbook would probably have been used at Covent Garden in 1741, when Blunt's undressing onstage was omitted. In the

promptbook, however, the stage-direction for his undressing is left in. Langhans also suggests that Cross may have worked from an older prompt copy, perhaps one prepared by John Stede for Lincoln's Inn Fields in the 1720s (p. 9). We cannot be sure, then, of the date that the alterations recorded in the promptbook were made; but it is reasonable to conclude that they were made by 1740, and possibly some years earlier.

13 *The Rover : or, the Banish'd Cavaliers. A Comedy, With the Alterations, As it is now reviv'd and Acting at the Theatre-Royal in Covent Garden* (London, 1757).

14 *Love in Many Masks: As Altered by J. P. Kemble, from Mrs Behn's Rover, and first acted at the Theatre Royal in Drury Lane, March 8th, 1790* (Dublin, 1790).

15 Elizabeth Howe, *The first English Actresses* (Cambridge, 1992), p. 54.

16 *London Daily Post and General Advertiser*, 9 and 10 March 1741. The letters concern the revival due to open on 16 March. The number for 9 March carries a letter addressed to Ryan (and probably written by him), praising the play but suggesting that it would be more decent if Blunt went offstage to undress. The following day, Ryan's reply appeared, welcoming the chance to point out that this alteration was already planned.

17 *The London Chronicle: or, Universal Evening Post*, 22–4 February 1757. There were further complaints in later issues. This critic's strictures are discussed in Leo Hughes, *The Drama's Patrons*, pp. 127–9, and in C. H. Gray, *Theatrical Criticism in London to 1795* (New York, 1931), pp. 135–6.

18 Woffington was famous for her playing of Sir Harry Wildair in Farquhar's *The Constant Couple*, a role she took over from Robert Wilks. Jordan also played Sir Harry Wildair. Woffington's acting is described in Thomas Davies, *Memoirs of the Life of David Garrick Esq.* (London, 1808), I, pp. 340–3; quoted in David Thomas, *Theatre in Europe: a documentary history. Restoration and Georgian England, 1660–1788* (Cambridge: Cambridge University Press, 1989), pp. 383–4. See also Doran, *Their Majesties Servants, or Annals of the English Stage, from Thomas Betterton to Edmund Kean* (London, 1865), ch. 28. For Jordan's career see the entry under her name in Philipp Highfill, Kalman Burnim and Edward Langhans, eds., *A Biographical Dictionary of Actors, Actresses, Musicians, Dancers, Managers and Other Stage Personnel in London, 1660–1800* (Carbondale and Edwardsville, 1973–87, 12 vols.).

19 As altered by Kemble, Behn's play fits nicely as a type of eighteenth-century comedy: it can be seen as an example of what R. D. Hume calls humane comedy, characterized by its arousal of benevolent good will, with some elements of reform comedy. See R. D. Hume, 'The multifarious

forms of eighteenth-century comedy', in G. W. Stone ed., *The Stage and the Page: London's 'Whole Show'; in the Eighteenth-Century Theatre* (Berkeley, LA and London, 1981), pp. 3–32.

20 Sarah Ward acted in London and the provinces, and was praised for her acting in 'some sentimental parts of genteel comedy'. See Highfill, Burnim and Langhans, *A Biographical Dictionary*, vol. 15, p. 271.

21 See Lynch, *Box Pit and Gallery*, p. 139.

22 See Ben R. Schneider, 'The coquette-prude as an actress's line in Restoration comedy during the time of Mrs Oldfield', *Theatre Notebook* 22 (1967), 143–56, table 1.

23 See Pearson, *The Prostituted Muse: Images of Women and Women Dramatists 1642–1737* (London, 1988), p. 254. Pearson suggests that while men like Southerne and D'Urfey present strong feminist themes in their plays, women's work is distinguished by its irreverence towards male characters: 'Women are more likely to mock men, even their nominal heroes.'

24 Colley Cibber, *An apology for the Life of Colley Cibber: with an historical view of the stage during his own time* [1740], ed. B. R. S. Fone (Ann Arbor, 1968), p. 75.

25 A *Rhapsody on the Stage*, published in 1746, claimed that: '*Wilks with genteel and unaffected air / In gay Sir Harry Charm'd th'attentive fair.*' Quoted in Highfill, Burnim and Langhans, *A Biographical Dictionary*, vol. 16, p. 120.

26 *Tyranny Triumphant* (1743), quoted in Highfill, Burnim and Langhans, vol. 16, p. 120.

PART II ❧ POETRY

6 Aphra Behn: poetry and masquerade

PAUL SALZMAN

> In Gentle Numbers all my Songs are drest:
> And when I would Thy Glories sing,
> What in Strong Manly Verse should be exprest
> Turns all to Womanish Tenderness within
> 'To the Unknown Daphnis'[1]

When Aphra Behn went on her spying mission in 1666, like all good agents she had a number of different names. For Lord Arlington, the Secretary of State in charge of intelligence, whose office supplied her with a memorial outlining the information she was to extract from William Scot, she was Mrs Affora.[2] Her assumed identity was marked by the name Astrea, a romance name possibly acquired during an earlier romantic alliance with Scot in Surinam, an alliance also marked by the name Celadon, which was given to Scot by the hostile governor of Surinam, William Byam, in his account of the aftermath of the affair in a letter to Sir Robert Harley.[3] In her letters back to Arlington's office, Behn used a code which substituted numbers for various words, such as 156 for England or 27 for army. Behn was 160.[4]

When she entered the world of literature, Behn announced her arrival as both a military campaign and a spying mission. In the prologue to her first play, *The Forc'd Marriage*, staged at the Duke's Theatre in 1670, Behn announces that a significant gender division has been challenged:

> Women those charming Victors, in whose Eyes
> Lie all their Arts, and their Artilleries,
> Not being contented with the Wounds they made
> Would by new Stratagems our Lives invade.[5]

The prologue goes on to introduce an image that must have been particularly revealing to those who knew of Behn's undercover work:

> Today one of their party Ventures out,
> Not with design to conquer, but to scout.
> Discourage but this first attempt, and then
> They'll hardly dare to sally out again.
> The Poetess too, they say, has Spies abroad,
> Which have dispers'd themselves in every road,
> I'th' Upper Box, Pit, Galleries; every Face
> You find disguised in a Black Velvet Case.
> My life on't; is her Spy on purpose sent,
> To hold you in a wanton Compliment.   (pp. 285–6)

The masquerade is linked to the spy in this passage, which casts a soon to be familiar slur associating playwright and prostitute (the latter signified by the mask).[6] This image, spoken by a male actor, is disarmed by a female actor, who continues the prologue:

> He tells you tales of Stratagems and Spies;
> Can they need Art that have such powerful Eyes?
> Believe me, Gallants, he'as abus'd you all;
> There's not a vizard in our whole Cabal.   (p. 286)

The vizard has already been assumed by the playwright in splitting her prologue between the sexes in an attempt to disarm the criticism directed at a woman for broaching the boundaries of the male profession of letters. Behn masquerades, at the beginning of her dramatic career, as both male objector and female defender. She was later to introduce a much-remarked split within her own self-projection of the female writer: referring in the preface to *The Luckey Chance* (1685), to 'my Masculine Part the Poet in me' (p. 187). In a discussion of Behn's plays, most particularly *The Rover*, Elin Diamond suggests that

> In Behn's texts, the painful bisexuality of authorship, the conflict between (as she puts it) her 'defenceless' woman's body and her 'masculine part' is *staged* in her insistence, in play after play, on the equation between female body and fetish, fetish and commodity – the body in the 'scene'. Like the

actress, the woman dramatist is sexualized, circulated, denied a subject position in the theatre hierarchy.[7]

There is a greater self-consciousness and self-control than this, it seems to me, in Behn's 'staging' of her poetry, where she is equally compelled to enter a world dominated by male writers working in specifically misogynistic forms. This is most evident in the satirical poetry of the Restoration, and in the bawdy lyrics of writers like Rochester and Sedley.[8] Angeline Goreau, among others, notes 'the physical repulsion that feminine sexuality inspired in the male poets of Aphra Behn's generation'.[9] At times, it is true, Behn's poetry simply seems to reflect a watered down version of this perspective, with the benign view of the seducer in 'Song: Cease, Cease Amynta to Complain' and the homage to Rochester in 'On the Death of the Late Earl of Rochester'. (It was, one should remember, Rochester who wrote 'That whore is scarce a more reproachful name / Than poetess', a taunt echoed by Robert Gould specifically to attack Behn: '*Punk* and *Poetess* agree so pat, / You cannot well be *This* and not be *That*'.)[10] But she also writes counter poems, such as 'To Alexis in Answer to his Poem Against Fruition', a sharp portrait of the rake's unstable insatiability, which wittily overturns the misogynistic attitudes of the male poet. Even sharper is the critique inherent in her version of the impotence poem which a number of male writers produced, where, for Behn, the astonished woman's disappointment is more important than the man's anger. Such an unsettling of Restoration lyric conventions could be seen to culminate in Behn's analysis of female passion in 'On Desire', and most notably in her unfixing of sexual categories in 'To the Fair Clarinda, Who Made Love to Me, Imagined More Than Woman', which offers a potential lesbian solution to the Restoration male sexual marauder. As well as these genres, Behn's political poetry, pretty much neglected by recent criticism, is engaged in a complex negotiation of the possibilities of female involvement with Restoration debates over succession and the future nature of the state.[11]

For Catherine Gallagher, 'Aphra Behn is in the business of selling', and she offers 'playful challenges to the very possibility of female self-representation'.[12] The competitive world of professional playwright may well have involved Behn in the marketplace in a direct way, but in her poetry she offers a much more complex instance of challenges to 'the very possibility of female self-representation'. In order to understand this process, I have turned to recent work on theories of femininity and masquerade, which have had a notable effect on film theory, because such approaches to the question of gender allow for an account which recognizes how Behn was approaching questions of subjectivity within her poetry. These in turn reflect the social tensions aroused by the position of women in Restoration society.

The impetus to this work on masquerade and femininity has been a revaluation of an essay by Joan Riviere, 'Womanliness as Masquerade', first published in *The International Journal of Psychoanalysis* in 1929. Riviere discusses a case of an 'intellectual woman', who assumed a particular mask (or performance) of femininity, especially during her engagement in 'masculine' activity, such as lecturing.[13] Riviere begins by stating that 'women who wish for masculinity may put on a mask of womanliness to avert anxiety and the retribution feared from men' (p. 35). While to some extent Riviere fixes masculinity and femininity within the boundaries imposed upon them by the conventions of psychoanalysis under the aegis of Freud, her conception of the masquerade opens up a space which unsettles some of the certainties associated with the categories of sexual difference:

> Womanliness therefore could be assumed and worn as a mask, both to hide the possession of masculinity and to avert the reprisals expected if she was found to possess it – much as a thief will turn out his pockets and ask to be searched to prove that he has not the stolen goods. The reader may now ask how I define womanliness or where I draw the line between genuine womanliness and the 'masquerade'. My suggestion is not, however, that there is any such difference; whether radical or superficial, they are the same thing.   (p. 38)

Stephen Heath has noted that it is at this moment that Riviere allows for the possibility of a much more radical questioning of the boundaries of masculine and feminine than her framework might have indicated: 'In the masquerade the woman mimics an authentic – genuine – womanliness but then authentic womanliness is such a mimicry, is the masquerade ("they are the same thing"); to be a woman is to dissimulate a fundamental masculinity, femininity is that dissimulation.'[14]

For Luce Irigaray, the masquerade of femininity became a strategy which might unsettle patriarchal order:

> But on the exchange market – especially, or exemplarily, the market of sexual exchange – woman would also have to preserve and maintain what is called femininity. The value of a woman would accrue to her from her maternal role, and, in addition, from her 'femininity'. But in fact that 'femininity' is a role, an image, a value, imposed upon women by male systems of representation. In this masquerade of femininity, the woman loses herself, and loses herself by playing on her femininity.[15]

There has been some debate over whether Irigaray, or for that matter Riviere, *can* be read as unsettling the question of gender through masquerade.[16] The film theorist Mary Ann Doane, for example, has moved away from her early valuation of Riviere. In her influential essay 'Film and the Masquerade', first published in 1982, and intersecting with the debate on spectatorship, Doane characterized the masquerade in this way:

> The masquerade, in flaunting femininity, holds it at a distance. Womanliness is a mask which can be worn or removed. The masquerade's resistance to patriarchal positioning would therefore lie in its denial of the production of femininity as closeness, as presence-to-itself, as, precisely, imagistic.[17]

In her later essay, 'Masquerade Reconsidered', Doane questioned the fact that in Riviere, and also in Irigaray, 'masquerade specifies a norm of femininity', and she notes that 'masquerade is not theorized by Riviere as a joyful or affirmative play but as an anxiety-ridden compensatory gesture, as a position which is potentially disturbing, uncomfortable, and inconsistent, as well as psychically painful for the woman'.[18]

The particular problems of the concept of masquerade associated with the debate over female spectatorship are not so evident in a consideration of a writer like Behn. Similarly, the very constrictions imposed by the tendency for even a feminist psychoanalysis to reinvoke a normative

femininity may be turned to advantage through examining Behn's historical context, which offered a particularly restrictive set of gendered expectations for a woman writer who was not content with the private and
sanctified realm of a matchless Orinda. It is in this context that Heath's
reclamation of a truly disruptive reading of masquerade in Riviere's work
is particularly relevant to an understanding of Behn's poetry as it entered a
masculine, not to say misogynistic, society:

> she puts on a show of the femininity they demand, but inappropriately,
> keeping her distance, and returns masculinity to them as equally unreal,
> another act, a charade of power. But then masculinity is real in its effects,
> femininity too, the charade is *in* power . . . this woman's life is marked by
> power and its effects, is caught up in the definitions of
> masculinity/femininity, the identifications of the man and the woman.[19]

One of Behn's earliest published lyrics, 'Damon being asked a reason for
Loveing', which appeared in *The Covent Garden Drollery*, a miscellany
Behn herself probably edited, in 1672, is, at first glance, a typical example
of the easy pastoral love poetry which Behn produced with considerable
facility. Spoken by Damon, the poem seems to mimic the male voice of so
much pastoral poetry:

> *Phillis*, you ask me why I do persue,
>   And Court no other Nymph but you;
> And why with eyes, sighes, I do betray,
>   A passion which I dare not say:
> His cause I love, and if you ask me why,
> With womens answers, I must reply.   (p. 10)

What, exactly, is a woman's answer to the 'reason' for loving? It transpires,
in the second stanza, that lack of reason is the basis:

> You ask me what Arguments I have to prove
>   That my unrest proceeds from Love:
> You'l not believe my passion till I show,
>   A better reason why tis so;
> Then *Phillis* let this reason serve for one,
> I know I love, because my reasons gon.   (ibid.)

The equation of woman with the absence of reason, made by Damon in this poem, becomes rather more paradoxical in the posthumous publication of a version of the poem in 1707 in *The Muses Mercury*, with some interesting variants, which seem to have some authority as deriving from Behn's manuscripts (see Todd, pp. xliii–iv). In that version, the last line of the first stanza reads 'And with a woman's Reason, I reply' (p. 462). By the end of the poem, Damon complains that it is the apparent indifference of Phillis that causes him to ask a woman's question; this indifference is without reason – so he claims – but it is not unreason itself, for Damon himself, at the very end of the poem, withholds reason:

> Thus you no reason for your coldness give,
>   And tis but just, you should believe;
> That all your beauty unadorn'd by art,
>   Have hurt, and not oblig'd my heart.
> Be kind to that, return my passion too,
> And I'le give reason's why I love you so.   (p. 11)

Damon is, in fact, passion at this stage of the poem, and Phillis is coldness/reason withheld, which is, in a sense, reason itself. As Behn assumes the mask of the male lover in this poem, she inserts the woman's answer into his lips, and asks, in a particularly unsettling form, a woman's question about passion. This question veers away from the dichotomizing that informed the prologue to *The Forc'd Marriage* which I quoted at the beginning of this essay; a traditional dichotomizing that returns in the epilogue to that play, spoken 'By a Woman': 'You to our Beauty bow, we to your Wit'.[20] In 'Damon being asked a reason for Loveing', the categorizing of wit versus beauty, male versus female, is altered within an apparently bland device of ventriloquism. Damon speaks for Phillis in the poem, and voices her critique of a naive opposition: 'You say . . . That neither witt nor beauty in her dwell, /Whose lover can no reason tell' (p. 10). Behn asks who is allowed to speak within this lyric convention, and she does so, not always by speaking as a woman, but also by speaking through (behind) the male lover.[21]

Throughout her collection *Poems upon Several Occasions* (1684), Behn juxtaposes voices (the seducer; the seduced), situations, tones and styles. Songs which had a particular dramatic context are detached from individualized speakers and reproduced as lyrics of conflicting sexual attitudes. In a particularly illuminating article, Bernard Duyfhuizen traces the metamorphoses of a seduction poem ('The Willing Mistress') through its appearance in *Covent Garden Drolery* in 1672, its dramatic use in Behn's play *The Dutch Lover* (1673), to several later versions, including an appearance in *Poems upon Several Occasions*.[22] In the course of these several transformations, Behn actually changes the speaker from male to female; the poem also, Duyfhuizen points out, bears some connections to Behn's troubled relationship with John Hoyle.[23] In the version in *Poems upon Several Occasions*, titled 'The Reflection: A Song', we are presented first with an objectified picture of the abandoned Serena as sorrow personified:

> Her Grief was swoln too high
> To be Exprest in Sighs and Tears;
> She must or speak or die. (p. 74)

The distancing does not last, as the woman *must* speak; what she speaks is the conquest of a male reason here seen as phallic, as invasive, as the male gaze:

> Alas how long in vain you strove
>   My coldness to divert!
> How long besieg'd it round with Love,
>   Before you won the Heart.
> What Arts you us'd, what Presents made,
>   What Songs, what Letters writ:
> And left no Charm that cou'd invade,
>   Or with your Eyes or Wit. (p. 75)

The invasion of wit here is *reflected* by the ironically named Serena, who ends in the posture of abandonment: 'I lay me down and dye.'

The effect of 'The Reflection' is complicated by its close juxtaposition (in *Poems upon Several Occasions*) with another song taken from one of Behn's plays: 'The Counsel'. This was first 'sung' by the page Abevile in *The Rover II* (1681), but, detached from his particular voice, it seems a seduction poem (in the *carpe diem* mode) offered by Behn as an example of the very male aggression (invasion/attack) which leads to the situation depicted in 'The Reflection':

> A Pox upon this needless scorn:
> *Sylvia* for shame the Cheat give o'er:
> The End to which the Fair are born,
> Is not to keep their Charms in store:
> But lavishly dispose in haste
> Of Joys which none but Youth improve;
> Joys which decay when Beauty's past;
> And who, when Beauty's past, will love? (p. 79)

This may well be seen, in Heath's terms, as returning masculinity to the (supposed) male reader in a charade of power, given that Behn mimics the masculine as well as the feminine writing position. The sexual aggression in 'The Counsel' begins with 'A Pox', the expletive that Behn collapses into its 'real' context in a different poem, which takes the masculine tone, but not the masculine voice; 'A Letter to a Brother of the Pen in Tribulation' pokes fun at 'Damon' (sometimes identified as the playwright Edward Ravenscroft), who is doing 'Pennance' in a sweating tub: a 'cure' for the pox. Behn's voice here is ironic, and she writes just like one of the boys: ' – Pox on't that you must needs be fooling now. / Just when the Wits had greatest need of you' (p. 73). As the poem proceeds, Behn apparently sympathizes with Damon's plight and his supposed anger, and concludes by suggesting the trapped rake's curse against women:

> Now I could curse this Female, but I know,
> She needs it not, that thus cou'd handle you.
> Besides, that Vengeance does to thee belong,
> And 'twere Injustice to disarm thy Tongue.
> Curse then, dear Swain, that all the Youth may hear,
> And from thy dire Mishap be taught to fear.
> Curse till thou hast undone the Race, and all
> That did contribute to thy Spring and Fall. (p. 73)

Behn here displaces the traditional position of the woman (who curses) on to the man, who is a victim of the woman who can 'handle' him. His tongue is, in fact, disarmed; Behn allows him no voice with which to curse 'the Race' of women who have thus taken revenge, who have reduced a potent spring to a detumescent fall.

Along with the transposed voice, Behn also offers a transposed gaze, for a great many of her poems utilize a form of blazon directed at the male body. Of particular interest is a poem that forms part of a series dealing with a frustrated love affair with 'Lysander', a figure who has not been identified.[24] In 'To Lysander at the Musick-Meeting', Lysander's body is described in terms which are reminiscent of the clichés of the blazons that described so many female bodies ripe for enjoyment:

> I saw the Softness that compos'd your Face,
> While your Attention heightened every Grace:
> Your Mouth all full of Sweetness and Content,
> And your fine killing Eyes of Languishment:
> Your Bosom now and then a sigh wou'd move,
> (For *Musick* has the same effects with Love.)
> Your Body easey and all tempting lay,
> Inspiring wishes which the Eyes betray,
> In all that have the fate to glance that way:
> A careless and a lovely Negligence,
> Did a new Charm to every Limb dispence. (p. 94)

Lysander's 'easey and tempting' body produces a desire that Behn was to make the subject of one of her later poems, 'On Desire', a pindaric which, perhaps only fortuitously, concludes with an image of a Lysander who seeks out a desire seen as a weakness: 'And tho with Virtue I the world perplex, / *Lysander* finds the weekness of my sex' (p. 284). To negotiate an economy of desire which positions the woman as either passive object or insatiable temptress, Behn offers the image of woman as commodity back to the male 'negotiator', placing herself in a position of equality in the power relations that are carried out. This is evident in another Lysander poem, 'To Lysander on some verses he writ, and asking more for his Heart than 'twas worth', which uses the image of the marketplace to destabilize the function of woman as object of exchange:

Take back that heart, you with such Caution give,
   Take the fond valu'd Trifle back;
I hate Love-Merchants that a Trade wou'd drive;
   And meanly cunning Bargains make. (p. 92)

The love-merchants' trade could be seen to involve the counters of the literary economy as well, as Behn is attempting to create a space for herself in the trade of love-merchants who deal in the repertoire of poems of desire:

I care not how the busy Market goes,
   And scorn to Chaffer for a price:
Love does one Staple Rate on all impose,
   Nor leaves it to the Traders Choice. (p. 92)

Behn enters the poetic love-market by offering up the positions and representations of male and female desire as masks which may be assumed, removed, even metamorphosed into their opposites. What we might call literary market forces determine the modes available to Behn, but she is able to counteract some of the centrifugal force of this masculine economy by the *excessive* production of gendered positions. It is rare for Behn to posit a poetic stance outside such forces, although this is perhaps evident in 'The Golden Age', a 'paraphrase' of part of Tasso's *Aminta*. The effect of this ambivalent, 'utopian' poem has been effectively described by Kate Lilley: 'As she strategically manoeuvres between text and intertext, Behn stages an uneasy rapprochement between a woman's strategic entrepreneurial self-marketing in the world of men, and the dream of original, atemporal, polymorphous but feminized pleasure and self-sufficiency'.[25] More often, Behn shifts the current poetic modes from within.

Perhaps the most famous example of this is 'The Disappointment', written in what was virtually a special male Restoration genre: the impotence poem. It is particularly interesting that this poem was first printed in Rochester's *Poems on Several Occasions* (1680), and was often ascribed to him.[26] That this could be seen as a Rochester poem indicates, perhaps, the fine line Behn treads when she shifts the focus away from the man's obsession with the visible object of his self-frustration to the woman's response. Behn moves away from her French source in this refocusing (see Todd, pp. 392–4), but also moves away from the phallic aggression and self-flagellation evident in the genuine Rochester impotence poem, 'The Imperfect Enjoyment', which includes what is in some ways a set-piece in such male poems: the railing against the penis: 'Worst part of me, and henceforth hated most'.[27] In 'The Disappointment', the phallus is indeed veiled, and symbolically 'discovered' by the disappointed, naive Cloris:

> Her timerous Hand she gently laid
> (Or guided by Design or Chance)
> Upon that Fabulous *Priapas*,
> That Potent God, as Poets feign,
> But never did young *Shepherdess*,
> Gath'ring of Fern upon the Plain,
> More nimbly draw her fingers back,
> Finding beneath the verdant Leaves a snake.   (p. 68)

The gently mocking tone of Behn's poem is evident here, as the potent god of poets like Rochester is deflated by a literary mockery of phallic desire. For Rochester, the impotence motif leads from self-disgust to a sexual disgust turned upon the woman. That Behn's poem could be placed within Rochester's own collection indicates how she was forced to counter a resistance to a female poetic voice that could even extend to this peculiar version of male appropriation. Such an act has to ignore a telling moment in the last stanza of 'The Disappointment', when the narrator makes her female perspective and identification clear: 'The Nymph's Resentments none but I / Can well imagine or Condole' (p. 69).[28]

  If we turn to Behn's political poetry, it is evident that the assumption of a public voice involved an intersection with the gendered voice examining sexual identity, and the repercussions of an ideological position. Steven Zwicker has stressed that all poetry in the Restoration involved 'the polemicized nature of literary language, literary subject, and literary authority'.[29] Behn, in her public poetry and her satire, is engaged in a fairly constant Tory stance – although Behn's own position in relation to Catholicism remains in doubt, her support of James was consistent.[30] Catherine Gallagher has pointed to the significance of Tory ideology for a large number of women writers in the late seventeenth century (she concentrates on Margaret Cavendish and Mary Astell, but her argument is clearly relevant to Behn), noting 'that Toryism and feminism converge because the ideology of absolute monarchy provides, in particular historical situations, a transition to the ideology of the absolute self'.[31] Behn was, however, able to conceive of female subjectivity beyond the process of absolute monarchy, as a poem like 'The Golden Age' makes clear ('Monarchs were uncreated then, / Those Arbitrary Rulers over men', p. 31), just as, in her revised version of her commendatory verses to Thomas Creech on his translation of Lucretius, she was able to express a more dramatic questioning of 'poor Feeble Faith's dull Oracles' (p. 29) than she had in the first version, which prefaced the translation in its second edition. In the revised poem to Creech, Behn is able to express more directly the epicureanism that the translator of Lucretius perhaps did not want to record so directly; here Behn allies herself with the 'philosophy' of Rochester, at the very moment when she also interprets the translation as giving women access to a knowledge which is denied to them because of their ignorance of Latin and Greek.

Therefore, the expression even of Behn's more direct support for James necessitated a deliberate assumption of a voice (which might be called the panegyric), which was far from uniform, even within the public poems, and which certainly coexisted with satirical poetry of a more complex and questioning nature. Again, Steven Zwicker has stressed how the unsettled nature of later Restoration politics influenced writers:

> To write on affairs of state in the later seventeenth century was invariably, perhaps inescapably, to participate in rhetorical masquerade; to write at all was to face a language in which the central terms of public life, politics and religion, had become instruments of disguise.[32]

'Ovid to Julia' is a good example of Behn writing oblique political commentary in the manner of Dryden; the fact that this was an anonymous poem (printed in a different form as 'Bajazet to Gloriana' in *Poems on Affairs of State*, 1697) indicates that it treads on slightly dangerous ground in its treatment of Mulgrave's courtship of Princess Anne (James's daughter), and in its references to Monmouth.[33] In the poem, Behn speaks through the voice of the exiled Ovid (an overly ambitious Ovid who stands, indirectly, for Mulgrave), but this is an Ovid who uses the language of the many abandoned female lovers in Behn's poetry: 'I bring no Forces, but my sighs and tears, / My Languishments, my soft complaints and Pray'rs' (pp. 183–4). 'Languish' is a word Behn frequently associates with the posture of the helpless female victim – earlier on in the poem the 'expecting Nymphs' have often 'languish'd for the Author of their flame' – but within this poem, *Julia* is the agency of destructive passion. In a clear reference to Monmouth, male aspirations to sovereignty via sexual (or any other) conquest are mocked: 'How ev'ry Coxcomb aim'd at being Crown'd' (p. 183). The final image is of the triumphant Julia, inserted into the dominant position through Behn's manipulation of Ovid's male voice:

> Your Slave was destin'd thus to be undone.
> You the Avenging Deity appear,
> And I a Victim fall to all the injur'd Fair. (p. 184)

This oblique treatment of political concerns contrasts with the major public poems of celebration. Behn wrote a pindaric poem on the death of Charles II; a consolatory poem to his widow; a long and complex pindaric celebrating the coronation of James; a poem celebrating James's wife Mary's pregnancy, which anticipated the birth of a male heir to the throne; a poem celebrating the birth of the child who became the Old Pretender; and finally, after resisting the request of Burnet to celebrate the arrival of William and Mary, a poem congratulating Mary on her arrival in England. Behn's loyalties to the Tory cause are evident throughout these public poems, but with the exception of the pindaric on Charles's death, the poems concentrate on the female figures involved in the struggle over sovereignty in England during the 1680s. The role of queen was particularly problematic after the Exclusion Crisis and during James's brief reign. Behn's pindaric on Charles's death mourns the king as an 'Earthly God' (p. 191) and concludes by celebrating James as a newly risen sun. But in the poem written to Charles's widow Catherine, Behn turns to the image of the queen's two bodies as a way of conceptualizing both Catherine's female self (involved in loss and mourning) and her sovereignty, which perhaps has echoes of the way Queen Elizabeth shifted between her female body and male sense of sovereignty:

> Your *Valu'd* Loss a *Noysey Grief* disdain'd
> Fixt in the *heart*, no outward sign remain'd;
> Though the *soft Woman* bow'd and dy'd within;
> Without, Majestick Grace maintain'd the *Queen*!　　　　(p. 198)

Here Behn reverses the traditional sense of the sovereign's two bodies, as the female body is internalized, and the visible majestic body represents sovereignty.[34] Thus, Behn's other formulations of the internalized split involved in being a woman writer ('What in Strong Manly Verse should be exprest / Turns all to Womanish Tenderness within') are transposed into a sense of how the Queen is able to achieve a self which is simultaneously the repressed feminine and the visible body of office. Behn does then go on to see Catherine as a figure of the virgin Mary mourning Christ on the cross, a hagiographic move of particular audacity.

　　Behn celebrated James's coronation with her longest and most ambitious pindaric poem. In it, she turns from James to his Queen, Mary, and calls for a Muse which might help her to evoke the figure of Mary as Laura (a name evocative of her family's association with the great Italian poets):

> Bless the *soft Muse* that cou'd express
> *Beauty* and *Majesty* in such a dress,
> As all the World *Adoring* shall confess!
> Oh *fond seducer* of my *Nobler part*,
> 　　Thou soft insinuating *Muse*　　　　(p. 201)

Beneath the elaborate praise for James, and for the carefully enumerated figures in the coronation procession, the figure of Mary stands as a product of a poetic persona imagined by Behn as the welcome seducer, as a figure of feminine softness, and therefore, as offering a subterranean lesbian image of the source of the panegyric itself. Accordingly, when Behn writes a poem congratulating Mary on her pregnancy, she actually imagines a conception fathered, not by James, but by God:

> Heav'n has, *at last*, the Wond'rous WORK achiev'd.
> Long did th'ALMIGHTY pause, and long debate;
> For MONARCHS are not fashion'd at a Heat.　　　　(p. 294)

The italicized '*at last*' is perhaps not very tactful, but Behn goes on to celebrate the arrival of a Prince in an audacious piece of anticipation that was criticized by John Baber in his poem addressed to James on the birth of his son. Behn produced her own congratulatory poem, which again was addressed to Mary, not to James, as well as a fierce satirical attack on Baber, 'To Poet Bavius', which takes Baber's poem apart almost line by line.[35] Behn offers an attempted counter to the growing pressures on James and Mary, which were to lead, ultimately, to their departure from England in 1688. She does this by elevating Mary to a divine status which is also bound up in her production of the required heir. Reading the satire on Baber beside the poems to Mary produces a quite dizzying sense of generic switching, especially when Behn takes Baber to task for a generic move which she herself displays:

> And had not thy Unlucky *Rhiming Spirit*,
> Writ *Satyr* now, instead of *Panygerick*:
> Vile Pointless *Satyr*, thou might'st still have been
> A poor forgotten Drone without a Sting:
> And without notice follow'd still the King.   (p. 300)

The tension between satire and panegyric is undermined by Behn's manipulation of both forms. This whole process culminates in Behn's final political poem, just before her death. In response to a request by Gilbert Burnet to react positively to the new regime, Behn wrote a pindaric which clearly expressed her dismay at the loss of James, albeit in politic terms:

> Tho' I the Wond'rous Change deplore,
> That makes me Useless and Forlorn,
> Yet I the great Design adore,
> Tho' Ruin'd in the Universal Turn.   (p. 310)

Behn suggests that Burnet is the appropriate writer to celebrate the change of fortunes, and she refuses his request. However, while Behn did not write a poem for William and Mary, she reconsidered her response to Burnet and wrote one to Mary alone. In singling out Mary, Behn was able to fall back upon the consolation that she was James's daughter – 'Great

Caesar's Off-spring' (p. 307) – although this turns upon the paradox that the political confusion can only be resolved by a fundamentally divided loyalty. Once again, Behn turns to the idea of a gendered image of the queen, this time not split into the sovereign's two bodies, but rather seen as a unity of wit and beauty, mind and body, sovereignty and femininity:

> All Natures Charms are open'd in your face,
> You Look, you Talk, with more than Human Grace;
> All that is Wit, all that is Eloquence,
> The Births of finest Thought and Noblest Sense,
> Easie and Natural from your Language break,
> And 'tis Eternal Musick when you speak;
> Thro' all no Formal Nicety is seen,
> But Free and Generous your Majestick Meen,
> In every Motion, every Part a Queen;
> All that is Great and Lovely in the Sex,
> Heav'n did in this One Glorious Wonder fix.   (p. 306)

Behn is thus able to trace the dynastic change solely through a concentration on a female line (having had to set aside that much-celebrated son and heir), and it is only the woman who can reconcile 'the differing Multitudes', as Mary is seen, ultimately, as figuring Moses returned from the Mount, 'Eyes all shining with Celestial Flame' (p. 307). Responding to political crisis, Behn evokes the Queen as both male prophet and epitome of female perfection: 'Your Form and Mind, no One Perfection want, / Without all Angel, and within all Saint' (p. 306). The problematic representation of a gendered poetic voice crosses over between the public poetry and the love poetry, as Behn now moves between a masquerade of 'womanliness' and of sovereignty simultaneously, just as the poetic voice offers itself up as an uncertain panegyric.

It is in this context that I want to conclude by citing 'To the fair Clarinda, who made Love to me, imagin'd more than Woman', a poem which critics have begun to see as Behn's most radical questioning of the conventions of gender within a poetic tradition. Carol Barash has noted that, in this poem, 'the relationship between the speaker and Clarinda is framed and defined by a world in which gender opposition is the law'.[36] The figure of Clarinda unsettles the gender oppositions of poetic convention, beginning with the address of the speaker to the object of desire:

> Fair lovely Maid, or if that Title be
> Too weak, too Feminine for Nobler thee,
> Permit a Name that more Approaches Truth:
> And let me call thee, lovely Charming Youth.   (p. 288)

Barash points out that 'If Clarinda *is* both maid and youth, both Hermes and Aphrodite, then men and women can no longer be understood as oppositionally "nymph" and "swain".'[37] Barash sees Clarinda as figuring forth an image of 'the female sexual body [as] snakelike, phallic, or – to be precise – clitoral', an interpretation echoed by Bernard Duyfhuizen.[38] Behn writes 'For who, that gathers fairest Flowers believes / A Snake lies hid beneath the Fragrant Leaves' (p. 288). Behn's imagery seems a deliberate rewriting of 'The Disappointment', where Cloris might, like a shepherdess, 'More nimbly draw her Fingers back, / Finding beneath the verdant Leaves a snake' (p. 68).[39] In 'To the fair Clarinda', Cloris is specifically recalled (Clarinda is 'Soft *Cloris* with the dear *Alexis* joined'), and in that sense the clitoral image overwrites, rather than displaces, the phallic at this moment in the poem. Barash notes that, 'Paradoxically, this love poem to another woman is more clearly encoded in terms of male and female oppositions than any of Behn's heterosexual love poems. The more rigidly gender and sexuality are mapped onto real physical bodies, the more manipulable and unstable the categories "male" and "female" become.'[40] This is most evident when the poem concludes with an image of the hermaphrodite unravelling into its component gendered selves:

> When e'r the Manly part of thee, wou'd plead
> Thou tempts us with the Image of the Maid,
> While we the noblest Passions do extend
> The Love to *Hermes*, *Aphrodite* the Friend.

The image of the hermaphrodite had been used throughout the sixteenth and seventeenth centuries to characterise the female who trangresses gender as monstrous.[41] Here, Behn undoes the monstrous: 'For sure no

Crime with thee we can commit'. The fact that Hermes attracts love and Aphrodite friendship suggests that Behn recognizes the fragility of this deconstruction of the pressures of gender in the Restoration political and poetic context. Nevertheless, the escape from sexual predation offered by Clarinda points to the culmination of Behn's masquerade of gender throughout her poetry, as she searched for the possible representation of a female sense of self.

NOTES

1 Unless otherwise noted, all of Behn's poetry is quoted from Janet Todd's edition: *The Works of Aphra Behn*, ed. Janet Todd (London, 1992), vol. 1.

2 Significantly, Arlington did not call her Mrs Behn, even though she must have married the enigmatic man who provided her surname fairly recently; for the latest speculations about the shadowy Mr Behn, see Jane Jones, 'New light on the background and early life of Aphra Behn', this volume.

3 See Angeline Goreau, *Reconstructing Aphra: A Social Biography of Aphra Behn* (Oxford, 1980), p. 68. Astrea and Celadon are names taken from d'Urfé's pastoral romance *l'Astrée* (1607–21), although Todd suggests that Behn may more generally have had in mind the 'ambivalent virginal and fecund goddess of justice, once identified with Elizabeth I' (Todd, p. ix).

4 For a full account, including the documents, see W. J. Cameron, *New Light on Aphra Behn* (Auckland, 1961); see also the accounts in Behn's biographies, esp. Goreau, chap. 7, and Maureen Duffy, *The Passionate Shepherdess: Aphra Behn 1640–89* (London, 1977), chaps. 7 and 8.

5 Montague Summers, ed. *The Works of Aphra Behn* (Oxford, 1915), vol. 3, p. 285; further references to this edition.

6 See in particular Jacqueline Pearson, *The Prostituted Muse: Images of Women and Women Dramatists 1642–1737* (Brighton, 1988); and the discussion of the prologue in Catherine Gallagher, 'Who was that masked woman? The prostitute and the playwright in the comedies of Aphra Behn', *Women's Studies*, 15 (1988), 26–7.

7 Elin Diamond, 'Gestus and signature in Aphra Behn's *The Rover*', *ELH*, 56 (1989), p. 535.

8 For an excellent discussion of the satire, see Felicity Nussbaum, *The Brink of All We Hate: English Satire on Women 1660–1750* (Lexington, 1984), chaps. 2–4.

9 Goreau, *Reconstructing Aphra*, p. 66; see also Pearson, *The Prostituted Muse*, *passim*.

10 See Pearson, p. 9.

11 This neglect of Behn's public and political verse mars Dorothy Mermin's otherwise interesting analysis of her emergence as a poet, along with Katherine Philips and Anne Finch; Mermin even states that 'Philips, Behn, and Finch, like the make coterie poets before them, wrote in and of small private worlds', which may be true of Philips and Finch, but certainly not of Behn; see Dorothy Mermin, 'Women becoming poets: Katherine Philips, Aphra Behn, Anne Finch, *ELH: A Journal of Literary History*, 57 (1990), p. 341.

12 Gallagher, 'Who was that masked woman?', p. 41.

13 References to Joan Riviere, 'Womanliness as a masquerade', in *Formations of Fantasy*, ed. V. Burgin, J. Donald and C. Kaplan (London, 1986), p. 35.

14 Stephen Heath, 'Joan Riviere and the masquerade', in *Formations of Fantasy*, p. 49.

15 Luce Irigaray, *This Sex Which Is Not One*, trans. Catherine Porter (Ithaca, 1985), p. 84.

16 See, for example, John Fletcher, 'Versions of masquerade', *Screen* (1990), 43–70; Clare Johnston, 'Femininity and masquerade: *Anne of the Indies*', in *Jacques Tourneur*, ed. C. Johnston and P. Willemen (Edinburgh, 1975), 36–44.

17 Mary Ann Doane, *Femmes Fatales: Feminism, Film Theory, Psychoanalysis* (London, 1991), p. 25.

18 Ibid., p. 38.

19 Heath, 'Joan Riviere and the masqueradè', p. 56.

20 Summers, *Works of Aphra Behn*, p. 381.

21 Damon's 'passion which I dare not say' is echoed in 'That which I dare not name' in 'Song: I led my Silvia to a Grove'. The metamorphoses of this poem are analysed by Bernard Duyfhuizen, who considers the shift, in variant versions, between male and female speakers in this seduction poem, in '"That which I dare not name": Aphra Behn's "The willing mistress"', ELH, 58 (1991), 63–82.

22 Ibid., *passim*.

23 For Hoyle, see especially Duffy, *The Passionate Shepherdess*, chap. 14; Goreau, *Reconstructing Aphra*, pp. 189–206.

24 Another good example is 'In Imitation of Horace', a version of Odes i.v which reverses the object of the blazon from female to male.

25 Kate Lilley, 'Blazing worlds: seventeenth-century women's Utopian writing', in *Women, Texts and Histories 1575–1760*, ed. Clare Brant and Diane Purkiss (London, 1992), p. 126.

26 See David M. Vieth, *Attribution in Restoration Poetry: A Study of Rochester's 'Poems' of 1680* (New Haven, 1963), pp. 85–9, 448–50.

27 *The Complete Poems of John Wilmot, Earl of Rochester*, ed. David M. Vieth (New Haven and London, 1974), p. 39.

28 On this point, see also Carol Barash's important account of the poem, 'The political possibilities of desire: teaching the erotic poems of Behn', in *Teaching Eighteenth-Century Poetry*, ed., Christopher Fox (New York, 1990), pp. 164–72.

29 Steven N. Zwicker, 'Lines of authority: politics and literary culture in the Restoration', in *Politics of Discourse*, ed. Kevin Sharpe and Steven N. Zwicker (Berkeley, 1987), pp. 231–2.

30 On Behn's Catholicism, see Gerald Duchovnay, 'Aphra Behn's religion', *Notes and Queries*, 221 (1976).

31 Catherine Gallagher, 'Embracing the absolute: the politics of the female subject in seventeenth-century England', *Genders*, 1 (1988), p. 25.

32 Steven N. Zwicker, *Politics and Language in Dryden's Poetry* (Princeton, 1984), p. 35.

33 See Germaine Greer, ed., *The Uncollected Verse of Aphra Behn* (Stump Cross, 1989), pp. 174–9.

34 For the doctrine of the queen's two bodies, see Marie Axton, *The Queen's Two Bodies* (London, 1977); for Elizabeth, see Philippa Berry, *Of Chastity and Power: Elizabethan Literature and the Unmarried Queen* (London and New York, 1989).

35 For annotation, see Todd, *Works*, p. 439 and especially Greer, *Uncollected Verse*, pp. 204–9.

36 Barash, 'Political possibilities of desire', p. 173.

37 Ibid., p. 174.

38 Ibid.; Duyfhuizen, 'That which I dare not name', p. 79.

39 The recasting of the snake image is discussed in the context of Behn's revision of pastoral conventions by Elizabeth Young, in 'Aphra Behn, Gender and Pastoral', *Studies in English Literature*, 33 (1993), 523–43.

40 Barash, 'Political possibilities of desire', p. 174.

41 Philippa Berry cites Stubbs's reaction to gender disturbance in *The Anatomy of Abuses* (1583): 'Hermaphroditi: that is, Monsters of bothe kindes, halfe women, halfe men' (p. 69).

7 'For when the act is done and finish't cleane, / what should the poet doe, but shift the scene?': propaganda, professionalism and Aphra Behn

VIRGINIA CROMPTON

I ⌒

The majority of Behn's political poems, in which anti-Stuart material is resisted and Stuart absolutism is promoted, were written between 1679 and 1689, the last decade of Stuart monarchy. During this decade Stuart ideology was undermined through the ingenious use of fiction and argument in relation to a bizarre succession of semi-fictitious 'events', epitomized by the 'Popish Plot' and the warming-pan scandal. The Popish Plot involved many individuals and rumours, sham-plots and counter-plots, central to which was the allegation that members of the queen's Catholic household intended to kill the King. The Glorious Revolution was precipitated by the birth of the Prince of Wales and the subsequent warming-pan scandal which consisted of rumours that James II was not the father of the prince, or that Mary of Modena had feigned her pregnancy and smuggled a baby into the bed in a warming-pan, or that the prince had died after a few weeks and been replaced. The ability to convince the public that events had taken place or might take place was seen to be crucial to effective government and to its hold on power.

Owing to the widespread use of anonymity during the Restoration, particularly in the publication of political writing and pamphlets, the extent of Behn's contribution to Stuart propaganda cannot be known. A reference in 'A Letter to Mr Creech at Oxford, Written in the last great Frost' suggests that Behn produced propaganda for Charles II in the last years of his reign. She describes a coaching accident that took place after visiting the King to collect payment for 'Tory Farce, or Doggerell':

> From *White-Hall* Sir, as I was coming,
> His Sacred Majesty from Dunning;
> Who oft in Debt is, truth to tell,
> For Tory Farce, or Doggerell . . .[1]

'Tory Farce' by Behn is well known but there are few examples of pamphlet propaganda of the sort suggested by the above quotation. Exceptions include two editions of Behn's Broadsheet ballad, entitled *Song. To a New* Scotch *Tune* (1681) (Behn, 1, no. 47), on the subject of James Scott, Duke of Monmouth, Charles II's eldest illegitimate son. Monmouth, 'England's Darling',[2] had forfeited his court position through close association with Lord Shaftesbury, who was promoting him as the Protestant alternative to Charles II's heir, his Catholic brother, James, Duke of York. Although the 'Exclusionists' generated an impressive popular following in the wake of the Popish Plot, their political campaign collapsed in Oxford in 1682. In Behn's poem, Monmouth is depicted as the innocent shepherd Jemmy, 'a Lad, / Of Royal Birth and Breeding'. Despite his enviable charms, 'ev'ry Grace Exceeding', and idyllic lifestyle, Jemmy's Eden is polluted: 'A Curse upon Ambition: / The Busie Fopps of State / Have ruin'd his Condition'.

This ballad was included in the second edition of *Female Poems on Several Occasions by Ephelia* in 1682 and reprinted again in Behn's *Poems upon Several Occasions* in 1684, the third of three 'Jemmy' poems in this miscellany.[3] The first, 'Song to a Scotish tune' (Behn, 1, no.4), was originally printed in 1672 in *The Covent Garden Drolery*. The ballad is narrated by Jemmy's lover, a shepherdess, who 'could not say him nay'. In the first two stanzas, the narrator describes their pastoral bliss, but in the final stanza, war intrudes into the idyll and, inverting the 'swords into ploughshares' prophesy, the narrator laments Jemmy's transformation from shepherd to soldier:

His Sheep-hook to a Sword must turn;
  Alass! what shall I do.
His Bag-pipe into war-like sounds,
  Must now exchanged be,
Instead of Garlands, fearfull Wounds:
  Then what becomes of me.   (no.4, lines 27–32)

At the time of its first publication in 1672, this poem would have reminded readers of Monmouth's impressive military service during the campaign in the Low Countries of the early 1670s. By 1684, however, Monmouth had been implicated in the scandalous opposition activities of the 1680s, including the Rye House Plot of 1683. In the altered political context of 1684, the 'war-like sounds' suggest Monmouth's association with increasingly aggressive opposition tactics. The final lines now question the future of those who have been seduced by Monmouth into opposition politics.

The most detailed of Behn's Monmouth ballads, 'Silvio's Complaint: A Song, To a fine Scotch Tune' (Behn, 1, no.38), has only survived in *Poems upon Several Occasions*.[4] In this poem, Silvio-Monmouth, in effect a fallen angel, regrets his false ambition through a developing refrain which climaxes in his despair: 'See how my Youth and Glories lye, / Like Blasted Flowers i'th'Spring: / My Fame Renown and all dye, / For wishing to be King'. The accompanying verses describe the causes of his corruption and the extent of his loss. In the first five stanzas, Silvio mourns his wasted innocence, beauty, his lost loves and talents, 'for Pow'r Debaucht'. In the sixth stanza, Silvio accuses 'Old *Thirsis*' of his corruption: 'Old *Thirsis* be accurst: / There I first my peace forsook, / There I learnt Ambition first'.[5] In the final verses, he abandons his hopes and cautions youth to 'Shun Ambitious powerful Tales: / Destructive, False, and Fair'. It is possible that all three poems had been available in broadsheet editions. Political ballads were a popular source of information and commentary, and on occasion appeared remarkably influential.[6] Thus these romantic ballads provide the vehicle for Behn's popular political commentary.

A poem printed as a broadsheet in 1685 entitled *Rebellion's Antidote: Or a Dialogue Between Coffee and Tea* (Behn, 1, no.54) may be an example of Behn writing political 'doggerell' in collaboration with 'JCB'.[7] The poem consists of an insubstantial dialogue between 'Tea' and 'Coffee' about the horrors of 'Rebellion, Treason, and Sham-ploting Sin' which are to be cured by a dose of 'twist', a mixture of tea and coffee (*OED*). Behn may have produced any number of such verses, either published anonymously or subsequently lost. This poem seems unsophisticated, yet is typical of Restoration ephemera. Coffee houses, in particular, were recognized meeting places for political debate and there are many references to tea and coffee in Restoration political verse.[8] Whilst the textual context is relatively accessible, the political context is less obvious. Published in 1685, *Rebellion's Antidote* may have been written in response to the Monmouth Rebellion, yet the political references are so glib and simplistic that it is difficult to interpret the poem as anything other than loyalist effusion.

Behn's revision of the text for Francis Barlow's edition of *Aesop's Fables* (Behn, 1, no.72) in 1687 provides a second example of co-authored propaganda. During the 1680s, Barlow produced ingenious visual propaganda, notably packs of playing cards which depict the events of the decade.[9] His playing cards are apt vehicles for political commentary since card games themselves mimic political intrigues. Barlow first published his engravings of *Aesop's Fables* in 1666 accompanied by Thomas Philipott's English text.[10] By 1687, when Barlow commissioned Behn's verses and reprinted his engravings, he was experienced in the production of visual propaganda, and Behn's reworking of Philipott's material reflects this interest. Copies of Philipott's original are available and a comparison with Behn's adaptation reveals her particular interests and priorities.[11] Behn's efforts are most clearly employed in abbreviating Philipott's rambling stanzas into six lines of verse, four describing the fable and a couplet for the moral. However, the changes also show that she aimed to secularize religious references, politicize the moral commentary and introduce Restoration diction.

Above all, Behn uses the fables to comment on Monmouth's career: by 1687, he had been dead for two years. On James II's succession, Monmouth invaded England, landing in Lyme Regis on 11 June 1685. He proclaimed himself king at Taunton on June 18, but was captured on the 6th of July, following the battle of Sedgemoor, and executed for treason a few days later. The Monmouth ballads, written between 1672 and 1685, reveal Behn's sustained interest in Monmouth's ambiguous political position as Charles II's favourite son and the focus for opposition intrigue. In her adaptations of Philipott's text, Behn reflects on Monmouth's tragedy. For example, Fable xii tells the story of a youth who tries to kill a dove, but is fatally wounded by an adder while hunting. In his moral, Philipott had discussed the vulnerability of the poor to tyrannous government: 'Thus Povertie its right hath oft forgone, / When by injurious greatness trod upon.' Instead, Behn refers to Monmouth: 'The young usurper. who design'd t'invade, / An others right, himselfe the victime made.' Throughout her version, Behn uses Monmouth's 'late pittyed president' (i.e. 'precedent') to warn against 'false ambition' (Fable xxiv). Other allusions to Monmouth include the effects of 'dire ambition' on 'The fond aspiring youth' of Fable xxxv; the 'Mercy extended' to 'the ungrateful men' of Fable l, a comment on Charles II's toleration of his son's behaviour, despite his continued association with the opposition; the 'western warr' for Monmouth's west country uprising in Fable li; and the lure of 'fancy'd Crownes' which led the 'young warriour' of Fable lxxx to his ruin.

Behn's adaptations are clearly designed to represent Stuart royalist politics. For example, she alludes to disloyal statesmen, one of whom was probably Shaftesbury, in Fable lxxii, and the corrupt trials of the Popish Plot in Fable xliii; she expresses support for the King in opposition to parliament, as in Fable xxii. As Behn champions the monarchy rather than parliament, so she favours the rich above the poor. Unlike Philipott, Behn seldom expresses sympathy for poverty. Fable xxviii offers a rare (and surprising) exception: an Ape 'implord, the fox her bum would vaile, / With a proportion of his useless Taile'; the fox refuses. In this instance, Behn accuses the 'Ill natured Rich' of enjoying the poverty of others, although she more commonly cautions the 'Rurall Swain' against the 'pomp & noys' of high society (Fable xlviii) and the worthlessness of 'all the Luxuries of Courts' (Fable vii). Thus, in the majority of these fables, Behn advises the people to learn from Monmouth's example and remain content with their lot: she warns against political activity and social ambition.

Versions of *Aesop's Fables* were popular during the seventeenth century: Wing's short-title catalogue lists sixty-five editions from 1641–1700.[12] Five years after the Behn-Barlow edition, Roger L'Estrange published *Fables from Aesop and other Mythologists* (1692) in which the narration of each fable is likewise concluded by a 'Moral Reflexion' expressing his political and philosophical views. In both these cases, the 'translators' have introduced political material into the original text. Furthermore, *Aesop's Fables* was a standard teaching text which, L'Estrange claimed, was 'universally read and taught in all our schools'.[13] Thus the politicization of Behn's and L'Estrange's translations offered an opportunity to indoctrinate the youth of the higher ranks with Stuart royalism. L'Estrange advertised the educational benefits of his innovative prose translation in the Prefaces to his 1692 and 1699 editions; Behn's version, with parallel texts in English, French and Latin, is clearly excellent teaching material.

The printing and binding of Behn's 1687 edition of *Aesop's Fables* is of an exceptional quality: extant copies are beautifully bound, the illustrations are remarkably fine.[14] The edition was likely to have been expensive, and was presumably intended for wealthy readers. Stuart interpretations of political events are presented in the context of enduring literature, rendered desirable through the extravagance of the gorgeously produced text. Scholars have argued that opposition politicians exploited pictorial propaganda with greater skill than their Stuart royalist counterparts (George, p. 53). This edition of *Aesop's Fables* reveals that Behn collaborated with Barlow to explore an area of effective propaganda production that was humorous, memorable and accessible to both literate and non-literate 'readers'.

II ⟨∾⟩

In 1688 and 1689, Aphra Behn published broadsheet poems to the influential pamphleteers, Roger L'Estrange and Gilbert Burnet, entitled *A Poem to Sir Roger L'Estrange On his Third Part of the History of the Times. Relating to the Death of Sir Edmund Bury-Godfrey* (1688) and *A Pindaric Poem to the Reverend Doctor Burnet on the Honour he did me of Enquiring after me and my Muse* (1689) (Behn, 1, nos.82 and 87). Behn, Burnet and L'Estrange certainly knew of one another and may all have been personally acquainted. Burnet discussed Behn in letters to his moral protégée, Anne Wharton, Rochester's niece; Behn and Wharton had exchanged letters and poems following Rochester's death, before which Burnet had secured Rochester's famous death-bed conversion;[15] Burnet and L'Estrange refer to each other in their various tracts and memoirs; and L'Estrange licensed several of Behn's works. Behn's poems to L'Estrange and Burnet offer insights into the production of political poetry in general, assist in understanding Behn's politics in particular, and shed light on her own work as a propagandist. In her poem to L'Estrange, she discusses his work in relation to the Popish Plot crisis; in her poem to Burnet, she discusses Burnet's involvement with the Glorious Revolution. Therefore these poems tackle the nature of propaganda in relation to the main political events of the decade. Behn's poems *To L'Estrange* and *To Burnet* were written within a few months of one another, are concerned with an issue vital to government, and address the most prominent propagandists of the Stuart and Orange courts.

A Poem To Sir Roger L'Estrange, On his Third Part of The History of the Times. Relating to the Death of Sir Edmund Bury-Godfrey, commemorated the publication of the third part of L'Estrange's *History of the Times*, which discussed the Popish Plot. L'Estrange was personally affected by the plot and subsequent political crises in various ways, not least by the lapsed Press Act. This may well explain the industry with which L'Estrange produced pamphlets during these years. Violet Jordain has estimated that from 1679 to 1681 there were at least 64,000 copies of pamphlets bearing L'Estrange's name in circulation in London, while, between 13 April 1681 and 9 March 1687, L'Estrange published 931 editions of his newspaper, *The Observator*.[16] In his 'Preface to the Reader' published with collected papers from *The Observator* in 1683, L'Estrange claims he worked 'for the *Enformation* of the *Multitude*' because of 'The *Needfullness* of some *Popular Medium* for the *Rectifying* of *Vulgar Mistakes*, and for the *Instilling* of Dutyfull, and *Honest Principles* in the *Common People*, upon That *Turbulent* and *Seditious Juncture*' (L'Estrange, pp. 1–3).

In his Preface to *The History of the Times*, L'Estrange discusses the extent of his personal resolution and hardship:

> I contracted a horror for this villainous cheat (the Plot) from the very
> spawning of it, and in the same moment an ambition above all things
> under the sun, to have some hand in breaking the neck on't. From that
> time to this, I have barred myself the benefits of ease, liberty, con-
> versation and effectually all the comforts of humane life in order
> to this end.   (Kitchin, p. 338)

The History of the Times was L'Estrange's final narrative concerning the
Popish Plot, written in retrospect and unconstrained by the threat of violence from the aggressive citizens which had, he claimed, caused him to
write cautiously at the time: 'there was no launching out into the abyss of
the Plot mystery without certain ruin, but coasting and slanting, hinting
and trimming was the best office a body could perform in that season'
(Kitchin, p. 241). Typically, L'Estrange draws the reader's attention to the
matter of style: 'there's no Other way of Conveying the True Sense, &
Notion of Things either to their Affections, or to their Understandings,
then by the Palate' (L'Estrange, p. iii). L'Estrange argues that political
writers must separate presentation from content in order to influence the
public. He admits that effective propaganda requires compromise: 'slanting, hinting and trimming'.

   In *To L'Estrange*, Behn pays tribute to L'Estrange's efforts to reverse
the tide of public opinion following the '*Vice* and *Villany*' of the Popish
Plot. She describes the events that took place during the sustained period
of political crisis following Titus Oates's allegations and Edmund Bury
Godfrey's mysterious death. She explains the widespread support for the
opposition as a product of misinformation and argues that the public were
'misled' by 'corrupted' institutions (n.82, lines 15–20). 'Rescuing the
World from stupid Ignorance', L'Estrange has made the truth visible:
'*Truth*, which so long in shameful Darkness lay, / Raises her shineing
Head'. Indeed, the celebration of L'Estrange is indivisible from a celebration of truth: '*Truth*, the *first-born of Heaven!*' The hyperbolic religious
diction is typical of Behn's panegyrics, and is often used to represent
values that are absolute, rather than relative. For example, in her poems
on Charles II's death and James II's accession, Behn represents monarchs
as divine figures because, in the Stuart tradition, monarchy is determined
in essence and kings are kings by divine right, rather than by agreement.[17]

She uses religious diction to insist that L'Estrange is absolutely right.

It is fundamental to Behn's poem that L'Estrange has shown that Titus Oates lied, and that the lies are seen to be the cause of the crisis: 'Detecting *Knaves*, who willingly mistook, / It shews the *Source* from whence the Mischief broke' (no.82, lines 75–6). Both Behn and L'Estrange present 'history' as an objective category that resists its own political content through recourse to the ideal of 'truth'. Behn traces the social chaos to the influence of 'Unknown *Religions*'. Friendships are undermined by religious arguments and sons argue against their fathers: 'And *Friends* to *Friends*, *Parents* to *Sons*, were Foes'. In keeping with Stuart doctrine, the relationship of father and son is essential to, and symbolic of, the relationship of king to subject.[18] Once this bond is broken, social order is inverted: 'The Inspir'd *Rabble*, now wou'd *Monarchs* Rule'. Thus this description of disorder is also an interpretation of its causes. As the poem progresses, the references become more particular. Behn comments specifically on Monmouth's popular following, based in Wapping:

> From *Wapping-Councils*, all *Decrees* went out,
> And *manag'd* as *they* pleas'd the Frantick Rout:
> Then *Perj'ries*, *Treasons*, *Muthers*, did ensue,
> And total *Dissolution* seem'd in View.   (no.82, lines 32–5)

The antagonistic relationship of son to father is epitomized by the relationship of Monmouth to Charles II. Monmouth's refusal to respect his father is simultaneously a refusal of the subject to respect the monarch: this disobedience within the royal family itself compounds the problem of government, threatening the nation with 'total *Dissolution*'.

Social disorder results in Viscount Stafford's execution which Behn represents in terms of Christ's crucifixion: 'a shameful Death, / To Undeceive the *World*. . . / And like a *God*, dy'd to redeeem *Our Faith*'. Behn describes this violent anarchy as insanity: 'The *World* ran *Mad*, and each distemper'd *Brain*, / Did *strange* and *different Frenzies* entertain'. Indeed, those who 'th'*Infection* shun' are most likely to be persecuted, prosecuted, and executed. Disorder, represented as a disease, is the result of lies. Truth is therefore the cure. Behn praises L'Estrange for his inspired and enchanting treatment:

You, *Mighty* Sir, stretch'd your all *Conquering Hand.*
You tun'd your *Sacred Lyre*, and stopt the Rage,
Of this abandon'd, this distemper'd Age.
By the soft force of *Charming Eloquence*,
You eas'd Our *Fears*, and brought us back to *Sense.*   (no.82, lines 64–8)

Here Behn emphasizes the style of L'Estrange's work. In order to restore health, L'Estrange must overcome his frenzied patient: his propaganda is represented as a 'sacred lyre' and the skilful presentation with which he wins reluctant readers is '*Charming Eloquence*'.

Behn's representation of L'Estrange's writing is entirely consistent with L'Estrange's self-representation. In the first edition of *The Observator*, 13 April 1681, L'Estrange explained that, "'Tis the *Press* that has made 'um *Mad*, and the *Press* must set 'um *Right* again. The Distemper is *Epidemical*; and there's no way in the World, but by *Printing*, to convey the *Remedy* to the Disease' (L'Estrange, p. 14). Again, in the 1683 Preface, he wrote:

> The *Common people* are *Poyson'd*, and will run *Stark Mad*, if they be not *Cur'd*: Offer them *Reason*, without *Fooling*, and it will never *Down* with them: And give them *Fooling* without *Argument*, they're never the *Better* for't. Let 'em *Alone*, and All's *Lost*. So that the *Mixture* is become as *Necessary*, as the *Office*.   (L'Estrange, p. 5)

Here, then, the representation of opposition to government as sickness can itself be seen as a component of Stuart propaganda. Behn and L'Estrange share their theoretical perspective: both acknowledge the tact and care with which the presentation of propaganda is composed. In Behn's poem, the scene of conflict exists between the political context (a form of mental sickness) and L'Estrange's writing (a treatment that restores health). 'Truth' is not L'Estrange's only weapon and the style of his writing is openly manipulative – musical, charming and easing. Behn's confidence in the truth places this use of style beyond question.

III ও

In 'Propaganda and the Revolution of 1688–89', Lois Schwoerer has argued that William of Orange's unresisted invasion of England, known as the Glorious Revolution, could not have been achieved without William's sophisticated propaganda campaign.[19] She notes, for example, that William included printing presses amongst the equipment he brought to England with his fleet (Schwoerer, p. 856). In October 1688, William distributed two pamphlets, his *Declaration of His Highness William Henry, Prince of Orange, of the Reasons Inducing Him to Appear in Armes in the Kingdom of England for Preserving of the Protestant Religion and Restoring the Lawes and Liberties of England, Scotland, and Ireland* and its sequel, the *Second Declaration of Reasons*, issued two weeks later. The *Declarations* were printed in Amsterdam, Edinburgh, The Hague, Hamburg, London and Magdeburg in English, Dutch, German and French. William used them as his official vindication and they were given to all but the English and French ambassadors at the Hague. Copies of the *Declaration* were sent to towns throughout England: English booksellers were invited to sell copies for their own profit; they were sent through the penny post and William's allies received up to three thousand copies each to distribute amongst their friends.

Although many councillors were involved in composing these tracts, Gilbert Burnet was personally responsible for the style of both English translations, and his careful revisions (which are preserved in Dutch archives) 'resulted in one of the most effectively written tracts that appeared in the entire campaign' (Schwoerer, p. 852). Amongst the material included in the *Declaration* was the controversial rumour that the Prince of Wales was an impostor: 'To crown all those evil councellors . . . published that the Queen hath brought forth a son . . . not only we ourselves but all the good subjects of the Kingdom do vehemently suspect that the Pretended Prince of Wales was not borne by the Queen' (Schwoerer, pp. 854–5). Burnet's *An Enquiry Into the Measures of Submission to the Supream Authority: And of the Grounds upon which it may be lawful or necessary for Subjects to defend their Religion, Lives and Liberties* (1688)[20] weighs the matter of monarchy and law at length, concluding finally that royal prerogative is beyond the law. Yet, although Burnet appears sympathetic to the principles of monarchy, he revokes his loyalty to the Stuarts in the final page:

And yet even [Regal Dignity] is prostituted, when we see a *young Child* put in the Reversion of it, and pretended to be the *Prince of Wales*: concerning whose being born of the *Queen*, there appear to be not only no certain Proofs, but there are all the Presumptions that can possibly be imagined to the contrary.   (Burnet, p. 132)

In Burnet's pamphlets, then, the alleged pretence of the Stuarts to produce a male heir is the *sole reason* for the dissolution of the subject's allegiance to the King.

The birth of the Prince of Wales was the turning point both for internal opposition and for the heirs presumptive, William and Mary. Behn published at least three unequivocally pro-Stuart broadsheet poems on the occasion: *A Congratulatory Poem To Her Most Sacred Majesty, on the Universal Hopes of All Loyal Persons for a Prince of Wales* (1688), *A Congratulatory Poem to the King's Most Sacred Majesty, On the Happy Birth of the Prince of Wales* (1688), and *To Poet Bavius; Occasion'd by his Satyr He Writ in his Verses to the King, Upon the Queens being Deliver'd of a Son* (1688) (Behn, 1, nos.83, 84 and 85). In these poems Behn goes out of her way to exhibit loyal reactions to the pregnancy and birth. Over this issue, Burnet and Behn produced public political texts in direct opposition to one another, representing positions that seem politically incompatible. Nonetheless, Behn's poem to Burnet the following year indicates dialogue and limited reconciliation.

In *A Pindaric Poem to the Reverend Doctor Burnet on the Honour he did me of Enquiring after me and my Muse*, Behn appears to decline Burnet's commission of a poem on William's succession. The implied commission itself might seem surprising since Behn's Stuart loyalty was well known through her work; yet her politics probably attracted Burnet, who certainly recognized the value of unexpected conversion.[21] In replying to Burnet's suggestion, Behn reviews his achievements, again exploring a propagandist and his work. However, *To Burnet* reflects the profound change in Stuart fortunes and in this second analysis of propaganda the relationship of texts to their readers is problematic. Although Behn deals with similar elements, content and style now sit in an uneasy configuration. In *To L'Estrange*, Behn recognized that L'Estrange manipulated his readers in order to restore political stability; when the system that is represented is absolute (i.e. divinely right), then the propagandist is like-wise right. In *To Burnet*, Behn has transformed the moral structure: there is no sense of truth, neither in Burnet's 'wond'rous Pen', nor in Behn's 'Opinions' (no. 87, lines 11 and 18). Behn praises Burnet's skill in repre-senting a political position. The matter of right and wrong, which had been invested with religious imagery and significance in *To L'Estrange*, is transformed in *To Burnet* to a difference of opinion.

Behn described L'Estrange's style as 'Charming Eloquence' and she utilized similar diction in her treatment of Burnet's successful propa-ganda, suggesting the process of seduction:

> With Pow'rful Reasoning drest in finest Sence.
>   A thousand ways my Soul you can Invade,
> And spight of my Opinions weak Defence,
>   Against my Will, you Conquer and Perswade.
> Your Language soft as Love, betrays the Heart,
> And at each Period fixes a Resistless Dart,
>   While the fond Listner, like a Maid undone,
> Inspir'd with Tenderness she fears to own;
> In vain essays her Freedom to Regain:
> The fine Ideas in her Soul remain,
> And Please, and Charm, even while they Greive and Pain.
>
> (No.87, lines 16–26)

Behn claims that Burnet's influence is as insidious as seduction and as irre-versible as lost virginity. The propagandist penetrates the political subject, who is ruined in the process: there is no marriage, the propagan-dist offers no political contract. Behn implies that Burnet's language improperly impregnates his readers. Whilst L'Estrange's writing is restorative, Burnet's propaganda is represented by the suggestive context of pleasure and corruption.

The trope of seduction also enables Behn to refer to William's inva-sion of Britain. William had insisted that he would not cross the Channel without an invitation and was considerably embarrassed when James II's first attempt to escape was foiled and he returned to London.[22] William attempted to appear non-aggressive, yet he arrived with an army; the con-frontation with James further undermined his self-representation as an uncontested hero. Behn's amorous language evokes militaristic equivalences, images of moral compromise, treachery and captivity. Thus the metaphor of sexual penetration utilizes military vocabulary: 'you can Invade,' 'my . . . weak Defence', 'you Conquer' (no.87, lines 18–24). Later in the poem, Behn returns to Burnet's skill as a political writer, once again in terms that are both eulogistic and equivocal:

> Oh Strange effect of a Seraphick Quill!
>   That can by unperceptable degrees
> Change every Notion, every Principle
>   To any Form, its Great Dictator please:
> The Sword a Feeble Pow'r compar'd to That,
>   And to the Nobler Pen subordinate;
> And of less use in *Bravest* turns of State:
> While that to Blood and Slaughter has recourse,
> This Conquers Hearts with soft prevailing Force:
> So when the wiser *Greeks* o'recame their Foes,
> It was not by the Barbarous Force of Blows.
> When a long ⌐en Years Fatal War had fail'd,
> With luckier Wisdom they at last assail'd,
> Wisdom and Counsel which alone prevail'd.   (no.87, lines 70–83)

The apparent celebration of Burnet's writing provides Behn with another opportunity to comment on William's opportunistic tactics through the example of the Trojan war. The analogy purports to illustrate the power of non-violence – 'soft prevailing Force' – yet Behn effectively implies that William's 'luckier Wisdom' was, like the Trojan horse, deceitful and, like the Trojan horse, the means for subsequent violent attack. Behn places 'Wisdom and Counsel' in opposition to 'the Barbarous Force of Blows', the discussion of which was a pressing issue in 1688.

In all this, the propagandist seems to be something of a magician who can dissolve 'every Notion, every Principle', presumably the dissolution of the political certainty that L'Estrange had restored. Behn's appreciation of Burnet's power is suggestively critical: she admires his achievements, yet describes him as the 'Great Dictator' (no.87, line 69), a resonant phrase following the rejection of James's absolutism (and possibly suggestive of Cromwell as well). Burnet manipulates political

consciousness 'by unperceptable degrees ... To any Form'. Behn is implying that Burnet's success is itself dangerous. In order to release the nation
from the supposedly tyrannical power of the monarchy, the entirely arbitrary force of the 'Great Dictator' has been empowered. The propagandist, Behn warns, cannot even be restrained by the 'Feeble Pow'r' of the
army. In the final lines, Behn compliments Burnet in an apparently conventional manner:

> 'Tis you that to Posterity shall give
>   This Ages Wonders, and its History.
> And great *NASSAU* shall in your Annals live
>   To all Futurity.
> Your Pen shall more Immortalize his Name,
> Than even his Own Renown'd and Celebrated Fame.
>
> (no.87, lines 98–103)

This compliment contains direct comment on the significance of Burnet's
propaganda, and William's political debt to Burnet. Behn suggests that
William is constructed in Burnet's writing; his textual representation is
more significant than his real life. In contrast to *To L'Estrange*, in which
Stuart ideology is represented as truth, Behn depicts the new order as a
fiction in her poem *To Burnet*. Behn represents William's invasion and the
establishment of contractual monarchy, 'This Ages Wonders' (no.87,
line 100), as the miraculous construction of power from representation. In
Behn's terms, Burnet has rendered the 'real' difference between monarchs
and subjects obsolete: his propaganda had recreated power.

IV   ∽·

Political texts were discredited when their writers were seen to be mercenary: political writers could not provide 'disembodied' commentary, or
flattering publicity, without promoting their own political character. In
this respect, the deposition of James II created severe difficulties for professional Stuart writers, such as Behn, whose loyal personae would be
compromised if they addressed verse to William and Mary. This problem
had obviously been faced by writers throughout the seventeenth century.
In *To Burnet*, Behn explores her future as a professional writer, and more

particularly as a political propagandist. Alongside her assessment of Burnet's achievements, she contemplates the necessity of political and professional compromise. As the title indicates, Behn wrote *A Pindaric Poem to the Reverend Doctor Burnet, on the Honour he did me of Enquiring after me and my Muse* in order to clarify her position as a political writer in relation to a representative of the new government.

Although Burnet's invitation to Behn to write for William has not survived, her reply implies that he complimented her work and offered her professional support. Nonetheless, Behn reminds Burnet that his victory is her defeat; his successful propaganda has directly undermined her work: 'But yet how well this Praise can Recompense / For all the welcome Wounds (before) you'd given!' (no.87, lines 27–8). The Orange succession not only invalidates Behn's Stuart poetry, but also poses a problem for her future work. She goes on to explore the application of a system of relative values, that she must now accept, through the metaphor of currency:

> But since by an Authority Divine,
> She is allow'd a more exalted Thought;
> She will be valu'd now as Currant Coyn,
> Whose Stamp alone gives it the Estimate,
> Tho' out of an inferiour Metal wrought.   (no.87, lines 39–43)

'She', Behn's Muse, like a coin, will take her value from the imprint of Burnet's approval, just as the value of money is determined by the stamp on the coin, rather than by the metal from which it is made. The financial image conveys the professional dilemma she faces: whether to adapt her political message in order to receive payment, or to remain faithful to an obsolete currency.

Behn dwells on her chance for self-promotion. She represents Burnet's commission and patronage as an opportunity to establish her neglected reputation:

> So fam'd by you my Verse Eternally shall live:
> Till now, my careless Muse no higher strove
> T'inlarge her Glory, and extend her Wings;

> Than underneath *Parnassus* Grove,
> To Sing of Shepherds, and their humble Love;
> But never durst, like *Cowly*, tune her Strings,
>   To sing of Heroes and of Kings.   (n.87, lines 32–7)

This passage is surprising, not least because Behn had written a considerable number of court poems and many plays and pastoral poems that dealt with political issues, heroes and kings. The reference to Cowley is particularly perplexing since Behn had recently translated Cowley's verse: her version of Cowley's political poem 'Sylvae' was published in July 1689, shortly after her death. Indeed, in 1680 Dryden commented on Cowley's influence on Behn in his preface to *Ovid's Epistles*, in which Behn's translation of 'Oenone to Paris' appears.[23]

Although Behn distances herself from Cowley in this quotation, she proposes the comparison. Since *To Burnet* deals with professional and political integrity, Behn's oblique allusion may be understood in relation to Cowley's wavering Stuart allegiance during the Protectorate, specifically his decision to compromise his political position. In 1656, Cowley returned to Britain following his long royalist exile and published his volume, *Poems*, in which he accepted the authority of the Protectorate and the inevitability of political compromise.[24] Cowley had persistently represented royalist politics in his poetry during the 1640s, and wrote fiercely political works, such as *The Puritans Lecture*, *The Puritan and the Papist* and *The Civil War*.[25] Having shared the conditions of exile for several years, Cowley was a complex and politically ambiguous figure for Restoration poets.[26]

In his 'Preface' to *Poems*, Cowley describes the death of his Muse in the 'sharp *winter*': writing in exile is impossible. Cowley explains his decision to return from exile and publish:

> . . . it is so uncustomary, as to become almost *ridiculous*, to make *Lawrels* for the *Conquered*. Now though in all *Civil Dissentions*, when they break in to open hostilities, the *War* of the *Pen* is allowed to accompany that of the *Sword* and everyone is in a maner obliged with his *Tongue*, as well as his *Hand*, to serve and assist the side which he engages in; yet when the event of battle, and the unaccountable *Will* of God has determined the controversie, and that we have submitted to the conditions of the

Conqueror, we must lay down our *Pens* as well as our *Arms*, and we must march out of our *Cause* it self, and dismantle that, as well as our *Towns* and *Castles*, of all the *Works* and *Fortifications* of *Wit* and *Reason* by which we have defended it. *We* ought not sure, to begin our selves to revive the remembrance of those times and actions for which we have received the *General Amnestie*, as a favour from the *Victor*. The truth is, neither *We*, nor *They*, ought by the *Representation* of *Places* and *Images* to make a kind of *Artificial Memory* of those things wherein we are all bound to desire like *Themistocles*, the *Art* of *Oblivion*.   (Cowley, p. 9)

Here, then Cowley acknowledges military defeat and offers not only to abandon the propaganda war, but also to realize the defeat of royalist ideology: 'dismantle... all the *Works* and *Fortifications* of *Wit* and *Reason*'.

Both Behn and Cowley divide poetry into the political and the aesthetic, and in both cases they aspire to political writing. Thus Cowley chooses to abandon the defunct political system rather than produce escapist art, 'the *Art* of *Oblivion*'. Likewise, Behn aspires to the production of poetry 'of Heroes and of Kings', rather than that of 'Shepherds and their humble love'. In this context, then, Behn had not previously imitated Cowley since she had yet to abandon royalism in favour of the new order. *To Burnet* explores precisely this possibility: will Behn produce nostalgic work or will she move with the times? Burnet's commission appears to offer Behn an opportunity to compromise, like Cowley, and the prospect of guaranteed success.

In representing this professional dichotomy, Behn divides herself into poet and Muse. This convention is present in many of her court poems and here Behn uses the division to differentiate between the professional writer and the political subject. The poet, the 'I' of the poem, discusses current events with the pragmatic objectivity of the professional writer; in contrast, the Muse is a political idealist, emotionally committed to the past. In these passages, the narrator of the poem distances herself from the Muse and thereby is able to discuss the professional/political dilemma without rejecting the possibility of compromise. In a sense, this division of self indicates that professional interests have already been separated from political beliefs. There is, nonetheless, a sense of co-operation between the halves of the split self, so that the poet urges the Muse to adapt, and the Muse tries in vain to oblige; the poet appears to be paralysed:

> But oh! if from your Praise I feel
>   A joy that has no Parallel
> What must I suffer when I cannot pay
>   Your Goodness, your own generous way?
> And make my stubborn Muse your Just Commands obey.
>   My Muse that would endeavour fain to glide
> With the fair prosperous Gale, and the full driving Tide
> But Loyalty Commands with Pious Force,
>   That stops me in the thriving Course.
> The Brieze that wafts the Crowding Nations o're,
>   Leaves me unpit'y far behind
>   On the Forsaken Barren Shore,
> To Sigh with Echo, and the Murmuring Wind;   (no.87, lines 44–56)

Behn represents herself trapped between political commitments and a prosperous future. The 'I' of this passage recognizes and desires all the conventions of polite society – she is pleased by praise, she wants to respond in kind – yet the 'stubborn' Muse exists beyond convenience and pragmatism. Burnet's 'Just Commands' are over-ruled by the 'Pious Force' of past allegiances.

The final stanza dispenses with the split self: Behn is 'Useless and Forlorn', 'Ruin'd in the Universal Turn' (no.87, line 87 and line 89). Yet this ending may be something of an invitation to Burnet. Behn reflects on the pressures of poverty and propaganda, and suggests these forces work together;

> Nor can my Indigence and Lost Repose,
> Those Meager Furies that surround me close,
>   Convert my Sense and Reason more
>   To this Unpresidented Enterprise,
>   Than that a Man so Great, so Learn'd, so Wise,
> The Brave Atchievement Owns and nobly Justifies.   (no.87, 90–5)

Perhaps Behn is suggesting that she can be bought.

Unfortunately, no evidence has yet been recovered that determines whether Behn's poem to Mary was published before *To Burnet*. If it was, then Burnet must have been soliciting a poem specifically for William, Behn having already diluted her loyalism. However, Behn may have written the poem to Mary as a result of Burnet's commission and published the poem *To Burnet* to clarify the extent of her political compromise. Although the events of 1688 forced Behn into a degree of political inconsistency, she seeks to preserve the appearance of political integrity, without which her political verse would have little worth. *To Burnet* might be read as a vindication of her decision to accept the new government, through the images of the violated political self and divided poet-Muse. Presumably, Behn negotiates her political and professional self-representation in order to establish a pragmatic future.

The utmost importance of professionalism to Behn is revealed by her renegotiation of court alliance in *A Congratulatory Poem to her Sacred Majesty Queen Mary upon her Arrival in England* (Behn, 1, no.86). Narcissus Luttrell's copy of Behn's final state poem is dated 26 February 1689, William and Mary's coronation took place on the 11 April 1689, and Behn died five days later, on the 16 April 1689. In this poem Behn reassesses and qualifies the ambitions and politics expressed in her other court poems. Although Behn did not survive many days into the reign of William and Mary, this poem does not anticipate such an abrupt and absolute resolution to the problem of her loyalty and employment. It is in no sense a defeatist poem and there is no suggestion that Behn found the possibility of retirement, exile or death an acceptable solution to her political and professional crisis. In fact, she tests the position she developed in the Jacobite state poems, confronting fully the difficulties of uniting professionalism and integrity.

Behn adopts a similar tone in the final lines of 'A Satyr on Doctor Dryden,' (Behn, 1, no.71) in which she reflects upon Dryden's timely conversion to Roman Catholicism during James II's reign. Using the metaphor of the Israelites, which Dryden used extensively and with enormous success in *Absalom and Achitophel*, Behn accuses Dryden of opportunism. This poem includes several harsh descriptions of Dryden, from 'a grey old hedge bird' to 'A lewd old Atheist' with 'an impious ulcerated mind' (no.71, lines 6–7 and line 14). Yet the poem concludes with pragmatic, if cynical acceptance:

and when another Moses shall arise
once more I know thou'lt rub and clear they eyes
and turn to be true Israelite againe
for when the act is done and finish't cleane
what should the poet doe but shift the scene.   (no.71, lines 29–33)

Dryden is 'constant to the times' (no. 71, line 23) and Behn seems to be saying that there is no such thing as political integrity. If Dryden is inconsistent, then he is no more than a professional writer, simply representing the changing 'scenes'.

NOTES

1 *The Works of Aphra Behn, vol I, Poetry*, ed. Janet Todd (London, 1992) no. 55. Hereafter cited as Behn, I, and included in the text. All references to Behn's poems are cited by their number in this edition.

2 From the title of another ballad on Monmouth published in 1681: *England's Darling; or, Great Britain's Joy and Hope in that noble Prince, James, Duke of Monmouth*.

3 See Mary Ann O'Donnell, *Aphra Behn: a Bibliography of Primary and Secondary Sources* (New York, 1986), pp. 83–9 and pp. 255–6. Hereafter cited as O'Donnell and included in the text.

4 Todd notes that the repetitive 'Scotch tune' reference in the titles of all three poems contains a pun on Monmouth's surname, Scott, in 'Spectacular deaths: history and story in Aphra Behn's *Love-Letters, Oroonoko* and *The Widow Ranter*' in *Gender, Art and Death* (Cambridge, 1993), pp. 32–62 (p. 37).

5 Although Shaftesbury is often held responsible for Monmouth's political betrayals of his father and uncle, Monmouth himself blamed Halifax for his disgrace and challenged him to a duel in 1681. After Shaftesbury's death, Charles and James had Sir Thomas Armstrong executed as an outlaw (i.e. without trial) in 1683 for corrupting Monmouth. See Frances Estelle Ward, *Christopher Monck, Duke of Albemarle* (London, 1915) p. 133 and J. R. Jones, *Country and Court: England, 1658–1714* (London, 1978; repr. 1986) p. 223.

6 The potentially high political impact of popular ballads is explored in C. M. Simpson, *The British Broadside Ballad and its Music* (New Brunswick, NJ, 1966), pp. 449–55, in relation to Thomas Wharton's *Lillibulero*. For a comprehensive collection of popular and satirical verse of this period,

see *Poems on Affairs of State*, 7 vols., ed. George de F. Lord (London and New Haven, 1968–71).

7 See Janet Todd and Virginia Crompton, 'Rebellion's antidote: a new attribution to Aphra Behn', *Notes and Queries* n.s. 38 (1991), 175–7.

8 It is possible that coffee represented the opposition and tea the Stuart loyalists. Shaftesbury's political meetings were famously associated with the Green Ribbon Club coffee house. Tea was less readily available, although it was certainly drunk at court. For example, when James, Duke of York and Mary of Modena lived in exile in Scotland in 1680, they took tea with them and it was admired as a novelty. See Carola Oman, *Mary of Modena* (Bungay, Suffolk, 1962), p. 70. For other examples of the significance of tea and coffee, see Todd and Crompton, p. 176, and Behn, 1, 407–8.

9 See David Kunzel, *The Early Comic Strip* (Berkeley, CA, 1973), pp. 130–48, and M. Dorothy George, *English Political Caricature to 1792: A Study of Opinion and Propaganda* (Oxford, 1959), pp. 46–51. Kunzel reproduces many of Barlow's cards. Hereafter cited as Kunzel and George and included in the text.

10 See *Aesop's Fables* (London, 1666).

11 For further observations, see Germaine Greer (ed.), *The Uncollected Verse of Aphra Behn* (Stump Cross, 1989) pp. 191–6, and Behn, 1, 427–32. Both Greer and Todd have footnoted Behn's version with reference to Philipott's original.

12 Donald Wing, *Short-title Catalogue of Books printed in England, Scotland, Ireland, Wales and British America and of English Books Printed in Other Countries, 1641–1700*, 3 vols. (1952), revised by John J. Morrison (New York, 1988).

13 George Kitchin, *Sir Roger L'Estrange: A Contribution to the History of the Press in the Seventeenth Century* (London, 1913), p. 392. Hereafter referred to as Kitchin and included in the text.

14 I have examined three copies in the British Library, two copies in the Cambridge University Library and a copy in the Wren Library, Trinity College, Cambridge. Several extant copies of the 1687 edition include varying numbers of pages from the 1666 edition, suggesting that Barlow had at least sold part of the first edition unbound. It appears that the same plates were used for Behn's text: Philipott's lines were erased and Behn's verses engraved in their place. Therefore a mixed edition is not unsightly. The two authors can be distinguished easily by the number of lines in the verses since all Behn's adaptations are six lines long. During this period such a publication would initially be sold unbound.

15 In December 1682, Burnet wrote to Anne Wharton, 'Some of Mrs Behn's songs are very tender, but she is so abominably vile a woman, and rallies not only in all religion but in virtue in so odious and obscene a manner, that I am heartily sorry she has writ anything in your commendation.' See Maureen Duffy, *The Passionate Shepherdess: Aphra Behn 1649–1689* (London, 1977; repr. London, 1989), p. 205.

16 See Roger L'Estrange, *Selections from The Observator*, introduced by Violet Jordain (Augustan Reprint Society, no. 141, 1970), pp. i–xiv. Hereafter cited as L'Estrange and included in the text.

17 For example, see *A Pindarick on the Death of our late Sovereign*, lines 47–52 (Behn, 1, no. 65).

18 See Sir Robert Filmer, *Patriarcha* (London, 1680; repr. Cambridge, 1991).

19 Lois Schwoerer, 'Propaganda in the revolution of 1688–89' in *American Historical Review*, 82 (1977), 843–74. Hereafter cited as Schwoerer and included in the text.

20 Reprinted in Gilbert Burnet, *A Second Collection of Several Tracts and Discourses Written in the Years 1686, 1687, 1688, 1689* (London, 1689), pp. 119–32. Hereafter cited as Burnet and included in the text.

21 Burnet had published an account of the deathbed conversion of Rochester, the Restoration atheist and libertine, entitled *Some Passages of the Life and Death of the right honourable John Earl of Rochester who died 26 July, 1680* (London, 1680). The text aroused considerable public interest.

22 James left London soon after the news of William's invasion. William was warmly received in London when he arrived. However, James was caught as he tried to leave the country and returned to William by over-helpful subjects. William, who was staying at Windsor, ordered James to London (Foxcroft, pp. 256–7).

23 It is possible that Behn's disassociation is an obscure literary joke. In a translation of Horace in celebration of Pindar, Cowley wrote: 'Lo, how th'obsequious *Wind*, and swelling *Ayr*/ The *Theban Swan* does upwards bear / Into the *walks* of *Clouds*, where he does play, / And with extended *Wings* opens his liquid way. / Whilst, alas, my *tim'erous Muse* / *Unambitious* tracks pursues; / Does with weak unballast wings, / About the *mossy Brooks* and *Springs*; / About the *Trees* new-blossom'ed *Heads*, / About the *Gardens* painted *Beds*, / About the *fields* and flowry *Meads*, / And all *inferior beauteous things* / Like the laborious *Bee*, / For little drops of *Honey* flee, / and there with *Humble Sweets* contents her *Industrie*.' Here, then Cowley has translated Horace's comparison of his modest verse to that of Pindar (the Theban swan). Behn's reflection on Cowley appears to parallel this passage. See Cowley's Pindaric ode, 'The Praise of Pindar' in Abraham

Cowley, *Poems: Miscellanies, The Mistress, Pindarique Odes, Davideis, Verses Written on Several Occasions* ed. by A. R. Waller (Cambridge, 1905), pp. 178–9, lines 36–50. It is even possible that the reference to Roman elections echoes Cowley. In his essay 'Of Liberty', Cowley describes Roman candidates canvassing votes before the election, and argues that to obtain votes they flattered the population: 'Behold the Masters of the World begging from door to door.' He claims that ambition and power enslave the individual. See Abraham Cowley, *The Essays and Other Prose Writings*, ed. Alfred B. Gough (Oxford, 1915), p. 110. Hereafter referred to as Cowley and included in the text.

24 In 1688, Behn wrote an elegy on Edmund Waller, who, like Cowley, wavered in his commitment to the Stuarts (Behn, 1, no. 81). Behn identifies strongly with Waller; she describes his work as a formative influence: 'wondrous Bard, whose Heav'n-born *Genius* first / My Infant *Muse*, and Blooming *Fancy* Nurst' (no. 81, lines 25–6).

25 See Alan Rudrum, 'Energies in reaction', *TLS*, no. 4562, 7 September 1990, p. 953 and Alastair Fowler, 'A new fashion in love,' *TLS*, no. 4717, 27 August 1993, pp. 3–4.

26 Cowley attempted to live up to the uncompromising allegiance expected of Stuart courtiers in attendance at the exiled court of Henrietta Maria and Charles Stuart. Having returned to England, he declared his intention to retire to America. Although he actually made his peace with Cromwell's government, Cowley tried to conform to royalist ideals. See Raymond A. Anselment, *Loyalist Resolve: Patient Fortitude in the English Civil War* (London and Toronto, 1988), pp. 155–84.

8 Aphra Behn: the politics of translation

ELIZABETH SPEARING

Aphra Behn lived in a period when translation was a prestigious activity. A great variety of instances and discussions of translation offered aesthetic and intellectual excitement to her and her contemporaries. During Behn's most productive period, Dryden, the greatest writer of the age, was almost constantly engaged in thinking about translation, both writing about it and practising it. Abraham Cowley's *Pindarique Odes*, published in 1656, would have been the latest thing at a formative stage of Behn's development, and, together with their short preface, must have contributed powerfully to an association of translation with poetic innovation and creativity. To an intelligent woman, almost certain to have had little Latin and less Greek, translation would have been associated with access to the ideas and literature of classical paganism and with the possibility of escape from the strongly and perhaps stiflingly Christian framework of the vernacular writings most readily available to her.[1] Translation was a controversial subject, with its own growing list of manifestos and *artes poeticae*; there were not only those who objected to the wider accessibility of pagan works, there was also disagreement about the very nature of 'translation'. A list of the titles of a volume of poems will often reveal a careful distinction made among translation, imitation and paraphrase, and a preface of Henry Higden's suggests informed readers eager to categorize and criticize: 'Well then, *A Modern Essay* let it be, for as a *Translation* I could not, and as a *Paraphrase* I would not own it: if I have ventured on something between both, I hope it may be the less censured.'[2] Yet such distinctions were not always drawn, and the range of activities conducted under the general heading of translation was so wide that it can be difficult to determine whether a particular text should be considered as a translation or as an 'original' work.

This situation was not of course new, for the 'originality' of earlier authors as diverse as Chaucer, Malory and Shakespeare is at least equally hard to define, given their dependence on pre-existing sources; but the heightened interest in conceptualizing translation in the later seventeenth century meant that such questions then arose more sharply. Accusations of plagiarism were common, and it is probably not by chance that a female author should be especially liable to such accusation,[3] for, as we shall see, the politics of translation are intricately interwoven with sexual politics.[4] From Genesis on, both secondariness and deceptiveness have more often been attributed to women than to men, and I shall argue that in Behn's case the politics of translation include not merely her response to or addition of overtly political content, but also a distinctive, and distinctively feminine, participation in power-relationships involving text and reader.

This is not the place to embark on a detailed account of the view of various seventeenth-century theorists of translation,[5] but a basic dichotomy existed between those who believed in the exact fidelity to thought that both Denham and Dryden referred to as 'servile' translation (and Robert Lowell as taxidermy),[6] and those who believed it more important to be faithful to the 'soul' or 'spirit' of the original, a belief which would make literal translation impossible. When the work under consideration is in verse, the problem is particularly acute; Sir John Denham went so far as to say that '. . . it is not his [the translator's] business alone to translate Language into Language, but Poesic into Poesie; & Poesie is of so subtle a spirit, that in pouring out of one Language into another, it will all evaporate; that if a new spirit be not added in the transfusion, there will remain but a *Caput mortuum* . . .'[7] Of Behn's translations, that to which Denham's statement applies most aptly is probably her version of Cowley's *Of Plants*, Book VI. She revered Cowley's achievement as a poet and, no less important, shared his political opinions; and the outcome is a remarkably accurate and resourceful rendering of his Latin hexameters into English heroic couplets. Here, despite her alleged ignorance of Latin,[8] it is scarcely possible to distinguish Behn's 'spirit' from Cowley's; but a more revealing illustration of her practice as translator will be found in her treatment of a more neutral source.

Consideration of late seventeenth-century theories of translation in relation to the works of Aphra Behn is of limited usefulness. Most such theories concern the Englishing of classical texts; and apart from 'paraphrases' of Horace and Ovid, Behn is translating writers of her own century, and works very different from those considered by such theorists as Dryden and Roscommon. It is unlikely that readers of *The Island of Love* would have been mentally comparing Behn's text with the original and wondering whether they were looking at metaphrase, paraphrase or imitation, nor is there any evidence that Restoration critics considered its original author, Paul Tallemant, the Ovid of his time. Most of Behn's translation was from French (a language of which she seems to have had an excellent knowledge), and much of it from prose; in this area she herself added to the body of seventeenth-century comment in her preface to a work by Fontenelle[9] where she makes some rather surprising statements, and some which do not necessarily conform with her actual practice. Speaking only of modern European languages, Behn considers French 'of all the hardest to translate into English', Italian being the easiest; this is partly caused by a lack of affinity between the French and English nations, partly by the fact that French had 'suffered more changes this hundred years past' than other languages; newly introduced French words were not yet acceptable in English and 'it runs a little rough in *English*, to express one *French* Word, by two or three of ours'. On the other hand, she suggests that French style is such that it is natural to abbreviate it in English: the French 'confound their own Language with needless Repetitions and Tautologies; and by a certain Rhetorical Figure, peculiar to themselves, imply twenty Lines, to express what an *English* Man would say, with more Ease and Sense in five; and this is the great Misfortune of translating *French* into *English*: If one endeavours to make it *English* Standard, it is no Translation. If one follows their Flourishes and Embroideries, it is worse than *French* Tinsel.'[10] Here it is tempting to see less a considered literary opinion of the works she was translating than an impersonation of a chauvinist, anti-French attitude which can be found running through English writing from Shakespeare's *Henry V* and Fanny Burney's *Evelina* to the contemporary *Sun* newspaper. Whatever the faults of Tallemant's allegories, tinsel decoration was not one of them, nor does Fontenelle indulge in periphrastic ornament, and, as will be seen, the alleged ratio of twenty French lines to five English ones is more or less reversed in Behn's versions of Tallemant.

The writers of commendatory poems prefacing Behn's translation of Balthazar de Bonnecorse's *La Montre*[11] show just how different the task Behn was undertaking here could be considered from that of translating the giants of Greek and Latin literature:

> But why should you, who can so well create,
> So stoop, as but pretend, you do translate?
> Could you, who have such a luxuriant Vein,
> As nought but your own Judgement could restrain;
> Who are, yourself, of Poesie the Soul,
> And whose brave Fancy knocks at either Pole;
> Descend so low, as poor Translation,
> To make an Author, that before was none?
> Oh! Give us henceforth, what is all your own!
> Yet we can trace you here, in e'ery Line;
> The Texture good, but some Threds are too fine:
> We see where you let in your Silver Springs;
> And know the Plumes, with which you imp his Wings.   (Charles Cotton)

> We owe to thee, our best Refiner, more
> Than him, who first dig'd up the rugged Ore
> . . . .
> While the rude Heap, which lay before unform'd
> To Life and Sense, is by they Spirit warm'd.   (Geo. Jenkins)

'G. J.' is even more outspoken in condemning Bonnecorse: great France will look on with envy as Behn outdoes their greatest wit, 'Witness *La Montre*, from their Rubbish rais'd.'

Prose works translated by Aphra Behn include Bonnecorse's *La Montre*, Fontenelle's *Histoire des Oracles* and *Entretien sur la pluralité des mondes*, *Agnès de Castro* by Jean Baptiste de Brilhac and an incomplete version of La Rochefoucauld's *Maximes* (*Seneca Unmasqu'd, or, Moral Reflections from the French*). Several of Behn's poems are also translations or paraphrases. Some of the plays, too, owe a debt to French originals;

Langbaine lists under Behn's name *The Emperor of the Moon* as 'taken from *Harlequin, Empereur dans le Monde de la Lune*' and Sir Patient Fancy as 'Part ... taken from ... *Le Malade Imaginaire*'.[12] The works to be examined in this essay are her 'translations' of Tallemant's *Le voyage de l'Isle d'Amour* and *Le Second Voyage de l'Isle d'Amour*.[13] The Abbé Paul Tallemant (1642–1712) wrote these works at an early age and gained admission to the Académie when he was only twenty-four. His extremely successful career as a writer and preacher seems to have owed as much to his influential connections and the charm of his character as to any literary distinction. The *Voyages* recount in allegorical form the experiences of a young man as he falls in love for the first time, is heartbroken, disenchanted, learns to amuse himself cynically with women, and finally renounces love in favour of military glory. The two works, each taking the form of a letter to a friend, are in prose interspersed with verse, the latter sometimes representing the outpourings of the lover, sometimes the description of an allegorical place or figure (the City of Discretion, the Princess Hope), sometimes a song or speech delivered by such a figure. They aroused admiration in their own time, and in 1915 Montague Summers still called *Le Voyage* 'a dainty fantasy' and commented that Tallemant's 'neat and elegant' poems never failed to please,[14] but it is now hard to praise Tallemant's work with much warmth, and indeed a French scholar and admirer of Behn, Bernard Dhuicq, has recently assessed the relative value of these texts and Behn's translation of them in terms not essentially different from those used about *La Montre* and its translation: 'elle apporte en effet, dynamisme, couleur et relief à un modèle mièvre et pauvre'.[15] The seventeenth century in France is known as a period of *épuration*, when literary language became more abstract, precise and restricted in vocabulary. Such characteristics, a source of power, intensity and excitement in a tragedy by Racine, have a very different effect in Tallemant's love-allegory, where the result of abstraction is pallor rather than intensity, and human nature is almost purified out of existence. As in the drama of Corneille and Racine, physical contact is banished from the stage; human passion is translated into a specialized verbal code, free of colloquialism and of the bodily connotations of everyday language. Even before the seventeenth-century refinement, English translators had tended to make their French originals more concrete and richer in social detail.[16] Behn certainly does so in these two works, and if Tallemant had read her versions he would surely have been shocked at their lack of decorum and of *bienséance*, their mingling of a wide range of different linguistic registers, of Englishness and classicism, and of imagery taken from many different sources.

I shall begin with Behn's version of the first *Voyage. Poems on Several Occasions: with A Voyage to the Island of Love* is the only contemporary volume of poetry which (apart from commendatory verses) was entirely written or translated by Behn; it was published in London in 1684. In both French and English an unhappy lover (Tircis in Tallemant, Lysander in Behn) writes to his friend Lycidas to describe how his voyage to the country of Content was interrupted when he and some other passengers went ashore on an enticing island called the Isle of Love; he continues with an account of his relationship with the charming Aminte (Aminta). One feature that emerges at once from comparison is Behn's addition of references to a wide variety of concrete human activities unmentioned by Tallemant; and among these the struggle for various types of power is prominent. In this quite literal sense, she transforms her source into a more political text. Relatively early in his journey, the lover reaches the city of Hope, situated on the river of Pretension, and meets the Princess Hope. Behn's river suggests a more dangerous ambition than successful love:

> 'Tis treacherously smooth and falsly fair,
> Inviting, but undoing to come near;
> 'Gainst which the Houses there find no defence,
> But suffer undermining Violence;   (679–82)

and four lines of French verse saying only that Princess Hope doesn't keep her promises, encourages lovers to persist, and raises false expectations of longer life, are developed by Behn into twenty-four lines where Hope is seen in political terms, and terms which do not only have general application, but must have been particularly familiar to her British contemporaries:

> Great in Pretension, in Performance small,
>   And when she Swears 'tis Perjury all.
> Her Promises like those of Princes are,
>   Made in Necessity and War,
>   Cancell'd without remorse, at ease,
>   In the voluptuous time of Peace.   (720–5)

Tallemant gives Hope two petitioners, 'dont l'un aimoit en un lieu si haut, qu'il n'osoit en rien attendre de bon; & l'autre avec même dessein esperoit tout de sa fortune' (p. 18). Here Behn particularizes as well as politicizing: the first lover aims so high that 'even to Hope, for him, was Impudence' (742), and Hope's reply identifies him, tacitly yet unmistakeably, with John Sheffield, Lord Mulgrave, a man whose arrogance was often commented on, and who had recently been deprived of his offices and sent away from court for wooing the Princess Anne, then third in line to the throne (and eventually queen):

> Were she the Heir to an illustrious Crown,
> Those Charms, that haughty meen, that fam'd renown,
> That wond'rous skill you do in Verse profess,
> That great disdain of common Mistresses;
> Can when you please with aid of Billet Deux,
> The Royal Virgin to your Arms subdue . . .   (759–64)

But the character described at greatest length is a third figure, and one added to the text by Behn herself. So great was her interest in James Scott, Duke of Monmouth and illegitimate son of Charles II, that she introduced him repeatedly into her writing (including another 'translation', her paraphrase of Ovid's epistle of Oenone to Paris[17]); she was clearly struck, not just by his looks and his charm, but by the glamour of his youth at court, and his sordid downfall after the failure of the political ambitions which Shaftesbury had encouraged. (He was to make a final attempt at power which led to his execution the year after this volume was published.) Monmouth features here as a 'young Hero',

> Conducted thither by a Politick throng,
> The Rabble Shouting as he passed along,

accompanied by a 'faithless Flatterer',

> Who in return, calls him, *young God of War!*
> The *Cities Champion!* and his *Countries Hope*,
> The *Peoples Darling*, and *Religious Prop.*
> *Scepters* and *Crowns* does to his view expose;
> And all the Fancied pow'r of Empire shows. (785–94)

Such additions of contemporary English political material stand out in sharp contrast to the impression of complete political neutrality given by the abstraction of Tallemant's French. Within this abstraction, it is paradoxically impossible to be a royalist because it is impossible to be anything else: absolutism allows no public sphere within which party politics could be acted out. Behn's version reflects the more open English scene, within which politics are part of the normal range of human activities and are indeed open to violent controversy, and it is possible to be, like Behn herself, a partisan royalist.

Lysander's first sight of the Island of Love had already included 'an old Batter'd Fop' tricked by

> . . . a fair she, that has a Trick in Art,
> To cheat him of his Politicks and Heart;
> Whilst he that Jilts the Nation ore and ore,
> Wants sense to find it in the subtiller *W—re*. (195–8)

Behn's Cythera includes those for whom the winning of sexual dominance is inextricably mixed with the winning of political power ('The Royal Virgin to your Arms subdue . . .'), and those whose vanity can be exploited by a power-hungry flatterer. It even includes those features of the Restoration political scene, a crafty cabal and a yelling mob.

For Behn, then, national politics merge readily into sexual politics; and both are closely connected with religion, a fire zone for power-struggles in the seventeenth century, and often inseparable from politics at every level. While lodged at Jealousie, the tortured lover is no longer in his right mind; Behn's 'translation' of the words 'je devins emporté, méfiant, soup-çonneux' (p. 29) includes,

> And obstinate as new Religion,
> As full of Error, and false Notion too,
> As Dangerous, and as Politick; (1535–7)

and later, in the Temple of Love, a Priest of Hymen is in attendance, but, we are told, very rarely called upon. Priests are then blamed for the introduction of 'the Marriage-cheat' (1702 ff.). Marriage is seen as an evil institution, against the natural law of Heaven, and it is presented in straightforwardly political terms: a means of enslaving people and of confining wealth (and therefore presumably power) to a ruling class. Conventional morality is further undermined when the lovers, proceeding from an exchange of hearts in the Temple of Love to the Bower of Bliss, are stopped by Honour, described first as a phantom, then as an idol with numerous worshippers (1779–1819). It was a commonplace of the Golden Age ideal that civilization distorted natural sexual relations, that 'What Nature made to be possest, / Mistaken Honour, made a Theft';[18] Dryden introduces the same idea in the opening lines of *Absalom and Achitophel*, but it is entirely lacking in Behn's original. Once more, Behn is quite strongly anti-clerical; she relates the religion of honour to the many sects of seventeenth-century England, pulling the reader into the text as witness: 'And as in other Sectuaries you find, / His Votaries most consist of Womankind' (1809–10). As with the questioning of marriage, the method is to assert that something which is generally accepted as natural and unquestionable has a specific historical origin and derives from the self-interest of a particular group of persons. The normal value-system is completely inverted: youth is debauched and beauty ruined not by sexual indulgence, but by the constraints imposed by the false notion of honour.

From the very beginning Behn tends to add a sexual colouring to her source, even in places where the French offers no foothold for any such addition. One of her earliest expansions occurs in describing the storm which blows the travellers to the island. Tallemant has 'Nous vogâmes paisiblement', 'un orage furieux' arises and for five hours blows them off course, then the sun shines once more. His prose account takes less than eight lines and contains only three adjectives and two adverbs relating to the weather; there are no references to people, their feelings, or their behaviour. In contrast, Behn, using a method often referred to as 'paraphrase', where the sense of a few lines of the original is first given and then expanded upon,[19] develops the calm, the ensuing storm and the change back to fair weather into a baroque extravaganza. In her forty-three lines (74–116) she introduces imagery which humanizes and eroticizes the elements in a most sensational manner; before the storm 'The ruffling Winds were hush'd in wanton sleep'; afterwards the exhausted waves, like a successful but weary rapist, 'O're-toil'd and Panting, Calm and Breathless lay'. She intensifies the storm ('The billows all into disorder hurl'd, / As if they meant to bury all the World'), and prolongs it, describing it in relation to the anger of the gods and the terror of human beings. At the same time, the crisis is used to comment satirically on human behaviour; the voyagers 'Load the angry Skyes' with repentance, and, in a line anticipating Pope in the neatness with which it turns on an implied relative, they 'make those vows, they want the pow'r to keep'. Such additions of sensuality and satire are entirely characteristic of Behn's rehandling of Tallement.

Tallemant had managed to compose two pieces which were about sex but devoid of sensuality. The lover's first sight of Aminte is presented in six lines of pallidly tasteful abstraction and cliché:

> Car tout ce qu'a d'apas la brillante Jeunesse,
> Tout ce qui peut d'un coeur attirer la tendresse,
> La Fraicheur, l'Embon-point, la douce Majesté,
> De la bouche & du teint la charmante beauté,
> Des Roses & des Lis le meslange agreable
> Rendoient de ses beaux yeux le charme inevitable.

Behn has twenty-three lines, divided into two sections, and transforms this lifeless catalogue into the sensuous evocation of a speaking, moving beauty. Where Tallemant is discreetly vague about any of the woman's charms below neck-level, Behn's second section is more suggestive:

> **THE CHARACTER**
> Such Charms of Youth, such Ravishment
> Through all her Form appear'd,
> As if in her Creation Nature meant,
> She shou'd a-lone be ador'd and fear'd:

Her Eyes all sweet, and languishingly move,
Yet so, as if with pity Beauty strove,
This to decline, and that to charm with Love.
A chearful Modesty adorn'd her Face,
And bashful Blushes spread her smiling Cheeks;
Witty her Air; soft every Grace,
And 'tis eternal Musick when she speaks,
From which young listening Gods the Accents take
And when they wou'd a perfect Conquest make,
Teach their young favourite Lover so to speak.

II
Her Neck, on which all careless fell her Hair,
Her half discover'd rising Bosome bare,
Were beyond Nature form'd; all Heavenly fair.
Tempting her dress, loose with the Wind it flew,
Discovering Charms that wou'd alone subdue,
Her soft white slender Hands whose touches wou'd
Beget desire even in an awful God;
Long Winter'd Age to tenderness wou'd move,
And in his Frozen Blood, bloom a new spring of *Love*　　　　　(252–74)

This recalls pictures of ladies by Kneller and Lely; it emphasizes the sexual attractiveness of a woman for the benefit of a male spectator, who has to be intrigued and aroused by the strip-tease performance implied by the partial uncovering of the bosom and the unspecified charms revealed when the wind blows her dress aside (the word 'discover' is used twice). The primary appeal is visual, as in such a portrait, but it also implies movement and the sensation of touch; 'Le charme de ses beaux yeux' in Tallemant becomes in Behn's first section, 'Her Eyes all sweet, and languishingly move'; the 'rising' of her bosom suggests movement, her garments move in the wind; even her hands seem about to move. The picture not only moves itself, but, in the final lines, moves a fictive spectator.

Behn has always had a reputation as a writer who not only wrote about sex but also stirred up erotic fantasies in her readers. This was the impression made by *A Voyage to the Island of Love* on her friend and admired fellow-translator Thomas Creech;[20] in a long commendatory poem published in the same volume, he moves quickly from Behn as Muse to Behn as provider of ammunition for Cupid. This translation, says Creech, disarms men, making them ready to yield to the first beauty they meet, and offers 'sweet destruction' to previously chaste women. The reader, he claims, shares the erotic experience of Behn's lovers:

> In the same Trance with the young pair we lie,
> And in their amorous Ecstasies we die,

and the cool are irresistibly aroused to passion:

> Within their Breasts thy warmth and spirit glows,
> And in their Eyes thy streaming softness flows;
> Thy Raptures are transfus'd through every vein,
> And thy blest hour in all their heads does reign;
> The Ice that chills the Soul thou dost remove,
> And meltst it into tenderness and Love.

In recent years we have become more aware that, in a situation where most writers are male, female writers tend to be defined by their femaleness, and that male comments on female writing may respond stereotypically to the sex of the writer rather than the sex in her writing. Although it is certainly true that Behn's translation introduces a strongly sensual element, I am less certain that the reader is simply carried away, as Creech suggests, by the effect she produces. Behn adds sensational detail to her original, but does so with the conscious, and consciously indecorous, ingenuity that belongs to the baroque or mannerist mode. Once this is recognized, the witty exaggeration in her version become more noticeable, and the process of 'working up' effects comes to seem as prominent as the effects themselves. The terms used about the first of these two translations by Behn herself in a letter to her printer Tonson suggest the production and enjoyment of conscious artifice rather than the sharing of sensations: asking him to pay her an extra five pounds, she comments, 'you can not think wt a preety thing ye Island will be, and wt a deale of labor I shall have yet with it'.[21] Her ideal reader will not necessarily be moved only in the same way as the 'awful God' in the passage quoted above; the god too is part of the artifice she has fashioned.

   We need to recognize that there is something paradoxical in Behn's role as translator. She enters into the text adopting the masculine subject-position of her French original, yet the very completeness of her imper-sonation turns it into a piece of acting, a masquerade. Any translation can be said to involve some degree of role-playing: Stephen Greenblatt has written about Wyatt as translator, 'He could, of course, play with masks – the translations are all an elaborate kind of masking . . .'.[22] In all but the most literal of translations, there will be some kind of cohabitation of the translator with his source. Roscommon realized this when recommend-ing to the would-be translator the choice of 'a *Poet* who *your* way do's bend',[23] and Dryden stressed the importance of considering the source poet's 'genius and distinguishing character';[24] but however compatible poet and translator, however much effort is made towards convergence, a translation is likely to reveal something of the translator's 'distinguishing character'. Total self-effacement on the translator's part is scarcely possi-ble; thus the relation between the translator and his or her original is, in the broadest sense, political, in that it involves a shifting balance of power. This may be completely overt, as in the case of one modern translator of French and German novels into English, who stated that for him the greatest pleasure of translation lay in the sense of absolute domination he gained over his originals.[25] The activity of earlier male translators has similarly been seen in terms that imply a struggle with the source for mastery: 'wrenching transformation' or 'brutal rewriting', to quote two phrases applied to Wyatt's versions of Petrarch.[26] In the case of a female translator, the power relation is more likely to be veiled and complex, and, if she is writing for money, she will be under a particular obligation to please, and thus to adopt a seductive rather than a dominant approach.[27] (That Behn did translate for money, while at the same time feeling concern for the aesthetic quality of her work, is made clear in the letter to Jacob Tonson quoted above.) A clue to her understanding of the situation may be found in the 'Character' of Aminta already quoted. This implies a political analysis of the love relation in which what will satisfy a desire gendered as masculine *must* be a performance. The god is male and domi-nant; his favourite is of unspecified sex, but is submissive, and therefore gendered feminine. The favourite has to learn to speak in a certain way in order to please the god; it is a matter not of spontaneous passion, but of learning a part. As a female translator, Behn is in a position analogous to the favourite's. The politics of translation thus become, for her, a form of sexual politics; and this emerges more clearly from her version of the second *Voyage*, to which I now turn.

This return to the Isle of Love takes the form in Behn's version of a reply to the first letter by its recipient, now spelled 'Lycidus', and giving his name to the translation.[28] *Lycidus, or, The Lover in Fashion . . . Together with a Miscellany of New Poems by Several Hands* was the last volume containing poems by Behn to be published in her lifetime, and appeared in 1688, the year before her death. The collection as a whole contains a number of poems which suggest a coterie playing with sexual roles and sexual ambiguity. The volume includes Behn's 'To Amintas, upon reading the lives of some of the Romans' ('For neither sex can here thy fetters shun': Amintas would have been equally irresistible to Lucretia and to her ravisher), and 'To the fair Clarinda, who made Love to me, imagin'd more than Woman'.[29] Of the compositions by other hands, Daniel Kendrick's commendatary poem exclaims of Behn, 'Ah, more than Woman! more than man she is', and a Pindarick by a Lady on Behn's *Poem on the Coronation of James II* praises the fact that it '. . . did at once a Masculine wit express, / And all the softness of a Femal tenderness'; Behn excels man 'Not in soft strokes alone, but even in the bold'. The penultimate poem, immediately preceding 'To the fair Clarinda', is by a lady who professes to offer her heart to Astrea, since her lover has proved ungrateful. Three poems are addressed to 'Antonia', one of them presumably by a woman ('But humbler I with Blushes do confess'). 'Antonia' is admired as 'heroick', capable of guiding women to Amazonian glory; scorning the arts of her sex, she is praised for her wit and rhetorical powers ('A wit uncircumscrib'd by femal rules, / That nice, that dull, excuse for silent Fooles'). She and 'The fam'd *Astrea*' are the only two such gallant maids produced by the present age. The third poem also admires 'Antonia' on the slightly surprising grounds of believing that had she been Portia, she would have been right in there with Brutus, thrusting her dagger through Caesar's heart; it goes on to make explicit this suggestion of sexual ambiguity: 'Thy soul all Man; soft Woman all thy Form. / At once his Arms possess, who thee embrace, / A Heroin *Venus*, and a Love-sick *Mars*'. The appearance of *Lycidus* in the context supplied by these poems underlines the difficulty of establishing a clear boundary between translation and other forms of literary activity. Restoration books of poetry often include translations alongside 'original' compositions; and *Lycidus* can be better understood when seen in the context of the whole volume in which it was first published. *A Voyage to the Island of Love*, for all its elements of political satire, is set in what is fundamentally the golden Arcadian world which is also a theme of several poems appearing in the same volume. *Lycidus*, as Behn's subtitle suggests, evokes a sophisticated, amoral society; no longer in love, the characters amuse themselves by impersonating lovers, and Behn herself becomes involved in an intricate masquerade in which, as translator, she plays a masculine part, without ever pretending that it is anything but a part.

As in the preceding translation, Behn usually expands Tallemant's material, and again that expansion includes a certain amount of social context. This time, however, the social setting has a more theatrical air: it is often strongly reminiscent of a comedy of manners. Whereas in Tallemant the young lover proceeds in a more or less abstract fashion on his allegorical course, Behn shows his development into a foppish, complacent gallant. Advice to see all beauties while loving none is expanded into a lively catalogue of women, each offering a different pleasure. The state of being out of love is entirely agreeable; the pleasures without the pains, love has become a civilized arrangement which paradoxically makes possible the delights of that pre-civilization Golden Age of sexual freedom to which Behn repeatedly refers in her writing. In this city the God of Love is no longer a tyrant:

> Here 'tis with Reason and with Wit he Rules,
> And whining Passion Ridicules.
> No check or bound to Nature gives,
> But kind desire rewarded thrives. (p. 315)

Behn changes the names of the two women wooed from the pastoral Sylvie and Iris to a Bellinda and a Bellimante of Restoration comedy. A little guardian Cupid sounds like a rake's manservant, giving incongruously worldly advice to his charge; he refers to the allegorical figure Respect as 'Sir *Formal*, . . . a very great favorite of the Lady's, who is always in fee with them as a Jilt with a Justice; who manages their Fools just as they wou'd have 'em' (p. 321). Whereas the French lover (still the Tircis of the first *Voyage*) sets out alone on his second journey, Lycidus, his English counterpart, is an actor in the human comedy, who embarks on his voyage in the company of an 'abundance of young Heirs, Cadets, Coxcombs, Wits, Blockheads, and Politicians, with a whole Cargo of Cullies . . .' (p. 300): in short, the *dramatis personae* of contemporary society or a contemporary stage. Behn's Isle of Love even has writers of satires and lampoons; the lover soon resolves 'to be no longer a *Mark-out fool* for all the Rhiming Wits of the Island to aim their Dogrel at' (p. 308). The relationships and scenes of comedy are embedded in the text, with Behn often expanding her original into a sketch in which psychology and scene could have been developed for the stage. Where Tallemant's lover merely recognizes his successor in Amynte's[30] favours as a man he had seen in the town of Les Rivaux, Lycidus recognises this figure as not just 'one of my Rivals, but most intimate Friend' (p. 308). And when the lover wisely decides to abandon this woman and pursue two others, Behn introduces potential 'scenes' which do not exist in the French; the two women knew each other, for example, 'convert, and play'd and walkt together', but Lycidus is so discreet that they are not jealous; 'when I hapned to be with 'em both I carried myself so equally Gallant that both commended my conduct and imagin'd I did it to hide the secret passion I had for herself' (p. 334).

In both French and English the text of the second *Voyage* is actually about dissembling, the process of learning to put on an act or a mask. The lover is encouraged to woo two women simultaneously, then declare himself to both in the language of passion; Behn's version makes plainer than the French the role-playing involved and the narrator's awareness of it: 'To gain my wisht end I talkt of a flame, / Of sighing, and dying, and fire' (p. 322). The sense of skilled and experienced control of technique in this and other poems in the work supports the impression of love as a sophisticated game of charades requiring skill and self-mastery to be properly enjoyed. One village on the allegorical map is that of Intelligence, where lovers indulge in 'all that soft Love can permit' (p. 323), but all communication between them is by a secret language of signs and half-words; an abundance of artifices makes life agreeable. The Lover keeps up a

pretence to two women, wooing one while enjoying the other: 'I accustomed myself to counterfeit my Humour, whenever I found it convenient
for my Advantage: Tears, Vows, and Sighs cost me nothing, and I knew all
the Arts to jilt for Love, and could act the dying Lover' (p. 325). The mild
pretence of 'Enfin apres avoir assez fait le langoureux' (p. 147) is rendered
specifically in terms of theatre: 'In fine, after I had sufficiently acted the
Languishing Lover, for the accomplishment of all my Wishes, I thought it
time to change the Scene' (p. 326). Lycidus had even looked in the glass,
and found himself 'as fit for Conquest, as any Sir *Fopling*, or Sir *Courtly
Nice* of 'em all' (p. 313).

Behn's Lycidus is more fully characterized than her Lysander of the
first *Voyage*; no longer merely A Lover, he might be a soldier (he hopes to
see his friend Lysander 'the next Campagne as absolutely reduc'd to
reason as myself'); he knows that he is young, rich, witty and handsome,
with all the qualities that 'subdue the Hearts of all the Fair' (p. 299).
Impersonating him, Behn enters into the theatricality of the world represented. With him, she assumes a distinctively masculine persona, in a way
the French original does not, to generalize about the roles of the sexes in
love and to express a sense of common cause and camaraderie with other
men. Behn assumes the detached tone of a man of the world whose experiences with the opposite sex have left him cynical about the human race and
bitter towards women. The work is distinctively baroque in its layers of
artifice: Behn is pretending that she is a man who is pretending to be dying
of love. Her art as translator becomes at once that of a dramatist and that
of an actress in a breeches role.

I have noted above the difficulty of drawing a sharp distinction
between translation and other types of literary activity; and it is interesting to see that a kind of transvestite ventriloquism can also be found not
only in her plays, where it is required by the genre itself, but in an earlier
work of hers which was not a translation. 'A Letter to a Brother of the Pen
in Tribulation'[31] is a dramatic monologue addressed to a fellow-writer
who has been forced to undergo treatment for venereal disease. Here
Behn adopts with great gusto the verbal costume of a man of the world,
swearing with the best of them ('Damn'd Penetential Drink . . . Pox on't
that you must needs be fooling now' [11, 13]), referring to woman as if

she were a man and blaming 'that Sex that has Confin'd thee so' (28) and 'this Female' (41) as the source of the recipient's sickness. It would be a mistake to suppose that such ventriloquism on Behn's part is a true adoption of masculinity. It is in part, no doubt, a reflection of the deceptiveness that Steven N. Zwicker has seen as characterizing not only Restoration politics and political language, but also the 'deep structure' of the whole culture of the period in which she was writing. He refers, for example, to 'epic whose most characteristic expression is in travesty and translation', to 'the emergence of new genres that take deception as their subject and whose function is to act as screen and mask', and to 'the transformation of old genres to accommodate the need for indirection and masquerade'.[32] More particularly, though, I would suggest that Behn's enthusiastic adoption of male roles can usefully be seen as belonging to *sexual* politics. Recent theorists have extended Joan Rivière's 'conception of womanliness as a mask'[33] to suggest that an 'excessive' or 'quoted' masculinity as well as femininity may be a means by which woman can defend herself in the field of sexual politics. Mary Ann Doane has written,

> As both Freud and Cixous point out, the woman seems to be *more* bisexual than the man . . . Male transvestism is an occasion for laughter; female transvestism only another occasion for desire. Thus, while the male is locked into sexual identity, the female can at least pretend that she is other – in fact, sexual mobility would seem to be a distinguishing feature of femininity in its cultural construction.[34]

There is perhaps an analogy between the self-conscious elaboration of effects that we have found in Behn's translations from Tallemant and this more general notion of feminity as a masquerade. In the heightening that Behn introduces into this rather pallid French work, as a sort of cosmetic effect, there is a central element of role-playing, even self-mockery, and this is as much a political phenomenon as the wearing either of lipstick or of jeans and shirt.

Behn adopts an exaggeratedly masculine persona from the beginning of the supposed letter from Lycidus to Lysander. As Lycidus she claims to have seen witty, handsome men, 'with the advantage of a thousand happy Adventures', who are finally fit only for a hospital. Women are not content with mere reciprocity in love,

> . . . but they would compel us all to Present and Treat 'em lavishly, till a Man hath consumed both Estate and Body in their Service. How many do we see, that are wretched Examples of this Truth, and who have nothing of all they enjoyed remaining with 'em, but a poor *Idaea* of past Pleasures, when rather the Injury the Jilt has done 'em, ought to be eternally present with 'em. Heaven keep me from being a Woman's Property. There are Cullies enough besides you or I, Lysander.
>
> (pp. 299–300)

The ensuing account of his first love affair after landing on the Isle of Love is presented as a parodic acceleration of fashionable literary love. The blushes like the morning, sighs like gentle perfumed winds, wounds from azure eyes, are all run through with wry detachment. 'In fine . . . I compared her to all the Fopperies, the Suns, the Stars, the Coral, and the Pearl, the Roses and Lillies, Angels Spheres, and Goddesses, fond Lovers dress their Idols in. For she was all fancy and fine imagination could adorn her with, at least, the gazing Puppy thought so' (p.301). The 'gazing Puppy' here is the speaker, observing himself. The French is the work of a male writer who, though he might be supposed to be detached from such feelings by his religious vows, is nevertheless at the same stage of life as his literary persona, and does not distance himself from the feelings recounted in the text as the older female writer does. However, she detaches herself not in her own person, but as a man who has learnt from his masculine experience.

The letter-writer goes on to express a traditional view of the power relationship between young women and their lovers. Their behaviour shows his weakness and his mistress's strength:

> . . . using all the Arts of her Sex, both to ingage and secure me, [she] play'd all the Woman over: She wou'd be scornful and kind by turns, as she saw convenient . . . I watch'd, and waited like a Dog, that still the oftner kick'd wou'd fawn the more.
>
> Oh, 'tis an excellent Art this managing of a Coxcomb, the Serpent first taught it our Grandam *Eve*; and *Adam* was the first kind Cully: E're

since they have kept their Empire over Men, and we have, e're since,
been Slaves . . . She saw me young enough to do her Service, handsom
enough to do her Credit, and Fortune enough to please her Vanity
and Interest: She therefore suffer'd me to Love, and Bow among
the Crowd, and fill her Train.   (p. 301)

Not only the generalizing of the situation but the placing of it in a social
context is an addition of the translator's. So too is the occasional insertion
of colloquial metaphors to contrast with the conventional poetic love
metaphors: the indecorum makes us question the validity of the emotions
and of the style in which they are being described. The lover indeed
suffers figuratively the fate of the realist Sancho Panza (and we may be
meant to recognize the allusion): 'Thus was I tost in the Blanket of Love,
sometimes up, and sometimes down' (p. 301).

When the narrator begins to discover what everyone else already
knew, his language becomes likes that of a young gallant in a comedy,
including exclamations which have no source in the French: 'and [I] like a
keeping Cully, lavish'd out my Fortune, my plenteous Fortune, to make
her fine to Cuckold me. 'Sdeath! how I scorn the Follies of my Dotage; and
am resolv'd to pursue Love for the future, in such a manner as it shall never
cost me a Sigh . . .' (p. 303). At such points, the reader almost expects
Lycidus to exit stage left. As he agonizes further over the suspicion of the
woman's unfaithfulness, Lycidus accuses himself of 'a thousand weaknesses below the Character of a Man' (p. 308). Knowledge of the truth
inspires a rage which 'made me say things unbecoming the Dignity of my
Sex, who ought to disdain those faithless Slaves, which Heaven first made
to obey the Lords of the Creation' (p. 309). Tallemant's Tircis shows no
such male chauvinism, but puts his feelings in terms that have no reference to gender: 'ma rage me fit dire des choses qu'elle seule est capable
d'inspirer' (p. 108).

Both English and French lovers are now made to pronounce themselves no longer of a humour to swell the floods with their tears (though
Behn's mocking parody is more protracted), but when they resolve to
amuse themselves with uncommitted relationships, and the respective
narrators explain the acting of the part of afflicted love, Behn's version is
much more fully developed. As at other points, her 'translation' becomes

almost a dramatic monologue, in strong contrast to the merely explanatory quality of her French original:

> . . . & ie pris enfin une habitude de contrefaire mon humeur quand bon
> me sembloit, les larmes ne me coustoient plus rien, & ie sçavois faire le
> miserable quand la fantaisie m'en prenoit. (pp. 145–6)

> Who the Devil wou'd not believe me as much in love now as I ever was
> with *Silvia*: my heart had learn't then all the soft Language of Love which
> now it cou'd prattle as naturally as its Mother Tongue; and sighing and
> dying was as ready for my mouth as when it came from my very heart;
> and cost me nothing to speak; Love being as cheaply made now by me
> as a barter for a Horse or a Coach; and with as little concern almost: It
> pleas'd me while I was speaking, and while I believ'd I was gaining the
> vanity and pleasure of a conquest over an unvanquisht heart. (p. 324)

The theatricality of *Lycidus* is, I think, beyond question, and I would
argue that it involves a specifically transvestite impersonation; Behn as
translator 'pretends that she is other' to borrow Doane's phrase, and in
this way participates all the more fully in a culturally constructed femininity. We have seen that in both *A Voyage to the Island of Love* and *Lycidus*,
where she adopts the persona of a male narrator, Aphra Behn's presence is
shifting and elusive. She takes on a literary equivalent of the adaptability
expected of any woman in seventeenth-century society; the politics of
translation intersect with sexual politics to produce a masquerade in
which the translatress's power may be at its greatest when it is most completely dissembled. In a passage inserted into what is probably the closest
of all her translations, that of Cowley's *Of Plants*, Book VI, she writes,
addressing the laurel,

> I by a double right thy Bounties claim,
> Both from my Sex, and in *Apollo*'s Name:
> Let me with *Sappho* and *Orinda* be
> Oh ever sacred Nymph, adorn'd by thee;
> And give my Verses Immortality. (lines 590–4)[35]

A sidenote adds, 'The Translatress in her own Person speaks'; but the
translatress need not speak in her own person, or claim the total appropri-

ation implied in '*my* Verses', in order to enter into the delicate power-relations implicit in the translated text.

NOTES

1 Behn's sense of her exclusion from the opportunities offered by a classical education is strikingly conveyed by her poem 'To the Unknown Daphnis on his Excellent Translation of *Lucretius*'. See *The Works of Aphra Behn*, ed. Janet Todd, vol. 1 (London, 1992), poem no. 11. All quotations from Behn's verse, except those from verse in *Lycidus*, are from this edition, and poems are identified by the numbers given therein.

2 Henry Higden, *A Modern Essay on the Thirteenth Satyr of Juvenal* (London, 1686).

3 As indicated in her Post-script to *The Rover*.

4 Similarly, authorship even of translation of the Psalms was denied to the Countess of Pembroke; see, Ben Jonson as reported by Drummond of Hawthornden (*Ben Jonson*, ed. C. H. Herford and Percy and Evelyn Simpson, 11 vols. (Oxford, 1925–52), 1.pp. 204–5).

5 For such an account see Muneharu Kitagaki, *Principles and Problems of Translation in Seventeenth-century England* (Kyoto, 1981). The leading theorists besides Dryden include Sir John Denham ('To Sir Richard Fanshaw upon his translation of *Pastor Fido*', 1648, and the preface to *The Destruction of Troy*, 1656), and Wentworth Dillon, Earl of Roscommon (*An Essay on Translated Verse*, 1684).

6 Preface to *Imitations* (London, 1962). In the twentieth century, the opposite extreme of literalism is represented by Vladimir Nabokov; see the preface to his translation of Pushkin's *Eugene Onegin* (New York, 1964).

7 Preface to *The Destruction of Troy* (London, 1656).

8 Dryden wrote in the Preface to *Ovid's Epistles*, '. . . that of Oenone to Paris is in Mr Cowley's way of imitation only. I was desir'd to say that the Authour who is of the Fair Sex, understood not Latine. But if she does not, I am afraid she has given us occasion to be asham'd who do' (*Of Dramatic Poesy and Other Critical Essays*, ed. George Watson, 2 vols. (London, 1962), 1.p. 273).

9 *Entretien sur la pluralité des mondes* (Paris, 1686), published two years later in London as *A Discovery of New Worlds. From the French, Made English by Mrs A. Behn. To which is prefixed a Preface, by way of Essay on Translated Prose* . . . Quotations are from this edition.

10 For further comment on Behn's theory and practice of translation, see Margaret Turner, 'A note on the standard of English translations from the

French, 1685–1720', *Notes and Queries* 199 (1954), 516–21; Bernard Dhuicq, 'Aphra Behn: Théorie et pratique de la traduction au xvııème siècle', *Franco-British Studies* 10 (1990), 75–98; and Kitagaki, *Principles and Problems*.

11 Balthazar de Bonnecorse, *La Montre or the Lover's Watch* (London, 1686); reprinted 1696 and subsequent reprintings with Behn's novels as *The Lover's Watch & The Ladies Looking-Glass to dress herself by*.

12 Gerard Langbaine, *The Lives and Characters of the English Dramatick Poets* (London, 1699), p. 9.

13 These were published together in Paris in 1675 as *Le Voyage et la Conqveste de l'Isle d'Amour. Le Passe-partovt des Coeurs*. Mary Ann O'Donnell, *Aphra Behn: An Annotated Bibliography of Primary and Secondary Sources* (New York and London, 1986), suggests that this is likely to have been the edition used by Behn. *Le Voyage de l'Isle d'Amour* had appeared in *Recueil de quelques pièces nouvelles et gallantes* (Cologne, 1663). French quotations here are taken from this 1663 edition for the first *Voyage*, and from the 1675 edition for the second. Tallemant's first *Voyage* ends with an account of Aminte being snatched from the arms of Tircis by Destiny in terms too abstract for it to be clear how Destiny effects this. Aminte reappears at the beginning of the second *Voyage*, having forsaken Tircis for Another. Behn either intended to make changes in the personae of her second voyage, or was not yet familiar with the second part of Tallemant's text; her Aminta dies in Lysander's arms and, possibly as a result of earlier misunderstanding, she changes both lover and beloved for her second *Voyage*.

14 *The Works of Aphra Behn*, 6 vols. (London, 1915), VI.p. 223.

15 Dhuicq, p. 79.

16 See, e.g., A. C. Spearing, 'Marie de France and her middle English adapters', *Studies in the Age of Chaucer* 12 (1990), 117–56.

17 Todd, no. 6.

18 See Behn's 'The golden age. A paraphrase on a translation out of French' (Todd, no. 12), st. VIII–IX.

19 See Oldham, 'David's lamentation for the death of Saul and Jonathan, paraphrased' for an example of this type of 'translation'. Compare also Behn, 'A paraphrase on the Lords Prayer' (Todd, no. 58).

20 Creech (1659–1700) was a Fellow of All Souls', Oxford, and famous for his translations of classical writers. See Behn's 'To the unknown Daphnis on his excellent translation of *Lucretius*' and '*A Letter to Mr Creech* at Oxford, written in the last great Frost' (Todd, nos. 11 and 55).

21 Cited by Kathleen M. Lynch, *Jacob Tonson, Kit-Cat Publisher* (Knoxville, 1971), pp. 99–100.

22 *Renaissance Self-Fashioning: From More to Shakespeare* (Chicago, 1980), p. 120.

23 Wentworth Dillon, Earl of Roscommon, *An Essay on Translated Verse* (London, 1685), reprinted in *Irish Writings from the Age of Swift*, vol. 8, ed. Robert Mahony (Dublin, 1978), 95.

24 In *Of Dramatic Poesy*, ed. Watson, ii.p. 21

25 Oral remark by Douglas Parmée, translator of Flaubert's *Education sentimentale* and Fontane's *Effi Briest*.

26 Greenblatt, *Renaissance Self-Fashioning*, p. 148; Thomas M. Greene, *The Light in Troy: Imitation and Discovery in Renaissance Poetry* (New Haven, 1982), p. 261.

27 An interesting example of her acting out of seductive femininity in a form that amounts to parody is found in the 'Epistle to the Reader' prefacing her play *The Dutch Lover* (London, 1673), in which she begins by addressing the 'Good, Sweet, Honey, Sugar-Candied Reader', and proceeds to profess her female ignorance: she refers to 'Logick etc. and several other things (that shall be nameless lest I mispell them)', and to the 'Dramatique' poets '(so I think you call them)' (*Works*, ed. Summers, i. pp. 221–2).

28 *Lycidus* is quoted from *The Works of Aphra Behn*, ed. Summers, vi.

29 Todd, nos. 78 and 80.

30 Behn has had to introduce a Silvia for this role as Aminta had died at the end of the first Voyage.

31 Todd, no. 23.

32 'Politics and literary practice in the Restoration', in *Renaissance Genres: Essays on Theory, History, and Interpretation*, ed. Barbara Kiefer Lewalski (Cambridge, Mass., 1986), p. 274.

33 'Womanliness as a Masquerade', in *Psychoanalysis and Female Sexuality*, ed. Hendrick M. Ruitenbeek (New Haven, 1966), p. 220.

34 'Film and the masquerade: theorising the female spectator', *Screen* 23.3/4 (Sept/Oct 1982), 74–87, p. 81.

35 'Orinda', Katherine Philips (1631–64), was, like Behn, a translator as well as a poet. Her translations of *Pompée* and *Horace* (the former successfully staged in Dublin with a prologue by Roscommon) are close to Corneille in both thought and expression. In 'La Solitude de St Amant Englished' (a 'parallel text' printing) her choice of diction and almost slick rhyming make the tone less fresh and uncontrived-sounding than that of the original (*Poems . . . to which is added . . . Pompey & Horace; with several other translations out of French*, London, 1667).

9 'But to the touch were soft': pleasure, power, and impotence in 'The Disappointment' and 'The Golden Age'[1]

JESSICA MUNNS

Introduction ∾

Aphra Behn contributed largely to the Restoration's sexual discourse and in this essay I discuss two of her poems in relation to a proliferating literature of sexual anxiety focused on masculine sexual impotence. 'The Disappointment' (1680) is a translation/adaptation of the French poem, 'Sur une Impuissance' (1661) by de Cantenac, significantly altered by Behn as she looks at masculine sexual impotence from a female perspective. The title quotation of this essay is taken from 'The Golden Age', (1684), loosely based on the prologue to Tasso's *Aminta* (1573), in which, I shall argue, Behn offers a route through cultural anxieties centering on the erect or the 'soft' penis read as signs either of male enmeshment in productive labour or inadequacy.[2]

In the seventeenth century, as Roger Thompson has noted, 'masculine impotence or at least inadequacy was a[n] . . . obsession'.[3] It is an obsession, of course, which has by no means been limited to the seventeenth century. Masculine impotence provides the stock motif of many cuckolding tales, which frequently link masculine impotence with wealth. The acquisition of wealth, as in Chaucer's *Merchant's Tale*, is often associated with age, age is associated with sexual decline, and the public power of the older man is undermined by his private inability to satisfy the youth and beauty his money can purchase. In Restoration literature, alongside these traditional figurations of the power of wealth and the impotence of age, increased anxieties over the relationships between sex, marriage and wealth produce new variants on the theme of impotence – new sites of impotence – and new figurations of what it is about wealth, apart from age, that produces impotence.

Giles Slade has investigated the combined figure of rake and eunuch – above all Wycherley's Horner – to argue that 'the centrality of impotence to Restoration discourse of all types, derives . . . from the upheavals following the Civil War which challenged cavalier gender ideology and led to a pervasive insecurity about what masculinity was'.[4] Undoubtedly, the civil war legacy of social and political insecurity challenged traditional concepts of authority and, since political authority was male, masculinity. As J. G. A. Pocock points out, 'seventeenth-century men were still pre-modern creatures for whom authority and magistracy were part of a natural and cosmic order', and for whom the 'unimaginable fact [was] that between 1642 and 1649, authority in England had simply collapsed'.[5] Slade suggests that the demoralizing effects of the defeat, exile, and imprisonment of the cavaliers influenced further generations of young men brought up meditating on their fathers' defeat and resenting the new powers that masculine defeat and absence had given their mothers.[6] Slade is surely correct in identifying the Restoration as a society in 'crisis' over 'masculinity', and in reaction to a period during which the traditional male ruling class was defeated. I would like to suggest, however, that this societal 'crisis' responded not only to the immediate past of cavalier defeat (and the ever present traditions of misogyny), but also to the anxieties of a society in transition from feudal aristocracy to bourgeois capitalism.

In particular, a cavalier/aristocratic and libertine ethos of careless and free sexuality becomes implicated in the nascent workings of a market economy that both endorses the free-flow and exchange of goods and also recommends frugal hoarding and careful expenditure. Richard Braverman examines the relationships between sexual spending and economic thrift in his discussion of Etherege's lyric 'Cease Anxious World'. Braverman draws attention to the lyric's anxiety as it propounds a 'cavalier . . . antipathy to . . . productivity and frugality, countering it with a libertine economy of excessive [sexual] expenditure'. Braverman concludes, however, that the cavalier's 'witty triumph beyond the anxious world of the actual economy is at the same time a measure of his declining status in a society in which real property was more potent than wit'.[7]

Jean-Joseph Goux's discussion of what makes the penis transform into the phallus is relevant to the ideology of cavalier excessive sexual expenditure described by Braverman.[8] For Goux there is a 'structural, genetic, functional correspondence between gold and the penis' and both can become a privileged 'general equivalent' – the Gold Standard, the Phallus. With reference to the privileged status of gold, Goux cites Marx's thesis that gold functions as 'something that can be done without, that does not enter into the satisfaction of immediate needs as an object of consumption nor into the immediate process of production as an agent'. Gold is, in Goux's words, 'pure superfluity, excess par excellence'.[9] For Goux, the penis can similarly transform because it also represents a kind of surplus-value, it is 'the site of unproductive expenditure, that which surpasses immediate needs; it is the site of surperfluous (and deferrable) expenditure'.[10] As such a site of excessive expenditure, the penis/phallus fulfils the ideological needs of the cavalier 'antipathy to productivity and frugality'.

For many Restoration writers, however, processes elevating either gold or the penis to a 'general equivalent' above 'immediate needs' have become grounded. The relationship between gold and the penis is present but problematic, sometimes directly and uncomfortably related and not necessarily indicating freedom from need. It was possible to imagine the penis as a site for *productive* expenditure, even labour. Penniless gallants not only work for cash payments but also supply impotent city husbands with needed heirs becoming tools in the sexual and fiscal economy of others.[11] The language of love in Restoration comedies frequently draws on the language of commerce – not least in the various famous 'proviso' scenes.[12] The relationship between sex, marriage and money, or sex, marriage and the processes of exchange are not new or unique to the Restoration, but systems of sex-money-stock-property exchange have become central, widespread, and are an integral part of a very political discourse of impotence, incapacity, and sexual avoidance. The productive labour of the penis can then evoke the Earl of Rochester's aristocratic distaste for those who 'Drudge in fair Aurelia's womb / To get supplies for age and graves' (17–18).[13]

If masculine sexual potency is equitable with productive labour, coinage, and use-value, then masculine potency and its dominant sign, the phallus, have also become implicated in activities associated with commerce and therefore potentially degrading to a gentleman. The 'purity' of sexual excess – gentlemanly largesse – is in danger of commodification, and with this danger the status of the phallus as a 'general equivalent' is destabilized. Non-productive sex, such as the supremely unproductive expenditure of premature ejaculation, or even the failure to achieve erection, become newly problematized sites of concern which are investigated in the 'imperfect enjoyment' genre.[14]

Imperfect enjoyment: 'The Disappointment'. ❧

In male 'imperfect enjoyment' poems, the embarrassment of male sexual inadequacy often mingles with mock-heroic raillery, such as addresses to the 'base mettell hanger by your Master's Thigh! / Eternall shame to Prick's heraldry' (1–2), or reminiscences, as in Rochester's in 'The Imperfect Enjoyment' (1680), of past better encounters when 'This dart of love . . . / With virgin blood the thousand maids have dyed' (37–8).[15] In Sir George Etherege's relatively decorous poem, also entitled 'The Imperfect Enjoyment' (1662), the mock-heroic note is struck as the failed encounter is expressed in terms of siege warfare with the male lover falling 'Dead at the foot of the surrendered wall' (30).[16] The male failing is attributed to female beauty – 'You'd been more happy had you been less fair' (50) – and prudery – 'condemn yourself, not me; / This is the effect of too much modesty' (41–2). Both excuses draw on conventional constructions of femininity, modest and fair, to explain why the equally conventionally constructed male, vigorous and over-powering, has failed. In both Etherege's and Rochester's poems, a mock-heroic language translates shame into comedy and evokes as well as cancels the traditions of male supremacy. The genre moves uneasily between chivalric glorification and shame, between memories of a better past and the imperfect present, and between self-disgust expressed as mockery and forms of exculpation. In Behn's 'The Disappointment', however, the narrative of masculine conquest temporarily suspended by impotence is reworked into an uncompromising narrative of female frustration.

Behn's poem, situated in an eternal pastoral is not concerned with the past, and her characters of nymph and swain, Cloris and Lysander, do not bring histories to their encounter.[17] Her poem is less concerned with explaining (away) the male failure than with describing its effect on his female partner. An evocation of female desire replaces the conventional enunciations of male expectation as 'The Disappointment' dwells as much upon Cloris' feelings of aroused desire (stanza 6 is devoted to the topic) as those of her lover, and emphasizes *her* 'disappointment' rather than that of her amorous but incapable swain. In contrast to Cloris's 'Resentments' (131), in Rochester's poem his partner, like Bellamira in Sir Charles Sedley's 1687 play of that name, is rather charmingly understanding.[18] When her lover prematurely ejaculates all over her body, 'Smiling, she chides in a kind murmuring noise / And from her body wipes the clammy joys' (19–20).

Sperm, even if premature and clammy, is still equated with 'joys' and the lady is not so much disappointed as desirous of 'more' (22).[19] The lines in which she asks for 'more' are admirably tactful as she indicates that premature ejaculation is to 'love and rapture's due' (23) – rather than a sign of incapacity. She is not repelled but merely asks, 'Must we not pay a debt to pleasure too?' (24). She is, as it were, an uncritical consumer who is prepared to regard the premature ejaculation as a preview portending further and more mutual pleasures. She is flatteringly confident that her lover has 'more'; nevertheless, her insistence, however charming, that she is still waiting to be paid her measure of sperm and pleasure surely articulates the male fear that *their* 'love' and 'rapture' are not enough for women. It is this apprehension that Rochester's poem both articulates and seeks to cancel.

In Behn's poem premature ejaculation also takes place, but not over the woman's body, rather it is Lysander who feels the consequences of his failure as 'The Insensible fell weeping in his Hand' (90). The relocation is relevant; there are no soft female murmuring noises, no gentle wipes of 'clammy joys', and no requests for 'more'. The male failure is situated in the male body and is regarded as final. Moreover, Behn's Cloris is not sweetly understanding but horrified. When she investigates her lover's limp penis, she rapidly withdraws her fingers as if 'Finding beneath the verdant Leaves a snake' (110). Male imperfect enjoyment poems take off at this point in the narrative of sexual disaster to address their penises, to remind them of past glories and threaten dire punishments.

The form, in fact, is pre-eminently about the penis, who becomes a character, an old friend but recalcitrant and problematic. The vagina, if it is mentioned at all, as in Rochester's poem, is crudely denominated a 'cunt' (40, 43), or as in the anonymous poem already cited, 'One Writing Against his Prick', is a 'Port hole' (14) – basically an empty inert space which it should be possible to penetrate.[20] In 'The Imperfect Enjoyment' Rochester even de-genders the 'cunt' since his imperial penis would 'carelessly invade/ Woman or man/ . . . Where'er it pierced, a cunt it found or made' (41–3). Harold Webber argues that in Rochester's sexual universe, 'men make women, the penis representative of a phallic power that alone establishes gender'.[21] These lines, however, which are indifferent both to procreation and the pleasure of the partner, do not so much create women with their awkward wombs, but specifically, 'cunts' as neutral gender-indifferent spaces.

Behn reverses the usual centre of the genre from the penis to the vagina, for her Cloris does not just possess a convenient orifice but a luscious vagina described in (clichéd) religious terms as an 'altar' and a 'paradise' as well as a 'fountain where delight still flows' (45, 47, 49). Cloris's vagina is also sensitive and responds to her emotions. Unlike Rochester's friend, when her lover fails her, she undergoes an immediate cessation of desire which Behn describes with anatomical precision: 'The Blood forsook the hinder Place / And strew'd with Blushes all her Face' (116–17). Lysander's feelings are described as those of 'Rage and Shame' (97), and are self-absorbed and self-directed. Cloris's feelings are similarly confused but different. She feels a mixture of 'Disdain and Shame' (18), disdain presumably for her lover's incapacity, and shame at having participated in this fiasco. And, given the centrality of rape in Restoration discourses of masculine sexuality, there can be few more humiliating suggestions than the idea that it is male incapacity and not male rampant vigour that speeds the nymph's steps with 'Fear and Haste . . . o'er the Fatal Plain' (130).

The shift from penile absorption to a centering on the female experience is strengthened at the end when the author intervenes to state that

'The *Nymph's* Resentments none but I / Can well Imagine or Condole' (131–2), while Lysander's 'Griefs' are described as unknowable (133–4). In place of the male poems' emphasis on the male anatomy and sperm as virtual capital – unfortunately wasted, gratuitously expended in 'clammy joys', and a debt not paid – Behn's poem shifts the emphasis to the failure to respond and exchange pleasure for pleasure. The usually cancelled female body is articulated, as are the female physical and emotional sensations of aroused and unsatisfied desire.

Behn's version of the genre is, indeed, a species of table-turning as she gives expression to the fears of inadequacy and weakness the form inscribes but usually seeks to mediate and dissipate through humour, crudity and deflection. In the lines which describe Cloris touching her lover's limp penis, the author humorously refers to the 'fabulous Priapus, / That potent god, *as poets feign*' (105–6, emphasis added), to reveal that the poets, indeed, lie. The military language of sexual conquest is reversed; the plain is 'Fatal' precisely because it is *not* fatal; no maidenhead has been vanquished, and if neither combatant has been triumphant, it is Cloris who is up and running while Lysander lies 'fainting on the Gloomy Bed' (120). In Behn's poem the unproductive penis cannot be converted in some other currency of masculine authority. It is neither a well-worn sword nor a blunted battering ram; it is not a surly old pal or a disdainful aristocrat; Lysander merly has an 'insensible' and 'weeping' penis and has failed his mistress. In a subversive revision of the Edenic myth, the penis is a snake from which the nymph recoils and which brings neither knowledge nor pleasure. Masculine impotence is the failure to satisfy female desire and defeat cannot be laughed away, braided into memories of past victories, or, as in the French original, cancelled out by subsequent success.[22]

In the light of Behn's uncompromising poem of female frustration, male fears that their power and autonomy is threatened by penile insertion into the demanding and draining vagina/womb are highlighted. Compared to failure, power is sustained *in absentia* – unconsumed but also unproved. Giles Slade points out that the combination of the figures of rake and eunuch is significant and argues that the compensatory behaviours of the rake are an expression of an utter lack of confidence by contemporary men in their own manhood.[23] But the eunuch, or male who refuses/denies sexual activity is not simply the lacking figure for which the age found compensation in the rake. The eunuch, or the male who takes unto himself the position of the eunuch, is taking up a compensatory position which manifests power through indifference to female demands. To pleasure a woman plays into her market; to deny her pleasure conserves the male spermatic treasury. As Goux argues, 'the eunuch (the entrepreneur, or producer) subserviently catering to the tyrant's (the consumer's) will to *jouissances*, is in fact the tyrant of the tyrant, though the latter believes he remains the master'.[24] To maintain a position outside the circle of desire, as Pierre does in Thomas Otway's *Venice Preserv'd* (1682) when he refuses sexual intercourse with his mistress but allows her intercourse with her lover, who is also his political opponent, is a position of control. It is, however, a wounded position and control of the sexual economy is bought at a high price. The phallus/penis equation has acquired not so much a slash as question marks, phallus? penis?

Perfect enjoyment, 'The Golden Age'. ~

A solution sought to the conundrums of sexuality, its shifting sites of power, and its implication in a material and social economy of hoarding and spending, was to imagine a golden past when issues of power, authority, and wealth were unknown and when sexuality implied only pleasure – an era, in fact, which if golden was free of gold or guilt. Behn's poem 'The Golden Age' depicts just such an Ovidian era of ease, natural bounty and pleasure. 'The Golden Age' investigates the links between male codes of behaviour, wealth, property, authority, labour and sexual desire, and offers a vision of felicity when all re/productivity was achieved 'Without the aids of men' (35). For although Behn assumes a male voice when she invites a young woman to reassume the Golden Age and confess freely to those desires which 'we can guess' (171), she creates here a very explicitly female paradise.

'The Golden Age' can be seen as positing an alternative rather than a contradictory vision of sexuality to that of 'The Disappointment'. Both are pastorals, but the pastoral of 'The Golden Age' is more complete and carries implications not only of the mutuality of desire but the mutuality and permeability of gender itself. Behn's Golden Age is also an era in which all the institutions which instantiate masculine power are unknown, unformed, and in which, consequently, concepts of shame which, above all, govern female sexuality are unknown and unformed.

In 'The Disappointment' Cloris' resistance to Lysander is minimal, 'She wants the pow'r to say – *Ah! What d'ye do?*' (20). Nevertheless, her eyes are 'bright and severe' indicating that 'Love and Shame confus'dly strive' (21–2) and she refers, if not very seriously, to her *'Dearest Honour'* (27) as something she cannot give to Lysander. In 'The Golden Age' the nymphs are less inhibited; the 'Nymphs were free, no nice, no coy disdain, / Deny'd their Joyes, or gave the Lover pain' (97–8). The only resistance they put up is 'kind' (99), and their physical reactions of 'Trembling and blushing are not marks of shame' (100). The blushing that first indicated Cloris' sexual arousal and was then displaced to her face to signal her shame and anger, is here only to be read as arousal. Love thus uninhibited by societal conventions, 'Nor kept in fear of Gods, no fond Religious Cause, / Nor in Obedience to duller Laws' (109–10) produces *jouissance*, entirely satisfactory and orgasmic 'Joyes which were everlasting, ever new' (107). The sensations of pleasure and joy are resituated to a non-teleological world of passionate sexuality which is without the taint of shame or the contamination of relations and exchanges in power, wealth, and status.

In Behn's poem, the counter-forces to such a vision of felicity are described through negation in stanzas 3 to 9. The Golden Age is depicted as an era without labour (stanza 3), without war and ambition (stanza 4), without property (stanza 5), and without honour (stanza 8). In the Golden Age there were no rulers, for 'Monarchs were uncreated then' and therefore there were no 'Arbitrary Rulers' and no 'Laws' (4: 51–3). Religion, seen as setting 'the World at Odds', too was unknown and unneeded (4: 54), and there was also no need for laws protecting property right for 'bounteous Nature' provided plenty for all (4: 58–64) and 'Right and Property were words since made' (5: 65). A detour in stanzas 6 and 7 returns the reader to 'The flowry Meads the Rivers and the Groves' (6: 84), asserts the freedom of sexual pleasure in the Golden Age (6: 84–116) prior to 'Politik Curbs' that 'keep man in', and stanza 7 concludes by wondering who but the 'Learned and dull moral Fool / Could gravely have foreseen, man ought to live by Rule?' (7: 112, 115–16).

In a subtle and insightful essay, 'Contestations of Nature', Robert Markley and Molly Rothenberg provide one of the few close readings of this poem. They argue that in 'The Golden Age' Behn's commitment to a patriarchal and aristocratic Tory ideology work against her desire to create a paradise of untrammelled and female sexuality and they point to places where Behn's poem 'discloses contradictions within contemporary constructions of nature, politics, gender, and identity'.[25] Without wishing to impose an ahistorical 'feminism' or a forced consistency on a poem as densely located along complex lines of ideology, my reading of the poem differs from theirs. I wish to suggest that the poem, particularly as seen in the light of my discussion above, offers a subversive vision of female sexuality and desire freed from either the power of the phallus or the failure of the penis.

According to Markley and Rothenberg, Behn 'can neither locate historically nor define theoretically a structure of causation' for the Fall she describes.[26] The logical arrangement of negative elements in the poem, however, is suggestive of a pattern of causation if not historical location. First labour, then war and monarchy, then property, and then honour, are isolated and condemned. As Markley and Rothenberg stress, this pastoral harbours a lie, the lie that, for instance, Raymond Williams argues Ben Jonson's 'To Penshurst' or Thomas Carew's 'To Saxham' harbour with their mystifications of property and status and erasure of labour.[27] Indeed, Markley and Rothenberg argue that Behn recapitulates 'self-aggrandizing and aristocratic values' in her description of the prelapasarian swain as 'Lord o'er his own will alone' (4: 57).[28] The erasure of labour is, indeed, vital to this, as to many other pastoral poems, since labour unsuitable to the gentle, instantiates just those status differentials, marked by property and wealth, that, however improbably, are being denied. This erasure is achieved by the insistent and visionary depiction of nature so bounteous that labour, and the demarcations of property productive of wealth and status are redundant.

There is nothing original in this pattern, Behn draws both on her original, Tasso's *Aminta*, and, surely on Ovid, as well as the long traditions of Classical and libertine evocations of 'soft' pastoral. With labour erased, what Behn can then depict is a world where the ease and autonomy associated with aristocracy is experienced by all. For in no way is Behn's poem a 'proletarian' pastoral glorifying shared labour and a simple diet of acorns. What she evokes is world where war, which depends on the property claims produced by labour, and which in turn produces its own ideology of masculine honour is unknown and, where, therefore, both honour and masculinity, creations of the fallen world are irrelevant.

Behn distinguishes between this 'natural' aristocracy in which swains are lords of themselves and all that they survey, and the postlapsarian world where the processes, initiated by labour, have produced a condition of mercantilist struggle marked by invasion and the capture and hoarding of what once was general. It is within these terms of the fallen world as a world of economic struggle where 'Pride and Avarice become a *Trade*', carried on by wars which '*barter'd* wounds and scarrs', seen as '*Merchandize*' (5: 67, 69, 70 emphasis added), that Behn locates the fall of sexuality and the commodification of woman. Behn employs an economic register in her description of the way in which honour inhibits female sexuality, and, in the process, also demystifies honour.

Behn associates honour with the concept of sexual shame for women, 'Honour! thou who first didst damn, / A Woman to the Sin of shame' and, in the process, honour robbed 'us of our gust' (8: 117–18, 19). Specifically, what honour taught woman was to commodify herself by making herself articially beautiful and hard to obtain. The idea is carried in an image of loosely free-flowing hair imprisoned;

> The Envious Net, and stinted order hold,
> The lovely Curls of Jet and Shining Gold,
> No more neglected on the Shoulders hurl'd:
> Now dressed to Tempt, not gratify the World,
> Thou Miser Honour hoard'st the sacred store,
> And starv'st thyself to keep thy Votaries poor.   (123–7)

Markley and Rothenberg comment on these lines that the woman's 'pre- and post-lapsarian bodies are commodified' since the 'Curls of Jet and Shining Gold define her in economic terms prior the commercial interest of "Miser Honour".'[29]

In many ways this reading is correct, and it might be more consistent to compare the black and blonde curls of the Golden Age to tar or straw. The mention of precious objects, however, is commonplace in pastorals and Land of Cokaigne narratives of pre-commercial paradises. Objects, such as jewels, or activities, such as leisure, which register as economically significant in our fallen world, are referred to in paradise texts to stress, as in this text, their unregarded nature in the prelapsarian state. There is always a double inscription at work which presents as a wonder the devaluation of objects or activities which can only be wondered at because they have value. So that even if the curls recall 'Jet' and 'Gold', the point of these terms of value is, surely, that in the happy primal state they lie 'neglected on the Shoulders hurl'd', and only in the fallen world, are they stored in 'stinted order'.[30] Descriptions of the curls as a 'sacred store', reference to lovers as 'Votaries' (137), or to love as a 'sacred Gift' (9: 142) might also be felt to be inappropriate to a pre-religious era. In the prelapsarian world Behn imagines, however, that which has now been mystified and made rare to become objects of *unsacred* barter or 'Theft' (9: 144), was once both numinous and freely given.

The connection between honour and commodification, indicated by the term 'Miser Honour', is strengthened as the poet banishes honour from sites of poverty 'Shepheards Cottages' (150), and tells it to 'Deal and Chaffer in the Trading Court / The busie Market for Phantastick Things' (154–5). The lines of connection drawn here are interesting. Honour was frequently subject to satiric attacks, but usually in terms of its 'Phantastick' qualities, such as adherence to a mere word, rather than its integration into a system of trade, exchange and barter. Indeed, honour was attractive (and satires on honour as 'phastastick' are often, in fact, commending it) precisely because it did *not* have a negotiable exchange-value. There is a courtly and aristocratic disdain at work in this poem, as nature's largesse and excess are celebrated, which we would expect from a high Tory poet. There is also a radical and subversive note implicit in the categorical connections between masculinity, property, and the ideological reification of consumerism as honour.

Such reification is impossible in the Golden Age since effortless consumption is the norm in a world of plenty. The landscape description with which 'The Golden Age' opens stresses the lush and endlessly renewing vegetation which invites the 'endless' enactment of love.

> . . . an Eternal Spring drest ev'ry Bough,
> And Blossoms fell, by new ones dispossest;
> These their kind Shade affording all below,
> And those a Bed where all below might rest.
> The Groves appear'd all drest with Wreaths of Flowers,
> And from their Leaves dropt Aromatick Showers,
> Whose fragrant Heads in Mystick Twines above,
> Exchang'd their Sweets, and mix'd with thousand Kisses.   (1: 5–12)

And if lovers are in constant activity under the trees, above them gentle breezes waft perfumed air over the birds, who spend their time in 'Love and Musick' (2: 25–30).

Markley and Rothenberg argue that this is no 'pristine wilderness but an idealized vision of a bucolic English countryside that has already been acted upon (implicitly) by labor'.[31] The Englishness of the countryside is, I think, questionable, and labour is explicitly banished as the poet notes that it is Spring who dresses the boughs and that 'the willing Branches strove / To beautify and shade the Grove' (1: 13–14).[32] This is absurd, but this is paradise and, as suggested earlier, the erasure or displacement of labour is an essential element that enables the erasure of all the other troubling signs that mark the fallen world and which connect sexuality with an economy of power, status and wealth. For Markley and Rothenberg, the dispossession of falling blossoms by new ones suggests 'a violent renewal dependent on usurpation' marking the 'irruption of an economic and political lexicon ('affording', 'Exchang'd', 'Sacrifice') into an otherwise idyllic and historical description of nature'.[33] The idea of an endlessly self-renewing nature which denies seasonal alteration is a dream at least as old as Homer's Garden of Alcinious. The point of the 'Eternal Spring' (1: 5), so dear to the European imagination, is, surely, that the dispossession of nature, which in the 'real' world signals the hard winter and dearth to follow, is in the happy garden of the Golden Age without fear.

'Eternal Spring' is contrasted with the 'real' world of withering beauty and 'Eternal Night' in the concluding stanza in which Sylvia is urged in Catullian terms to seize the day. Here there is indeed confusion since the Sylvia so abruptly introduced is urged to 'Assume' the 'Golden age' in an era then explicitly described as driven by short time, decay and change – an era, in fact, in which the free sexuality of the Golden Age cannot function. The dispossession of nature, however, is a transformed sign in the Golden Age, precisely marking not usurpation and loss but an extraordinary plenty. Similarly, the exchanges that take place in the branches of 'Sweets' for 'Sweets', and 'Kisses' for 'Kisses', form a continuous and, in a sense, meaningless exchange of sameness. Implicitly, these exchanges are opposed to the more usual forms of barter which depend on the existence of tables of equivalence – kisses for coins, virginity for marriage, money for goods. The language of exchange and dispossession that Behn uses marks not the irruption of an 'economic and political lexicon'; but the distance between our fallen usage and understanding and that lost, best age when all the signs for things we hoard, fear, or covert had free and joyous connotations. Above all, sexuality contaminated and repressed by the economy of thrift and possession in the fallen world, is freed from economic connotations.[34] This is effected largely by replacing the penis from the processes of reproduction with images of a non-penetrative but fecund sexuality.

Despite the poem's sensual recreation of the pleasures of uninhibited heterosexual activity, a compelling strain of imagery suggests that this golden age and land is polymorphous in its sexuality, and unaware of and indifferent to sexual difference. In stanza 3, as in the Ovidian, 'soft pastoral' versions of the golden age, the land is described as without husbandry. The earth is unpenetrated, 'The stubborn Plough had then / Made no rude Rapes upon the Virgin Earth' (31–2). Not only virgin, but also mother, the earth produces 'Without the Aids of men' (34). Behn's earth virgin-mother is self-generating and contains without masculine intervention the principle of all sexuality: 'As if within her Teeming Womb / All Nature, and all Sexes lay' (35–6). What Behn offers here is a female reinscription of the traditional masculine vision of a land made perfect by its ability to reproduce itself in the absence of women.[35] But where that vision is of an asexuality sustained by a mystical misogyny associating heterosexuality with defilement, Behn's vision is rather of a displacement of an economic defilement of sexuality which then liberates heterosexuality, all sexuality, into free play and pleasure.

In response to Behn's vision of a spontaneous and polymorphous reproduction of nature, Markley and Rothenberg argue that women, 'are written out of this myth of undifferentiated procreation'. To be more accurate about the processes of procreation, they argue, and present 'a positive image of unrepressed female desire' would be in seventeenth-century terms to 'confront the consequences of their sexual activity: pregnancy, the bearing of fatherless children, and the resultant challenges to the hereditary distribution of wealth, power and prestige'.[36] But it is not so much that women – or men – are been written out, but rather the cultural practices relating sexuality to the laborious drudgery of reproducing the social economy which are denied through the relocation of reproduction to one virgin womb. Since this womb functions without the intrusion of the penis what is being written out are those 'consequences' which in the fallen world the penis gathers to itself as the phallus. This is visionary, unreal, and in many ways a lie; however, it is a productive lie enabling the celebration of sexuality and procreation without reference to an economy of commodification, which as I have argued, the entire poem locates as repressive of female desire.

The idea of a spontaneous and non-phallic sexuality is developed in the last lines of the third stanza, which describe the benevolence of the snakes in the paradise. In 'The Disappointment' Cloris withdrew her hand in horror, as from a snake, when she felt Lysander's limp penis. In 'The Golden Age', however, snakes signify neither sin nor masculinity, neither shame nor disdain, and neither the rampant nor the failed penis. Rather, the snakes–penises are revealed as charming toys with which the 'Nymphs did Innocently play' since 'No spightful Venom in the wantons lay; / But to touch were Soft, and to the sight were Gay' (3: 46–8). Divorced from the economy of masculine power, the 'Soft' penis is not a mark of male shame and failure. It contains no 'Venom' – that problematic sperm – and it is not the object of female scorn but a thing of tactile pleasure and visual beauty, precisely because it has been removed from reproductive labour and positioned outside a phallocentric system. It does not need to be erect and to penetrate since earth does it all, all alone and on *her* own. In the ideal world Behn has depicted, all the masculine economies of wealth, social position, and sexual domination are bankrupt, or rather they are not yet bankrupt because, happily, they only exist within the sign system of the fallen world. Swain and lord are interchangeable terms, 'Conquerors' are 'Charming' (6: 104) not violent and take only what is freely given, and the processes of veiling, hiding, stinting and storing (8: 126, 128, 132, 136), which commodify and repress female sexuality are unknown.

In 'The Golden Age', Behn avoids the contradictory significations that associate pleasure with debt, ejaculation with spending and waste and insert sexuality into a material and ideological economy of male power which is then threatened and contaminated by heterosexuality. The passionate physicality of Behn's visionary world of aroused sensual/sexual pleasure may be dependent upon displacing reproduction to the fantasy of spontaneous birth but it also disables the misogyny which is so much a part of sexual discourse which seeks to refuse commodification.[37] The excess associated with aristrocratic ease is retained but feminized as it lies within the 'Teeming Womb' of the virgin earth mother. The vexed anxieties of denying the penis or fearfully entering the devouring and reproducing womb and either revealing its inadequacies or participating in laborious processes are replaced by images of soft playfulness. In the 'Golden Age', love/sex is polymorphous, 'uncontroul'd (7: 105), and entirely free from the systems of homologous exchange between wealth, status and sexuality which so troubled the age. The clitoris, surely implied by the 'young opening Buds' which 'each moment grew' (3: 42), suggests a spontaneous pleasure and renewal dissociated from reproductive labour. 'Right and Property', reduced to 'words', are unknown (65–6), and 'Snakes securely' dwell 'Not doing harm, nor harm from others felt' (3: 44–5) as Behn imagines an uneconomic era of mutuality and unrationed ever renewable pleasure. It is a world where man's penis is not yet a phallus.

NOTES

1 I am grateful to my colleagues Dianne Sadoff, David Suchoff, Susan Kenney and Gita Rajan, and to my sister Penny Richards, for their thoughtful reading of this essay which has benefited from their comments. I am also grateful to Janet Todd for her editorial suggestions.

2 The dates given are publication dates. 'The Disappointment' was first published without attribution in *Poems on Several Occasions: By the Right Honourable, the E of R-*, [Antwerpen] 1680. It was reprinted with variations

in Behn's *Poems Upon Several Occasions: with a Voyage to the Island of Love* London, 1684. 'The Golden Age' appears in the same collection. All citations from Behn's poetry are taken from *The Works of Aphra Behn*, ed. Janet Todd, vol. 1, *Poetry* (Columbus, 1992). Unless otherwise stated, emphasis is as in the text.

3 Roger Thompson, *Unfit for Modest Ears: A Study of Pornographic, Obscene and Bawdy Works Written or Published in England in the Second Half of the Seventeenth Century* (London, 1979), 1.105.

4 Giles Slade, 'The two-backed beast: eunuchs and priapus in *The Country Wife*', *Restoration and Eighteenth-Century Theatre Research*, second series, 7, 1 (1992), 23–43, 23.

5 J. G. A. Pocock, *Virtue, Commerce, and History: Essays on Political Thought and History. Chiefly in the Eighteenth Century* (Cambridge, 1985), p. 55. The recycling of Sir Robert Filmer's pre-war *Patriarcha* (1680), as well as the considerable outpouring of patriarchal sermons, might also be taken as manifestations of crisis and anxiety over masculinity and political authority.

6 Giles Slade, 'The two backed beast', 25, 27.

7 Richard Braverman, 'Economic "art" In Restoration verse: Etherege's 'Cease Anxious World', *Philological Quarterly*, 69, 3 (Summer 1990), 383–8, 384, 386. The recognition that wit (and birth) are not enough forms the basis of Susanna Centlivre's comedy, *A Bold Stroke for a Wife* (1718) which traces a conflict between various available modes of masculinity on a continuum from frugality to expenditure.

8 For a discussion of the penis/phallus equation see Jane Gallop, *The Daughter's Seduction: Feminism and Psychoanalysis* (Ithaca, New York, 1982), 97. See also Gallop's essay. 'Phallus/penis: same difference', in *Men by Women, Women and Literature*, vol. 2, n. s., ed. Janet Todd (New York and London, 1981) 243–51.

9 Jean-Joseph Goux, *Symbolic Economies: After Marx and Freud*, trans. Jennifer Curtiss Gage (Ithaca, New York, 1990), pp. 27–28.

10 Jean-Joseph Goux, *Symbolic Economies*, 28–9.

11 The reversal of positions was noted in earlier works responding to social reconfigurations in terms of a market economy. In a review of Douglas Bruster's *Drama and the Market in the Age of Shakespeare* (Cambridge, 1992), Peter Bradshaw notes, 'Bruster writes that wives' conjugal duties were seen on and off the stage as a form of sexual labour, which the complaisant cuckold could lease to other men for financial advantage. Thus the eroticism of the pagan 'horn of plenty' is transmuted into a cuckold's horn of profitability', *Times Literary Supplement*, 12 February

1993, 12. For dramas in which women buy male sexuality, see, for instance, John Dryden's *The Wild Gallant* (1669), Aphra Behn's *The Rover* (1677), and Thomas Otway's *The Souldiers Fortune* (1680).

12 Otway's *Friendship in Fashion* (1677), offers a representative example as a male character explains that men defame women 'to beat down the Market' and a female character warns that men should take care 'lest you over-reach yourselves, and repent of your purchase when 'tis too late' (2. 127, 220–2). See also his brutally financial 'proviso' scene between Sylvia and Courtine in *The Souldiers Fortune* (1680).

13 John Wilmot, Earl of Rochester, 'Song' (1680) from *The Complete Poems of John Wilmot, Earl of Rochester*, ed. David M. Vieth (New Haven and London, 1968). All citations from Rochester's work are taken from this edition.

14 See Richard Quaintance's essay 'French sources of the imperfect enjoyment poems', *Philological Quarterly*, 42 (1963). 190–9.

15 Anon, 'One writing against his prick', *The Penguin Book of Restoration Verse*, ed. Harold Love (Harmondsworth, 1968), 184.

16 *The Poems of Sir George Etherege*, ed. James Thorpe (Princeton, New Jersey, 1963). Etherege's poem is based on Charles Beys's 'La Iovissance Imparfaite. Caprice', published in *Les Oeuvres Poetiques du Sieur Beys* (Paris, 1652).

17 As Janet Todd points out in her notes to the poem, Behn alters the location and situation from the original which takes place in an urban bedroom while the young wife's husband is absent, *The Works of Aphra Behn*, ed. Janet Todd, 1, *Poetry*, 393.

18 Bellamira consoles her lover for his impotence by telling him that she likes him 'the better for it' since his failure is due to his faithful love for another woman (4. 6. 20–2), *Bellamira, or The Mistress*, in *The Poetical and Dramatic Works of Sir Charles Sedley*, 2 vols. ed V. De Sola Pinto (1928; rpt, New York, 1969).

19 As Dustin Griffin notes, 'cl~ ~my joys' is 'an elegant periphrasis . . . both apt and mock-formal' as the speaker begins to 'poke fun at himself', *Satires Against Man: The Poems of Rochester*, Berkeley, Los Angeles; London, 1973), 97. The formality of the mockery inscribes those expectations of control and success which have been so surprisingly denied.

20 Not only in 'Imperfect enjoyment' poems, but generally there are numerous derogatory references to the vagina; see, for instance, Rochester's description of Corinna as a 'passive pot for fools to spend in' (*A Ramble in St James's Park*, 102).

21 Harold Webber, '"Drudging in fair Aurelia's womb": Constructing

Homosexual Economies in Rochester's Poetry', *The Eighteenth Century: Theory and Interpretation*, 33, 2 (1992) 99–117.

22   In de Cantenac's poem, the lover returns the next day and satisfactorily makes love to his mistress.

23   Giles Slade, 'The two backed beast', 31.

24   Jean-Joseph Goux, *Symbolic Economies*, p. 209.

25   Robert Markley and Molly Rothenberg, 'Contestations of nature', in *Rereading Aphra Behn: History, Theory, and Criticism*, ed. Heidi Huttner Charlottesville and London, 1993); 301–21, 319.

26   Robert Markley and Molly Rothenberg, 'Contestations of nature', 307.

27   Raymond Williams, *The Country and the City* (London, 1973), pp. 27–34.

28   Robert Markley and Molly Rothenberg, 'Contestations of nature', 308–9.

29   Markley and Rothenberg, 'Contestations of nature', 314.

30   In Sir Charles Sedley's Golden Age poem, *The Happy Pair: or, A Poem on Matrimony* (1702), Adam is indifferent to the wealth that lies around him: 'The Daz'ling Di'mond wanted Influence / Pearls, like the Common Gravel, he contemn'd', (17–19), *The Poetical and Dramatic Works of Sir Charles Sedley*, vol. 1, 65–73.

31   Robert Markley and Molly Rothenberg, 'Contestations of nature', 305.

32   No one in their right minds would see an English spring as affording large opportunities for lolling easily beneath flowering trees. The landscape and the season are conventional and drawn from the Southern European pastorals and bucolics of Theocritus, Ovid, Virgil and Horace. For an example of a specifically English pastoral landscape, see Jonson's 'To Penshurst', which has its own and rather different political agenda.

33   Markley and Rothenberg, 'Contestations of nature', 305.

34   In Sedley's *The Happy Pair*, in the fallen world, contemplation of property produces impotence and 'when in Bed he should Embrace his Spouse, / Like a Dull Ox, he's still amongst the Cows' (267–8).

35   See Harold Webber's discussion of this trope in ' "Drudging in fair Aurelia's womb",' 112–13, which draws on James Grantham Turner's *One Flesh: Paradisal Marriage and Sexual Relations in the Age of Milton* (Oxford, 1987).

36   Robert Markley and Molly Rothenberg, 'Contestations of nature', 307.

37   See Felicity Nussbaum on the outpouring of misogynistic verse during the Restoration, *The Brink of All We Hate* (Lexington, Kentucky, 1984).

PART III ✧ FICTION

10 Who is Silvia? What is she? Feminine identity in Aphra Behn's *Love-Letters between a Nobleman and his Sister*

JANET TODD

> I have no Arts, Heav'n knows, no guile or double meaning in my soul, 'tis all plain native simplicity, fearful and timerous as Children in the Night, trembling as Doves pursu'd; born soft by Nature, and made tender by Love; what, oh! what will become of me then!

> She considers her condition in a strange Country, her Splendour declining, her Love for *Philander* quite reduced to Friendship, or hardly that; she was young, and eat and drank well; had a World of Vanity, that Food of desire, that Fuel of Vice: She saw this the Beautifullest Youth she imagin'd ever to have seen, of Quality and Fortune able to serve her; all these made her rave with a desire to gain him for a Lover, and she imagines as all the vain and young do, that tho no Charms had yet been able to hold him, she alone had those that would; her Glass had a thousand times told her so . . . [she] had a Heart to cast away, or give a new Lover; it was like her Money, she hated to keep it, and lavish'd it on any Trifle, rather than hoard it, or let it lie by: 'Twas a loss of time her Youth could not spare.[1]

The first passage is from the epistolary Part 1 of *Love-Letters between a Nobleman and his Sister*. It presents the apparently sincere letters of an incestuous couple, Philander and his sister-in-law, Silvia. Echoing the great illicit passions of Heloïse and the Portuguese nun, the heroine's love for her brother-in-law is strong enough to break all ties of family and society.[2] The second passage of consumption and expense is narrative comment on Silvia from the third Part of *Love-Letters*. It records the dwindling of passion into an expense of body to purchase 'any Trifle'. It transforms the heroine of romance into the anti-heroine of comedy.

199

Love-Letters, Aphra Behn's first and longest fictional work, is a heady mixture of history, propaganda, journalism, letters, farce and romance. From a reconstruction of a scandalous episode recorded in contemporary newspapers, the novel grew as the events of the mid-1680s unfolded, the final of the three parts being published in 1687 two years after the concluding event of the Monmouth Rebellion in which, as in the love affair, Philander played a central and treacherous part. Through the negotiation of fiction and history, third-person narrative and letter, the novel can be seen as a composite text: the real-life character of Henrietta is written as Silvia, presumed author of the letters which are shamly fictitious as French romantic epistles; she is then written as a character in fiction who proceeds to write herself as literary character when she takes up the pen within the third-person narrative. The practice is in keeping with an age that was keen to rewrite, from Shakespeare's plays to propagandist pamphlets, in the process wresting motifs from one political ideology or epistemology to another, forcing seemingly transparent texts to give up other obscurer meanings.

As history could be rewritten as literary genre, so genres could mutate, delivering both alternative visions and reinterpretations: the authenticity of Part I of *Love-Letters* does not merely contrast with the inauthenticity of Parts II and III but is undermined by it. The literary result of debasing realism is as outrageous as the scandal on which Part I was based: familial adultery of two aristocratic young people which reduced the lady to a commodity advertised for in the common press.[3]

Love-Letters reveals the systematic dismantling of the genre of romance through the strategies of correspondence and criticism. The novel goes on too long and the closure of romance is rejected by Parts II and III. If the original erotic letters were a repetition of Héloïse and the Portuguese nun, the final ones of Silvia are burlesque or pastiche, delivering comic inauthenticity. Through this change, the very act of correspondence, which seemed the quintessence of romance, becomes tainted; authentic feeling has been displayed and then subverted. It seems that incestuous adultery may lead to the adulteration of the genre of epistolary romance: genres transmute, are undone, and made inappropriate for a new disillusioned and debased era.

The generic instability of *Love-Letters* parallels the instability of personality in a novel that tells the story of development, degeneration, and growing self-awareness, in a context in which the moral discourse, occasionally put forward by the narrator of Parts II and III, has no more authority than any other.[4] In Part II the narrator does not so much take control as replicate the epistolary activity in the book. Everything narrated is reduced to a version to be interrogated and disputed. Where romance destroyed should deliver 'faithless men and ruin'd maids', in Eliza Haywood's formulation, *Love-Letters* ends provocatively with two rogues, the male one in the heart of society, the female in exile; patriarchy controls social not psychological outcome.

According to Stephen Greenblatt in *Renaissance Self-Fashioning* there was in the Renaissance an increased self-consciousness about the fashioning of human identity as a manipulable, artful process.[5] The fashioning of the female in Behn's novel occurs in a different context – the Restoration lacks the absolutes of the earlier period before kings could be judicially executed – and the difference in sex renders the fashioning less innocent than it was in Greenblatt's male examples, less concerned with integrity and self-worth than with the duplicity of the subordinate and the scandal of impersonation. Silvia's self-fashioning is performative, stagy, and sexually constituted.

Foucault and many others have argued that in the early modern period there was a new articulation of society through a sexual reconstruction of the world.[6] The material site of this sexualized order is the body, and especially the female body. As the eighteenth century progressed the woman would be increasingly constructed as both asexual and fetishized and the male would possess the constituting desire articulated as sexual. Created between 1684 and 1687 in the last few years of the Restoration, Behn's Silvia avoids the later construction; she has travelled beyond love and marriage both temperamentally and socially, and she therefore has no need of the eighteenth-century's fictional abstractions of virtue, virginity and chastity. It is the extraordinary achievement of Behn in her novel that the nobly born Silvia brings the reader to the point where it becomes utterly unimportant whether or not she has been bedding her man. Whig attitudes, commodity obsession, cynical concern for the self as consuming and empowered object alone, are all exposed in the presentation of Silvia who moves from a trangressing royalist to the shameless mirror image of Whig capitalist, going to market with herself.

Silvia, the central female character of *Love-Letters*, is transparently a portrait of the scandalous, full-breasted and irascible Lady Henrietta Berkeley.[7] Although research is revealing further connections between history and fiction, much of Silvia must be Behn's creation.[8] What is the concept of female self presented in the heroine or anti-heroine of the first work in which Behn could create a female self unconstrained by the conventions of theatre?

In Silvia, constructed by the author in the first-person letters and then constructed by herself with the author as commentator, the novel shows a woman learning with wonder that the femininity of softness and trembling doves she sets out with is a fiction and that she must author herself in another mode. Lines and gestures can be planned and learnt, used and abused, it seems. Energy is released as identity is destabilized and the individual practises self-presenting. The authentic and sincere simply do not belong in the energetic mirroring world which Silvia comes to inhabit and it is no surprise that the good siblings, Octavio and Calista, have to retreat to the singleness of the monastic life.[9]

It is fitting that Silvia's tutor in her transformation from naive girl to self-conscious adult employing the codes of femininity should be a man; the knowledge she requires is bound up with knowledge of men and her position within the patriarchal structures they create. But precisely because of her sex she will go beyond her mentor. The man can suffer or commit few irrevocable deeds, such as entering a monastery or mounting the scaffold. He finds many routes back to his starting place in family and society. But for the woman there is no such return, despite the fact that the body does not appear to register its own disgrace and undoing, as the feminine myths have supposed. After his sexual escapades Philander will always be a lord, Silvia is no longer a lady. Never an enlightened feminist, Behn notes but does not repine at this distinction: claims of social equality are as absurd in her world as claims of intellectual inequality. Philander does not in the end need to know as much about himself as Silvia.

Initially Philander is adult to Silvia as child. He is the libertine freethinker, the cynic who refuses any authority in love or politics. He preaches the demystifying Lucretian philosophy so seductive to the Restoration, which Charles Taylor describes as 'the notion that the metaphysical views which tie us to a larger moral order destroy our peace of mind, our psychic equilibrium, in the name of an illusion – that they impose extraneous demands which can only distract us from the true road to happiness and tranquillity'.[10] The philosophy which Behn saw as delivering energy and tragic charge rather than tranquillity especially fascinated her in the 1680s when she read Thomas Creech's translation of *De Rerum Natura* and she herself translated Fontenelle's *History of Oracles*. Fontenelle echoed the Lucretian notion that the belief in the gods' concern over us can only inspire human fear and he turned the rationalist historical gaze on the decline of one religious system, thus inevitably destabilizing the rise of Christianity as well. Lucretius also interrogated sexuality, and, while he advocated a frankness of sexual desire, he uncovered the mediating nature of sexuality leading to violence and power. Pleasure, he believed, was never pure but always included the desire to dominate.[11]

In pursuit of Lucretian demystification Philander insists on retreating from the honour code in which honour is signified by the man's physical bravery and the woman's chastity. He denies that his 'Reputation depends on the feeble constancy of a Wife', or that he can be persuaded ''tis Honour to fight for an unretrivable and unvalor'd Prize' (p. 18). The body will not be an absolute sign of anything. It becomes philosophically appropriate, then, that Philander should remain socially and sexually powerful despite proving himself both impotent and cowardly, as Silvia should appear sexually pure despite considerable sexual activity. Vows are but words for Philander who can betray his king, his prince, his wife and his mistress, but for the honourable man Octavio, his rival, 'Vow-Breach' is a betrayal of an authentic self; any stratagem is preferable to giving away 'thy pecious self by Vow' he says to a by-now-incredulous Silvia.

Politically Philander inhabits a Hobbesian world of individual desire and power. In the stated scheme of the book, when loyalty to the monarch is questioned, all authority is in doubt and God is dethroned.

The king, shorn of divine significance is indeed but a man. In this case why should not any individual be king?

> when Three Kingdoms shall ly unpossest, and be expos'd, as it were, amongst the raffling Crowd, who knows but the chance may be mine, as well as any others, who has but the same hazard, and throw for't; if the strongest Sword must do't (as they must do't) why not mine still?　(p. 45)

The only genuine ruler is individual appetite. The political and sexual cry is liberty, the excuse of the disobliged. Silvia will have little to do with state politics, but the message can be transferred from politics to social life, and Silvia, exiled without her clothes, will have been much disobliged.

Against the progressivism of the Christian political order Lucretian philosophy insists on the transitory but compulsory nature of states. In place of spirituality is inclination, the momentary sensual pleasure of sex, scent, music and rich texture. In debased form this becomes consumption. The ecstatic moment of sex is more important to Philander than enduring loyalty to a monarch on earth or hope of any 'gilded thing above'. But his moments need to be varied.

Since Philander exists only in the moment, he must hold any larger identity primarily in story. So he seeks narrative to affirm himself, the telling of the story of himself. Philander, with his sense of the timeless instant, begins the writing to the moment which makes writing almost stand in for action. In Part I, even while waiting for the love encounter, he wants the story of himself, the narrative or arrival, constantly needing himself affirmed through the history of present and past amours. Philander is an imaginist, requiring the fancy that can be employed in a new amour. He exists fully 'with bare imagination'. He is necessarily the master of discourse, an erotic fantasist whose sexual heat can accelerate through discursive stimulus until it must reach impotence in the body.

So what does the young Silvia, nicely reared in an aristocratic home amongst a noble family and a host of obedient servants, make of this powerful and unsettling personality, a man who has married her sister and been cuckolded by her? Would she suspect that his trivial motive in seducing her might be revenge? Or would she fear that incest for such a man might almost be a compulsion? Or would the novelty of the encounter erase all scruples? Will she be pupil as well as paramour?

As befits a young lady, Silvia in Part I begins in idealism. In an early letter she insists on the place of everyone in society and family. Honour can be invested in a name, she believes – the whole social structure demands it – and there is both futurity and posterity for the familial self. This conception invokes the Christian political scheme in which the king is there by heaven and law. He is delivered to the young woman as miraculous narrative, the Civil Wars becoming the romantic history of Charles II's famed escape. Silvia is absolutely ready to see personal and political in romantic terms, marriage and subjecthood as sacred. It is a vision that Philander will thoroughly counter.

His means will be sexual desire. But, never a simple essentialist, he knows and welcomes its implication in self-expression, fantasy and representation. According to La Rochefoucauld, whom Behn translated at about the time she was concluding *Love-Letters*, some would never have been in love if they had not heard love talked of.[12] Philander's first achievement with Silvia will be to raise desire of imitating his self-expressiveness.

So Silvia learns to write letters in which she raises as well as relates desire. As she moves further into expressions of herself, the learned repressions of her aristocratic feminine education are undone and sexual display replaces sexual recoil. In other areas, too, the language of drama legitimizes uncontrolled behaviour and she allows herself to rage because she has learnt the histrionic language and gestures of anger.

In the actual trial of Ford Lord Grey for his seduction of his sister-in-law, Henrietta Berkeley is constantly prevented from speaking. Self-expression seems, then, a revolutionary habit for a woman and, in giving her half of Part I of a book, Behn may be generously allowing Silvia what Henrietta was denied. But this is not the final effect of *Love-Letters* and in Part II, after the sexual act and the elopement, Silvia begins to wonder at the self that is being expressed. The mode of self-expression was appropriate only when there was a single self – in this case the desiring one – to express. But the divided self emerges as soon as desire is no longer singular and the loving expressive, as well as the theatrical raging, language is now

interrupted by moments of amazement at the multiplicity of the proliferating selves. The multivocal language normalizes multiple selves and the
notion of authentic self-expression appears decidedly limited.

Philander who had taught self-expression also teaches this limit. In
the epistolary form only absence can be encoded, along with memory of
presence. Once sex has occurred and entered the social, there is no further
use for the heated letter and little sense of authenticity or inauthenticity:
reader and writer learn to study linguistic techniques and verbal strategies
rather than luxuriating in their effect. The recipient of the letter has to
become not lover but critic. Where the two lovers were complicit in the
original discourse of the letters, after the elopement and Philander's
departure they pull away from each other. From then on they produce discourse inauthentically and individually, deforming the authentic genre of
the letter in which originally they began to write to each other. During
Part II doubts are even spread on the amorous sincerity of the letters of
Part I.

The erotic letter associated with the libertine royalist is transformed
into the compromised whiggish document of disloyal politics. It becomes
a commodity alienated and exchanged, and fluctuating in value. The close
relationship assumed for the true letter between letter and writer, words
and body, is subverted. The signature at the end of the letters now has no
authenticity, for the letters have become hypocritical. In another sense,
however, it is completely authentic, precisely revealing, to the one who
can properly read, the message of inauthenticity. In time the correspondence between Silvia and Philander becomes more and more literary,
more and more pastiche, with the result that it is pored over as an artefact
by the characters within the novel and then peters out.

The fate of letters resembles the fate of truth in the novel. Philander
has taught Silvia how to move from self-expression to the conscious creation of an image of herself in letters. The images in Part I, of the seductive body and of the loving writer, were aimed at raising desire. Later in
Part II Philander withholds himself as lover and creates himself as rake, his
two images ironically making two selves. Silvia belatedly sees Philander as
casting their affair in the libertine mode that she in her extreme youth had
not been able to recognize. The letters in which he reveals the division,

snatched, bargained over as they are, become the metonym for his inauthentic and circulating body. Through reading Philander's parallel
letters, Silvia understands his duplicity and learns double-dealing.

As she moves into new understanding, Silvia must then learn to read
as well as write, and to recognize that writing about the self is not
absolutely liberating – except as it reveals the ideologies which allow the
writing in the first place. Understanding must come from intellectual
effort: the cooling letter of Philander is read in different ways for different
messages and Silvia becomes anxious that her 'ill reading spoiled it'. To
compensate for the inadequacy of his letter she herself takes over its
writing, making scenes in which Philander and she act as she would wish.
She becomes the author of herself, re-enacting the love moments in little
dramas which require her to play various gratifying roles: the tragic
heroine, the victim, the passionate woman, and the Amazon. Where in the
epistolary Part i there was no mention of rereading letters for hidden messages, Silvia is now in Part ii a critic of her own epistolary performance. As
she recomposes her letters, she tries not so much to express some absolute
self and truth but to create the correct effect on the recipient. When many
hundreds of pages later she is described as an absolute cheat, the sincere
lover Octavio sees her charm inhering in her duplicitous words as much as
in her false body. So his curse on her is to be dumb, not ugly. She should be
condemned to try her 'Rhetorick' on heaven.

Philander sees life solely in terms of conquest and expenditure.
Conquest affirms his existence. Life becomes a hoard of riches needing to
be spent. Love may use up one object and require another. After his defec-
tion, when writing to Silvia he drops the language of love and substitutes
that of interest, suggesting to his cast-off mistress that the two of them
become confidantes, a sort of Valmont and Madame de Meurteuil of the
seventeenth century. Romantic love is the letting down of hair but, in the
sophisticated aftermath of love, the flowing hair should be put up;
Philander will turn from the long-haired cavalier into the short-haired
whiggish Roman. With loss of love the social self reasserts itself; the coun-
terfactual world he now creates must be imposed: Silvia should become
cheerful, gay and confident, instead of tragic and lovelorn. It is a long time
before she can achieve this degree of insouciance, but she does manage to

learn that the problem is her 'believing, easy Self' and she gives neither ease nor belief to the next lover, the hapless and sincere Octavio. Four hundred or so pages later she will manage to accept that she and Philander have become friends, but by then she has wit enough to ensure that she does not follow the trajectory of the Marquise de Meurteuil whose 'masculine' desire for mastery is thwarted by a final male move.

In her poem 'To *Lysander*, on some Verses he writ, and asking more for his Heart than 'twas worth', something of Silvia's progress with Philander in Books II and III of *Love-Letters* is succinctly captured. In the poem Behn reveals the process by which a woman is forced to play the feminine role, becomes an object, then learns to understand her potentially active role in this economy of desire:

> Take back that Heart, you with such Caution give,
>   Take the fond valu'd Trifle back;
> I hate Love-Merchants that a Trade wou'd drive . . . .

Neither the speaker of the poem nor Silvia tries to repudiate or retreat from this state of affairs, but understanding allows an ironic response and a knowing delivery of the last lines:

> Let us then love upon the honest Square,
>   Since Interest neither have design'd,
> For the sly Gamester, who ne'er plays me fair,
>   Must Trick for Trick expect to find.[13]

By the time Silvia captures and fleeces Alonzo, the last lover we hear about, she has thoroughly adopted Philander's libertine and sceptical views, living for the moment in aristocratic profligacy as perversely as the celebrated Earl of Rochester. She becomes aware of the misogyny which tended to mark the Restoration libertine and she counters it not with argument but with imitation: she turns into the female rake, seeking conquest not love.

Silvia is even quicker at learning the use of the sexualized body than at mastering effective rhetoric. She comes to put 'a price on beauty', not the correct one at first, but she soon understands the market. Her sexual allure is apparently an inexhaustible resource, now that she has come to apprehend the power and value of her charms.

At first she believes that her body has an intrinsic worth, but in time she discovers that, like any commodity, it is worth what the beholder sees in it. Gradually she understands that her charms are almost extraneous to her, and that she can use them for self-gratification. At the moment when she could be converted from beloved mistress into abandoned whore, she takes command of her bodily image and puts herself into circulation as potent woman.

Through the use of her body, Silvia learns the closeness of self-display to the self. There is no stress whatever on the female body's physical function of motherhood. The unborn child which is mentioned in the first deceiving interchange of letters between Silvia and Philander is never more than a sign of sex, the 'Pledge of our soft hours'; after her betrayal, it simply becomes an irritating reminder. It is so much a part of the past that she assumes it will inevitably become a new Philander who will simply duplicate the absent man; it has no claim whatever on her identity. Later, expecting the birth imminently, Silvia simply looks forward to being 'freed from the only thing that hinder'd her from giving herself intirely to her impatient Lover' (p. 316).[14]

The measure of the distance Silvia's body has travelled since she burnt and blushed for Philander is her last seduction of the hapless Octavio in Part III. Where in the disordered blood, the flushed face and the burning limbs he reveals the sincere responding body associated with femininity, she shows only self-control: her actions become like stage directions, her face is 'set' for seduction, and she falls on his bed 'as' unable to support the sight of his suffering. She even suffers a tear or two to run down her cheeks, the seemingly sincere tear that later sentiment would so glorify. When she tries to speak, 'she made her Sobs resist her Words; and left nothing unacted . . .' (p. 359). Despite his knowledge that it was his fortune that 'first won the dear Confession from thee, that drew my Ruin on', Octavio falls a 'shameful Victim to her Flattery'.

Once parted from the authentic and sensitive body, Silvia learns the body's limits as she had learn the limits of self-expression. The alienation is neatly portrayed when the body is shown to be silent on what the mind wants to know, having apparently no separate memory. When her servant and husband-of-convenience, Brilljard, finds her swooning, he takes advantage of her incapacity to begin a rape. Octavio enters and assumes the two are lovers. This leads Silvia to try to discover her state, even though she has no intention of anticipating Clarissa in taking responsibility for it: 'surveying of her self, as she stood, in a great Glass, which she cou'd not hinder her self from doing, she found indeed her Night Linnen, her Gown, and the bosome of the Shift in . . . disorder' (p. 156). The instrument of the mirror is needed to reveal herself to herself. Her dress tells her what may have happened to the body it covers and she adjusts her thoughts to accord with the revelation of her clothes, fearing that 'in that Trance some freedoms might be taken which she durst not confess'. Any more knowledge must come from artifice.

Silvia needs to affirm her existence not just with power over male sexuality, by raising desire, but by consuming male wealth. Away from the automatic comforts of home, she comes to realize that she is greedy and expensive and that the show of seductive femininity requires constant consumption on her part. When Octavio's elderly uncle pushes his advances on her, she loathes the man and yet his gay jewels sparkle in her eyes, 'so fond is Youth of Vanities, and she seeks to purchase an addition of Beauty at any Price'. Wealth is not a means of controlling the environment as much as an addition to the self. When she is about to leave the old man, she lets down to Octavio a night bag containing 'all the Jewels and things of Value she had receiv'd of himself, her Uncle, or any other'; her past is reduced to portable commodities. No wonder Octavio now judges he will soon have 'the Possession of Silvia'.

Where Silvia clearly learns from Philander in verbal and bodily expression, she necessarily has little guidance in the social one. Her liminal state is foreshadowed in an early letter she receives from her sister, Philander's wife. Where, after the incestuous love, Philander will simply be a philandering man, 'whose most inconstant Actions pass oftentimes for innocent Gallantries, and to whom 'tis no Infamy to own a thousand Amours, but rather a Glory to his Fame and Merit', Silvia will be a 'Prostitute' and a monster, the actor in 'a story . . . lewdly infamous' (pp. 312 and 74). Where he duplicates himself in his affairs, then, she must spiral downwards.

More even than Clarissa, Silvia loses class when she steps out of her father's house. She moves from being noble daughter to becoming beloved mistress and then betrayed whore, although even at the end of her history she rejects the word as too constricting and degrading. At the beginning of her story she had assumed that her class position was natural and inalienable and that no action could destroy it. In the crash of significances after the seduction, elopement and betrayal, she starts to understand the flimsiness of social status for a woman.

The noble daughter who could not look at a man becomes the free commoner who looks bold-faced at men and takes a servant for a lover. Just after her removal from her father's house without clothes or jewels, she had tried on other class identities. She became 'a fortune' which Brilljard, Philander's man, was rumoured to have stolen. This pretence allowed Brilljard to carry her into the chariot, mimicking a husband's action and later to acquire clothes for her in her new role. Silvia believes that this pretence has no effect on her status. But later, as mistress and servant scheme together, they become simply 'two young persons' as though rank were no longer of importance. In this situtation the maid can contemplate impersonating the mistress and the manservant plan to impersonate the master. As Silvia begins to write the deceiving letter that will allow the maid's impersonation, 'a certain Honour, which she had by birth, check'd the cheat of her Pen' (p. 208), but it was a short interruption.

Although periodically she may assert the lady over the servant, an equality has been created and Brilljard has a knowing look when he regards his 'mistress'. Once class is destabilized, only gender hierarchy is left and Brilljard 'began, from the thoughts she was his wife, to fancy fine enjoyment, to fancy authority which he durst not assume'. Sex quickly leads to ideas of dominance; at the end of Part III the 'frank' drinking of a bottle leads

> from one degree of Softness and gentle Force to another, and [Brilljard] made himself the happiest Man in the World; tho' she was very much disordered at the Apprehension of what she had suffered from a Man of his Character, as she imagined, so infinitely below her; but he redoubled

his Submissions in so cunning a manner, that he soon brought her
to her good Humour. (p. 373)

In other words the servant gains all that the noble Octavio has tried to buy
with his youth, beauty, status and wealth. Afterwards Brilljard uses the
authority of a husband and 'found her not displeased at his Services . . .'.
But, in case the reader should conclude that Silvia had a yearning for feminine submission, the narrator points out the element of blackmail in the
alliance: Brilljard knows too much. Language remains decorous but it
cannot hide the reality of prostitute and pimp.

In *Between Men* Eve Kosovsky Sedgwick notes how frequently the
woman's body mediates the relationship of unacknowledged desire
between men and how the homoerotic shadows the heterosexual
romance.[15] Silvia observes the phenomenon and struggles against it,
physically on occasion. Philander's letter of pleading to Octavio is as
impressive and seductive as his early ones to Silvia; through it he receives
money which is in a way payment for Silvia whom he will later call his 'celebrated mistress', as if she were indeed a prize possession that could be
stolen or bought from him.

When Calista and Silvia don men's clothes, it might be argued that
they take on some of the male freedom and subvert the gender economy of
desire which Sedgwick has described. But in fact Philander dresses his
women, turning each into a sort of pretty boy who will appear ravishing to
him. Calista ends up looking like her brother Octavio, and ultimately she
appears a mere mediator between the two male friends. When Philander
and Octavio finally fight over Silvia, they exclude her from the event,
declaring that they must go elsewhere since ladies' chambers are not the
place to adjust male debts. Nobody listens to Silvia, whose snowy arms
prove weak when men are intent on bonding: 'her Power of Commanding
she had in one unlucky Day lost over both those gallant Lovers'. The men
scorn her and insist that it is their friendship for which they fight. Each is
eager to forget Silvia and mention Calista, the purer lady who still has some
claim to sign for a man's honour. After Octavio finally exits from the drama
to enter a monastery, he concludes rather dubiously: 'a friend is above a
Sister, or a Mistress'. Such a view does not fit Silvia's sense of her own

importance and she keeps reinserting herself between men till in the end she manages to become both the desired man and the mediating woman.

Silvia, 'pleased with the cavalier in herself', is always less interested in the possibilities her masculine dress delivers than excited by the new power to raise desire through sexual ambiguity. Towards the end of her career she adopts men's clothes and thereby exchanges the experience of a woman for the inexperience of the boy she becomes. To Alonzo, the last of her gulls, she is simultaneously boy and woman, although she continues to raise desire, as Philander has taught her, primarily through the circulation of images of herself and by glimpses of femininity. Her image becomes so current and potent in society that Philander himself falls in love 'with the description of her', while by now he scorns the actual woman. But the show is really for Alonzo, the most arrogant of her lovers, who is already through gossip and rumour 'in love with what he has not seen'. After such stimulus to desire, Silvia has to avoid disappointment; consequently she sets off for the capture 'in perfect glory' and she continues to stage multiple selves with different costumes and discourses. She does, however, recognize that this multiplication diminishes her 'self'; but the raising of desire leaves little room for her own desire.

Unlike Clarissa, Silvia does not come to realize the untenability of the female identity outside the father's house; instead, in the bracing treacherous out-of-doors, she grows excited by the possibility of several identities: 'since I have lost my honour, fame, and friends, my interest and my Parents, and all for mightier love; I'll stop at nothing now' (p. 108). As she takes on roles and adds more and more men to her plots, she realizes that she has too much knowledge for a single self. If 'true love is all unthinking artless speaking, incorrect disorder, and without Method' according to the narrator, then Silvia can have little to do with it after the conclusion of Part 1. The loving and artless will appropriately exit in one single public extravaganza from a duplicating and duplicitous world with which they inevitably cannot cope.

The metaphor for Silvia's new state is of course the theatre and, like the actress, she clearly uses her body as an instrument. Life becomes a play where each line is composed in response to the one before. Silvia spoke with all her 'female Arts, and put on all her Charms of Looks and smiles,

sweetned her mouth, soften'd her Voyce and Eyes, assuming all the tenderness and little affectations her subtil Sex was capable of . . .' (p. 195). As
Behn puts it in 'Seneca Unmasqued', she learns to 'Vizard' her sentiments.

The peculiar theatricality of Silvia is inevitably connected with the
innovation of the Restoration: women on the professional stage for the
first time in England. For fourteen years before writing *Love-Letters*,
Behn had been creating female theatrical images for a theatre that was
involved with the court and court politics as never before or since, and it is
not surprising that her metaphor for female identity and authority within
the shifting social world of the Restoration should be theatrical. The
actress plays not for immediate gratification, for physical fulfilment of
desire, but for effect, for power over others. If gratification occurs, this is a
bonus: Silvia learns, then, that she has 'a secret joy and pleasure in gaining
conquests, and in being adored'. She thus uses her mirror as the actress
uses hers, as a capitalist and politician, not as a narcissist.

Silvia learns her craft almost as soon as she realizes Philander's
treachery. She writes a letter that imitates a tragedienne's rage:

> Thou that betray'd thy Prince, abandon'd thy Wife, renounc'd thy Child,
> kill'd thy Mother, ravisht thy Sister, and art in open Rebellion against thy
> Native country . . . thou hast made a very Fiend of me, and I have Hell
> within; all rage, all torment, fire, distraction, madness.   (pp. 218–19)

The enjoyment of the rhetoric and the performance eases her into the
next character:

> I will expose my self to all the World, Cheat, Jilt, and flatter all as thou
> hast done, and having not one sense or grain of Honour left, will yield
> the abandon'd body, thou hast rifl'd to every asking Fop: Nor is that all,
> for they that purchase this, shall buy it at the price of being my *Bravos*:
> And all shall aid in my revenge on thee.   (p. 219)

The result of this 'rant' is ease. From then on she is almost always self-
conscious in her roles, although not always aware of the self-reflexive
power of acting: 'feigning the lover possessed her with a tenderness
against her knowledge and will'.

Where Philander sought validation of himself in narrative – which

in fact contradicted the emphasis on the moment which was his philosophy – Silvia needs to affirm her identity by splitting herself, by creating
more and more identities. The romantic single identity becomes a
promiscuous pastiche; by the end of her history she is not so much 'feminine' as the conduit for society's various fantasies of the feminine. The
histrionic self-presentation of femininity cannot easily be assimilated into
civilization and culture beyond the stage: the revelation that it is a
confidence trick must be repressed. In the end, then, Silvia and her skills,
though multifariously desired, are cast out and exiled: Behn perceives that
Don Juan can return to society instead of entering hell, but his feminine
counterpart cannot.

Despite the emphasis on staging femininity and constructing an
appearance of sexual desire and desirability, in much of Behn's writing
sexual desire is still revealed as a kind of compulsion. It was presented in
this way when the noble Silvia was persuaded out of her comfortable status
and home at the end of Part 1. But, as the book continues, compulsion
becomes a deeper matter, and at times both body and mind seem to follow
helplessly into destructive moves which both disapprove. 'Inclination' is
often beyond expressed desire, a kind of self-destructive perversity at odds
both with sexual desire and 'sober choice'. When she has won back the
rich and loving Octavio after a mistaken reversion to a lukewarm
Philander, Silvia is suddenly compelled to visit the latter against all sense:

> she check'd this Thought as base, as against all Honour, and all her Vows
> and Promises to the brave *Octavio*; but finding an Inclination to it, and
> proposing a Pleasure and Satisfaction in it; she was of a Nature not to
> lose a Pleasure for a little Punctilio of Honour. (p. 363)

The narrator helps her to some justification: 'she believed it more to the
Glory of her Beauty to have quitted a hundred Lovers than to be abandoned by one' and she therefore uses 'her Cunning to retrieve, what it had
been most happy for her, should have been for ever lost'. But Silvia goes
further along her perverse course and she submits to the violence of
Philander's rage, accepting crude terms; she 'bends like a Slave for a little
Empire over him; and to purchase the Vanity of retaining him, suffers
herself to be absolutely undone'. Even as she packs to flee with the imperi-

ous Philander, she knows that self-interest argues against the move and that she will be ruined. Yet her expression of freedom seems to demand this very self-destructiveness.

More philosophically honest than Philander, Silvia accepts the irrationality and perversity of some of her most self-destructive acts and avoids taking serious refuge in the dignifying notion of fate. When she sighs, 'What strange Fate or Stars rul'd my Birth, that I shou'd be born to the ruine of what I Love, or those that Love me?' (p. 294) the narrator notes the theatricality of the sigh: 'At this rate they passed the night . . .' But, without the astrological and physical notion of compulsion, Silvia is left with no explanation of her perversity. Her response, when she has to face its consequences, is to abandon all pretence of rational self-control and turn her rage on herself. The realization that she has lost Octavio and, more importantly, his fortune, by her own perverse pursuit of Philander reduces her to the 'fury of a bacchanal, [more] than a woman of common sense and prudence'.

These periodical rages and failures of self-control or -mastery in Silvia help to indicate the limits of an individualism which otherwise might appear triumphant in her presentation. For all the apparent delight in energy and the zest for masquerade, Behn's *Love-Letters* does not suggest that the ideology of the individual is entirely true and that there really are free choices to be made outside history, society and the unconscious levels of the psyche. A tension of the self is born in Silvia of the effort at rational self-interest subverted by stronger urges.

Because the readers must respond to the energy of this tension, they join the narrator of Parts II and III in being accomplices of the deceitful and predatory Silvia and Philander who drive their victims into the monastery and onto the scaffold. The cynicism and knowledge of fraud which both Silvia and the reader achieve make for an essentially comic vision in which romance is transformed not into tragedy but into pornography, spectacle, and bedroom farce.

Love-Letters celebrates and unmasks energy and energetic masking. Silvia reveals a mixture of flexible selves: she believes in the possibility of rigorous self-interest and submits to the uncontrolled impulse. She imagines she can shape herself simultaneously as lady and whore. She desires money but will not hoard, spending to affirm an aristocratic identity in a world where her class status is suspect. Refusing the negations of Christianity, its emphasis on something and somewhere else, she avoids any transcendence and inwardness, wanting gratification here and now; if the self as commodity is the price for this, she will happily pay it. In the end she has mutable identities so inauthentic that they achieve a kind of authenticity. At the same time she refuses feminine contingency and suggests that in the last resort sex, status and luxury can be dispensed with; 'she had not a heart that any love, or loss of honour, or fortune could break'. Perhaps this may be the source of the reader's inappropriate sympathy.

NOTES

1 References to *Love-Letters* are to volume 2 of *Works of Aphra Behn* (London, 1993); the first quotation is from p. 24 and the second from pp. 394–5.

2 *Lettres portugaises* were translated into English by Roger L'Estrange as *Five Love-Letters Written by a Cavalier* (1678).

3 The advertisement appeared in *The London Gazette* for September 1682.

4 For a discussion of the morally ambiguous narrator of *Love-Letters*, see Jacqueline Pearson, 'Gender and narrative in the fiction of Aphra Behn', *Review of English Studies* n.s., vol. 42, February 1991, 40–56 and May 1991, 179–90.

5 Stephen Greenblatt, *Renaissance Self-Fashioning: From More to Shakespeare* (Chicago, 1980), p. 2.

6 See Michel Foucault, *The History of Sexuality*, vol. 1 trans. Robert Hurley (New York, 1978). See also Jon Stratton, *The Virgin Text: Fiction Sexuality & Ideology* (Brighton, 1987), p. vii.

7 The term 'full-breasted' occurs in the early versions of the advertisement in *The London Gazette* but was dropped from later issues.

8 For the connections between *Love-Letters* and the historical records, see the notes to volume 2 of *Works of Aphra Behn*.

9 On a superficial level the tricky nature of social identity was clear in the trial that was the immediate stimulus of *Love-Letters*. Here identity was assumed to be stable but momentarily confused and it was the business of the court to sort it out. Was Henrietta Berkeley primarily a daughter or a wife? Ought she to speak as one of these? Ought she to express her

trangressing self at all? When in a startling development a husband was produced, did this annihilate status as noble daughter and dependent girl? Who was the husband? If Turner, which Turner? What status had he? Was he a gentleman? In other words, who was his father? Could he be a husband or was he a bigamist? Were the letters produced at the trial historical documents or fictional works? Was the trial subverted by drama? Were people authentic or playing parts? See the extracts from the trial in the Appendix to *Works of Aphra Behn*, vol. ii.

10 Charles Taylor, *Sources of the Self: The Making of the Modern Identity* (Cambridge, 1989), p. 345.

11 See for example: 'Lovers' passion is storm-tossed, even in the moment of fruition, by waves of delusion and incertitude. They cannot make up their mind what to enjoy first with eye or hand. They clasp the object of their longing so tightly that the embrace is painful. They kiss so fiercely that teeth are driven into lips. All this is because their pleasure is not pure, but they are goaded by an underlying impulse to hurt the thing, whatever it may be, that gives rise to these budding shoots of madness.' *The Nature of the Universe*, trans. Ronald Latham (Penguin, 1951), pp. 163–4.

12 'Seneca Unmasqu'd', no. 344, *The Works of Aphra Behn*, vol. iii.

13 *Works*, vol. i. pp. 92–3. See a fuller discussion of this poem in the introduction to Paul Salzman, ed., *Selected Works of Aphra Behn*, forthcoming from Oxford University Press.

14 Nothing is heard of the child after its birth. Calista, also pregnant by Philander, does not even wish to look on her child.

15 Eve Kosovsky Sedgwick, *Between Men: English Literature and Homosocial Desire* (New York, 1985).

11 Slave princes and lady monsters: gender and ethnic difference in the work of Aphra Behn

JACQUELINE PEARSON

Although the discourse of racial difference in Aphra Behn's *Oroonoko* has been much examined and debated, it has not been sufficiently noted how persistently Behn uses images of racial and cultural difference throughout her work.[1] These images not only interest her for their own sake, as a source of dramatic contrasts; they are also of strategic use as an instrument for exploring related but separate discourses of gender and class difference. As Kristina Straub has demonstrated, one notable aspect of the discourse of racial difference in the Restoration and eighteenth century is its tendency to be recycled as part of other related discourses of class, sexuality or gender difference. Any group of marginalized low-status people tends to be seen in images of other groups of the marginalized and low-status. Straub cites a number of examples, for instance, where actors, either individually or as a group, are derogatorily described in images of racial otherness. Actors, 'Like wand'ring Arabs, shift from place to place', and Thomas Betterton, the most famous Restoration Othello, is, obscenely and slanderously, described in 'A Satyr of the Players' in the sexual act, fucking 'like any Moor'.[2]

In passages like this, one marginalized and demonized group is described in terms of another: and such accounts can become still more explosive when a third term, that of gender, is added. In an anonymous satire, 'A Session of the Poets' (1676), for instance, Behn, 'poetess Aphra', is depicted claiming her own rights to the poet laureateship. She 'swore by her poetry and her black ace / The laurel by a double right was her own /

For the plays she had writ and the conquests she'd won'.[3] The 'black ace' certainly, as Maureen Duffy points out, images the female sex organs. This passage thus economically links in a single image ideas of transgressive female sexuality, transgressive female authorship, the theatre, and racial difference. Such a combination can obviously be an effective weapon in the armoury of an 'establishment' satirist defending 'high' culture against infiltration by class, racial, and gender outsiders. But very different things might happen when a member of a marginalized low-status group herself accepts the identification with analogous dispossessed aliens, and uses this identification to disrupt received stereotypes of class, of race, and of gender.

Behn's female characters, traditionally viewed as low-status on the grounds of gender, do tend to identify themselves, either overtly or by implication, with ethnic outsiders, those cast as low-status by virtue of race or nationality. Hippolita in *The Dutch Lover*, a seduced and abused woman, figures her sense of her alienness within Spanish society by adopting the role not only of a courtesan but of a Venetian courtesan. In *Oroonoko* Behn implicitly identifies white women with Black slaves, and her own white female narrator with the Black slave protagonist: both are in an anomalous and self-contradictory position with regard to status and authority, he as a prince but also a slave, she as a member of a ruling elite but also a woman.[4] By such identifications, Behn opens up for questioning all her culture's stereotypes of gender, race, and power. We need, of course, to remember that 'Behn could only constitute herself through available cultural discourses', and not expect from her a late twentieth-century vocabulary of political correctness.[5] If we keep this in mind it is possible to see Behn working within, but also against, inherited stereotypes of racial, as of gender, hierarchies. I want to examine Behn's treatment of relations both between white and non-white races, and also between culturally different whites (and, in the case of *Oroonoko*, non-whites). In order to introduce Behn's treatment of racial and cultural difference, I shall first explore briefly a range of texts, and then look in more detail at the second part of *The Rover*, *The Revenge*, *The Dutch Lover*, *Abdelazer*, and finally *Oroonoko*.

Behn's own class and ethnic origins are obscure, but it may be that she was brought up in Surinam, she certainly spent some of her young adulthood in continental Europe, and it now seems probable that her husband was a Dutch or German captain who dealt in slaves.[6] Many of her plays and prose tales are set in continental Europe and in America, usually with convincing local detail, and sometimes giving central place to images of racial and cultural difference. Despite her Tory patriotism, she is less likely than some of her contemporaries to subscribe to a jingoistic Little Englandism, and is knowledgeable about political and religious practices in other countries, showing a wide sympathy for different social mores and values.

At its simplest, ethnic difference appears in Behn as a direct correlation for gender difference. Sometimes this appears in profoundly optimistic images, at a level which may be read as personal and/or political, of the possibility of arriving at harmonious relations between self and Other without erasing difference. In the first part of *The Rover* (1677), to take a relatively straightforward example, all the central romantic relationships consist of a Spanish woman and an English man, and the difference in nationality lightly and effectively dramatizes not only the potential Otherness of men to women, but also the fact that this very Otherness is what makes possible harmonious heterosexual relations. In this play, as in others, like *The Feign'd Curtizans* (1679), or *The Young King* (1679), where the love of the Dacian Cleomena for the Scythian Thersander will bring political as well as personal harmony, ethnic difference tropes gender difference: and, by presenting the ethnic Other positively, sympathetically and unstereotypically, Behn opens the door for similar potentially oppositional ways of presenting femaleness, suggested by such images as women's adoption of transvestite disguises in *The Rover* and *The Feign'd Curtizans*, and by Cleomena's military prowess in *The Young King*.[7]

Indeed, so firm is her troping of a harmonious heterosexuality as national, racial or cultural difference that the overcoming of obstacles to union is often achieved through the pretence of such difference where it is not actually present: thus Arabella Fairname in *The Wandring Beauty* masquerades as a Welshwoman in order to flee a forced marriage and win a man who will love her and not only her money, Alonzo masquerades as the Dutchman Haunce van Ezel to rescue Euphemia from a forced marriage in *The Dutch Lover* (1673), Don Carlos tricks an old merchant into giving him his wife by assuming the identity of the Grand Turk in *The False Count* (1682), and in a play which both uses and satirizes this plot-scenario, Cinthio and Charmante win the women they love by pretending to be lunar royalty in *The Emperor of the Moon* (1687).

Behn is, of course, realistic enough to note that the gender differ-ence troped by ethnic difference does not always guarantee the harmo-nious heterosexuality which the comic conclusion promises. In *Agnes de Castro* the love of the Portuguese prince for a Spanish lady leads to tragedy. *Oroonoko* depicts a society acutely aware of race, class and gender hierarchies, where racial difference renders an effective relationship between the African prince and his platonic '*Great Mistress*' (v.p. 176) the white female narrator impossible, even as the narrator sees Oroonoko as in some respects her double, and their edgy, divided relationship is effec-tively but pessimistically dramatized through absences and aporias.[8] In *The Widdow Ranter* the cross-racial love between the English general Bacon and the Indian Queen is again impossible within Virginian society (though the parallel plot centred on the assertive and independent Ranter translates racial difference into gender terms in a much more optimistic way).

Finally the second part of *The Rover* (1681) rewrites the world of its predecessor in an altogether darker mode, and while in the first part national difference seemed to guarantee a harmonious heterosexuality, the second part dramatizes ethnic difference through more troubling images.[9] This is particularly obvious in the case of the two 'Lady Monsters' (1.p. 148), who provide images for an extreme in gender, racial, religious, and even biological Otherness, since they are Mexican Jewish heiresses, one 'an overgrown Giant', the other 'little, and . . . deform'd' (1.p. 124). Behn deals with these characters quite sympathetically, giving them some poignant lines ('I to be happy, must be new created', 1.p. 156), and allowing them to emerge victorious over their foolish suitors, who are in any case seen as no less monstrous than they, one a 'Mouse', not a 'Man' (1.p. 156), and another 'a bearded *Venus*' (1.p. 186). The 'Monsters' provide grotesque comedy in keeping with the harlequinade element in the play, but more seriously they are also allowed to suggest the monstrousness of a system of money marriages in which women attain significance only in terms of their financial value.

Images of monstrousness are not confined to these two figures, in any case, but take on class as well as gender and race resonances. The heiresses are 'Monsters of Quality' (1.p. 124), and the repetition of a favourite Behn word identifies them with Spanish, and by implication all, 'Women of Quality', who suffer 'too much Constraint' simply by virtue of their sex (1.p. 131). Later Willmore imagines a woman going to bed with a man who is as decrepit as a 'dismember'd Carcase', and yet still thinking him perfect because he is 'of Quality' (1.p. 132). Behn, usually less critical of class than of race or gender stereotypes, here allows herself to question the romanticization of class privilege which is a significant part of her discourse elsewhere.

Finally, the monstrousness of the 'Lady Monsters' is also used to make political points about Europe during the Interregnum. They are said, for instance, to be worth enough to 'purchase all *Flanders* again from his most christian Majesty' (1.p. 124), so that Spanish hegemony in the low countries is attacked as monstrous: and Willmore's 'better to be Master of a Monster, than Slave to a damn'd Commonwealth' (1.p. 165) by implication extends the image of monstrosity to Cromwellian rule and the deposition of the true king in England. For two such minor characters, the 'Lady Monsters' are not only treated with sympathy as individuals, but are also the vehicle of images of monstrosity which ultimately apply not to women, foreigners, Jews or the deformed, but to foolish men, oppressive hierarchies, and unjust political systems.

Behn is a typical Restoration writer in that her work frequently uses and restructures older texts,[10] adapting them to her own purposes and especially, as Susan Staves has suggested, 'shift[ing] the emphasis toward the woman'.[11] This is particularly true of *The Revenge; or, a Match in Newgate* (1680), an anonymous play now widely believed to be the work, in whole or in part, of Behn.[12] This play seems on the surface to accept stereotypically negative associations of ethnic – and other – kinds of Otherness, but also to use these in a way which is not stereotypical.

The Revenge revises Marston's *The Dutch Courtesan*, sometimes quite closely in terms of both plot and language, but with major subversion and reworking of the title character. The common associations of Dutchness for Marston's audience would include gluttony, avarice, drunkenness and stupidity: Behn's audience would add to this the fact that the Dutch had been recent enemies and were still commercial rivals, and were associated with such alleged atrocities as Dryden had chronicled in *Amboyna; or, the Cruelties of the Dutch to the English Merchants* (1673) and Behn would touch on in *Oroonoko*. Marston's Franceschina, a professional prostitute, is lustful, cruel, devious and untrustworthy; a stereotypical ethnic Other. The badge of this Otherness is a grotesque stage-Dutch accent, which immediately demonstrates her difference from, and opposition to, the other characters. Behn revises Corina as a seduced maid, a suffering victim as much as a manipulating revenger, and shifts sympathy significantly away from the male characters.

Within such a radical revision, Franceschina's Dutchness, especially in Martson's grotesque imagining of it, is unrecuperable and must simply be abandoned: it is incompatible with a sympathetic reimagining of Corina. At the same time, she continues to be surrounded by images of ethnic otherness – which, as we have already seen, Behn tends to identify with heterosexual desire. Her brothel is compared to Flanders, which Englishmen should 'love' and hope that 'war should be maintain'd there, lest it should be brought home to their own doors' (p. 355), and her clients run a gamut of ethnic otherness which images Corina as a high-powered merchant not so much selling herself as trading in the rich and exotic – 'English and French merchants of the best rank, jews of the richest tribes, Irish lords, Scottish earls, and, lastly, the Dutch agent...' (p. 372).

Images of ethnic Otherness and the negative overtones that they traditionally carry tend in the play, as in this last instance, to be reassigned to the male characters. As in the second part of *The Rover*, 'monster' is a key word, applied to the practical joker Trickwell (Cocledemoy in Marston's version, p. 353),[13] and also surfacing in his story of 'the Gravesend monster' (p. 380): Trickwell, an anarchic, amoral force, also assumes national or cultural otherness in disguise, speaking 'broken French', or appearing in 'northern or . . . Welsh' dialect (p. 371). Wellman, who has seduced and abandoned Corina, is described by Friendly (Marston's Malheureux) as having, 'Indian-like' exchanged 'real

Gold for shining gingling Bawbles' (p. 363). If, as seems likely, this is a reminiscence of Othello's lament that in murdering Desdemona he has, like 'the base Indian', thrown away 'a pearl . . . / Richer than all his tribe' (v. ii. 348–9), it shows Behn's alertness to images of racial and cultural difference even as she seems to have erased them; it also demonstrates Behn's depiction of the men, not the women, as truly the moral aliens.

If in some respects *The Revenge* by abandoning the central image of ethnic difference seems to accept its traditionally negative resonances, it at least uses these resonances to reclaim the woman and to draw attention to the causes of her vengefulness, her seduction and abandonment by Wellman. An earlier play, *The Dutch Lover* (1673), shows Behn questioning the stereotypes commonly associated with Dutchness even as she seems to use them.[14] Haunce van Ezel, the title character, is a typical clown-role: Euphemia manages to avoid a forced marriage with him to marry Alonzo who she loves, while Haunce's intellectual and cultural inferiority is translated into class terms as he is tricked into a low-status marriage with one of Euphemia's maidservants. And yet, in this dark comedy with its emphasis on violence and deception, Haunce as Other is the least threatening to the women of the play's male characters. On one occasion, indeed, he actually saves Hippolita from rape, and his *'great Dutch Knife'* is hilariously and suggestively contrasted with the small dagger of the would-be rapist (1.p. 278): this episode at least presents Haunce in a surprisingly positive light, and so does his good-humoured philosophy at discovering he has been tricked into marrying a servant.

Indeed in this play it seems that it is ethnic sameness, troped as family relationship, rather than difference that poses the most sinister dangers to the happiness of the characters: this is figured especially as the incest that seems to threaten the supposed brother and sister Silvio and Cleonte, and does actually, unknown to them, threaten the real brother and sister Alonzo and Clarinda. As in Gothic novels by women in the late eighteenth and early nineteenth centuries, which are in some ways the true successors of Behn, the real dangers to women are firmly inscribed within ordinary social and family life, not outside it. Haunce duplicates the stereotype of cultural difference as grotesque comedy, but at the same time he also represents exogamous possibilities which are the only keys to happiness for the play's characters.

Behn of course foregrounds issues of racial as well as of cultural difference, focusing upon relationships between white and Black as well as between different European nations. *Oroonoko* and 'The Unfortunate Bride' have significant Black characters. In the very short short story 'The Adventures of the Black Lady' the protagonist Bellamore is, presumably, only 'black' in the usual seventeenth-century meaning of the word, dark-haired and dark-eyed. But her name, while representing 'bell'amora', 'beautiful love', can also be read as 'bella mora', 'beautiful Moor'. Pregnant, unprotected, unmarried and consequently persecuted in Restoration society, she is thus identified by implication with the position of Blacks as outsiders.

Behn, obviously, inherited a received language which associated racial difference with 'cruelty', 'lasciviousness', 'credulity', 'jealousy', 'treachery', and even devilishness, but she revises this language as often as she uses it straightforwardly.[15] Even where she seems to use it most simply, there may be hidden countercurrents: I have already suggested elsewhere that the 'Blackamoor Lady' (v.p. 410) Moorea in 'The Unfortunate Bride' is developed so simply and uncharacteristically as a stereotypical villainess – a 'Devil' (v.p. 410), 'black in her mind, and dark, as well as in her body' (v.p. 411) – because the narrator is aware of an anxious sense of identity with her, as both struggle to take control of male texts.[16] An apparently wholly negative and stereotypical depiction of the racial Other at more profound level, it seems, turns a mirror to the Self.

Another Behn character who seems to provide a traditionally negative view of racial difference is the eponymous anti-hero of *Abdelazer; or, the Moor's Revenge* (1677). After *The Dutch Lover*, *Abdelazer* was Behn's next play: clearly at this stage in her career she was particularly preoccupied with images of racial and cultural difference. *Abdelazer* is an unusual play – Behn's only tragedy – and it is hard to see what attracted her, usually so critical of stereotypes of race and gender, to its source, *Lusts Dominion; or, the Lascivious Queen*,[17] which presents them in the extremely simple forms of the lustful Moor and his accomplice and then victim, the 'lascivious [white] queen' of the subtitle. Behn's play is consummately theatrical, a 'magnificent tapestry . . . in colours strong and daring':[18] it offers marvellous opportunities for music, spectacular sets and scenery, and elaborate costumes. And yet to a superficial examination it certainly seems puzzlingly anomalous among Behn's plays in its presentation of racial and gender Others, since, like its original, it seems to use the identification to demonize both the Black and the woman. It could be argued that here as in *The Revenge* Behn slants the emphasis toward the women characters, that she alters somewhat the original stereotyping by a fuller and more psychologically acute analysis of individual character, especially in the case of Abdelazer himself, or even that she mocks stereotypes of racial difference by ironic exaggeration, and takes a subversive delight in gleefully chronicling the careers of bad women, as she does in *The Fair Jilt*. And yet she alters the plot of *Lusts Dominion* less than one might have expected, following it closely in almost every material respect.[19] Can *Abdelazer* be regarded simply as a potboiler which duplicates the simple stereotypes of its predecessor?

It could rather be argued that in terms of language Behn to some extent destabilizes the discourse of white superiority of *Lust's Dominion*. While Mary Pix, for example, tends to use traditional associations of 'black' with assertive female sexuality, revenge, guilt, and hell (see *The False Friend*, pp. 10, 12, 59), Behn shows a marked resistance to these stereotypes of racial difference and to the reassuringly simple contrasts between self and other that they offered to those safely within the dominant culture.[20] Where in *Lusts Dominion*, for instance, Eleazar believes his wife is as 'chaste as the white moon' (p. 112),[21] Behn's Abdelazer removes the automatic association of whiteness with light, purity and heaven and simply believes that she is 'chaste' (ii.p. 21), and while the King in *Lusts Dominion* offers his mistress to 'circle this white forehead with the crown' (p. 135), in *Abdelazer* he promises to 'circle thy bright Forehead' (ii.p. 50). Whiteness is no longer simply equivalent to chastity and beauty: even the Black Abdelazer has 'Beauty' (ii.p. 10), a fact that destabilizes not only racial but gender oppositions. Behn resists the stereotypical associations of blackness and whiteness, and in her hands both concepts become more complex than the stereotypes allow, even, like gender difference, more socially constructed than biologically given. For instance, Behn significantly expands on Abdelazer's vengeful resentments against the

Spaniards, who dethroned and murdered the king his father, and who now rule the land of which he believes himself rightful king. He acts as he does not because Blacks are naturally evil, but because of his dispossession within Spanish society.

In at least one other important respect, it seems to me, it would be misleading to view *Abdelazer* as a play which simply recapitulates racial stereotypes. Restoration tragedy was fundamentally dependent on clear binary oppositions and on the straightforward implementation of stereotypes (which explains Thomas Rymer's rage at Shakespeare for not in *Othello* adhering to the received stereotypes of the bluff honest soldier and the lascivious Black).[22] Although in the last act of *Abdelazer* Behn sticks quite close to the plot of *Lusts Dominion*, in one respect she alters quite radically its implications. *Lusts Dominion* works in terms of binary oppositions – white/Black, male/female, good/bad. Its ending clarifies these oppositions in a total separation of black and white – even the wicked queen, since she is white, is reformable in spite of her adultery and murder, whereas Eleazar must die, and the last lines of the play proclaim the banishment from Spain of 'all the Moors', now defined as a monolithic group, all 'black' and therefore 'barbarous' (p. 192).

However if the last act of *Lusts Dominion* works to clarify and separate the terms of these binary oppositions, the conclusion of *Abdelazer* works to complicate and subvert them, to blur distinctions, to identify rather than contrast apparent opposites. Behn's play contains no wholesale demonization and banishment of the Black characters: indeed, the happy ending is possible because of the disinterested benevolence of a 'good' Moor, who warns Philip and the Cardinal to flee, and later risks his life to rescue them.[23] The moral distinction between Black and white is thus much less absolute than it is in the earlier play. In addition, the fifth act is filled with images of reversal and especially gender reversal, which suggest that the distinction between male and female is also less clearcut than her material might suggest. Abdelazer woos Leonora in language 'Soft as the Whispers of a yielding Virgin' (II.p. 87), he fears his compassion will make him 'turn Woman' (II.p. 88), Philip in prison compares himself to 'the sad *Andromede*' awaiting rescue by Perseus (II.p. 92), and he compares Zarack, who has come to kill him, with the 'dear Conqu'ress' of a 'Love-sick Youth' (ii.p. 93). Binary oppositions of race, gender, even class are destabilized, as Alonzo is ennobled and 'made . . . equal' to the Princess Leonora so that their marriage becomes possible (ii.p. 97).

This destabilization of binary oppositions leads us, I think, to the heart of Behn's discourse of racial and cultural difference and its useful-ness to her as part of gender and class discourses. A number of feminists, most notably Hélène Cixous in *La Jeune Née* (1975), have shown how the 'patriarchal value system' depends on binary oppositions, and that 'each opposition can be analysed as a hierarchy where the "feminine" side is always seen as the negative, powerless instance'. Cixous opposes to this patriarchal binary system 'multiple, heterogeneous *difference*'.[24] So does Behn: by destabilizing binary oppositions she effectively deconstructs her own text, replacing its stereotypes with a rich sense of race, class and gender difference as reciprocal metaphors.

While plays with European settings by other near-contemporary women writers like Susanna Centlivre tend to contrast British characters with a fairly monolithic concept of the 'foreign', always to the advantage of the former,[25] Behn instead creates broad canvasses emphasizing mul-tiple difference. *The Dutch Lover*, for instance, does not contrast Englishmen with 'foreigners', but offers a wide range of ethnic posi-tions, including Spaniards, Germans, the Dutch, Englishmen, Venetians, and the inhabitants of Flanders. Moreover, ethnic positions are oddly fluid: the Dutch Haunce van Ezel is half Spanish (as well as 'half Man, half Fool' i.p. 262), the Flanders colonel Alonzo discovers that he is really Spanish, Spanish Hippolita adopts disguise as a Venetian, and Spanish Alonzo disguises himself as a Dutchman. The epi-logue even compares the play itself, and its author, to 'the *German* Princess' (p. 329), Mary Carleton, herself probably a similar user of dis-guised nationality and an imposter who claimed aristocratic European rank but was executed for theft in 1673. Ethnic fluidity is also echoed elsewhere in the text by gender and class fluidity: Hippolita appears in male disguise ('My Soul . . . is all Man', i.p. 293), and Silvio is revealed as not a low-status bastard son but of 'Quality' (i.p. 319). There is even an edgy, half terrifying, half comic, sense that still more fundamental kinds of fluidity are possible: Alonzo is 'transform'd from Man to Beast' (i.p.

260), and Haunce too fears that he will be 'transmigrated into some strange Shapes anon' (1.p. 323).

The Dutch Lover, then, resists binary opposition which will identify women with the 'negative, powerless instance', replacing it with 'multiple, heterogeneous difference' in terms of ethnicity, but also class and gender, and deriving a great deal of comic and disturbing energy from a sense that identity is essentially fluid, contingent, dependent upon how it is situated and how it is named. The happy ending is, indeed, only possible because of this contingency. In ethnic terms, no nationality is given privileged status, and indeed ethnicity is revealed as an artificial construct, easily mimicked and easily revised.

Similar processes are at work in a more serious mode in the novella *Oroonoko*. At its simplest, the discourse of race here erodes the traditional opposition between the civilized (white) and uncivilized (black) by a range of strategies. The most striking is a simple but effective pattern of reversal by which the Black prince Oroonoko is made to seem the 'civiliz'd' one, with 'nothing of Barbarity in his Nature' (v.p. 135), while his white betrayers are 'wild', capable of 'absolute Barbarity' (v.p. 207). This renegotiation of the limits of civilization and barbarism may also have offered strategic tools to Anglophone Blacks when they themselves began to write: Olaudah Equiano, for instance, describes in quite a similar way how to his African eyes it was the whites who seemed 'savage' and 'brutal'.[26]

This simple reversal may, however, be replaced by the wholesale dismantling of binary oppositions in favour of multiple heterogeneous difference. As in *The Dutch Lover*, there are important moments when a simple binary opposition is replaced by a whole range of ethnic and racial positions – whites in England; whites in Africa; whites in Surinam; blacks in Africa; blacks in Surinam; native Americans, who are not treated monolithically but belong to different tribes with different customs and languages; whites who have gone native to trade with them (one of whom is a 'perfect *Indian* in colour', v.p. 184). There are crucial moments in the text, which I shall illustrate in the next paragraph, where binary opposition is disrupted by the timely intervention of a third term.[27] There has been a certain amount of uneasy commentary on the fact that, although Imoinda is allowed to be a fully African woman even to the extent of having tribal tattoos (v. p. 174), Oroonoko in order to be the hero has to be Europeanized, presented as 'more civiliz'd, according to the *European Mode*' (v.p. 161), and given not only mastery of European languages and cultures, European manners and a European tutor (v.p. 135), but even European facial features (v.p. 136).[28] This could be viewed, however, not as an eradication of Oroonoko's Otherness, an essentially racist reiteration of a single, Anglocentric, standard of civilization, but as a replacement of the binary opposition between black and white, barbarous and civilized, with a freer and more complex range of alternatives. Oroonoko is not so much a black white man as a character who is used to destabilize such essentially oppressive binary oppositions.

It is also important to note that in *Oroonoko* the whole action is not viewed throughout by the medium of a privileged white gaze, but we are also allowed to see the whites through the eyes of Blacks and native Americans as well as vice versa.[29] In a particularly striking example, the female narrator, her brother and maid visit an Indian village accompanied by Oroonoko and a white trader who has spent many years among the Indians: at least four different ethnic/cultural possibilities confront each other. We first see the Indians through the eyes of the white visitors, but this immediately shifts to showing us the white visitors through the eyes, and the language, of the Indians (v.pp. 185–6). The effect is a defamiliarization of white elite-class behaviour, clothes, and assumptions. It is by no means certain in this scene that the 'naked' Indians are less civilized than their white visitors, '*Things*' who cannot even speak their language, and are comically described as wandering through the tropics 'dress'd . . . very glittering and rich' (v.p. 185). *Oroonoko* is the most complex of Behn's texts in the treatment of racial difference, with its reversals of traditional stereotypes, its dismantling of binary oppositions, and its command of a range of ethnically different viewpoints which work to unsettle the apparently self-evident assumption of white superiority.

Behn's texts may recuperate femininity and cultural difference by identifying them, or may go even further by eroding the very foundations of the binary habits of thought through which a white aristocratic patriarchal culture excludes its Others and maintains itself in power. At its simplest she may mock her culture's traditional views on difference, whereby stereotypical 'Others' are created, by revealing the civilized nature of the supposed savage and, more painfully, the savage nature of the supposedly civilized, as in *Oroonoko*, or even by outrageous overstatement, as in *Abdelazer*. She also, at her most radical, dissolves binary oppositions of self/alien, male/female, upper class/lower class, to produce disturbing but exhilarating texts like *The Dutch Lover*, where the fluidity of class, cultural, and gender boundaries, and of identity itself, offers infinite possibilities for fruitful change.

NOTES

Unless otherwise stated, the place of publication is London. References to Behn's works are, unless otherwise stated, to Montague Summers ed., *The Works of Aphra Behn* (1915).

1 Recent examples include Ros Ballaster, 'New hystericism: Aphra Behn's *Oroonoko*: the body, the text, and the feminist critic' (in Isobel Armstrong ed., *New Feminist Discourses: Critical Essays on Theories and Texts* (1992, pp. 283–95); Laura Brown, 'The romance of empire: *Oroonoko* and the trade in slaves' (in Felicity Nussbaum and Laura Brown eds., *The New 18th Century* (1987, pp. 41–61); Moira Ferguson, *Subject to Others: British Women Writers and Colonial Slavery, 1670–1834* (1992, pp. 27–49); Heidi Huttner, 'Aphra Behn's *Oroonoko*: the politics of gender, race, and class' (in Dale Spender ed., *Living by the Pen: Early British Women Writers*, 1992, pp. 39–51).

2 Kristina Straub, *Sexual Suspects: Eighteenth-Century Players and Sexual Ideology* (Princeton, NJ, 1992), pp. 161, 26.

3 Cit. Maureen Duffy, *The Passionate Shepherdess* (1977), p. 155. This satire is too early – post-November 1676 according to Duffy – to refer to Behn's most famous exploration of racial difference, *Oroonoko* (1688): but the image could be inspired by the appearance of *Abdelazer*, probably in September 1676.

4 See Pearson, 'Gender and narrative in the fiction of Aphra Behn' (*RES* vol. XLII., nos. 165–6, 1991), pp. 184–5, 187.

5 Deborah C. Payne, '"And poets shall by patron-princes live": Aphra Behn and Patronage' (in Mary Anne Schofield and Cecilia Macheski eds., *Curtain Calls: British and American Women and the Theater, 1660–1820*, Athens, Ohio, 1991), p. 117.

6 See especially Jane Jones, 'New light on the background and early life of Aphra Behn' (*Notes and Queries* 235 (1990), pp. 288–93).

7 I am well aware that the image of transvestite disguise is much more

complex and unstable than this might suggest: see Pearson, *The Prostituted Muse: Images of Women and Women Dramatists 1640–1737* (Brighton, 1988), esp. pp. 100–18.

8 See Pearson, 'Gender and narrative', pp. 185, 187–8.

9 See Pearson, *The Prostituted Muse*, p. 166.

10 E.g. *The Town-Fop; or, Sir Timothy Tawdry* is based on George Wilkins' *The Miseries of Enforced Marriage* (1607), but also uses Beaumont and Fletcher's *The Maid's Tragedy*. Behn knows Molière (*Le Malade imaginaire*, *L'Amour medecin* and *Les Femmes savantes* are used in *Sir Patient Fancy*, *Les Précieuses ridicules* in *The False Count*), *The Young King* adapts material from Calderon's *La vida es sueño* as well as from Beaumont and Fletcher's *Love's Cure; or, the Martial Maid*; etc.

11 Susan Staves, *Players' Sceptres: Fictions of Authority in the Restoration* (Lincoln, Nebraska, 1979), pp. 172–3.

12 F. M. Link, *Aphra Behn* (New York, 1968, p. 90) considered Behn's authorship of *The Revenge* 'as near a certainty as one can get'.

13 References to *The Revenge* are to R. Dodsley, *A Select Collection of Old Plays*, vol. XII, 1744.

14 For mid-17th-century stereotypes of Dutchness see Andrew Marvell, 'The character of Holland' (1653): '*Holland*, that scarce deserves the name of *Land*, / As but th'Off-scouring of the *British Sand* . . . / This indigested vomit of the Sea, / Fell to the *Dutch* by just Propriety' (H. M. Margoliouth ed., *The Poems and Letters of Andrew Marvell*, Oxford, 1970, 1.p. 100): and *Dutch Boare Dissected; or, a Description of Hogg-land* (1664) – 'A Dutchman is a lusty Fat two-legged Cheeseworm. A Creature that is so addicted to eating Butter, drinking Fat Drink and Sliding that all the world knows him for a slippery fellow' (cit. Rodney Bolt, *Amsterdam*, 1992, p. 84).

15 Rana Kabbani, *Europe's Myths of Orient* (1988), p. 19; Eldred Jones, *Othello's Countrymen: The African in English Renaissance Drama* (1965), pp. 22, 79.

16 Pearson, 'Gender and narrative', pp. 49–50.

17 This play, first published in 1657, is now generally thought to be *The Spanish Moor's Tragedy* by Dekker, Haughton and Day, performed 1599–1600. This should not, however, be too readily accepted: the 1657 text at least seems to contain a number of echoes of Shakespeare's Jacobean tragedies, which may render this identification suspect.

18 Summers, vol. II, p. 5.

19 The only major difference in plot-detail, apart from those I deal with in the text, is that in *Abdelazer* the Queen-Mother dies, murdered on the

orders of her Black lover, while in *Lust's Dominion* she escapes and survives to repent: Behn is prepared to allow a sexually autonomous woman the dignity of being a tragic hero, while her predecessors are not.

20 For further exposition of this point, see Pearson, '"Blacker than hell creates": Mary Pix rewrites *Othello*' (forthcoming).

21 Quotations from *Lusts Dominion* are from W. Carew Hazlitt ed., Dodsley's *A Select Collection of Old English Plays* (1875), vol. xiv.

22 See Gary Taylor, *Reinventing Shakespeare* (1990), pp. 33–9.

23 In *Lusts Dominion* Zarack also releases Philip and the Cardinal, but only because he is bribed to do so.

24 Toril Moi, *Sexual/Textual Politics* (1985), pp. 104–5.

25 The kind of play I have in mind is exemplified by Centlivre's *The Wonder: a Woman Keeps a Secret* (1714), which contrasts in a fairly simple way the oppression and confinement (of women and of lower class men) in Portuguese society with the freedom both are allowed in Britain, where 'Duty wears no Fetter, but Inclination', for the English are a race 'in Love with Liberty' (iii.pp. 8, 13). Behn occasionally aims for local moments of this kind: at the end of *The Rover*, for example, Willmore is made to criticize Spanish confinement of women, for he is 'of a Nation, that are of opinion a Woman's Honour is not worth guarding when she has a mind to part with it' (i.p. 103). However, the general effect of this play, unlike Centlivre's, is not simply a rather smug demonstration of the superiority of English cultural formations over those of the Mediterranean world.

26 *The Interesting Narrative of the Life of Olaudah Equiano or Gustavus Vassa, the African, Written by Himself* (orig. 1789: ed. Paul Edwards, 1967, p. 27).

27 I do not mean to imply that this dismantling of binary opposition by the introduction of a third term is a gender-specific literary device (are there any?), simply that it is particularly strategic for women writers (and, possibly, writers from other marginalized groups) as a way of dismantling an opposition which names them as perpetually Other. Male writers might use similar techniques: Shakespeare's *Titus Andronicus* demonizes the Goths and the Black Aaron in exactly similar ways, and in *Othello* Iago, a world-class 'Other', despises both the Black Othello and the Florentine Cassio. Generally speaking, though, such devices often seem to recapitulate rather than challenge ideas of Otherness, and neither Shakespearian example seems to me as forceful as Behn's deconstruction of binary opposition.

28 See, e.g. Ferguson, *Subject to Others*, pp. 36–7.

29 For a fuller illustration of this point see Pearson, 'Gender and narrative', p. 186.

12 *Oroonoko*'s blackness

CATHERINE GALLAGHER

The hero of Aphra Behn's *Oroonoko; or the Royal Slave* is not just black, but *very, very* black. His blackness is, moreover, luminous, beautiful, wonderful. *Oroonoko* emphatically breaks the traditional Western metaphoric links between black skin and moral degeneracy, a connection that Behn herself had assumed in an earlier story. I want to explore this extraordinary blackness. It has, I believe, three layers of significance: it celebrates a certain textual effect produced by print, which *Oroonoko* allies with heroic authorship; it emblematizes the hero's kingship; and it is a metonymic sign of his commodification. These three layers – textuality, kingship and commodification – are bonded together by their paradoxical recognition and denial that blackness means racial difference. That is, each level seems to contain and displace an acknowledgement of the racial significance of blackness. I hope to show that, at each level, the racial meaning is displaced by the author's fascination with disembodiment and her attraction to dispossession.

On several occasions during her career as a playwright, Behn had complained about the difficulty of communicating with her audience through the gross medium of actors on stage. In contrast, she had extolled the wonders of print for what she considered its relative thinness of obstructive mediation. In her tales, too, we can see evidence that print's seeming disembodiment, its mobility and even its potential anonymity gave it a magical quality. The reproduction and sale of the *identical text* in numerous copies provided proof of her ideas' transcendent non-materiality, their escape from the physical accidents of place and time,[1] and therefore of their substantive likeness to the immaterial and immortal mind they represented.

Of course, such a notion of a transcendent text, elevated above all materiality, preceded print; but print paradoxically gave material evidence for a text surpassing all copies. The potential for seemingly infinite reproduction obviated the possibility of equating the text with any, or for that matter, all of its instantiations. Behn apparently imagined that, through such wide dissemination, her ideas can be anywhere and yet nowhere in particular. Like other seventeenth-century writers,[2] she seems fascinated with not only the appearance of the anonymous hand but also the gap between the physical act of writing and the immaterial result. She confesses, for example, the haste of the book's composition in the dedication to *Oroonoko* – 'I writ it in a few hours . . . I never rested my pen a moment'[3] – even as she contrasts the ephemeral, bodily labour to the eternal, static, spiritual product: '[poets] draw the nobler part, the soul and mind; the pictures of the pen shall out-last [the drawing] of the pencil, and even worlds themselves'. Here the author reminds us that writing is not really a graphic art. The black ink that outshines the 'pencil' marks of the visual artist signifies the incorporeal and eternal, not only because it 'draws[s] the nobler parts', but also because the text perpetuated in print seems to rise above its own graphics. The blackness of ink, therefore, seems to indicate a state beyond its own visibility.

That Oroonoko's blackness is associated for Behn with this inky abstraction is an inference I draw from several pieces of evidence. First, Behn had, in an earlier story, linked black skin with anonymous writing. In 'The Unfortunate Bride; Or, The Blind Lady a Beauty', Behn's narrator – herself a rather shady character – claims that much of her information comes indirectly from a black woman, Mooria, who not only longs to be the object of the hero's love but also steals his letters to his mistress and forges new ones to drive the lovers apart. The story makes the lady's blackness a metaphor for her 'dark designs' and for her means of accomplishing them: stealing the writings of others and rewriting them 'in a disguised hand'. The black lady, in other words, is an inky creature who separates people from their written representations and plunges them into obscurity. She is more designing than the narrator and more adept than any other character at achieving her designs by textual misrepresentation.

Although there are several such women in Behn's stories, who manipulate the action by disguising their 'hands', Mooria is the only one who *embodies* this form of power. The darkness of her skin is associated with invisibility and magical powers of transformation; that is, her skin colour is a metaphor for the disembodying and hence anonymous potential of writing. The very ink that allows graphic representation and hence the dissociation of bodies and language, seems to cover the body of Mooria herself, making the same association between black bodies and writing that was figured in the novelty inkwells wrought in the shape of African heads in a somewhat later period.

Since Mooria's skin seems an emblem of the disembodying power of writing, for which the blackness of ink is a related sign, we might also see in her a figure for the 'anonymous hand' par excellence: print, the medium of the story's dissemination. Print intensified anonymity simply by increasing standardization, making the graphemes relatively interchangeable regardless of their origin, and by wide dissemination, which broke the link common in scribal culture between texts and specific places where they could be read. The more identical copies of a text there were, the less it seemed to occupy any particular location, and hence the less it seemed any body's physical emanation. The figure of the black woman, then, combines the blackness of racial difference, the obscurity of the narrative 'I' in this particular story, and the potential erasure of the writer, which might in turn call to mind the 'anonymous hand' of publication.

In the character Mooria, therefore, Behn had already used dark skin to signify a certain impersonal textual effect. Bearing this in mind, we can go on to look at the internal evidence linking Oroonoko's blackness to the wonder of print. But the first thing that might strike us as we move from a consideration of 'The Unfortunate Bride' to an analysis of *Oroonoko* is that the later story associates the blackness of the character not with authorial obscurity but with authorial transcendence.

In this regard, *Oroonoko* seems the polar opposite of 'The Unfortunate Bride'. The narrator not only claims her authorial identity and her personal experience of the events, but also gives herself an important role in the story and hence a sustained presence.[4] She identifies herself as Aphra Behn, a writer already known to the public as a playwright, one whose established reputation should guarantee the story's veracity. She even discusses her next play, stressing that it, like *Oroonoko*, is at least to some extent based on her life experience.

This stress on the work as an expression of the author's authentic identity has a parallel in the metaphoric use of blackness. Whereas in 'The Unfortunate Bride' the narrator's anonymity seemed intensified by the 'dusky' obscurity of Mooria, in *Oroonoko*, the gleaming blackness of the eponymous hero corresponds to the narrator's heightened presence. If Mooria's colour emphasized her invisibility and that of the narrator, Oroonoko's radiates a light that illuminates the narrator's identity. He is blacker than the black lady, indeed he is blacker than anybody, but that does not make him 'dusky'. Instead, it makes him brilliant: 'His face was not of that brown, rusty black which most of that nation are, but a perfect ebony or polished jet' (pp. 80–1). He is not a *brown* black, but a black black. Behn's distinction between brown blacks and black blacks departs from the usual conventions of representing sub-Saharan native people, who, according to Winthrop Jordan, were normally all described as absolutely black: 'blacke as coles', as one voyager to Guinea put it a century earlier.[5] By making complete blackness a distinguishing characteristic of the noble Oroonoko, Behn attached a positive aesthetic value to the colour: the brown blacks are dull, but the shiny black black reflects light.[6] Even when dressed in slave's clothes, Oroonoko's gleaming blackness 'shone through all' (p. 108). The lustrous quality of the hero's blackness, which is 'so beyond all report', requires the eye-witness reporting of a known author; Aphra Behn, therefore, must emerge from her obscurity and explain the circumstances of her witnessing.

As a character, she is, indeed, paralleled with Oroonoko.[7] Like him, she arrives a stranger in Surinam, but is immediately recognized as superior to the local inhabitants; like him, she appears a shining marvel when she travels to the Indian village; and like his, her words are always truthful. As narrator, she repeatedly identifies herself as the well-known author, Aphra Behn, in order to vouch for the otherwise incredible brightness of Oroonoko. There is, then, a close connection between Behn's sustained authorial presence in this book, unprecedented in her works, and the black hero's lustre; as the story moves forward, a mutual polishing takes place in which narrator and hero buff off each other's obscurity. Although in the beginning Oroonoko had the misfortune 'to fall in an obscure world, that afforded only a female pen to celebrate his fame' (p. 108), by the end the narrator presumes to hope 'the reputation of my pen is considerable enough to make his glorious name to survive to all ages' (p. 141).

Hence through an intensification of blackness, hero and narrator emerge into the light. This process can be read as a celebration of the bright, transcendent possibilities inherent in print. Oroonoko resembles the mystical body of the text;[8] his blackness is a luminous emanation of authorship, which gleams forth from multiple inscriptions.

Such an interpretation of this 'admirably turned' (p. 80) ebony figure is quite consonant with one of Oroonoko's most-remarked features: the fact that he is densely over-written. Indeed, the narrator seems quite self-consciously to present her hero's story as a layering of narrative conventions. The early part of Oroonoko's story depends on references to the theatre and on the self-conscious employment of courtly intrigue conventions to familiarize and authenticate the action. And the brief idyll of the middle section is similarly realized through reference to a literary model; when Oroonoko and his wife Imoinda are reunited, Oroonoko's English protector and putative master, looking on, 'was infinitely pleased with this novel' (p. 112).[9] One could continue to multiply the evidence, for the last half of Oroonoko's history is particularly thickly encrusted with tragic references and is highly wrought in the histrionic codes of heroic drama.[10]

This dense literary artificiality has exasperated some modern readers of *Oroonoko* and has been the chief evidence in the twentieth century for the story's inauthenticity.[11] The stress on Oroonoko's conformity to literary conventions, however, was probably intended to make him seem believably noble. The narrator proves the hero's greatness by showing how closely he adhered to heroic models. The sense that Oroonoko was made up of myriad literary conventions would have made him familiar and hence credible to contemporary readers, for real heroic action was necessarily imitative.[12] The resolute intertextuality of the narrative, then, was not a failure of imagination, but rather a proof that the author deserved fame because she had a property, a legitimately heroic story, which was recognizable as such only because it conformed to other such representations.

We can read Oroonoko's gleaming blackness, then, as a celebration of inscription without turning it into a self-reflective modern text. However, a danger lurks in such a reading. If Oroonoko's blackness becomes mainly an allegory of textuality, even with such historical and formal qualifications as have been introduced, we will lose sight of the phenomenal wonder that empowers the text in the first place. Unless we acknowledge that Oroonoko's blackness refers to racial difference and indeed is dependent on a stock response of racial prejudice in the reader, we cannot explain what was supposed to be so wonderful about him and so meritorious in the author. The reader is frequently invited to marvel at the fact that Oroonoko, *although black*, behaves just like a perfectly conventional European tragic hero. Hence the first full description of Oroonoko relies for its sense of the marvellous on the very racial prejudice it seems to be in the process of dispelling:

> His nose was rising and Roman, instead of African and flat. His mouth, the finest shaped that could be seen; far from those great turned lips, which are so natural to the rest of the Negroes. The whole proportion and air of his face was so noble, and exactly formed, that, bating his colour, there could be nothing in nature more beautiful, agreeable and handsome . . . Nor did the perfections of his mind come short of those of his person; for his discourse was admirable upon almost any subject; and whoever had heard him speak, would have been convinced of their errors, that all fine wit is confined to the white men, especially to those of Christendom; and would have confessed that Oroonoko was as capable even of reigning well, and of governing as wisely, had as great a soul, as politic maxims, and was as sensible of power, as any prince civilized in the most refined schools of humanity and learning, or the most illustrious courts. (p. 80)

Oroonoko is a wonder because blackness and heroism are normally thought to be mutually exclusive qualities; indeed, the passage asserts that they normally *are* mutually exclusive. It is only in his differences from other Africans that Oroonoko achieves heroism, but it is in his blackness that his heroism partakes of the marvellous. His is a 'beauty so transcending all those of his gloomy race, that he struck an awe and reverence, even in those that knew not his quality; as he did in me, who beheld him with surprise and wonder' (p. 79). Thus his colour, as a sign of racial difference, is the very thing reminding us that all of his features are different from those 'which are so natural to the rest of the Negroes.'

Oroonoko's blackness must therefore be seen at once as authentically and unnaturally African. It is the exotic trait that makes his story worth writing, the feature that makes him unprecedented as hero and hence a wonder. However, it is also the feature that necessitates such an energetic marshalling of heroic literary precedents. His blackness is presented as something the hero and writer must overcome, something that 'naturally' threatens to become the condition of his obscurity. Simultaneously, it is presented as that which makes him worthy of fame. The author's virtue lies in so densely packing Oroonoko with heroic reference as to prove him wonderful; that is, to make his very blackness shine. Hers is an especially great achievement because in English stories blackness doesn't normally shine. Blackness as racial difference, therefore, at once helps explain why Oroonoko's colour gleams with 'unnatural' intertextuality and reveals how such gleaming redounds to the glory of the author.

Oroonoko's blackness is consequently to be read as a 'natural' physical indication of racial difference, even inferiority, textually transubstantiated into a wonderful sign of heroic distinction. It is thus highly appropriate that descriptions of Oroonoko's and his wife Imoinda's heroic bodies should emphasize their artificiality; they are not so much bodies of flesh and blood as pieces of polished handiwork. 'The most famous statuary could not form the figure of a man more admirably turned from head to foot' is the sentence that precedes the description of Oroonoko's colour as 'not of that brown, rusty black which most of that nation are, but a perfect ebony, or polished jet', with 'the white of [the eyes] being like snow, as were this teeth' (pp. 80–1). Readers are being called on here to put the actual African bodies they might have seen (the *brown* black ones) out of their imaginations and substitute for them statues of ebony and ivory. Indeed, when Oroonoko alights at Surinam dressed in his 'dazzling habits' to be gazed at in his journey by the whites and the merely 'brown' blacks, he resembles nothing so much as a magus statue. The common brown Africans eventually greet him as 'King' and even, in a scene that fuses Christ child and magus, fall to worshipping him as divine when he finally arrives at his destination.

Imoinda's body is also artifactual, but in a slightly different way. At first she is described merely as a female version of Oroonoko, but the allusions are appropriately classicized to accommodate a female divinity: 'To describe her truly, one need say only, she was female to the noble male; the beautiful black Venus, to our Young Mars' (p. 81). Like his, her features are to be imagined as European, and the description of the pair of lovers might well have evoked images of Jonson's *Masks of Blackness*, or of the actors and actresses in black face and lavish costumes who played the 'kings' and 'queens' of Africa and India in the Lord Mayors' Pageants.[13] Such figures would have been quite appropriate to the court intrigue section of the novel. However, after Imoinda has been sold into slavery, had her name changed to Clemene, as Oroonoko has his changed to Caesar, and emerges into our view through the eyes of the white colonists, her body undergoes a fabulous transformation:

> Though from her being carved in fine flowers and birds all over her body, we took her to be of quality before, yet, when we knew Clemene was Imoinda, we could not enough admire her.
>
> I had forgot to tell you, that those who are nobly born of that country, are so delicately cut and raced all over the fore-part of the trunk of their bodies, that it looks as if it were japanned; the works being raised like high point round the edges of the flowers.　(p. 112)

This abrupt scoring of Imoinda's body, so strongly and clumsily marked in the text ('I forgot to tell you') coincides with the narrator's re-vision of her as at once slave and romantic heroine, 'Clemene' and Imoinda. Appropriately, Imoinda's body is not just transformed textually, through metaphor, but is supposed to have been transformed materially into an artificial decorative object of exotic origin; she is 'japanned', like a highly varnished and intricate piece of oriental carving. And yet she isn't quite statuary in this description because the plasticity and pliancy of actual flesh, as well as its susceptibility to wounding, scarring and discolouration are invoked by the description. Finally, the reference to 'high point' makes Imoinda's flesh onto its own laced clothing.[14] Her body becomes a fabric representing other things; it is, if I may be allowed one pun, all texture.

The descriptions thus stress the exotic artificiality of both Oroonoko and Imoinda, but the artifactual nature of Imoinda presents sublimation, the process of becoming art, as an ordeal through which a body passes. That is, the reader's experience of flesh is not altogether banished from Imoinda's description, as it is from Oroonoko's. Even more obtrusively than Oroonoko's, Imoinda's is a body of representation. However, we are required, in this revision of her half way through the story, to imagine her skin as the material out of which the representations are made. Oroonoko, on the other hand, is a completed representation; the African body is useful to his description only as contrast. Imoinda reminds us that such refinement uses up bodies. Consequently, her image directs us to a consideration of the full relationship between Oroonoko and the commonplace 'brown' Africans in the novel.

The overwrought artificiality of Oroonoko, symbolized by the gleaming blackness of his body, not only sets him apart from his countrymen but also suggests the two ways in which he absorbs and represents them: through kingship and commodification. On an abstract level, one could point to a structural homology between Oroonoko's unnatural blackness and kingship as it was conceived from the late Middle Ages through the seventeenth century.[15] Just as Oroonoko can be seen as the mystical body of the text, that which outlives myriad graphic instantiations to become the repository of overlapping forms of heroism; and just as his heroism, like the book's textuality, both depends on and is poised against the blackness of print and the blackness of racial difference (both, in turn, concepts abstracted from physical objects); so kingship was perceived as a mystical body standing above and incorporating all bodies in the realm but also outliving them and thus proving the realm's continuity through time.

In Ernst Kantorowicz's well-known account of this concept, the mystical body of the king both depends on physical bodies and is contrasted to them.[16] Since all the realm's bodies are imagined to be incorporated in one, with the king as the head, all are imagined to be, in some sense, the bodies of the king; and yet in no physical body, not even his own, is true kingship completely contained, for the king's physical body, subject to decay and death, merely represents the immortal kingship that temporarily inhabits it. How the king's physical body represented kingship was a subject of some debate, especially in the years preceding and following the regicide, which Parliament justified by claiming in effect that *it* was the mystical body of the king, and Charles I's body was that of an enemy to the 'real' sovereign. Such a radical splitting off of the actual and mystical bodies, however, was abnormal, and the explicit ideology of a high Tory like Behn would have held that the king's actual body, as long as it breathed, was the sacred and unique incarnation of the realm's mystical incorporation. Nevertheless, the king's two bodies were conceptually separable, and in *Oroonoko* they emphatically come apart so that the body of kingship itself, like the text, achieves a kind of incorporeality.

The narrator often refers to Oroonoko's kingship as if it were comparable to normal European models. In the initial description quoted earlier, for example, her stress on his heroism culminates in the greatest wonder of all, which her European readers would have found most difficult to believe: 'That Oroonoko was as capable even of reigning well, and of governing as wisely . . . as any prince civilized in the most refined schools of humanity and learning, or the most illustrious courts.' It is not surprising that such an ideal of princely capability would be figured in a bloodless statue of a body, one contrasted to living bodies and made imperishable through metaphors, for Behn represents in this figure not just a king, but kingship. As a specimen of a mere African king, we are given Oroonoko's grandfather, who is 'a man of a hundred and odd years old' (p. 79), but who, far from having any marks of immortality about him, is senile and sexually impotent. Moreover, and most tellingly, the actual king's body is indistinguishable from the bodies of his subjects; to get his first glimpse of Imoinda, he dresses himself as the 'slave and attendant' of a 'man of quality' (p. 84), and is wholly successful in this disguise. In contrast, Oroonoko, as we've seen, had a 'beauty so transcending all those of his gloomy race, that he struck an awe and reverence, even in those that knew not his quality' (p. 79). This king's body, then, is to be imagined as one of that mass of brown black bodies that Oroonoko's unnatural blackness is defined against.

Even though the king's actual and mystical bodies seem thus separated in Oroonoko's home kingdom, Oroonoko's blackness is nonetheless defined against the mass of African bodies as an abstracted essence of them, as if his blackness were the sum and intensification of their less perfect darkness. The mystical body of kingship continues to represent even that against which it is defined, the physical bodies that constitute the realm, and the physical bodies are incorporated into the mystical body. Oroonoko's representation conforms to the imaginative pattern informing centuries of monarchist thought, pageantry, state organization, criminal law, family relations, and so forth; it was the common cultural property of the time.

Such a pattern of thinking, however, does not fully account for the representation of kingship in *Oroonoko*, for it does not explain why the salient physical attribute of the African bodies that is abstracted, refined, and intensified in Oroonoko's body should be their darkness. Of all the attributes of their bodies, why this one? In making her hero darker than his subjects, Behn departed radically from the traditional portrayal of the noble African or Moor,[17] who was often painted white. Of course, I've already partly answered this question in discussing textuality and racial difference, but neither of those issues comprehends Oroonoko's princeliness, his relationship to his subjects. Why should the sign of his kingship be a body from which everything that is African is explicitly banished except a hue that can only abstractly be described as 'black'?

The answer lies in the fact that Oroonoko's subjects, unlike those of a modern European king, are also his commodities. The narrator painstakingly explains that the word 'black' distinguishes the bodies of people who can be bought and sold from those of people who cannot. To a twentieth-century reader, the history of slavery makes this linkage obvious, but in the seventeenth century, before racial ideologies of slavery were developed, and in the midst of the racialization of the institution itself, it bore reiterating.[18] The word 'blacks' first appears in *Oroonoko* in contrast not to 'whites' but to natives of Surinam, who are 'a reddish yellow' (p. 76). These last, we are told, are not used as slaves because, through their fishing, hunting and industry, they supply the colony with such necessities that they must be lived with in 'perfect tranquillity, and good understanding' (p. 77).[19] Hence 'Negroes, black-slaves altogether', are imported. 'Black' as it is used here differentiates the body of the African from that of the Native American; it signifies that one has been made a commodity, and the other has not. Because this 'blackness' is the mark of commodification, we are then told, everything else about these bodies becomes indistinguishable:

> Those who want slaves, make a bargain with a master, or captain of a ship, and contract to pay him so much apiece, a matter of twenty pound a head . . . So that when there arrives a ship laden with slaves, they who have so contracted, go aboard, and receive their number by lot; and perhaps in one lot that may be for ten, there may happen to be three or four men; the rest women and children. (p. 78)

The twenty pounds paid, then, is for a 'black' person, regardless of any other physical characteristic. Gender, age, strength, size, beauty were all indifferent. Nor will any other colour suffice, as the case of the Frenchman, seized along with Oroonoko, but emancipated because of his colour, makes clear. 'Black' is a word that is used to describe a skin tone differing from all others that allows a body to have an abstract exchange value independent of any of its other physical qualities.

'Black', then, is connected to bodies but is also an abstraction from them signifying exchangeable value. It is not so much descriptive of the skin as of the difference between African skin and all other skin that has arbitrarily come to take on the meaning of exchange value per se. Hence the narrator immediately becomes chary of using it as a 'literal' term describing bodies. 'Coramantien', we are told, is 'a country[20] of blacks *so called*' (p. 78, emphasis mine), that is, a country of people one could call black and thus exchange for twenty pounds apiece. But this designation 'black', as we've already seen, is explicitly denied by the narrator to describe the literal colour of the African body, which in its physicality is merely brown. 'Black' identifies the commodity value of the slave body, its exhangeability for twenty pounds, as opposed to its physicality.

Thus the terrifying condition of slavery, having an African body that could be called 'black', is transfigured in this novel, into a gleaming vision of disembodied value in the figure of Oroonoko's kingly blackness.

Oroonoko's utterly unnatural body is the only one in which the word signifying exchangeability, 'black', and the actual colour of the body coincide. Only in his body is value realized as blackness. The intrinsic, non-negotiable kingship of Oroonoko is thus paradoxically figured in the same blackness that designates the principle of exchange itself.

The superimposition of kingship and exchange, odd as it might at first appear, was not in itself uncommon. Money, after all, was similarly a representation of exchange value underwritten by the idea of the English state's sovereignty, the mystical body of kingship. Although the relationship between the sovereign power and money was substantially revised in the course of the seventeenth century, and the last decade saw a strong parliamentary attempt to discount the 'extrinsic' value that money received from its association with sovereignty, the very agitation of the issue would have given the relationship a pronounced ideological importance.[21] What is odd about *Oroonoko*'s way of depicting this relationship is its insistence on the exchangeability of the subjects themselves for money. Exchange value and kingship are both realized in *Oroonoko* at the vanishing point of the African bodies, the moments when the king sells his subjects.

The kingship represented in Oroonoko, then, cannot be explained simply by noting that the king's mystical body underlay commerce; it is, rather, related to developments in the ideology of absolutism that reimagined the king's sovereignty as an absolute *property* right in the bodies of his subjects. It is to this notion of sovereignty that I will now turn.

The idea of property as an absolute right to dispose of something in any way one saw fit – to use it, destroy it, alienate it through exchange, etc. – was still not fully developed in English law in the seventeenth century. Nevertheless, such an idea of property underlay the vast expansion of trade during that century, and the desire of subjects to have greater dominion over their property came into conflict with what some saw as increasing claims of the crown for dominion. Conversely, some advocates of monarchical 'absolutism' argued that the secure property rights of Englishmen would prevent the king from becoming a despot, but even here the complete freedom of a subject to dispose of his own and the power of the monarch are counterpoised. To dissociate absolute individual property claims from the claims of absolute monarchy, however, would be mistaken, for the two were sometimes powerfully conjoined.[22] Indeed, never was the ideological connection closer than during the Exclusion Crisis of 1679–81, when the most famous work of Robert Filmer, *Patriarcha*, originally written in the 1640s, was published and widely cited to defend James's right to the throne. *Patriarcha* bases kingship itself on a God-given, patriarchal ownership of the bodies of the subjects. No matter how severely qualified by the customs and laws of modern nations, Filmer argued, the king's divine right derived ultimately from his private property right in these bodies, his right to dispose of them in any way he saw fit. Any legitimate limitation on this right, he argued further, was to be construed as self-imposed by the king.

As John Locke pointed out in the first of his *Two Treatises of Government*, Filmer's defence of absolutism essentially turned subjects into slaves:[23]

> This *Fatherly Authority* then, or *Right of Fatherhood*, in our Author's sense
> is a Divine unalterable Right of Sovereignty, whereby a Father or a
> Prince hath an Absolute, Arbitrary, Unlimited, and Unlimitable Power,
> over the Lives, Liberties, and Estates of his Children and Subjects; so
> that he may take or alienate their Estates, sell, castrate, or use their
> Persons as he pleases, they being all his Slaves, and he Lord or Proprietor
> of every Thing, and his unbounded Will their Law.[24]

It was Filmer, according to Locke, who thus pressed a claim of unlimited private property and Locke who refuted that claim in order to promote 'the older and more traditional constitutionalist or consent theory of government.'[25] Filmer made not only all property ultimately the property of the king but also all proprietors, arguing that they held their very lives as well as their livelihoods by a royal gift.

Without implying that Aphra Behn had actually read *Patriarcha* or that Filmer's formulations per se directly influenced her thinking, I would suggest that *Oroonoko*'s royalism, imagined as it is through the institution of slavery, is Filmeresque.[26] I would also venture, however, that because the tale depicts kingship as the absolute ownership of others, the essence of which is the right to exchange or destroy them, it is constantly rendering problematic the very thing it takes for granted: that someone can be owned, even by himself.

The narrator never claims that the subjects of the kingdom of Coramantien are slaves of their king, but the distinction between subject and slave is often blurred. The slaves Oroonoko trades in are supposed to be prisoners of war, in conformity with traditional European ideas of how slaves might legitimately be acquired. Because Oroonoko conquered them and could have put them to death, their lives are forfeit to him, and hence he can spare them and make them the property of others. Slavery, then, is legitimate because it is incidental to war. But Coramantien is also presented as a place where war is the only enterprise and slaves the only commodity,

> for that nation is very warlike and brave, and having a continual campaign, being always in hostility with one neighbouring prince or other, they had the fortune to take a great many captives; for all they took in battle, were sold as slaves, at least, those common men who could not ransom themselves. (pp. 78–9)

In this account, war seems incidental to the slave trade rather than vice versa. Moreover, as the story progresses, we are told often of attendants, mistresses, friends, and even wives who are sold as slaves. Although it is a dishonour for a subject to be sold into slavery, the king has a right to make such a sale, and we are told that every husband has the right either to take the life of his wife or to sell her. The kingdom is imagined to work on patriarchal principles closely resembling those that Filmer describes, with the members of each family living only by the father's sufferance, and the king, as the father of all, holding the same absolute power to dispose of all his subjects: 'for they pay a most absolute resignation to the monarch' (p. 83). The real status of a subject, therefore, is that he may at any moment be converted into a commodity.

Indeed, the proof of the monarch's power is precisely in such acts of alienation, for merely to keep and use a slave, as one would any other servant or subordinate, is not to assert fully one's right of ownership.

Hence, it is by virtue of having previously sold the slaves that Oroonoko encounters in Surinam that he is recognized as their king:

> . . . they all came forth to behold him, and found he was that prince who had, at several times, sold most of them to these parts; and, from a veneration they pay to great men, . . . they all cast themselves at his feet, crying out in their language, 'Live, O King! Long live, O King!' And kissing his feet, paid him even divine homage. (p. 109)

Kingship, the right of ownership, and the act of exchange entail each other so closely in *Oroonoko* that they are virtually identical. It is consistent with this logic that kingship should be painted black, the colour of exchange. It also follows that the representative of kingship, more perfectly and conspicuously identified by this colour than anyone, should ultimately be himself taken for a commodity in the very trade he practised.

If Oroonoko's abduction and sale seem inevitable, however, the logic of this version of absolutism must be deemed highly paradoxical. If absolute kingship is ownership, and absolute ownership is exchange, then the enduring, stable possession of a person, even of oneself, becomes a near impossibility. Sovereignty keeps sliding into self-alienation, and keeping someone entails the renunciation of property claims. Perhaps the most complex variation on this theme is the drama surrounding the possession of Imoinda, for in *Oroonoko* as in *The Luckey Chance*, the paradoxes of absolute property in persons become most starkly apparent precisely where, in the culture at large, the property relation would be deemed most 'natural': in the relation of husband and wife. Imoinda's possession is problematic from the outset. Plighted to Oroonoko, she is appropriated by his grandfather, the king, but the old man cannot consummate the relationship by 'possessing' her sexually. Aware of the king's impotence, Oroonoko continues to consider her his and succeeds in possessing her clandestinely, whereupon the lovers are discovered, and Oroonoko must flee.

Up to this point, the story is an utterly conventional intrigue plot, but here the slave market intervenes, giving the old man an unusual means of proving that Imoinda is actually his: he sells her. The act eventually, after Oroonoko's enslavement, reunites the lovers, but their second marriage, which takes place when they are both 'slaves in name only', exacerbates the problems of possession. For Imoinda and Oroonoko slavery means nothing but potential commodification; they are not forced to labour, and their activities are almost completely unrestricted. However, as long as they remain in Surinam, they are officially another man's property and hence vulnerable to sale. As soon as Imoinda becomes pregnant, this state of affairs becomes intolerable to Oroonoko, for the prospect of fathering a child while officially a slave, while his patriarchal right is legally violable, makes him suddenly aware that Imoinda's body is a medium for his self-alienation. By possessing her sexually he produces another property, a child, whom he cannot legally call his own. The reappropriation through revolt of Imoinda and all the Africans he formerly sold into slavery then seems exigent, and when this plan fails, Oroonoko's only means of keeping Imoinda and his child from the market is to 'free' them both from life altogether. Thus the integrity of Oroonoko's kingship is accomplished by the final 'carving' of Imoinda's body:

> . . . The lovely, young and adored victim lays herself down, before the sacrificer, while he, with a hand resolved, and a heart breaking within, gave the fatal stroke, first, cutting her throat, and then severing her, yet smiling, face from that delicate body, pregnant as it was with the fruits of tenderest love. (p. 136)

This quite literal defacing of Imoinda, the lifting of her still-smiling face, as if it were a mask or portrait, off her body is presented as the 'brave and just' (p. 135) liberation of her self from the body that was perpetually exchangeable. Oroonoko, the king of exchange, only keeps her and returns her to herself through this ultimate form of alienation.

Imoinda's severed face is not the first such mask we've seen in the book signifying integrity or self-possession, for the problem of owning in the tale extends even to one's relationship with oneself. The great Indian

warriors, for example, prove their fitness for leadership by defacing themselves.[27] The narrator described the contest for generalship this way:

> He, who is first . . . cuts off his nose, and throws it contemptibly on the
> ground, and the other does something to himself that he thinks surpasses
> him, and perhaps deprives himself of lips and an eye. So they slash on till
> one gives out, and many have died in this debate. And 'tis by a passive
> valour they show and prove their activity, a sort of courage too brutal
> to be applauded by our black hero; nevertheless, he expressed his
> esteem of them.   (p. 124)

   This bizarre chopping away of bits of one's body becomes, by the end
of the story, the heroic alternative to the alienation of marketplace
exchange, which appears to require whole bodies. Thus, although the
Indians' self-mutilation seems 'too brutal' at first to Oroonoko, he copies
it in the sacrificial transfigurations that are supposed to give him back his
kingly sovereignty. After being cornered by his pursuers, Oroonoko turns
on them:

> 'Look ye, ye faithless crew', said he, ''tis not life I seek, nor am I afraid
> of dying', and at that word, cut a piece of flesh from his own throat, and
> threw it at them, 'yet still I would live if I could, till I had perfected my
> revenge. But, oh! it cannot be; I feel life gliding from my eyes and heart;
> and if I make not haste, I shall yet fall victim to the shameful whip.'
> At that, he ripped up his own belly, and took his bowels and pulled
> them out . . .   (p. 138)

Later, in the actual execution scene, Oroonoko seeks the dismemberment
of his entire body, which appears all the more bloodless, inhuman, and
indestructible with each partition:

> And the executioner came, and first cut off his members, and threw them
> into the fire. After that, with an ill-favoured knife, they cut his ears, and
> his nose, and burned them; he still smoked [a pipe of tobacco], as if
> nothing had touched him. Then they hacked off one of his arms, and still
> he bore up, and held his pipe. But at the cutting off the other arm, his
> head sunk, and his pipe dropped, and he gave up the ghost, without a
> groan, or a reproach . . . They cut Caesar in quarters, and sent them
> to several of the chief plantations . . .   (p. 140)

Although this horror was aimed at 'terrifying and grieving' the slaves 'with frightful spectacles of a mangled king' (p. 140), it also creates the spectacle of the body of kingship, which appears most powerfully in such vanishing acts, when bodies seem at once reduced to mere things and transcended altogether. Now deprived of that which first constituted it – the ownership and exchange of others – Oroonoko's kingship becomes his godlike willing of the piecemeal alienation of himself. In this contradictory manner, he proves that he still owns it. Although the moment of death is noted ('his pipe dropped, and he gave up the ghost'), this anticlimactic act seems just another stage in the separation of his parts. Oroonoko undergoes an extraordinary self-division, only to become all the more singularly immortal, for 'he' is now unlocatable. The mystical body of kingship and the actual body of Oroonoko again become identical by the fragmentation and scattering of the latter. Just as the brown bodies reached their vanishing point in Oroonoko's black body of kingly and monetary representation, so his own body of representation reaches its vanishing point in this dispersion.

At this point in the text, the narrator makes her most striking appropriation in the form of a disclaimer: 'Thus died this great man, worthy of a better fate, and a more sublime wit than mine to write his praise. Yet, I hope, the reputation of my pen is considerable enough to make his glorious name to survive to all ages, with that of the brave, the beautiful and the constant Imoinda' (p. 141). Oroonoko's 'worth' demands more sublimity than she can summon, yet her own authorial reputation, itself a mystical body existing in and between texts, will be the support of 'his glorious name'. Ending the text with the word 'Imoinda' reminds us of Behn's special fitness to tell this love story, her femaleness, and yet the effect of authorship here transcends all such physical accidents even as it takes them into account. If Oroonoko scatters his members to maintain his integrity, Behn performs a similar act of disowning the story (insisting that it is really Oroonoko's and Imoinda's) to open a rhetorical space in which she can remind us of her authorship and the obligation it imposes. In her dedication of the book to Richard Maitland, she similarly at once claims and disclaims her product: ''Tis purely the merit of my Slave that must render [the book] worthy of the Honour it begs; and the Author of that of subscribing herself, My Lord, Your Lordship's most oblig'd and obedient Servant, A. Behn.'[28]

In this odd mixture of appropriation and disowning ("'Tis purely the merit of *my Slave* that must render' the book worthy of Maitland), the author trades in the 'parts' she claims are not exactly hers, and thus she avoids identifying herself with her commodity. Despite the insistent presence of the first-person narrator in *Oroonoko*, then, the phenomenon of authorship per se comes into view here as the principle of the exchange of representations. Behn merely transfers 'the nobler part' from one great man, Oroonoko, to another, Richard Maitland. Unlike Oroonoko's sovereign self or 'the beautiful and constant Imoinda', such representations are endlessly negotiable precisely because they are not really owned, and hence they make their vendor invulnerable.

NOTES

1 See Elizabeth L. Eisenstein's remarks on the preservative powers of print in *The Printing Revolution in Early Modern Europe* (Cambridge, 1983), pp. 78–88. She explains that wide dissemination became the means of making the text imperishable. 'The notion that valuable data could be preserved best by being made public, rather than by being kept secret, ran counter to tradition', she claims, and was still controversial in the eighteenth century. Behn, however, seems to have been quite secure in the belief that publication would make her words immortal.

2 It was not until the Restoration that writers began exploring the implications of the fact that authors communicated with their readers through print. Regardless of the fact that the technology was two hundred years old by 1660, Dryden seems to have been the first author to notice its impact. 'Dryden is among the first English writers to understand, at least implicitly, the conditions imposed on a literature that is primarily printed and read . . . where books and writing are the main instruments of transmission', claims James Engell in *Forming the Critical Mind: Dryden to Coleridge* (Cambridge, 1989), p. 22.

3 *Oroonoko and Other Stories*, ed. and introd. by Maureen Duffy (London, 1986), p. 25.

4 This is not unusual in stories about the wonders of the New World, where narrators routinely felt obliged to claim that they were eyewitnesses of the events they relate. Most of the evidence, though, does point to Behn's presence in Surinam in the early to mid 1660s. For presentation of this

evidence, see Rogers, 'Fact and fiction in Aphra Behn's *Oroonoko*', pp. 1–3.

5 Jordan, *White Over Black: American Attitudes Toward the Negro, 1550–1800* (Chapel Hill, 1968), p. 5.

6 In a footnote, Jordan names several later writers who celebrate 'the Negro's jet blackness', but Behn's is the earliest instance by over thirty years. Jordan, p. 10, n. 23.

7 For analysis of the narrator-hero relationship, see Martine Watson Brownley, 'The narrator in *Oroonoko*', *Essays in Literature* 4 (1977), pp. 174–81; Ferguson, 'Juggling the categories of race, class and gender: Aphra Behn's *Oroonoko*', pp. 165–6; Jacqueline Pearson, 'Gender and narrative in the fiction of Aphra Behn', part ii, pp. 184–90; Jane Spencer, *The Rise of the Woman Novelist*, pp. 47–52; and Starr, 'Aphra Behn and the genealogy of the man of feeling', pp. 362–8.

8 For a discussion of the parallels between kingship and textuality in the early modern period, see David Lee Miller, *The Poem's Two Bodies: The Poetics of The Faerie Queen* (Princeton, 1988).

9 'Novel' here can mean both 'novelty' and 'romantic tale'.

10 In 1696 Thomas Southerne turned the story into just such a play, which, in various versions, was a staple of the eighteenth-century repertory.

11 See, for example, Ernest Bernbaum, 'Mrs Behn's *Oroonoko*', in *Anniversary Papers by Colleagues and Pupils of George Lyman Kittredge* (Boston, 1913).

12 On *Oroonoko*'s relation to heroic drama, see Laura Brown, 'The romance of Empire: *Oroonoko* and the trade in slaves', in *The New Eighteenth Century: Theory, Politics, English Literature*, ed. Felicity Nussbaum and Laura Brown (New York, 1987), pp. 48–51.

13 For a description of the black-face characters in the Lord Mayor's Pageants, see Anthony Gerard Barthelemy, *Black Face, Maligned Race: The Representation of Blacks in English Drama from Shakespeare to Southerne* (Baton Rouge, 1987), chapter 3. For other possible references in Imoinda's iconography, see Margaret W. Ferguson, 'Juggling the categories of race, class, and gender: Aphra Behn's *Oroonoko*', *Women's Studies* 19 (1991), 181, n. 49.

14 The Reverend Richard Hakluyt, indeed, calls this kind of African body carving a form of 'branched damaske' and says that it takes the place of clothing. Hakluyt, *Principle Navigations, Voyages, Traffiques and Discoveries*, 4, p. 62. For other discussions of the insistent physicality of Imoinda and its hint of a conflict between the narrator and this black heroine, see Ballaster, 'New hystericism: Aphra Behn's *Oroonoko*; the body, the text and the feminist critic', in *New Feminist Discourses: Critical Essays on Theories and Texts*, ed. Isobel Armstrong (New York, 1992), pp. 290–3; and

Ferguson, 'Juggling the categories of race, class and gender: Aphra Behn's *Oroonoko*', pp. 170–1.

15 I am not arguing here that Oroonoko is supposed to be any particular king or all of the Stuarts collectively. My argument, rather is that Oroonoko, although he may indeed bring to mind certain Stuarts, is the symbol of an entity that is itself symbolic, Kingship, and that he represents a seventeenth-century revision of that entity. For arguments that detect likenesses with the Stuart kings, see George Guffey, 'Aphra Behn's Oroonoko: occasion and accomplishment', in *Two English Novelists* (Los Angeles, 1975), pp. 3–41; and Brown, 'The Romance of empire: *Oroonoko* and the trade in slaves', pp. 57–9.

16 I give in this paragraph a schematic summary of the intricate and complicated arguments described by Kantorowicz in *The King's Two Bodies* (Princeton, 1957).

17 See Barthelemy's discussion of the contrast between the heroic white Moor and the villainous black Moor in George Peel's *The Battle of Alcazar* (1589), pp. 75–81.

18 For various accounts of why and how Africans come to be the enslaveable race, see Winthrop Jordan, *White Over Black*, esp. pp. 91–101; Barbara Fields, 'Ideology and Race in American History', in *Region, Race, and Reconstruction*, ed. J. Morgan Kousser and James M. McPherson (New York, 1982); David Brion Davis, *The Problem of Slavery in Western Culture* (Ithaca, 1966), p. 178; and William D. Phillips, Jr, *Slavery From Roman Times to the Early Transatlantic Slave Trade* (Minneapolis, 1985), p. 184.

19 The narrator is not always perfectly consistent on this point. On at least one occasion she speaks of their 'Indian slaves', but she seems to use the term loosely in that case as a synonym for 'lowly servant'. She never describes the commodification of Indians.

20 In fact, 'Coramantien' was not a country at all but a port on the Gold Coast where the English had a trading station. According to Rogers, though, planters in America generally referred to Gold Coast Africans as 'Coramantiens' (Rogers, 'Fact and fiction in Aphra Behn's *Oroonoko*', p. 6).

21 For a discussion of the larger political implications of the debate over money at the end of the seventeenth century, see Joyce Oldham Appleby, *Economic Thought and Ideology in Seventeenth-Century England* (Princeton, 1978), pp. 236–41. She argues that 'Locke's denial of the extrinsic value of coin carried with it a limitation of government in economic affairs' (p. 237). She also quotes John Briscoe's 1696 attack on the state's power to fix the value of money, an attack phrased in language peculiarly relevant

to *Oroonoko*: '[as] it is a mark of slavery, so is it the means of poverty in a State, where the Magistrate assumes a Power to set what price he pleases on the Publick Coin: It is a sign of Slavery, because the Subject in such Case lives merely at the Mercy of the Prince, is Rich, or Poor, has a Competency, or is a Beggar, is a Free-Man, or in Fetters at his Pleasure' (p. 237).

22 The once widely held view that the Whigs represented the interests and ideology of trade while the Tories stood for an older aristocratic order that shunned commerce is no longer tenable. The most concise statements revealing the errors and simplifications of this position are J. G. A. Pocock's 'The mobility of property and the rise of eighteenth-century sociology' and 'Authority and property: the question of liberal origins', in *Virtue, Commerce, and History: Essays in Political Thought and History, Chiefly in the Eighteenth Century* (Cambridge, 1985). These show the strong connections between absolutist ideology in the seventeenth century and the spread of a notion of property as that which can be exchanged. To be sure, a certain kind of Tory ideology grew up in the 1690s and early eighteenth century, which vociferously opposed this idea of property, but Pocock, again, has shown that the Toryism of Harley and St John descends from theorists like Locke as opposed to absolutists. There is, then, no ideological contradiction between Behn's Restoration Court Toryism and her presentation of Oroonoko as a heroic warrier *and* slave-trader. The general intellectual history is complicated by the fact that slavery was sometimes identified as a characteristic of pre-commercial societies; slavery in *Oroonoko*, however, is not presented as a semi-feudal but as a fully commercial institution. That is, exchange, rather than mere ownership, is its essence.

23 Indeed, it gave them a status lower than that of slaves under English law, for even slaves were deemed to have something like a natural right to life, and in many of the English colonies (including Surinam) they could own property themselves.

24 *Two Treatises of Government: A Critical Edition*, ed. and introd. Peter Laslett (Cambridge, 1960), *First Treatise*, chap. ii, section 9, pp. 9–10.

25 James Tully, 'The framework of natural rights in Locke's analysis of property: a contextual reconstruction', *Theories of Property: Aristotle to the Present*, ed. Anthony Parel and Thomas Flanagan (Calgary, 1979), p. 119. For other contributions to the debate about sovereignty and the rise of absolute property, see Alan Ryan, *Property and Political Theory* (Oxford, 1984), pp. 14–48; J. G. A. Pocock, 'The mobility of property and the rise

of eighteenth-century sociology'; and G. E. Alymer, 'The meaning and definition of "property" in seventeenth-century England', *Past and Present* 86 (1980), 87–97.

26 Behn's articulation of kingship and property in subjects is similar to Filmer's although not necessarily derived from his. It isn't clear how widely influential *Patriarcha* was in the 1680s; but it certainly stands as a prominent landmark in the ideological terrain of the decade, which allows us to locate the general vicinity of Behn's tale. For a contrasting view of Oroonoko as the Lockean bourgeois subject, see Weston, 'The noble primitive as bourgeois subject', *Literature and History* 10 (1984), 59–71. For a discussion of a possible link between *Oroonoko* and a Hobbesian view of the world, see Starr, 'Aphra Behn and the genealogy of the man of feeling.'

27 For another discussion of mutilation and self-mutilation in *Oroonoko*, see Ballaster, 'New hystericism: Aphra Behn's *Oroonoko*', p. 292.

28 'The Epistle Dedicatory to the Right Honourable the Lord Maitland', in *Oroonoko, or The Royal Slave: A Critical Edition*, ed. and introd. Adelaide P. Amore (Lanham, MD, 1987), p. 3.

13 Confusing matters: searching the backgrounds of *Oroonoko*[1]

JOANNA LIPKING

Years of critical interpretation and student comment had blocked out in my mind what might be called the clichés about *Oroonoko*, the commonly observed features of the tale that have served in place of a single unified action, narrative form, or genre. Striking from the outset, surely remarkable for its time, is the easy, conversational narrator's voice that hurries us on, as it binds together 'wonders', reportage, notable displays of virtue and vice, and some subtle psychological probing. There are the two disparate locales, the stylized 'romantic' Africa with its model hero, ideal love, and court intrigues, and the more 'realistic' colony of Surinam, circumstantially described, possibly authentic, open to the anarchic and the sordid. Throughout, descriptions of all societies show a marked approving emphasis on traditional hierarchic order, which includes a matter-of-fact acceptance of slavery, creating the split identity of the 'royal slave'. Finally, amid faltering understandings and a comparatively untidy train of events, there is the horrific ending, with its climatic scenes of broken trust and physical dismemberment.

Wide-ranging reading in the backgrounds of *Oroonoko* for a projected edition did not dispel these impressions, but it softened their terms and oppositions. Repeatedly, other contemporary writings and pieces of information seemed to blur the lines or fill in the spaces between 'romance' and more realistic kinds of writing, between categories of persons, between high ideals and sheer brutality. Its hybrid nature needs recognizing, yet seen as a story of contrasts, *Oroonoko* seems to hold its own as a stirring but crude yarn with an altogether remarkable power to

259

resist penetrating readings, despite impressive amounts of critical ingenuity focused on it. We seem to stand outside the tale.

In this, Behn's work can be contrasted with *Robinson Crusoe*. The
adventures of the castaway Selkirk, some observations about the habits of
'homo economicus', and patterns of spiritual autobiography seem to carry
us directly to the heart of an amorphous book, though no doubt an insular
one. George Guffey's energetically argued case that Behn was drawing
attention to political events of the spring and summer of 1688, especially
the fragile circumstances of James II, his wife and heir, seems a similar
attempt to call Behn's story home, to give it a familiar framework and an
English home address.[2] But *Oroonoko* will not be called. The curiosity it
expresses and arouses about a new transatlantic world of human meetings
is too powerful, its facts about that world too often current. Some of the
works that provide its most interesting parallels are not English but
French, though some policies and attitudes seem identifiably English. In
any case, looking to this or any political analogy provides no guide to the
construction of the whole tale, which still appears arbitrary, patchy,
formula-ridden.

We are left still farther outside by the current approaches candidly
described in Margaret W. Ferguson's 'Juggling the categories of race,
class and gender.'[3] In this story, 'class' (mainly royalty or nobility) means
so much more than rank or privilege – Behn's word is 'quality' – that race
difference may fade from mind. 'Race' (or blackness) does not have its
fixed later meanings and associations, which can be seriously misleading,
while 'white' is not easily dissociated from its common synonym,
'Christian'. A focus on 'gender' with respect to women – not given the
central consideration given to manliness – leads to eroticized readings of
the tale or pits Imoinda against the woman narrator who has failed to consider her more attentively. The issues are not to be set aside, since Behn
gives them more thought and prominence than do writings by her male
contemporaries. In fact, there seems strikingly little precedent for the
presence of Imoinda as slave wife and partner, however subordinated. But
the abstract categories need to be brought to earth, grounded in Behn's
time and Behn's scenes.

This working report on how *Oroonoko* relates to and is illuminated by
contemporary writing, opinion, and fact is another way of beginning. The

works cited are often diverse, from distant parts of the library. Together they provide only a thin record of historical events, and, though patterns appear, individual passages are often too isolated – scattered through very long works – to be offered as representative. Moreover, they do not at all solve the intriguing questions about the work's origins, since they seem to provide powerful evidence for everything: that Behn used sources, that she followed received opinion, and that she was present in Surinam, that she was closely attentive to actual circumstances and falsified them boldly. All that can be concluded about the composition of the work is that, though apparently written in haste, it was probably put together very slowly. Yet consideration of this body of documents may move us from our own commonplaces about the story somewhat closer to the kinds of 'commonplaces' abroad or taking shape in Behn's world, from our sense of two sites and two styles toward a more complicated interbraiding. In place of dubious categorizing, we gain a deeper feeling for Behn's imaginative choices and her crafting.

Doubtless the most unchallengeable proposition is that Behn presents an ideal romance hero, displaying the strengths of the classical epic warrior as they were altered and augmented by the softnesses of seventeenth-century tastes in the heroic. Introducing her 'great man', she calls on her readers to respond with familiar unchecked emotion, to recognize and admire. In particular, Oroonoko is a strikingly close cousin of the Scythian prince Oroondates in La Calprenède's romance *Cassandra*, a work widely circulated in England in the translation of Charles Cotterell, master of ceremonies to Charles I and Charles II, with a dedication to the latter.[4] Given Behn's knowledge of romances, perhaps a broader canvassing of romance heroes is needed, but Oroondates' name, nature, and handling call for special notice.

By nature, of course, he is a paragon, his range of attributes signalled at once by his beauty and bearing and what they convey of his social elevation:

> his face was marvellously handsome; and through a beauty which had nothing of effeminate, one might observe something so Martial, so sparkling, and so Majestick, as might in all hearts make an impression

of Love, Fear, and Respect at once; his stature exceeded that of the tallest men, but the proportion of it was wonderfully exact, and all the motions of his body had a grace and liberty that was nothing common.   (p. 3)

The king's only son, he is bred to arms, performs prodigious single feats, and is worshipped by his men. Possessed as well of 'a soul capable of all gallant impressions' (p. 7), he has been carefully educated in wit, discourse, manners, morals. Returning after conquest, he is transfixed by love, which proves a concealed and static attachment to a woman who remains distant, but like Oroonoko he is so faithful and so afflicted – especially by a false death report – that his devoted male companions must intervene to counsel and divert him. Moreover, as a Scythian, Oroondates is an exotic, not Greek, Macedonian, or Persian, but from a distantly known people who have been 'held for barbarous, cruel, uncivil' (p. 8).

After such superlatives, absolute in their 'all' and 'nothing', it is no surprise that the characters respond to one another with sudden extreme emotion, in an idiom much like Behn's. They feel 'an excess of joy' (p. 13), are 'absolutely conquere'd (p. 23), avow feelings 'a thousand times' (pp. 40, 42). In some ways, however, the flight into romance is controlled by an allegiance to history. Like other romances, *Cassandra* is based loosely on the writings of classical historians. In his accompanying prefaces, La Calprenède expresses his regard for truth and probability, explaining that if he alters a little or diverges into epic style, he has avoided extravagance, and at least does not contradict his sources in 'those accidents that are feign'd' (p. 178). More important, he begins far into the middle of things, and before going on with his plot and branching subplots, told by the various involved lovers, he presents the hero's past life in a section titled 'The History of Oroondates' narrated by his squire. If the hyperbole above is mainly his, he also plays the historian, with a continuous 'I-you' relation to his listener and a measure of critical distance.

Like Behn's narrator, the squire is a reliable chronicler of the hero's achievements, 'having been present at the greatest part, and having learnt those from his own mouth, of which I could not be an eye-witness' (p. 7). Sometimes he is careful to give his physical location or explain what reports he has heard. Asides have a fairly spontaneous air, as he skips over duller matters or digresses, 'Nor can I forbear to tell you by the by' (pp. 35–6), stops to speculate or doubles back with 'I had forgot to tell you' (p. 22). Attesting to his master's high emotion, he is sometimes overwhelmed and breaks down, yet as a practical man who sees the disabling effects of excessive love, he also confides the strategies by which he has tried to control him. Romance, then, afforded Behn a model not only for her noble hero in war and love and friendship, but for her truth claims, her reportorial stance, and some part, at least, of her familiar extempore style.

Behn's prince is a far more adventurous choice of hero. Having been 'noble savages' of the classical world, Scythians continued to make their appearance in romance and plays. With her black-skinned West African, Behn crosses racial lines, breaks with the stereotyping and symbolic associations found in black villains of stage and story – including her own devilish Moorea in *The Unfortunate Bride* – and carries her hero far from battles and courts to a destiny registered mainly in ships' reports and colonial state papers. If her breadth of outlook wins approval, it is generally agreed that she has carefully modified her hero's Africanness to make him a more acceptable romance figure and has provided him with some distinctively European traits. In Laura Brown's summation, he is 'not only a natural European and aristocrat, but a natural neoclassicist and Royalist as well'.[5] The tone of much commentary is ironic, aloof.

But what is an African? We can easily pick out what seem anomalous features – the ideals and histrionics of an Oroondates, the Roman nose, the globes and compasses – but on what sort of figure do we pin them? The presumption is that we know what an African was and that Behn has given us a false one. No doubt she was Eurocentric, but that is hardly a singular fate. The centuries since are full of dubious images that run to type. Against what Africans are we testing hers?

In the distant past, of course, many non-Europeans, including Africans, were part of the Roman empire. If they were portrayed with classical features or compared to ancient Romans, that was the training of all educated observers. Behn might easily have seen illustrations of imposing plumed warriors or other classically modelled figures. Meanwhile, to the seventeenth-century travellers busy exploring trading opportunities along the Guinea coast, West Africans were diverse. Perhaps nothing short of slavery could have led modern readers to think that the inhabitants of a continent ought to be alike. Behn's contemporaries in the field discriminated eagerly, characterizing the people of each coastal district, each small anchorage. Their accounts are often derogatory; they were deeply repelled by funeral sacrifice and other 'heathen' practices and were often frustrated in their dealings with shrewd and experienced rulers and trading officials. Yet they regularly picked out kings, important men, and sometimes whole peoples who seemed in their eyes preferable and admirable, commending them for their European looks, virtues, and capabilities.

Gold Coast peoples in the vicinity of Behn's Cormantine – the established English trading station – were often praised for their looks, martial valour, intelligence, and civility in the English, Dutch, and German sources, which copied copiously from one another. The most interesting first-hand accounts, however, appear in some original French sources that do not have modern editions. The French expeditions were essentially directed from the court rather than by commercial companies, they reported back to that court, and they record what seem to have been notably polite and cordial encounters with the African elite. At times reality seems tinged with the idealizings of romance. The same aristocratic codes that produced *Cassandra* and the other romances, not *Robinson Crusoe*, produced a trade that was somewhat sporadic but accounts of social and diplomatic contacts that can show an extraordinary courtliness.

The most striking single passage appears in a 1671 report of a brief stop at the Gold Coast port of Commendo, whose Francophile king sought a French trading presence and sent several emissaries to France. The party was summoned to meet the local governor, who relayed the king's welcome and offered his services. As the unknown writer saw him:

> I admit I was surprised that I found in him nothing barbarous, but on the contrary, much humanity, and he received us very differently from all the others we had seen. I had been strongly impressed that in entering the Gold Coast, the people were more humanized than in other places; in

truth at the sight of him I thought highly of him, and if these people have engaging features, this man has more than all the Negroes combined. He is tall and well proportioned, all his limbs showing strength, without the unattractive flat nose or that large mouth that the other blacks have; his eyes were prominent, very open, brilliant, and full of fire. In all, one notices that his features are regular, and that they convey pride and much gentleness.[6]

Having entertained the travellers in his well-ordered small court, he pays a farewell visit to their ship, where he can't be persuaded to drink but enjoys speaking of his wars. As a suitable compliment, therefore, the French send him off with a five-canon salute.

A more prolonged display of civility met an early French slaving expedition to Allada, on the Slave Coast, in 1670. Along with courts far more splendid and feasts more lavish than would have been found in the smaller Gold Coast kingdoms, the travellers find good company. First entertained at the coast by a tall, hospitable prince 'of magnificent visage', they are carried on a rare visit inland to the court of his father, who has been educated in a Portuguese convent on São Tomé and is praised for his mental agility in terms that are best left untranslated: '*l'esprit vif*', '*la repartie prompte*', '*une humeur assez libre & enjouée*', '*comparaisons spirituelles & agreables*'.[7] Banqueting, conferences, and trading arrangements, all very formal and elaborate, continue over weeks. This happy demonstration of class solidarity has its own small crisis when the French discover that they have been sold eight of the king's wives, but they are able to mollify and cheer them by giving them command of all the women on board.

These were real Africans met on home ground – dominant, gracious, themselves apparently somewhat Eurocentric – not projections into vacant space. The same cannot be said of Behn's scenes of court life at Cormantine. Precisely the point of romance writers' shifting their tales to remote locales was that it left them free to invent, rather than being constrained by what their sources said or their readers might know of the kingdoms of Darius or Alexander. Only one study, by Katharine M. Rogers, defends Behn's portrait of Africa, arguing that its details are 'not so fantastic as they seem' and its 'major outlines' are 'accurate'.[8] Her account effectively counters later storybook images of a primitive or pastoral Africa, yet it constructs a single 'West African culture' that is a medley of unevaluated reports from earlier and later journeys, from old lore and modern scholarship on one locale. Her line of argument has not been pursued. For literary readers, the stylistic cues are so strong, the reminiscences of other loves and wars so obvious, that Oroonoko's early life is safely classed as a European genre piece, a superimposition.

To historians of West Africa, as well, Behn's kingdom seems some anyplace. She has imported a system of patrilineal descent, she supposes a marriage could be made by self-plighting, she interprets the ownership of women in narrowly and fiercely sexualized terms. One scholar offered a better plot: let Oroonoko poison his grandfather and inherit Imoinda automatically. Nonetheless they were firm on the need to distinguish which peoples and when, to expect complication in rules about kinship and incest, above all, to allow for the uncertainty of the sources. What seemed one clear conclusion, that body carving like Imoinda's was not found in the vicinity of Cormantine – perhaps Behn drew on older reports about the Gold Coast or contemporary reports of women form elsewhere, or Imoinda might have come from far inland – was waived aside by one scholar, who had herself come upon somewhat comparable practices among rural women unreported in more urban areas. As the reader comes to learn, while the conduct of trade was precise, down to the smallest unit of measure, other understandings were approximate. The best accounts, stockpiling rather than sifting information, may interpolate second-hand material, but even when contacts were direct, the Europeans relied on analogies that misled them, accepting rulers' sons as hostages, for example, when the nephews might be the political heirs, or entertaining as 'princes' in Europe persons who turned out to be of more ambiguous status. If these are the reports of Africa, who could say what tale heard on the far side of the world might emerge in England with a 'grandfather', an inspired invention of monogamy, and a leisurely hothouse harem?

By their nature, all the reports make Behn's love plot seem an especially airy fiction. Male travellers and traders in their contacts with male African officialdom never saw strong erotic or domestic ties, dwelling instead on African polygamy and sensuality, but that is weak evidence that nothing of the sort existed. New World slavery could scarcely provide a more unpropitious setting or a more cold-hearted set of records, yet among the scant documentary sources, a 1690 inventory of slaves on one estate includes several couples or families who were sold and remained together, and the 1679 travel log of slave trader Jean Barbot records the moving tears and embraces of a reunited family: 'I have seen nothing to equal the joy of that poor wretched man', he writes, or 'so much tenderness in a wife.'⁹ Early Caribbean histories include a sentence or two: Charles de Rochefort says that among themselves the slaves are passionate lovers, and the Dominican Du Tertre reports that their love for one another is 'very tender', so overseers must be careful when chastising a man's wife or children.¹⁰ In modern Suriname (as the name is now spelled), some of the stories of 'slavery days' carefully preserved in one large society of former runaways attest 'to the strength of romantic love among the early maroons'. (Curiously, one story tells of an eighteenth-century forebear who took away the wife of his less than potent 'grandfather'. Was there a pattern?)¹¹ These are mere twigs, not the warmly burning loves of *Oroonoko* or *Uncle Tom's Cabin*, but clearly the traders' descriptions of polygamy and sensuality left something out.

A last teasing detail is Behn's *otan*, her name for 'the palace of the king's women, a sort of seraglio'. Some scenes – of the irritable old king in his marble bath, or the dissimulations of his worldly courtiers – are so overcivilized and piquant that it has seemed likely that Behn was influenced by fashionable 'oriental' tales. In the annotations, *otan* has been traced to *oda*, Turkish for a room or chamber in a harem, and by the work's Ghanaian editor, K. A. Sey, to the Persian word *otagh*, meaning tent, room, pavilion. Yet a still closer term for house or apartment, generally transcribed *odan*, appears in four outdated Fanti dictionaries and one architectural study.¹² Behn apparently made up her stylized courtly Africa, but for now it seems wisest not to conclude that she made it of whole cloth.

Behn's 'realistic' New World scenes present the opposite problem, a huge overload of details that offer correspondences or possible correspondences with fact or received opinion. While scholars have combed the text for authentic details, and critics have adopted various argumentative stances, the standard older works on early slavery – by David Brion Davis, Elizabeth Donnan, Richard Price, the Bridenbaughs – cite Behn as a collateral source, noting her information on such matters as the contract sale of slaves in lots or the precaution of dividing them up. Some phrases have a specificity of no dramatic value: 'a bargain with a *master, or* captain of a ship', 'where they were to deliver *some part of* their slaves', 'they sold 'em off as slaves to several *merchants and* gentlemen'. What she says of slave names, cabins, holidays, noise and music agrees with other reports.

But Behn's story is nothing if not dramatic. If it is informed, it is also topical, emphasizing matters of high news value for her readers at home. We can match it with other reports not only to establish an external 'reality' she knew in detail, but to see what pieces of 'reality' she and others selected, saw in somewhat conventionalized ways, described in repeated phrases. Recent specialized research makes it easier to distinguish fact from formula.

One notable abuse was the kidnapping of free Africans. It was illegal, and it was also extremely short-sighted, since the Africans might be expected to retaliate against the fort officers or the next English ship, or simply to give their trade to the Dutch or other rival nations. Nonetheless, it went on, since the perpetual shortage of slaves in the colonies created a market of buyers who were eager to evade mercantilist regulations and were not sticklers for procedure. Africans in direct contact with the ships – traders, interpreters, pawns, passengers – were of course especially vulnerable. But one recurrent kind of story is of a group of Africans, of unspecified numbers, at an unspecified place, who come aboard a ship to trade or be entertained and are sailed off with. Du Tertre relays an episode he has heard that is only one sentence long but close in detail to Behn's: a captain lures some men into his boat with drink and gifts, and while they think only of enjoying themselves, the anchor is raised, they are seized and chained, and carried away into slavery (2: 494). A 1680 English pamphlet advocating stern measures against independent traders or 'interlopers' complains of their 'perfidious action' against 'some considerable Natives', when 'they forthwith caryed them away, and sold them at the

Plantations for Slaves'.[13] Later the Dutch captain William Bosman charges that the French made a regular practice of kidnapping traders who came on board, and Barbot says that it was done by 'many of the European nations' all along the coast, 'and when they come aboard their ships in a harmless and confiding manner, carried great numbers away to the plantations'.[14] While kidnappings of considerably smaller groups certainly occurred and were duly reported in the official papers,[15] Behn's scenario seems an elaboration of what was a recognized outrage, its numbers blown out of scale. The stealing of a prince and 'about an hundred' noble youths would have caused a major disruption at Cormantine, which does not appear in the extant fort correspondence, and when her captain realistically separates them for sale in lots, the young colony of Surinam could hardly have provided enough slave holders to sell them to.[16]

Once in slavery, slaves caught the attention of observers in certain limited ways. Sometimes these seem to adumbrate the later popular image of the noble African, though that is not how they are represented. First, Europeans were deeply struck by the slaves' willingness or determination to die. On the ships, the captains report, they drowned themselves or, like Oroonoko and his companions, refused to eat.[17] In the colonies, if treated harshly, they killed themselves, a matter of worry to Trefry when he goes after the runaways.[18] Observers were sometimes impressed by the attractiveness or personal dignity of individual slaves, or commented approvingly on their spirited group festivities, communitarian and domestic virtues, or capacity for fidelity to masters. Written for European audiences, these remarks often served to set off the faults of the colonists, who were criticized as narrowly acquisitive and morally lax. The liveliest reporter, Father Du Tertre, a veteran traveller who enjoys provocative anecdotes and paradoxical views, declares that the slaves live in a more Christian way than many of the French.[19]

Most obviously newsworthy, however, were slave escapes and rebellions. From a distance, the slave system appears a highly efficient machinery of repression, but up close it was managed only by constant anxious vigilance against the dangers mentioned in Behn's tale – shipboard mutinies, planned or spontaneous insurrections, large or small-group escapes, along with lesser resistances of every sort. Gold Coast slaves, whom the English called Cormantines or Cormantees and judged superior, played a prominent part in many of the serious uprisings during Behn's lifetime. In English Surinam during the 1660s, a Cormantine-led community of maroons was raiding plantations; two decades later, the Dutch had to recognize them by treaty.[20] In 1673 on Jamaica, about two hundred slaves from one plantation 'being most of them Coromantines (a Warlike nation in Guinea)' lodged themselves in the mountains, 'almost destroyed' their pursuers, and drew many more slaves to rebel and join them.[21] A failed insurrection in Barbados in 1675 was characterized by the governor as a 'damnable design' that had spread widely, 'especially amongst the Cormantin negroes . . . a warlike and robust people',[22] and the next year was reported, with some sensational detail, in a London pamphlet. A careful historical study of threatened slave plots in Barbados discloses many small correspondences with Behn's story: the plots originated on Saturday evenings and Sundays, often under cover of feasting; planters used white servants to keep watch over the slaves; the main body of the militia was comprised of poorer whites and was sometimes ineffectual; the slaves were mobilized by strong individual leaders. Moreover, the colony was regularly swept by panics, taking cruel preemptive action against plots that may not have existed.[23]

It was standard practice to mete out harsh and sometimes barbaric punishments to ringleaders, in the standard phrase, to 'terrify' the others. On the ships, some captains 'cut off the legs and arms of the most wilful, to terrify the rest'.[24] When the Barbados authorities saw insolence, 'four or five for examples sake were well whipped for terror to others' and one man burned alive; when they detected a conspiracy, some 'for a terror to others' were hung in chains to starve to death, others hanged, burned, or castrated.[25] By the Virginia code of 1705, runaway slaves who remained at large were to be dismembered or castrated, with the purpose of 'terrifying others from the like practices'.[26] To the Europeans' astonishment, however, slaves sometimes met these tortures with stoic impassivity. According to George Warren's report of early Surinam, returned runaways would 'manifest their fortitude in suffering the most exquisite tortures can be inflicted upon them, for a terrour and example to others without shrinking'.[27] Later descriptions of imperturbable individual deaths come to have a generic quality. Students of *Oroonoko* have culled various eighteenth-century instances, and for another case there are very telling accounts from far-flung newspapers, like in effect but using different details.[28] In 1688 it is too early to say that the slave trade had produced its own form of the heroic – here Behn was innovative – but in the colonial reports that were slowly collecting, there are patterns in observation, fashions in news.

An experienced professional writer, Behn could have known that she was tapping a vein of exciting, sometimes alarming reportage new to a sustained story format. Beside the ordinary operations of the slave system, however, the correspondences that can be gathered for inspection can seem a bit inconsequential. Even in these early decades, before attitudes were hardened, the vast indifference of a labour-supplying system is hardly to be described. Ships' reports give the numbers of slaves loaded and landed, tallying the large discrepancies. The colonial papers record in minute detail the tensions of colonists with the home governments or among themselves. The overwhelming silence and voicelessness on the slaves' side are broken by desperate acts, at which point observers turn from their own concerns to administer the necessary crowd control and blandly explain what the slaves think. They drown themselves in terror of Barbados, explains Thomas Phillips, supplying the 'reality': 'in reality they live much better there than in their own country; but home is home, etc.'[29] Resistance and rebellion might show that the slaves had an understandable desire for liberty, requiring counter-measures, or might equally show that they were perverse, unmanageable people fit only to be slaves. Their origins were forgotten; unless they led revolts, they went unnamed. Comparatively kindly characterizations in French sources are a miniscule part of works that are, as their titles show, travel books or natural histories, the brief remarks on slaves nearly lost amid elaborate descriptions of the odoriferous trees and the marmosets.

By contrast, Behn's unique 'middle passage' draws a connection between the powerful, patrician men met on the West African coast and the occasional impressive slave glimpsed in the colonies. Oroonoko remains in focus as an intimate, his friendship with the captain succeeded smoothly by the parallel new friendship with Trefry. Though his circumstances differ, he disembarks as a romance hero, an Oroondates, much as that prince came in disguise to the Persian camp, confiding his moving love story in scenes of sympathetic bonding and meanwhile, despite his unassuming manner, becoming the admired centre of the entire court and company. This model may explain the attractive but puzzling diffidence with which Oroonoko hides his birth from Trefry, dresses in coarse clothes for the populace, and greets the other slaves as their 'fellow slave'. In addition, Behn's 'royal youth' is conspicuously royal, defined as more than a civil ruler by the magnetized crowds, obeisant slaves, and gentleman planters who pay 'their court', as well as his creative power to draw different nations and races into cooperative relations.

If the prince and the narrator live remote from the work life of the colony, Behn's terms do not signal distance or inexperience but are simply the local language. Africans were commonly called 'Moors', as in Du Tertre's chapter heading, 'Of the Negro Slaves, vulgarly called Moors in France.' (In fact, some texts by non-travellers call black Africans 'Indians'.) A common European confusion about rank in Africa is reflected in the homage to Oroonoko as prince, great man, captain, king. The term 'slave' itself was loosely used, as it is here for indentured servants, so the status of Behn's 'Indian slaves, that rowed us' remains uncertain.

This fluidity of terms was accompanied by considerable fuzziness of opinion. If there was almost no articulate anti-slavery opinion in Behn's time, there were no sustained pro-slavery arguments either; the two would grow up together, in counterpoint. Slavery was an inherited institution, seen with the shrugging or split minds with which people commonly view injustices or cruelties. Along with kidnapped Africans purchased in good faith, observers uneasily noted the right of owners to possess any child – just like a cow or horse, remarks the Allada visitor (p. 437), or, in Du Tertre's simile, like a fruit that grows in their ground (ii: 504). Reports are entirely frank about the low drudgery and wretched conditions of the slaves, who are treated – say Ligon, Warren, Thomas Tryon, and others – like dogs or worse than dogs. For some this was a moral issue, for others mere fact. Characterizations of the slaves as naturally 'brutish', as people dehumanized by Africa or their owners, or as better than some or many planters may occur not only in different accounts but sometimes in different passages within the same work. That Behn too gives somewhat inconsistent impressions of the slaves and also the Indians may be one of the better arguments for her presence in Surinam. An armchair traveller or tale-teller at home might have wanted to arrange her material for clearer effect.

At certain points, however, we can observe Behn arranging her scenes. As hero and colonists come into conflict, two brief passages, satiric outbursts, present anomalous moments, not just elaborations or fancies but genuinely at odds with what anyone saw or thought. At these moments we see the author's shaping hand, her conceptions of freedom, a small organizing principle added to her tale.

The first occurs when Oroonoko's planned escape collapses and the slaves abandon him. In his passionate speech against slavery – delivered to the men only – he appeals broadly to the meaning of manhood and condemns the collective unworthiness of the colonists, disparaging them in various ways as less than men, below 'wildest salvages', identical with 'vilest creatures'. When the slaves capitulate, however, he comes up with the idea of their natural inferiority, not treated 'like dogs' but 'dogs' themselves. The despised Christians are still ranked below 'honest men', 'men of honour', but the slaves are lower still:

> he was ashamed of what he had done, in endeavouring to make those free, who were by nature slaves, poor wretched rogues, fit to be used as Christians' tools; dogs, treacherous and cowardly, fit for such masters, and they wanted only but to be whipped into the knowledge of the Christian gods to be the vilest of all creeping things, to learn to worship such deities as had not power to make 'em just, brave, or honest.

The one thing he can imagine that could make them yet more contemptible is their conversion to Christianity, creating a fourth, bottom category, a combined maximal worst.

Despite the unusual violence of this polemic, such play with ideas of hierarchy is familiar. Slaves might be held up as better and more moral than their Christian owners, and they might certainly be seen as worse, a servile order of people incapable of liberty. What is unprecedented is Oroonoko's idea of Christianizing as a further degradation, not a benefit, and his vision of slaves 'whipped into the knowledge of the Christian gods'. This is precisely what wasn't happening in the English colonies, which were notorious for keeping such 'knowledge' from their slaves. Of the early observers of Barbados, Ligon writes angrily that the slaves are denied Christianity, and Biet writes disapprovingly that religion goes unmentioned: 'The masters never think of their slaves' souls.'[30] The colonists adopted extreme measures to stop the Quakers from including slaves at meetings, and when ordered from home to convert their slaves, they balked, insisting that it 'would not only destroy their property, but endanger the island', since 'the converted negroes grow more perverse and intractable'.[31] Why then this angry flourish?

Like Oroonoko's earlier scorn for the captain and his gods, it is an arresting challenge to Behn's Christian readers to consider how hollow and repulsive their religion might seem to a man of active principle. There seems a second reason, however, in the image of slaves forcibly 'whipped'. The narrator herself is not a freethinker. On the contrary, she has herself provided religious instruction to the couple, the standard farsighted thing to do. When she satirizes the men of Byam's council, she stresses their blasphemy, and accompanies the general intimation that they are not 'worthy the name of men' with the specific one that they 'originally were such, who understood neither the laws of God or man'. This last pairing calls us back to Behn's early idyllic passage on the Indians' reliance on 'simple Nature', without religion, which would cost their 'tranquillity', or law, which would 'teach them to know offence'. Lacking such innocence, Europeans need both religion and law, church and state. In their hands, however, religion and law are turned into instruments of oppression, here in Oroonoko's vision of forced conversions, soon after in his condemnation by a kangaroo court.

In the second satiric passage we hear the narrator's anger, as she mocks the political authority and, with a judicial phrase, the legal pretensions of Byam's council:

> But calling these special rulers of the nation together, and requiring their
> counsel in this weighty affair, they all concluded, that (damn 'em) it
> might be their own cases; and that Caesar ought to be made an example
> to all the Negroes, to fright 'em from daring to threaten their betters,
> their lords and masters, and, at this rate no man was safe from his own
> slaves, and concluded, *nemine contradicente*, that Caesar should be hanged.

Counterparts of Byam's ragtag militia, these brawling apostles of order
are presented as ludicrous, 'special rulers' indeed. On the surface, their
fears, their line of reasoning, and their decision seem entirely ordinary.
According to English slave law – or, more accurately, piecemeal regulations and opinions gradually codified into law in response to circumstances[32] – a strong bill of particulars could be brought against Oroonoko.
He has fomented and led an escape of three hundred slaves, representing a
huge loss of property and a threat to peace and stability, for such 'ill examples', as Behn notes, might have 'very fatal consequences'. In the resulting
pursuit, the fugitives have mounted a resistance and 'killed some, and
wounded a good many'. After these offences against property, public
order, and the persons of whites, whipping of the ringleaders, or worse,
might be expected. Moreover, Oroonoko is now openly threatening to kill
the deputy governor. Nonetheless, as Behn constructs her colony,
Oroonoko remains a friend and ally and the council's sentence is a travesty.

Behn's theme is honour, honourable understandings, rather than
law. Initially Trefry calls Oroonoko's kidnapping 'dishonourable', 'a
perfidy', and he says nothing further to clarify his status as royal or free
and hence beyond the law. In some ways, however, Behn's telling seems at
least as alert to practical considerations as a more rigid and stereotypical
exercise of planter cruelty. That the planter elite react with calm uncon-
cern and may have abetted the escape is thoroughly implausible,[33] but
leniency need not be. Oroonoko leads a flight, not a revolt, unaccompa-
nied by theft or violence, and escape is only a pipe dream, for the slaves are
retaken at once. In the real colonies, where all kinds of short or long
absences were an everyday form of resistance, runaways' intentions and
how long they remained at large guided the handling of cases, and time
limits (generally in months) were specified in the statutes. The fears the

narrator reports, admittedly irrational, reflect the hair-trigger susceptibility of the Barbados colony to rumours, especially about armed slaves
poised to raid or with supposed designs on white women. On the scene,
the insistent low Byam is 'the only violent man' against Oroonoko.

Second and more basic, if they sometimes had to be controlled and
punished as persons, the prior bedrock principle was that slaves were
property. The reason why law developed slowly in the English colonies
was that it infringed on the property rights of owners, who were presumed
to exert sole control, whether kind or cruel. When statute law had to be
developed and rebellious slaves were punished or executed, additional
laws stipulated, first, that owners be reimbursed, and, second, that they be
penalized if they protected their slaves, a natural and common practice,
reimbursement or not, when slaves were in short supply. Trefry, not
Byam, is the owner here, and he comes as a 'mediator' to safeguard his
slaves and then brokers the treaty with Oroonoko. Byam is not only acting
in a way that is intrusive and ill-judged, he is specifically declared to be
propertyless: 'he had nothing, and so need fear nothing'. Moreover, in this
incipient jurisdictional tension, he does not behave as a responsible
official, punishing by example to affirm public order, but is fawning, over-
bearing, vindictive.

If the narrative to here is not unnuanced, it shows one feature obviously foreign to any colonial context: physical assaults by blacks are casu-
ally tolerated, even praised as brave, and one important principle is not in
force, the inviolable nature of white bodies. This principle served to
extend police control over all slaves as it deepened racial stratification,
protecting any and all whites in nearly any circumstance. In early Surinam
it might have been loosely understood, expressed in local rules, but by
1688 Barbados law is categorical about the penalties to follow 'if any
Negro or Slave whatsoever, shall offer any violence to any Christian, by
striking or the like'.[34] Here, after the fighting, Byam calmly gives orders to
'bury their dead'. Oroonoko and Tuscan are whipped not for their armed
resistance but for his 'revenge'. There is no suggestion that Imoinda be
punished for wounding Byam and others, only some regret that he didn't
die. When Oroonoko is driven to vow his own revenge, though 'he could
not hope to live', no one expresses misgivings or comments at all. His own

code of honour is not endorsed, but there is nothing to oppose it. Byam's office is recognized – notably by Oroonoko himself – but he has shown unacceptable deceit and cruelty, and no sense of horror at a black threatening or raising a hand against a white, let alone harming him, affords him any protection.

It is at this juncture, to save himself, that Byam in effect takes cover in administrative and legal procedure. His earlier written contract was a mere ruse. When this appeal to law doesn't work – Willoughby's royal appointment allows Trefry to claim that Parham is 'exempt from law' – he simply has Oroonoko abducted and executed, with 'inhuman' justices (who but he could have appointed them?) standing by. Having landed in a blaze of monarchial glory, Oroonoko is passed down through the social ranks, and at the very bottom, among men compared unfavourably to Newgate transports, is the law, aggressively used to compel and dominate.

Behn's style parodies Byam's slickness and the council's bluster. When Byam calls for advice, his 'weighty affair' is merely his need to evade what he has brought upon himself and to flatter his council's self-importance. Their '(damn 'em) it might be their own cases' seems a fair self-assessment in men no less rash, blind to Oroonoko, and comically unheroic. What has them so exercised, shocked into sudden unanimity, is not a genuine principle but a bugbear, followed by an overreaction. Their sweeping decision to 'fright' all slaves from 'daring to threaten their betters, their lords and masters' – using someone they do not own – shows nervous alarm and a pompous insistence on a superiority to which they are not entitled. Like everything else they do, it also seems bad governance, tending to make them not more but less 'safe'. Trefry's protective attitude and Marten's repudiation of 'terrifying' his slaves offer a better paternalistic model of slavery that was practised by some planters sufficiently capitalized to be humane.[35] The older principle of slave property is supported in Behn's story; the emerging one, sometimes at odds with it, of colony-wide police power is viewed with suspicion, and Trefry calls its planned use in this case a 'tyranny'; the added principle that raised white bodies above the least hint or threat of the violence freely visited on black ones is waived entirely. In practice, the early colonial experience was that Behn's benign vision of slave ownership was unworkable.

Read against the colonial records, the idea of imposed conversion seems just a brief polemical moment, while the more complex imposition of law, if perhaps not very 'realistic', shows not only a sentimental preference for the noble protagonist and his values but some degree of engagement with evolving concepts and practices. Both abuses can readily be seen to extend Behn's theme of honour, with its self-imposed ethical standards, its voluntary recognitions and agreements. Just as those high personal ideals are twisted into means of manipulation, so the most basic institutions in the hands of the wrong people are deformed into instruments of persecution.

That these entail punishments ('whipped', 'hanged') may also point us down, to the emphasis throughout the story on invasive physical acts. The most developed scenes are of fraud, betrayal of trust, but there has also been the steady menace of force, violation of bodily integrity. For Imoinda, defending herself gently and modestly, it has been the escalating sexual threats of an unwilling erotic captivity, the advances made to her as 'Clemene', the expropriation of her childbearing, finally the threat of rape and brutality that leads her to accept a smiling death. For Oroonoko, much less gently, it has been the 'indignity' of bondage and whipping. He never speaks out to invoke his princely status, but we may note how often he is bound, untied, and bound again, before and during the tortures, and how fiercely, from the core, he has always objected. History records slaves who met gruesome deaths defiantly and nobly, but none who offered to stand untied unless they were whipped.

His body, of course, is a royal one, though after all we have seen of his principles and varying impulses this resonates somewhat distantly. His aristocratic virtues are unrecognized by newer breeds of men. Perhaps it might be argued that this is a woman's work not because it shows special sympathy toward women or presents a love story where no one saw any such thing, but because it places such reliance on a fragile fabric of personal understandings and allegiances and conveys such profound mistrust of the categorical and unseeing. The well-meaning colonists seem caught as well. That they find no standing ground before a rapidly consolidating system suggests a highly interesting colonial story that Behn didn't mean to tell. There remains something curious about a narrative so sensitive to coercion, entrapment, helplessness, that doesn't turn for its central metaphor to plantation slavery, doesn't quite think beyond the common frame that slaves might be many things, but not free. Yet perhaps we are in a better position to consider at what points and in what ways *Oroonoko* does confront slavery. What lures us is partly the world it portrays. Discovering more of its contexts can only make it a richer story.

NOTES

1 My thanks to the members of the Fellows' Seminar on Race and Gender at the National Humanities Center, 1993–4, and especially to Edna G. Bay, Luise White, David W. Wills, and Maureen Warner-Lewis for their expert guidance and their willingness to discuss confusing matters and obscure sources.

2 Aphra Behn's *Oroonoko*: occasion and accomplishment', in *Two English Novelists: Aphra Behn and Anthony Trollope* (Los Angeles, 1975), pp. 3–41.

3 *Women's Studies* 19 (1991), 159–81.

4 *Cassandra: The Fam'd Romance*, partially translated in 1652, and in full in editions of 1661 (cited here), 1664, 1667 and 1676.

5 'The romance of empire: Oroonoko and the trade in slaves', *Ends of Empire: Women and Ideology in Early Eighteenth Century English Literature* (Ithaca, 1993), p. 36.

6 *Relation du voyage fait sur les costes d'Afrique*, in *Receuil de divers voyages*, ed. Henri Justel (Paris, 1674), p. 16. I am grateful to Doina Harsanyi for help in checking my translation.

7 [Sieur D'Elbée], 'Journal du voyage aux isles, dans la coste de Guinee', in J. de Clodoré, *Relation de ce qui s'est passé, dans les Isles & Terre-Ferme de l'Amerique* (Paris, 1671), p. 422.

8 'Fact and fiction in Aphra Behn's *Oroonoko*', *Studies in the Novel* 20 (1988), 3. Rogers posits (p. 9) that Behn did research.

9 G. Debien and J. Houdaille, 'Les origines des esclaves aux Antilles', *Bulletin de l'IFAN* B, 26 (1964), 166–94; 'Journal d'un voyage fait par Jean Barbot', ed. G. Debien, M. Delafosse, and G. Thilmans, *Bulletin de l'IFAN* B, 40 (1978), 327.

10 *Histoire naturelle et morale des Iles Antilles de l'Amerique* (Rotterdam, 1658), translated by John Davies as *The History of the Caribby-Islands* (London, 1666), bk 2, ch. 6; Jean Baptiste Du Tertre, *Histoire générale des Antilles habitées par les Francois* (Paris, 1667–71), 2, 499–500. By the colonial policies formalized in the French Code Noir, slaves were co-religionists, baptized and encouraged to marry.

11 Richard Price, *First-Time: The Historical Vision of an Afro-American People* (Baltimore and London, 1983), pp. 120, 115–16.

12 J. G. Christaller, *A Dictionary of the Asante and Fante Language* (Basel, 1881); J. B. Anaman, *Fanti and English Instructor* (Cape Coast, 1902); J. Delaney Russell, *Fanti-English Dictionary* (London, 1910); J. Berry, *English, Twi, Asante, Fante Dictionary* (Accra, Kumasi, London, 1960); Michael Swithenbank, *Ashanti Fetish Houses* (Accra, 1969). Professor Ivor Wilks, Northwestern University, recalls hearing the expression '*atina* people' (*atina-fo*) for female harem servants (letter of 5 December 1992).

13 *Certain Considerations Relating to the Royal African Company of England* (London, 1680), pp. 8–9.

14 *A New and Accurate Description of the Coast of Guinea* (1705), ed. John Ralph Willis, J. D. Fage, and R. E. Bradbury (London, 1967), p. 420, and see also pp. 475–6; *Barbot on Guinea: The Writings of Jean Barbot on West Africa 1678–1712*, ed. P. E. H. Hair, Adam Jones, and Robin Law (London, 1992), p. 239. So among the Suriname maroons, Richard Price heard enslavement described as a breaking of hospitality: 'The whites just came . . . sat down and ate with them, gave them drink, danced a lot, and then carried them off to the ships' (*First-Time*, p. 29, n. 23).

15 A small collection of cases is gathered by Colin Palmer in *Human Cargoes: The British Slave Trade to Spanish America, 1700–1739* (Urbana, 1981), pp. 25–6.

16 Richard Price in *The Guiana Maroons* (Baltimore, 1976), p. 7, estimates that at its peak in 1665, English Surinam had 'forty to fifty profitable sugar estates'. Behn's story is closer to a fifteenth-century Spanish case cited by Rogers, p. 7, than to any reported incident nearer her own time.

17 Thomas Phillips, 'A journal of a voyage made in the Hannibal of London, 1693–94', in Elizabeth Donnan, ed., *Documents Illustrative of the History of the Slave Trade to America*, 1 (Washington, DC, 1930), 402–03; *Barbot on Guinea*, p. 272.

18 Richard Ligon, *A True and Exact History of the Iland of Barbados* (London, 1657), pp. 50–1; see also George Warren, *An Impartial Description of Surinam* (London, 1667), p. 19; Rochefort, *Histoire*, p. 322.

19 2: 502. See also Antoine Biet's harsh characterization of Barbados colonists in *Voyage de la France Equinoxiale en l'isle de Cayenne* (Paris, 1664), chs. 31–32.

20 Price, *Guiana Maroons*, pp. 23–4.

21 From BL Add. MS 12431, quoted in Richard Hart, *Slaves Who Abolished Slavery* (Kingston, Jamaica, 1985), 2: 13–14.

22 *Calendar of State Papers, Colonial, 1675–76*, no. 690.

23 Jerome S. Handler, 'Slave revolts and conspiracies in seventeenth-century Barbados', *New West Indian Guide* 56 (1982), 19–22, 34–5. Analogous troubles on Antigua in the 1680s are analysed by David Barry Gaspar, *Bondmen and Rebels: A Study of Master-Slave Relations in Antigua* (Baltimore, 1985), pp. 174–80.

24 Thomas Phillips in Donnan, 1: 403; and see *Barbot on Guinea*, p. 775.

25 Handler, pp. 20, 24.

26 Quoted in William M. Wiecek, 'The statutory law of slavery and race in the thirteen mainland colonies of British America', *William and Mary Quarterly* 34 (1977), 271–2.

27 *Impartial Description*, p. 19. *Great Newes from the Barbadoes* (London, 1676) contains an anecdote of a defiant captured rebel, but otherwise I have not found written accounts of particular deaths before Behn wrote.

28 Wylie Sypher, 'A note on the realism of Mrs Behn's *Oroonoko*', *Modern Language Notes* 3 (1942), 404–5; Laura Brown, pp. 60–1; Gaspar, p. 23. See also Price, *Guiana Maroons*, p. 26.

29 Donnan, *Documents*, 1, 402.

30 Ligon, p. 82; Biet, p. 67. That slaves would have to be given English instruction as well as baptized was cited both by planters, who blamed the slaves' incapacity, and by their critics, who said the planters feared giving them means to rebel.

31 'Gentlemen of Barbados to the Lords of Trade and Plantations' in *Calendar of State Papers, Colonial, 1677–1680*, no. 1535; see also *C. S. P, 1681–85*, no. 59. On their persistent refusal, see Gaspar, pp. 132–4.

32 A comparative study of the Spanish, French and British colonies appears in Elsa V. Goveia, 'The West Indian slave laws of the eighteenth century', *Revista de Ciencias Sociales* 4 (1960), 75–106; on early English slave law I have relied especially on Richard S. Dunn, *Sugar and Slaves: The Rise of the Planter Class in the English West Indies, 1624–1713* (Chapel Hill, 1972), pp. 238 ff., and Gaspar, pp. 134ff.

33 See H. D. Benjamins, 'Nog Eens: Aphra Behn', *West-Indische Gids* 2 (1921), 537. A strong anti-Willoughby faction is easily imagined, however, since colonists of every political stripe wanted autonomy and resented government interference with their livelihoods.

34 Barbados Act for the Governing of Negroes, quoted in Alan Watson, *Slave Law in the Americas* (Athens, 1989), p. 68. Gaspar, p. 136, cites 1702 Antigua penalties if a white of any station 'be any Way hurt . . . by any Slave's Resistance'.

35 George Marten's substantial earlier holdings on Barbados are noted by Dunn, p. 68.

PART IV ❧ BIOGRAPHY

14 Private jottings, public utterances: Aphra Behn's published writings and her commonplace book[1]

MARY ANN O'DONNELL

No one has ever accused Aphra Behn of hypocrisy. Her dedication to the Stuart kings and the Tory cause has never been questioned, and her published writings never falter in her support of Charles II and his brother James II. Even the last two poems published in her lifetime, *A Congratulatory Poem to Her Sacred Majesty Queen Mary, upon Her Arrival in England* and *A Pindaric Poem to the Reverend Doctor Burnet*, although directed towards Whigs, have a Tory bite.

Her sardonic welcome to Queen Mary in March 1689, a few short weeks before death silenced her, is forced from a Muse 'Sullen with Stubborn Loyalty'.[2] Her follow-up poem to Burnet, addressing him as 'Reverend Doctor' even after he may have attained his bishopric, taunts the loyal follower of William of Orange by comparing his attempts at converting her, both spiritually and politically, to the actions of a swain in pursuit of other pleasures:

> Your Language soft as Love, betrays the Heart,
> And at each Period fixes a Resistless Dart,
> While the fond Listner, like a Maid undone,
> Inspir'd with Tenderness she fears to own;
> In vain essays her Freedom to Regain:
> The fine Ideas in her Soul remain,
> And Please, and Charm, even while they Grieve and Pain.[3]

285

Behn also compares the arrival of King William, referred to only as Nassau, to the entrance of the Greeks into Troy, and tells Burnet that "'Tis to your Pen, Great Sir, the National owes / For all the Good this Mighty Change has wrought'. With wry irony tinged with bitterness, she allows that

> great *NASSAU* shall in your Annals live
>   To all Futurity.
> Your Pen shall more immortalize his Name,
>   Than even his Own Renown'd and Celebrated Fame.[4]

Behn was never a trimmer – not in 1673 when she spoke out in *The Dutch Lover* against the 'long, lither, phlegmatick, white, ill-favour'd, wretched Fop' who condemned her play *a priori* 'God damn him, for it was a womans'.[5] Not in 1682 when she praised Henry Howard, then Earl of Arundel, for voting 'not guilty' in the trial of his uncle Stafford.[6] Nor in the last year of her life when she added the lines to Cowley's *Silva* about her double right to be counted among the poets who have earned the garland.[7]

Behn seemed aware of her impending death from mid-1688 and made some of her most openly personal statements at this time. For example, in a cancelled passage in her Dedication to Maitland in *Oroonoko*, Behn expresses her sympathy with the dedicatee's Catholicism,[8] an avowal later reinforced in her *Poem to Roger L'Estrange*, in which she mourns the death of Stafford, a Catholic, likens him to Christ at Golgotha, and declares that Stafford

> Calm as a Dove, receiv'd a shameful Death,
> To Undeceive the World, resign'd his Breath;
> And like a God, dy'd to redeem Our Faith.[9]

To the end, she remained in all her public pronouncements a loyal Tory.

Yet recent identification of Behn's handwriting in a manuscript miscellany of satirical poetry reveals that Behn knew of and collected the scathing satires of the period, not just verses skewering her political and literary adversaries, but verses attacking those whom she praised publicly.[10] Bodleian MS Firth c.16 collects some of the most scurrilous poems from 1682 to early 1689, especially from 1685 to 1688, many of which later appeared in various printed anthologies from 1688 to the early years of the eighteenth century – such collections as the *Muses Farewel to Popery* and the various *Poems on Affairs of State*.[11] But many have never been printed, and remain in unique copy in this manuscript or have survived in only a scattering of manuscripts.[12]

Bodleian MS Firth c.16 bears the title 'Astrea's Booke for Songs and Satyr's' on the front cover along with three dates superimposed on one another: 1685, 1686, and 1688.[13] The first hundred pages, written in a hand not Behn's, contain an admixture of poems dating from between 1682 and 1685.[14] After the first hundred pages, several other hands, including Behn's, started to record poems from 1685 to 1689 in chronological order. The collection may have been intended as a copy text for other manuscripts, but no similar manuscript has yet been located, or perhaps it served as a source for individually copied penny dreadfuls. The address on the front cover of the manuscript – the address of the Duke of Norfolk in Paris – suggests that it may have been a collection to be sent to the Duke while he was abroad, but since there is no evidence of when the address was written on the cover, its purpose remains a mystery.

The poems break into several sometimes overlapping categories. There are poems of political and religious satire, often the two together. A second group includes a large number of libellous commentaries on the sexual mores of prominent political, social, and court figures of the mid-1680s. A third category surveys the literary and theatrical scene, often with political satire or obscene commentary. The poems do not represent any one political point of view, but rather mix the views of the emerging Whigs and supporters of William of Orange with those of loyal Tories. The collection gathered in 'Astrea's Booke' does not seem to have served as a quarry for Behn's poetical miscellanies of the 1680s since only two poems from Bodleian MS Firth c.16 are printed in any of Behn's collections: Etherege's 'Song on Bassett', a card game, and 'Cato's Answer to Labienus'.[15]

The poetical miscellany that Behn and others gathered makes interesting reading when placed against the public writings of Behn for the same period and when considered in light of the persons with whom she was known to have associated.

For example, in 1684, Behn worked with Robert Wolseley,[16] who made a small name for himself by bringing out the posthumous edition of Rochester's *Valentinian*, which included both his own preface in praise of Rochester and Aphra Behn's first-day Prologue. The poet Anne Lee Wharton had thanked Behn and Wolseley for their tributes to her kinsman Rochester,[17] and may indeed have been responsible for both the performance of *Valentinian* by the United Company and for Wolseley's publication of it.[18] In fact, Wolseley may have been the link between the two women at this time, but aside from trading poems, the two women do not appear to have formed any relationship prior to Anne Wharton's death in 1685.[19]

While Wolseley was on friendly terms with Anne Wharton, his relationship with the notorious Wharton brothers, especially William, reached the level of angry lampooning by 1687. Eight of the poems in Bodleian MS Firth c.16 illustrate Behn's keen interest in the literary battles of Robert Wolseley and William Wharton.[20] The war of words ended in Wharton's death a week after he was wounded by Wolseley in a dull in December 1687.[21]

A Whig supporter of some literary pretensions, William Wharton was a younger half-brother to Sir Thomas Wharton, husband of Anne Lee Wharton.[22] As Robert Wolseley and William Wharton entangled themselves in poetic battle, another poetaster intruded on Wharton's side, identified in 'Astrea's Booke' as Sir H. Hub–d and in Behn's hand as Sir Harry Hubert.[23] This is most likely Sir Henry Hobart, 4th Baronet, a minor courtier who was also slain in a duel, in 1697.[24]

The source of the hatred between Wharton, Wolseley, and Hobart is not clear, even from the poems. The feud had been raging for at least two years since in one of the poems, Hobart mocks Wolseley and sets the time frame for the dispute: 'At last you've shown your two years brooding spight.'[25] There are allusions to Dryden and to an incident at Peter's,[26] and some veiled references to treason. The source could also have been political, stemming from Wharton's defeat for a seat in Commons in 1685, or even personal, related to Anne Wharton's death, also in 1685.[27]

Or the feud could simply have begun as a battle of literary wits. The final entry on the battle, 'The Quarrel', a poem probably by Dorset,[28] indicates that Wolseley was once Wharton's instructor in the fine art of libellous verse and then traces the enmity to Wharton's rebellion against his tutor. Dorset explains that public acclaim of Wharton's rhymes inflated Wharton's already large ego, creating a breach between the former collaborators.[29] No matter what the causes of the feud, the enmity festered for two years and the war broke out close to the date of the duel in late 1687.

The first poem, Wolseley's slap at Sir Harry Hobart, is entered in Hand A, but Behn has added the ascription not found in other manuscripts, 'by Mr Wolsely'. This attack is a sophomoric representation of him as the new 'Man of Mode', with the first line addressed to 'Right Heir to Fluter; Fop of the last Edition'.[30] The poems are mild when compared to the other satires recorded in 'Astrea's Booke'. Wolseley is linked to Dryden when addressed as 'Squab Puppy' and mocked for his large shape; Wharton is described as sickly, rickety, frigid. Wolseley is satirized as Rochester's echo, one who appropriated cast-off remarks and rhymes that Rochester did not see fit to use for his poem of praise to Anne Wharton and his preface to *Valentinian*. Wharton writes:

> And treat Departed Souls with Witts Ragoos
> Write Verses to ladies when they're dead
> And Prefaces which tire Men to read . . .[31]

The 'Ragoos' reference echoes Wolseley's line to Anne Wharton as he evokes sensory experience, particularly that of taste to elicit the power of her poetry:

> The Rich Ragoust, wit's too profuse expence
> A flavor gives that conquers human sense
> A taste[e] too high for weak man to digest
> *Ambrosia* 'tis, on which Immortals feast . . .[32]

Wharton's reference to 'Prefaces which tire Men to read' is a clear allusion to the Preface to *Valentinian*.

Dorset's 'The Quarell' sketches the duel between Bob Bavius and Will Maevius.[33] On the surface, Dorset's tone is lightly satiric, suggesting that this poem was written before the duel between Wolseley and Wharton. However, this poem is re-titled 'The Duel' in later reprintings and several images suggest that Dorset is alluding to a real duel. For example, Dorset pretends to eschew violence: 'Of Blood & wounds let bolder Poets Ring'. He describes the battle between Wolseley, 'the Mac Ninny of ye Age', and Wharton, 'such a wretched Rhymer', as a duel of quills that is joined by the unnamed Hobart, 'That sneering scribbling Country knight'. The darker side of Dorset's wit shows in the description of the battle:

> Angry at their revolt, wth passion wild
> Bob Bavius swore ne'r to be reconcild
> And with his Pens Butt end, knocks Poor Will downe.[34]

Since Wharton died of a wound to the buttocks, the reference to the 'Pens Butt end' is either fortuitous or a cruel trivialization of a death blow. With Wharton's death, Wolseley left the country, and the versifiers turned their interests to other matters.

Along with his poem on the Wharton-Wolseley quarrel and his 'Catalogue of Ninnies', other Dorset poems figure prominently in 'Astrea's Booke for Songs and Satyr's', including a rare Dorset translation, 'The Innocent Conjugates', ('Enflamed with Love and Led by blind desires' with Latin original), and three other poems associated with Dorset.[35] While writing his poems into her commonplace book, Behn and her co-scribes were also capturing some of the lampoons circulating on Dorset. And Behn was paying public homage to him in several published works.

Among the lampoons that date to 1682, Dorset is described as abandoned in London by Mall Howard, a well known bawd somehow connected to the sprawling Howard family.[36] Another poem probably also composed in 1682, 'A Letter to Julian' ('Julian how comes it of late we see'), links Dorset with Chumley, Fleetwood Shepheard, and Frazier as would-be wits.[37] Dorset is again linked to Capt. Robert Julian and identified as one of the libellous poets of the time in the well-known

'Julian's farewell to the Muses' ('Mine and the Poetts Plague consume you all'):

> Nay tho Inspired with more than delphick fame
> My great Maeceas Awfull Dorsett came
> And as a mark of his Censorious Witt
> Paid double fees for what himself had writt.[38]

As if in answer to the satire on what Dorset 'had writ', Behn cites him in *A Pindarick Poem on the Happy Coronation of His Most Sacred Majesty James II* as the first Peer, 'A Hero' bearing the ivory sceptre before Mary of Modena. Hailed as 'Eternal Wit', Behn writes, 'His looks made good to day, all he e're spoke or Write'.[39] Three years later, in 1688, Behn published in *Lycidus* her 182-line 'Pastoral Pindarick on the Marriage of the Right Honourable the Earle of Dorset and Midlesex to the Lady Mary Compton', a poem that dates to 1685, when Dorset married as his second wife the daughter of the third Earl of Northampton.[40] The poem, a pastoral dialogue between Aminta and Damon, is a wedding gift from Behn to Dorset, 'A rural Hymeneal song'. Had the poet in the voice of Damon 'been blest with Flocks or Herd', the gift would have been richer. As Damon notes: 'But I, alas! can only offer song / Song too obscure, too humble verse / For this days glory to reherse.'[41]

Behn's public statment to Dorset is a generous offering of her verse to a fellow poet, recognizing his art in several ways. For example, since the poem is included in *Lycidus*, it is notable that the shepherd Damon alludes to Dorset as 'Lysidus'.[42] On Dorset's poetry, Behn notes: 'Soft were the Songs, which from his lips did flow, / Soft as the Soul which the fine thought conceiv'd.'[43]

In this epithalamium, Behn adds one additional tribute to Dorset that ties Dorset to the well-known review of ladies seeking to replace the Duchess of Portsmouth as royal mistress, variously titled 'Colin' or 'Colon' or 'A Satyr on Several Women' ('As Colin drove his sheep along'). This 1679 satire was widely anthologized in manuscripts of the period, including the British Library Harleian MS 6913, in which it is attributed to Dorset as Lord Buckhurst.[44] Stopping short of placing it in Dorset's canon, Brice Harris notes the similarity between the Colin

poem and Dorset's 'Faithful Catalogue of our Most Eminent Ninnies'.[45]
However, Behn carefully links the 'Catalogue' to Dorset when Damon
wryly responds to Aminta's question: 'But who inspir'd you a
Philosopher?':

> Old *Colin*, when we oft have led our Flocks
> Beneath the shelter of the shades and Rocks
> While other youths more vainly spent their time,
> > I listen'd to the wonderous Bard;
> > And while he sung of things sublime
> > > With reverend pleasure heard.
> > He soar'd to the Divine abodes
> > And told the secrets of the Gods.[46]

Behn surely did not choose either 'Lysidas' or 'Colin' by accident, and the
addition of 'Colin' as Damon's philosophic guide links Dorset to the 1679
satire on the court women.

While some of Behn's strongest public statements were reserved for
the most prominent of court women, Mary of Modena, second wife of
James II, not even she was spared in the pages of 'Astrea's Booke'.
Although Behn had dedicated *The Second Part of The Rover* to James in
1681, while he was still Duke of York, and had again addressed him in her
*Pindarick on the Death of Our Late Sovereign with an Ancient Prophecy on His
Present Majesty*, the first time Behn addressed Mary of Modena was in the
Coronation poem, in which the poet seems not to have enough adjectives
for '*LAURA*! the Chast! the Pious! and the Fair!'[47] When Behn again
addresses Mary of Modena, in the *Congratulatory Poem to Her Most Sacred
Majesty on the Universal Hopes of All Loyal Persons for a Prince of Wales*, it is to
congratulate her on her pregnancy when all hope was lost that the Queen
might conceive and bear a healthy child.[48] This poem was quickly followed by the *Congratulatory Poem to the King's Most Sacred Majesty on the
Happy Birth of the Prince of Wales* and her attack on Baber *To Poet Bavius* for
the poem he published on the royal birth. But it is in the first poem that
Behn's rhetoric exceeds all previous paeans as she pictures Mary of
Modena as the second Virgin Mary and the son she will deliver as a second
Messiah:

> Like the first sacred Infant, this will come
> With promise laden from the Blessed Womb,
> To call the wand'ring, scatter'd Nations home.
> Adoring *PRINCES* shall arrive from far,
> Inform'd by *ANGELS*, guided by his Star,
> The New-born Wonder to behold, and greet,
> And Kings shall offer Incense at his Feet.[49]

At the same time that Behn is publishing these effusive natal celebrations, Behn's fellow scribes are adding to 'Astrea's Booke' two poems on the pregnancy and three on the delivery. From the placement of the two pregnancy poems, they were entered in the commonplace book around the beginning of April 1688, since they follow poems on the death of Samuel Parker, Bishop of Oxford, which occurred on 21 March 1688.

The title of the first of these diatribes sums up the entire poem and illustrates one of the many rumours circulating about the pregnancy: "The Miracle. How the Dutches of Modena being in Heaven pray[d] the Virgin Mary that the Queen might have a Son And how Our Lady sent the Angell Gabriel with her smok Upon w[ch] the Queen Conceived. To the Tune of thou hadst better bin starved att Nurse".[50] The second piece, 'Loretta & Winifred', is a rare item found so far in only two other manuscripts and probably never printed; it combines the mock-ironic aspects of a miracle of the Virgin along with the other rampant slander, that James was not the Prince of Wales' father.[51]

With the birth, a new round of slanders emerged. Among the very last of the poems entered into 'Astrea's Booke' are 'Tom Tyler' ('Old Storys of a Tyler sing'); 'An Excellent New Song call'd The Prince of Darkness' ('As I went by St. James's I heard a bird sing'); and 'The Audience' ('The Critticks that pretend to Sense').[52] Instead of transcribing poems such as Dryden's 'Britannia Rediviva', Behn's co-scribes were recording the poems that awarded paternity to the unfortunately named Papal Nuncio, Father D'Adda:

> A Prince cam[e] in the Nick of Time
> Blest Dadda 'tis a Veniall crime
> That shall repair our breach of state.[53]

'The Prince of Darkness' spreads the story that the baby was born to an unknown mother at Whitehall and smuggled into the delivery chamber for a fake birth, hence the subtitle of the piece: 'Showing how the three Kingdoms may be Sett on fire by a Warming Pan'.

Behn may have guessed that the birth of the Prince of Wales would begin the fall of the House of Stuart, since she must have realized the enormous popularity and credibility these rumour-filled poems had among the common people. But even with the tide shifting against Mary of Modena and James II, even with her health failing, Behn drew a strict line between private jottings and public utterance.

This careful delineation between private and public is seen just before her death when Behn dedicated one of her last works to Hortense Mancini, Duchess Mazarine, niece of the French Cardinal. This was a significant dedication since Mancini's moment at court had passed with the death of Charles, despite her kinship with Mary of Modena. Behn's *The History of the Nun* has the subtitle *The Fair Vow-Breaker*, ironic since Mancini had fled France to avoid the stifling religious hypocrisy of her husband and found refuge in the Court and the bed of Charles II, who as a penniless exile had been rejected as her suitor by her manipulative uncle.[54]

Behn's address to the Duchess raises two key issues – sex and class:

> I was impatient for an Opportunity, to tell Your Grace, how infinitely one of Your own Sex ador'd You, and that, among all the numerous Conquest, your Grace has made over the Hearts of Men, Your Grace had not subdu'd a more entire Slave.

This 'humble Declaration', according to Behn,

> has cost me a great deal of Inquietude, for that Fortune has not set me in such a Station, as might justifie Pretence to the honour and satisfaction of being ever near Your Grace, to view eternally that lovely Person, and here [i.e. hear] that Surprizing Wit.[55]

Yet the portrait of Mazarine that appears in the 'Astrea's Booke' is among the more vicious pictures in the manuscript. In 'On the Ladies of Honor. 1686', a poem so libellous that it appears only in a handful of other manuscripts and has never been printed, the satirist observes Mazarine's favoured sexual position and compares her to 'Cleaveland, or Sidley, or Ugly fac'd Nelly' and goes on to explain how after exhausting her lovers, Mazarine goes to the 'Bassett table' not to play cards but to select yet another lover.[56] She is similarly libelled in 'The Prophesie':

> When Mulgrave shall leave off his Lust & his Pride
> And Cornwall his Pimp F–k with none but his Bride
> Than Mazarines Lechery shall be deny'd
>   And Popery [Out of this Nation shall Run].[57]

Behn's passionate dedication is curiously at odds with the portrait of Hortense Mancini scattered among the verses in her commonplace book. A sadness haunts the portrait of the admirer trying to see the beloved and please her with a few choice words, almost a parody of the courtly love tradition made doubly ironic through its offer of affection to a beloved of the same sex. Here Behn's sense of being blocked from the centre of political and social power, of being pushed to the periphery by sex and class echoes the lines in her wedding verse to Dorset and again in the *Pindarick Poem on the Happy Coronation* where she expresses a muted outrage at her marginalization:

> Oh Blest are they that may at distance gaze,
> And Inspirations from Your looks may take,
> But how much more their happier Stars they Praise,
>   Who wait, and listen when you speak!
> Mine for no scanted bliss so much I blame,
> (Though they the humblest Portion destin'd me)
>   As when they stint my noblest Aim,
>   And by a silent dull obscurity
>   Set me at distance, much too far
> The Deity to view, or Divine Oracle to hear![58]

Behn's open expression of devotion to one of the same sex is not unlike her poem 'To the Fair Clarinda', and Maureen Duffy cites that poem and the dedication to Mancini as evidence that 'Behn's sexual ambiguity seems to have grown stronger as she got older'.[59]

Among the many literary figures with whom Behn associated and who appear in the pages of 'Astrea's Booke', John Dryden is the most famous. Among the many pieces related to Dryden, one of the most interesting carries marginalia in Behn's own hand not found in any other manuscript copy.

Printed versions of this poem carry the title 'A Heroic Scene', but in Behn's commonplace book it is headed with the stage direction 'Enter old Olivers Porter, in Bedlam with Olivers Poett & Olivers ffidler'.[60] The poem records a discussion among the Porter in a madhouse, Dryden (called Johnny or Oliver's Poet, so named for his early support of Cromwell), and L'Estrange (called Hog, Hodge, or the fiddler, so named because Cromwell in a visit once found L'Estrange playing bass violin at a musical gathering with several other men).[61] In the poem, both Dryden and L'Estrange quickly talk about their shifting allegiances, with Dryden noting that 'A windmill is not fickle, for we find / That it is always constant to the wind.' L'Estrange boasts that 'Long my sly pen serv'd Rome.' The poem is exceedingly clever with echoes and paraphrases of Dryden's writings.[62]

Behn's marginal comments, clearly her own responses to the poem, include her guess at the author and support Dryden and L'Estrange. The first two comments appear when the fiddler, L'Estrange, claims to have shifted to Cromwell at the fall of Charles I to serve the Protector as a spy. To these charges, Behn replies 'A damnd Ly'.[63] Behn's next comment 'all nonsense' mocks the Porter's response to L'Estrange's alleged movement from King to Cromwell to King to Pope.[64] As L'Estrange speaks of his public allegiance to the 'English church' ('for yet it is not time I should declare / Lest fools to whom I write should be aware'), Behn has inked in 'a sly knave ye poet' and added after completing the notation '& a plaguy guess',[65] suggesting that L'Estrange was a closet Catholic and that she knew it.[66]

Among the other marginalia, two relate to the Popish Plot. As the Porter supports Titus Oates, citing 'ten proclimations and four sennatts votes', Behn writes 'the more shame for em'. Then, as the Porter sneers that Sir Edmund Bury-Godfrey 'kill'd himself when he was dead', Behn naively or disingenuously writes 'why so?',[67] seemingly unaware of the popular charge that Godfrey committed suicide even though evidence indicated that he was strangled and then run through by his own sword after he died.[68]

Behn's speculation on the author comes with the Porter's comment: 'I amongst madmen am confin'd, 'tis true / But I have more solidity than you.' Behn's response asserts: 'Ye line betrays the Author'.[69] Oddly here Behn seems to suspect the author to be mad Nat Lee, one who would have known Dryden's works and style well, and this suspicion is repeated with a twist when Behn later writes: 'None but Shad= & ye mad man coud have given such a reason.'[70] At this point, Behn probably sensed Shadwell's hand in this satire, and with irony paralleled the free Shadwell and the insane imprisoned Lee.

At the end of the poem, after the Porter hits L'Estrange and Dryden with Nell Gwyn's Bible,[71] the Porter, left on stage alone, comments: 'And whom men hate with ruin they'll pursue', to which Behn adds: 'Exelent principles'.[72] Summing up the porter's speech in which he notes that all wants are satisfied by the state and

> vacant place is still suppli'd
> With persons that are duly qualifi'd
> No favor raises a desertless knave,
> Nor infamy, nor yet the gold he gave,

Behn has the last words: 'a speech very proper for a mad man'.[73] Behn's legacy is a running commentary on a lampoon of two men she knew well, L'Estrange and Dryden, and she makes an attribution to Shadwell along with it.

This poem is positioned just a few pages after Behn's hand appears for the first time in 'Astrea's Booke', as she begins to enter a series of attacks on Dryden's conversion to Catholicism. The first entry in Behn's hand in this commonplace book is the beginning of a satire on Dryden's conversion, 'Bays His Blind Side' ('From Father Hopkins whose Veines did inspire him'), which is cancelled after Behn realized that Hand A had copied it earlier. Then she entered Dorset's 'To Mr Bays 1685', ('Thou Mercenary Renigade, thou Slave'). Immediately following, Behn enters in her own hand 'Another on Mr Bays', the attack on Dryden that she is alleged to have written, a poem that carries an ascription to her in a British

Library manuscript and that both Montague Summers and Janet Todd have printed in her collected works ('Scorning Religion all thy life time past').[74] The variants between the poem as printed by both Summers and Todd assure that the poem in 'Astrea's Booke' is not a copy of or the source for the other two versions. Behn's hand is even, with no indication of composition *in situ*, and the poem can reliably be judged to have been copied from another source. Although Behn is writing this poem into her commonplace book along with a series of attacks on Dryden's conversion, she gives the piece the title 'Another on Mr Bays', a title that signals no proprietary interest or claim of authorship.

In addition to the other extant manuscript versions of this poem, two other, shorter pieces in manuscript either derive from this text or perhaps present an ur-text. Each is four-lines, and each is a unique witness without attribution.[75] The first appears in the British Library MS ADD 27408 (fol. 82[V]) as 'On Dryden':

> Of all religions present & all past
> Thou long hast raild & chose the worst at last
> Its like thy selfe for so thoud didst before
> Raile at all women & then chuse a whore

The second appears in British Library MS Harl. 7319 (p. 422) and is entitled 'To Mr Bayes'. It is attached to the end of the well-known satire on Dryden attributed to Tom Brown 'Traitor to God & Rebel to thy Pen' although the abrupt change of meter and style indicates that it is not part of the Brown piece:

> Quarreling all Religions past
> Espous'd the Romish at ye last
> Just the Old Trick! Just what he did before
> Rail'd at all Women, Marry'd to a Whore

The fact that at least two other versions of 'Scorning Religion all thy life time past' were circulating at the time raises some questions. The four-line versions appear to be some kind of song that served another writer as a source for the extended version. The longer version could be a pastiche of couplets and stanzas circulating at the time.

Whatever the compositorial mode, there is still no evidence that Behn is the author. Behn's relationship with Dryden is known to have been good through this period: Dryden has published her Englished version of 'Oenone to Paris' in his *Ovid's Epistles* in 1680, and even though he added to later editions John Cooper's translation of the same work, he never omitted Behn's paraphrase. In 1685, Behn wrote directly of Dryden in her dedicatory letter 'To Lysander', which precedes *Seneca Unmasqued*, her translation of the maxims of La Rochefoucauld in her *Miscellany*. After lauding Rochester, Mulgrave, and Scroope for their easy style, she goes on to praise 'the Charming and Incomparable Mr Dryden, where wondrous wit, and wondrous judgement meeting they have given him the Glory of having out-done all Ages past, and undone those that shall arrive'.[76]

Dryden also wrote a prologue and epilogue to *The Widdow Ranter*, which were published in folio in 1689 at least several months before the play itself was published.[77] The timing of Dryden's publication suggests that Behn may have known of Dryden's kindness before she died. And finally, there is a considerable evidence that Behn herself died a Roman Catholic although it is arguable that she was not a Catholic in 1686 when Dryden converted.[78]

The witness of Bodleian MS Firth c.16 argues against Behn's authorship of this particular satire on Dryden for four reasons. First, the existence of two other four-line variants suggests that the piece appeared first as a song by one or more hands. Second, no other identifiable work of Behn's appears in this collection.[79] Third, this is a copy of the poem from another written source although the source could be Behn's own composition. And finally, Behn shows no inclination to own this work: even in the privacy of her own commonplace book, she neither signs the poem nor titles it 'Mine on Mr Bays'. The cool detachment of 'Another on Mr Bays' distances Behn from the pride or the shame of composition.

Dryden's name appears throughout the commonplace book, notably in one sequence of four linked poems relating to Etherege: two verse letters from Etherege to the Earl of Middleton, Dryden's 'Letter to Sir G. Etherege at Rattisbone', and a parody of Dryden's letter.[80] This parody had to have been written after May or June, 1686, when Dryden's verse letter to Etherege was written,[81] and it vehemently attacks Dryden's conversion, which Dryden himself appears to have alluded to in his epistle to Etherege.[82] The inverted epistle goes on to mock Dryden's attack in Rose Alley and his pummelling in *The Rehearsal* and compares Dryden favourably to 'that Looby' Elkanah Settle. In the last two lines, Dryden is told to 'Flourish until that Fatal Hour / You hear the Belgic Lion roar'. Behn must have remembered this sharp image of William of Orange in the Spring of 1688, when in her *Congratulatory Poem to Her Most Sacred Majesty on the Universal Hopes of All Loyal Persons for a Prince of Wales*, she writes:

> Methinks I hear the Belgick *LION* Roar,
> And Lash his Angry Tail against the Shore.
> Inrag'd to hear a *PRINCE OF WALES* is Born:[83]

The list of contemporary poets and players, courtesans and courtiers who fill the pages of 'Astrea's Booke' is long. There is more to mine from this manuscript since the works are arranged chronologically, making it possible to look at some of what Behn was recording or reading while composing the works of her final years. Onc can only wish that Behn had spent more time writing comments in the margins and adding identities of authors almost certainly known to her. But in 'Astrea's Booke', she does allow us explore what she was thinking in the four years before her death.

NOTES

1 This expands the paper 'Mining the manuscript: Bod. MS Firth c.16 and contemporary literary criticism' given at the conference on 'Aphra Behn: politics and representation' at the University of East Anglia, 12–13 July 1991. I gratefully acknowledge the kind permission of the Bodley Library, University of Oxford, to quote extensively throughout this paper from Bod. MS Firth c.16.

2 Line 38. See Janet Todd, ed. *The Works of Aphra Behn*, vol. 1 (Columbus, 1992), pp. 304–7 and notes (hereafter cited as Todd); Germaine Greer, ed. *The Uncollected Verse of Aphra Behn* (Stump Cross, 1989), pp. 159–62 and notes (hereafter cited as Greer).

3 Todd, 1: 308.

4 Todd, 1: 309–10.

5 'An epistle to the reader', *The Dutch Lover* (London, 1673), A4ᵛ.

6 See the Dedication to Howard in *The City-Heiress* (London, 1682)

A2ʳ–A33ʳ. Behn identifies William Howard, Viscount Stafford only as the 'Great Sufferer' and does not directly supply the circumstances of the 'not guilty' vote. However, Henry Howard, Earl of Arundel and Lord Mowbray, was the only member of the Howard family to vote 'not guilty' when Stafford was tried before the House of Lords as one of the five Popish Lords implicated by Titus Oates and convicted by a vote of 55–31. It was Stafford who escorted Henry Howard when he was summoned to Parliament *in vitam patris* in January 1677/8. Stafford was Henry Howard's great-uncle.

7 Lines 586–94. See Todd, *Works*, 1: 325; Greer, p. 127.

8 The passage survives only in the Bodleian copy. See Gerald Duchovnay, 'Aphra Behn's religion', *Notes and Queries* 221 [n.s.23] (1976), 235–7.

9 *A Poem to Sir Roger L'Estrange on His Third Part of the History of the Times Relating to the Death of Sir Edmund Bury-Godfrey* (London, 1688), A4ʳ–A4ᵛ. Todd, 1: 291–3.

   See also M. A. O'Donnell, 'Aphra Behn', *Women Writers of the Seventeenth Century*, ed. Katharina Wilson and Frank Warnke (Athens, 1989) p. 343. Stafford was the known Catholic. If Behn were speaking from the Protestant point of view, it can be said that Stafford died to save that faith. But would Behn have then compared Stafford to Christ in the use of 'like a God' and in the next stanza where she terms Tyburn 'Golgotha'? One can only conclude that Behn was identifying with the religion of Stafford and may indeed have accepted L'Estrange as a Catholic. For further discussion see my 'Experiments in narrational stance, characterization, and tone in the prose fiction of Aphra Behn', Ph.D. Diss., Fordham University 1979, pp. 13–24.

10 See my 'Bodleian MS Firth c.16: A verse miscellany of Aphra Behn', *English Manuscript Studies: 1100–1700*, ed. Peter Beal and Jeremy Griffiths, vol. 2 (Oxford, 1990), pp. 189–222. There, I present a handwriting comparison and a bibliographical description of the physical manuscript along with some speculation on how and why it was put together. Appendices list the poems in the collection and modern printings of them.

11 For modern printings of some of these poems, see Howard H. Schless, ed. *Poems on Affairs of State*, vol. 3: 1682–5 (New Haven, 1968); Galbraith M. Crump, ed. *Poems on Affairs of State*, vol. 4, 1685–8 (New Haven, 1968); William J. Cameron, ed. *Poems on Affairs of State*, vol. 5, 1688–97 (New Haven, 1971); John Harold Wilson, *Court Satires on the Restoration* (Columbus, 1976); Margaret Crum, *First-Line Index of English Poetry, 1500–1800, in Manuscripts in the Bodlelian Library* 2 vols. (Oxford, 1969).

The volumes of the Yale *Poems on Affairs of State* will hereafter be cited as *POAS* with the volume number.

12 In the course of transcribing the poems for an edition, I have collated the poems against versions in over fifty other manuscripts and searched manuscript collections for unrecorded copies and printed books for published versions.

13 Harold Love groups this manuscript with several others under the rubric 'accession miscellanies', which he defines as 'collections that present retrospective surveys of the satire of a particular reign or reigns on the occasion of the beginning of a new one'. *Scribal Publication in Seventeenth-Century England* (Oxford, 1993), p. 269.

14 This hand, which I call Hand A, is the other predominant hand in the manuscript.

15 The correspondence between the text that Behn printed in *Lycidus* (1688) and the manuscript text of 'Cato's Answer to Labienus' suggests that the MS is the source of the printed version. This poem is attributed to Capt. John Ayloffe in the 1702 *POAS*, but the evidence points otherwise. First, I doubt Behn would publish a poem by a Rye House Plotter. Second, if she did, she would not take the care with the text that she did with this, noting in the 1688 publication that she was correcting the text since it was butchered in Higden's translations of the *Tenth Satyr of Juvenal* – a 1685 volume to which Behn also contributed a poem. Third, she speaks of the writer in the present tense in her advertisement about the poem in *Lycidus*, but Ayloffe was dead by then. In addition, a 1790 reprint of this poem attributes it to Robert Wolseley although ascriptions a hundred years after the fact are rarely reliable.

16 Wolseley's name also appears in older documents spelled 'Ouseley'. He was the son of Sir Charles Wolseley, a prominent Cromwellian. Wolseley may also be the author of one of the songs from *The Luckey Chance*, 'Oh! Love, that stronger art than wine.' *The London Stage* assigns it to 'Ouseley' with music by John Blow, based on its inclusion in *The Theatre of Music*, 4th book, 1687. The poem also appears in the Rosenbach Library MS 239/16 as 'A song by Col. Ousley'. The ascription does not appear in the 1687 printed text even though another of the songs is assigned to 'Mr. Cheek'.

17 Rather than being a response to Behn's Prologue, Wharton's 'To Mrs A. Behn, on What She Writ of the Earl of Rochester' ('In pleasing Transport rap't my Thoughts aspire'), is Wharton's thanks for Behn's eulogy 'On the death of the late Earl of Rochester' ('Mourn, mourn, ye Muses, all your loss deplore'). Wharton's poem to Behn was first printed in *A Collection of Poems by Several Hands . . .*, 1693. Behn printed her eulogy for Rochester

in 1685 in her *Miscellany* although it surely dates to the summer of 1680.

Behn printed 'Mrs Wharton to Mr Wolseley' ('To you, the generous task belongs alone') in *Lycidus*, 1688 and followed it immediately with Wolseley's 'Answer to the forgoing Copy' ('While soaring high above *Orinda*'s flights'). It is odd that Behn did not include Wharton's poem to herself in any of her published verse miscellanies even though she was aware of Wharton's unpublished piece and responded to it in 1684 in her *Poems upon Several Occasions*, 'To Mrs W. on her Excellent Verses Writ in Praise of Some I had Made on the Earl of Rochester' ('Enough, Kind Heaven! to purpose have I liv'd'). For an interesting discussion of Wharton's poem to Behn, see Maureen Duffy, *The Passionate Shepherdess* (London, 1977), pp. 194–8.

18 The first-day Prologue was published as a broadside along with an 'Epilogue by a Person of Quality' in February 1683/4. Luttrell dated his copy, now in the William Andrews Clark Library, '20 Feb. 1684/3'. Behn's Prologue was also reprinted in the 1685 edition of *Valentinian*, which contains Wolseley's anonymously published twenty-four page 'Preface concerning the author and his writings'. See my *Aphra Behn: An Annotated Bibliography of Primary and Secondary Sources* (New York, 1986), A16 and BB12.

19 I am most grateful to Susan Hastings for sharing with me her extraordinary knowledge of the Wharton family. For fuller information on the Whartons, and especially on Anne Wharton, see *The Surviving Works of Anne Wharton*, ed. Germaine Greer and Susan Hastings (Stump Cross Books, forthcoming).

20 The poems are 'A Familiar Epistle Directed to his Worthy Friend Sir Frivolous Insipid alias Sir H: Hub–d', by Mr Wolseley ('Right Heir to Fluter; Fop of the last Edition'), pp. 228–30; 'A Short Answer to a Laborious Triffle alias Bobbs Well Timed Epistle', by Harry Hubert ('Squab Puppy, who canst bark but never bite'), p. 231; 'A Familiar Answer to a late Familiar Epistle Humbly Addressed to the Best of Poets Alias the Worst', by Mr Wharton ('Welcome my honest long expected friend'), pp. 232–4; 'A Second Familiar Epistle . . . in Answer to His much Respected Friend ye Sieur Whiffle', by Mr Wolseley ('Daily disgracer of our English satire', pp. 234–8); 'A Postscript' ('Finish me one task more for Critic muse'), pp. 238–40; 'For Sir Frivolous Insipid' ('To thy first stanza, poetry laid by'), pp. 240–1; 'A Final Answer to All that the Laborius Triffle Has or May Write' ('That so much rhyme you in one month have writ'), pp. 241–3. The final poem 'The Quarrel', which is also known as 'The Duel', ('Of Chineus and Dametus sharper fight') is attributed elsewhere to Charles Sackville, 6th Earl of Dorset, and is recorded on pp. 243–5.

All but one of these were published in 1698 in *Poems on Affairs of State*. There is only one other complete transcript of these that I have so far located, Yale MS Osborn Shelves b 219, which probably served as the copy-text for the 1698 publication. Yale MS Osborn Shelves fb 108 contains three of the pieces; Folger MSS X.d.182–6 contain five.

21 Brice Harris cites the Gaol Delivery Records in *Middlesex County Records* (1892) in support of the date. The records indicate that the duel was fought on 9 December 1687, that Wolseley 'slew and murdered [Wharton], by giving him with a rapier a mortal wound in his left buttock', that Wharton died on 14 December, and that Wolseley was 'outlawed' for 'failing to appear to answer the indictment'. Harris, *Charles Sackville, Sixth Earl of Dorset: Poet and Patron of the Restoration*, Illinois Studies in Language and Literature 26, no. 3–4 (Urbana, 1940), pp. 11–12. Ebsworth dates the duel to December 1689 (see Schless, *POAS* 3:505), Ebsworth may have confused William with his more disreputable half-brother Col. Henry Wharton, who also died in a duel, in October 1689. See John Harold Wilson (*Court Satires of the Restoration*, pp. 292–4) on the Wharton family. Wilson records a reference in the *Hatton Correspondence* to an earlier duel, in February 1680, between a son of Sir William Poulteney and 'young Warcup' in which Henry Wharton was seriously injured.

22 Only a few pieces known to be his survive. See 'A New Ballad', 1683 ('Twere folly if ever') in *POAS* 3:505–10.

23 Bod. MS Firth c.16, pp. 228, 231.

24 See Cameron, *POAS*, 5:502n, where he notes that Hobart later became a prominent Whig leader of the Rose Club, in the mid-1690s. Wilson in *Court Satires* prints 'Julian's farewell to the coquets', dated September 1687, a poem also included in Bod. MS Firth c.16. This poem includes a passage on a Henry Hubbard, whom Wilson identifies as Henry Hobart (1658–98). The poem identifies him as one of the tribe of scribblers and lover of 'Doll' Mason, daughter of Sir Richard Mason and sister of the infamous Anne, Lady Brandon, cast wife of Charles Gerard, Lord Brandon. For more information on Doll Mason and her friendship with Anne Wharton, see Greer and Hastings, forthcoming.

    Another candidate is Sir Henry Herbert, Baron Herbert of Cherbury, who was also active in Whig circles until his death in 1691.

25 'A Short Answer', p. 231, line 2.

26 A coffee house frequented by Whigs. In 1682, after Ford Grey, Lord Grey of Werke, disarmed Christopher, Duke of Albemarle, in a duel, friends of Albemarle tried to provoke brawls with Grey's friends at Peter's. (Cecil Price, *Cold Caleb* [London, 1956], p. 73.)

27 A possible additional motive is supplied by a passage in Dorset's 'A ffaithfull Catalogue of Our Most Eminent Ninnies' (Bod. MS Firth c.16, pp. 201–14, lines 262–326; also in *POAS* 4:191–214). In this passage, one Herbert, whom the editor Galbraith Crump identifies on the basis of a manuscript annotation as Henry Herbert, later Lord Cherbury, is linked with Wolseley as sharing the same mistress, Lady Elizabeth Gerard, widow of the notorious drunk, fifth Lord Gerard. While the name 'Herbert' is clearly inscribed in 'Astrea's book of songs and satyrs' in Hand A, it is still possible that Hobart, not Herbert, was intended. See also above, n. 24, which discusses a link between Hobart and Dorothy Mason.

28 The poem is attributed to Dorset by Brice Harris, pp. 110–11. See also John Harold Wilson, *The Court Wits of the Restoration*, (1948; rpt. New York, 1967), p. 195, where he accepts Harris's ascription to Dorset, but confuses William Wharton with his father, Philip, Lord Wharton.

29 Not everyone had a high opinion of William Wharton's rhymes. In a diatribe dating to the Summer of 1686 addressed to the successor of the notorious Secretary to the Muses, Capt. Robert Julian, 'To Capt: Warcop' ('Here take this Warcop', Bod. MS Firth c.16, p. 70), we read a slap at Wharton, comparing him to one of Behn's poetical enemies:

> Baber has losst the Panigerick Straine
> And now to Balladmaking turnes his Braine
> Att wich Will Wharton long has Toyld in Vaine
> From that Dull Fop what Coud expected bee
> The Dullest of that senseless ffamely.

Warcop succeeded Capt. Robert Julian as Secretary to the Muses and purveyor of the kinds of poetry Behn and her colleagues were recording in 'Astrea's Booke'. Warcop is probably the 'young Warcup' involved in the duel in which Henry Wharton was injured (see n. 21). Wilson reprints the poem in *Court Satires*, pp. 159–66.

30 The next poem in the literary war follows a half-page intervention, and again it is written by Hand A, and again Behn's hand adds the attribution 'by Sr Harry Hubert' and the additional '3rd to Mr Wolsely'. This is followed by 'A Familiar answer to a late familiar epistle . . .', which Behn again notes 'by Mr Wharton', adding that this poem is 'To Mr Wolsely ye 2d' as if to indicate that it predates the preceding poem.

31 In 'A familiar answer to a late familiar epistle . . .', lines 65–6. I am most grateful to Susan Hastings for pointing out to me the reference to Wolseley's poem to Anne Wharton.

32 In Behn's *Lycidus* (London, 1688), H2ᵛ (p. 100).

33 This poem is copied in Behn's hand. Dorset's reference to Wharton as Maevius and Wolseley as Bavius may be the source of Behn's use of the opprobrius 'Bavius' for Baber in her answer to his *To the King, Upon the Queen's Being Deliver'd of a Son* the following year.

34 Bod. MS Firth c.16, p. 224, lines 43–5.

35 'The Opinion' ('After thinking a fortnight of Whig and of Tory'); 'Song' ('This making of bastards'); and 'To Mr Bayes' ('Thou mercenary renegade, thou slave').

36 The poems in Bod. MS Firth c.16 in which Dorset's pining for Mall Howard is satirized, all dating to 1682, are 'Song' also known as 'A court satire' ('Alas for poore St James Park') and 'Dorsetts lamentation for Moll Howards absence' ('Dorset no gentle Nymph can find'). For brief biographical sketches of Mall (or Moll) Howard, see Wilson, *Court Satires*, pp. 252–4 and Todd's edition of Behn's poetry (*The Works of Aphra Behn*, vol. 1), p. 458. Behn most likely is the author of the poem 'A Letter to the Earl of Kildare, disswading him from marrying Moll Howard'.

37 Bod. MS Firth c.16, pp. 10–11.

38 Bod. MS Firth c.16, p. 53, lines 31–4.

39 Lines 495–505. Todd, 1, 213; Greer, p. 48.

40 See Todd, 1:275–80 and notes.

41 Lines 171, 176–8. Todd, 1:280.

42 The spelling 'Lysidus' is used in the 'Voyage to the Isle of Love' attached to *Poems upon Several Occasions*. There Lisander writes to his friend Lysidus about his pursuit of Aminta, a name used again in this poem. The Lady Mary Compton is called 'Clemena', close to the name Behn used in 1688 for Imoinda in *Oroonoko*. Behn's reference to Creech as Daphnis in this poem is noted by Janet Todd, but not the reference as Lysidus. See *Works*, 1:433. Maureen Duffy, on the other hand, ignores Daphnis but identifies the shepherd Damon as Ravenscroft, Aminta as Behn, and Colin as Cowley. (*The Passionate Shepherdess: Aphra Behn 1640–1689* (London, 1977, p. 120.) For more on 'Colon', see below.

43 Lines 107–13. Todd, 1:278.

44 For modern printings see Wilson, *Court Satires* and *POAS 2*, 167.

45 Harris, pp. 82, 238.

46 Todd, 1: 278.

47 Line 41. Todd, 1: 201; Greer, p. 34. In the fifth stanza (lines 97–8), as Behn summons the Royal couple awake, she urges Mary 'Arise ! / From joys too fierce for any sense but Thine', or as Janet Todd notes (1: 202 and 418): 'Behn suggests that the pleasures of James' marital bed are so intense that only someone superhuman could endure them.'

48 The Queen had a history of miscarriages. Of her four live births, no child had survived to age four. It had been widely rumoured that in 1668 Lord Carnegy, Earl of Southesk, had deliberately transmitted venereal disease to James, then Duke of York, through Lady Southesk to avenge Lady Southesk's affair with James and to prevent any Catholic succession. See *POAS* 4:236–7.

49 Lines 13–19. Todd, 1: 294; Greer, p. 96.

50 First line: 'You Catholick Statesmen and Churchmen Rejoyce'; Bod. MS Firth c.16, p. 259. This was widely printed after the Glorious Revolution.

51 First line: 'Come al[l] tricking Papists, Abbess & Nun'; Bod. MS Firth c.16, pp. 261–2. The only other manuscript copies of this located so far are Bod. MS Douce 357 and BL Add. MS 29497.

52 Bodleian MS Firth c.16, pp. 295–6, 300–1, 301–3. All three are reprinted in *POAS*, 4, where 'The audience' is attributed to George Stepney.

53 'Tom Tyler', lines 13–15.

54 See Toivo David Rosvall, *The Mazarine Legacy: The Life of Hortense Mancini, Duchess Mazarine* (New York, 1969).

55 (London, 1689), A2ᵛ–A3ᵛ.

56 Bod. MS Firth c.16, p. 115, lines 5–14.

57 Bod. MS Firth c.16, p. 257, lines 5–14. This poem also is found in British Library MSS Harl. 6914 and 7317, Bodleian MSS Firth c.15 and Eng. poet. c.18, the Ohio State Choice Collection, and Yale Osborn fb 108. The poem was printed in 1689 in *The Muses Farewel to Popery*.

58 Lines 292–301. Todd 1: 208; Greer, pp. 41–2.

59 *The Passionate Shepherdess*, p. 277.

60 This poem is reprinted as 'A Heroic Scene' in Crump , *POAS* 4: 80–90 with most, but not all, the marginalia.

61 See *POAS* 4: 80, note at the subtitle.

62 Many of these echoes are recorded in the notes in Crump, *POAS* 4: 80–90.

63 Bod. MS Firth c.16, p. 105, lines 21, 24.

64 Bod. MS Firth c.16, p. 105, line 39. This marginal notation does not appear in *POAS* 4: 82.

65 Bod. MS Firth c.16, p. 107, lines 96–9. What appears to the editor of *POAS* as a cancellation of the last four words is actually an addition of these words over an underscoring.

66 See above for the discussion of Behn's attitude toward L'Estrange's religion.

67 Bod. MS Firth c.16, p. 108, lines 125–7.

68 In 1688, Behn published her *Poem to Sir Roger L'Estrange on His Third Part*

of the History of the Times; Relating to the Death of Sir Edmund Bury-Godfrey, praising L'Estrange's work. In this Third Part, L'Estrange again asserted, in the face of massive evidence to the contrary, that Godfrey had killed himself.

69 Bod. MS Firth c.16, p. 105, lines 41–2. This marginal notation is also not reported in *POAS* 4: 82.

70 Bod. MS Firth c.16, p. 107, lines 112–15.

71 Montague Summers identifies Oliver's porter as one Daniel, a very tall Irishman, who lost his mind in religious frenzy and ended up in Bedlam. Supposedly among his possessions was a Bible given to him by Nell Gwyn. *The Works of Aphra Behn*, 1: 456.

72 Bod. MS Firth c.16, p. 110, lines 215–16.

73 Bod. MS Firth c.16, pp. 110–11, lines 228–34.

74 This poem appears also in BL MS Add. 38671, where it is entitled 'A satyr on Doctor Dryden by Mrs Bhen' in what appears to be a near-contemporary hand. Montague Summers (*The Works of Aphra Behn* 5: 435–6), stating that his copy text derived from a transcript of a manuscript copy later lost, printed a 31-line version, and based on a reference in the *Historical MSS. Commission Third Report*, derives the title and states that a couplet is missing. Janet Todd has recently located Summer's probable source in the Westminster Diocesan Archives (see Todd, 1: xlvi, 231, and notes).

   The version in Bod. MS Firth c.16, inscribed in Behn's own hand, includes the missing couplet as does the version in BL MS Add. 38671. The two missing lines from Bod. MS Firth c.16 are

   > A lewd old atheist some religion owne,
   > Yet on (to show his judgement) worst than none.

   A copy of the page containing this poem from the manuscript is reproduced on p. 194 of my article in *English Manuscript Studies*.

75 I gratefully acknowledge the kind permission of the British Library to quote from BL MS Add. 27408 and BL MS Harl. 7319.

76 Todd, 4: 4. Behn's *Miscellany* was entered in the Term Catalogue for Easter 1685, several months before it was apparent that Dryden had converted. Even so, this is strong praise indeed and is never in later prefaces mitigated or repudiated.

77 See my *Aphra Behn*, A38.

78 See above, p. 286.

79 Sara Heller Mendelson (*The Mental World of Stuart Women* [Amherst, 1987], p. 174) attributes 'Caesar's Ghost' from this manuscript to Behn,

presumably on the basis of a cancelled signature at the end of the poem, but the evidence points to this poem being copied from another source. Indeed, the 'other source' could be Behn's foul papers, but nothing within the poem ties it to her.

80 The first three of these poems were widely circulated in manuscript and were printed in *The History of Adolphus* (1691), a fairy tale followed by an anthology of poems, probably compiled by George Granville since most of the poems are his. Along with the Dryden-Etherege poems there are ten of Behn's poems, two not previously published. Since Granville was a dedicatee of one of the last works published in Behn's lifetime, *The Lucky Mistake*, it may be speculated that Granville used Behn's commonplace book as his source for the Etherege-Dryden poems. Vinton Dearing in the textual notes to *The Works of John Dryden*, vol. III: Poems 1685–92, pp. 556–9, places Bod. MS Firth c.16 and *The History of Adolphus* in direct lines in the stemma.

The fourth poem, the parody 'To you who hang like Mecha's tomb' follows the first three in several manuscripts of the period and was printed in 1724. See James Thorpe, ed. *The Poems of Sir George Etherege* (Princeton, 1963), pp. 118–19.

81 James Anderson Winn, *John Dryden and his World* (New Haven, 1987), p. 611, n. 84. One of Dryden's sons was at this time working for Charles Middleton, 2nd Earl Middleton, Secretary of State for Scotland (Winn, p. 421), to whom Etherege had written his two verse epistles.

82 Winn, pp. 611–12, n. 85.

83 Lines 44–8. Todd, I: 298; Greer, p. 100.

15 New light on the background and early life of Aphra Behn[1]

JANE JONES

Aphra Behn gives some details about her family in *Oroonoko*.[2] Her father died at sea, on his way to become Lieutenant General of Surinam. His widow, with Aphra, her sister, and young brother continued to Surinam, and then returned to Europe without the wealth they had hoped to acquire. There are three known accounts of her origin by her contemporaries. One is in the preface to her works published in 1696[3] by 'One of the Fair Sex' 'She was a gentlewoman by birth, of a good family in the City of Canterbury in Kent, her paternal name was Johnson.' Another is in a marginal note to a poem *The Circuit of Apollo* written after Aphra Behn's death by Anne, Countess of Winchelsea:[4]

> Mrs Behn was daughter to a barber, who liv'd formerly in Wye, a little market town (now much decay'd) in Kent. Though the account of her life before her works pretends otherwise; Some persons now alive do testify upon their knowledge that to be her original.

The third is in Sir Thomas Culpepper's *Adversaria*:[5]

> Mrs Aphara Bhen was born at Canterbury or Sturry, her name was Johnson. She was foster sister to the Colonell her mother being the Colonell's nurse.[6] She was a most Beautifull Woman and a most excellent poet.

He refers to her again in *Adversaria*:[7]

> BEENE the famos female POET did 29 April 1689. Her mother was the Colonell Culpeper's nurse and gave him suck for some time. Mrs

310

Been was born at Sturry or Canterbury, her name was Johnson, so that
she might be called Ben Johnson. She had also a fayer sister maryed to
Cpt. Write their names were Franck and Aphra was Mr Beene.

The entry in the *Dictionary of National Biography* is by Sir Edmund Gosse,
and claims that a barber of Wye, John Johnson and Amy his wife baptized
a daughter, Aphra, on 10 July 1640.[8] An amateur historian[9] later checked
Wye Parish Register, and discovered there were no Johnson baptisms
between 1631 and 1665: the entry for 10 July 1640 actually reads 'Afara
the daughter of John and Amy Amis', and the father's trade is not shown.
He also checked the Burial Register and found that Afara the daughter of
John Amis was buried on 12 July 1640.

There is a recent biography *Reconstructing Aphra* by Angeline
Goreau.[10] She comments on the rarity and significance of the name
Aphra,[11] whereas Parish Registers show it to have been a vogue name of
the period, spread across all classes. Her description of Kent with 'its
gentle hills green in winter and summer' and 'the same families inhabiting
the same houses for generations'[12] suggests a superficial knowledge of an
often bleak county and its often mobile inhabitants. Her reconstruction of
Aphra's family, with the theory that Aphra was the possible illegitimate
daughter of Lady Willoughby adopted by the Johnsons could have been
suggested by her mis-reading of 'fayer sister' in Sir Thomas Culpepper's
note as 'foster sister'.[13]

There is another recent biography *The Passionate Shepherdess* by
Maureen Duffy.[14] She searched the Parish Registers of Canterbury,
Sturry, and surrounding areas for the baptism of an Aphra Johnson, and
finding one at Harbledown on 14 December 1640, the daughter of
Bartholomew and Elizabeth, assumed this must be the one, despite the
fact that, according to her, this Aphra Johnson was daughter to an
innholder.[15] Examination of the Marriage Registers[16] shows there were
other Aphra Johnsons in the area, and bearing in mind the great losses in
ecclesiastical records between 1640 and 1660, it is probable several more
went unrecorded. More accurate identification is therefore necessary.

Maureen Duffy claimed that Bartholomew Johnson acquired his
freedom of Canterbury by redemption in 1649 as an innholder.[17] Grants

of freedom are recorded in the Canterbury Burghmote Minute Books.
There is an entry dated 22 December 1648:

> It is ordered that if Bartholomew Johnson of this city barber shall pay
> unto Mr Chamberlane to the use of this citie the sume of £5 before the
> next Burghmote then he shall be admitted to the freedom of this city
> paying the fees accustomed.[18]

There is a further order to Bartholomew Johnson 'of this city barber'
dated 20 March 1648/9 for the sum of £10.[19] There is a final entry dated 24
July 1649:

> Whereas Bartholomew Johnson of this citie barber was by order of this
> Court of the 20th March last to have bine admitted to the freedom of this
> citie for the some of £10 if he should have paid the same within one
> moneth then next following the which he failed to performe and thereby
> lost the benefit of the said order. It is not withstanding now ordered by
> this Court that if the said Bartholomew Johnson shall paie unto Mr.
> Chamberlain to the use of this citie the sum of £7 of lawful Englishe
> money then he shal be admitted to the freedom of the same paying
> the accustomed fees.[20]

Maureen Duffy was mistaken. Bartholomew Johnson acquired his
freedom of Canterbury as a *barber*, not an innholder, and from being one
of several possible fathers of Aphra Behn, becomes the most likely candi-
date.

The Marriage Allegation for Bartholomew Johnson and Elizabeth
Denham shows a reasonably good signature on his part, and her mark -E-
on hers.[21] It states that Bartholomew Johnson, bachelor, a yeoman of
Bishopsbourne aged about twenty-three, whose parents are dead, is to
marry Elizabeth Denham, virgin, of Smeeth, aged about twenty-four, the
daughter of Francis Denham of Smeeth, at St Paul's Canterbury. It is
dated 25 August 1638, and they were married on the same day. It was cus-
tomary for a couple to return to the bride's home parish for the baptism of
their first child. Smeeth parish Records[22] show not only the baptism of
Aphra's sister Frances on 6 December 1638, but the reason for the hasty
marriage of the parents – Frances was obviously conceived out of wedlock.

Further back, an earlier Bartholomew Johnson baptized his family there – William on 2 February 1611/12, Joan on 22 October 1616, and very probably another child in the interim. The Bishop's Transcripts for 1614 and 1615 (the period when, according to the Marriage Licence, Bartholomew would have been born) are missing. Bartholomew Johnson senior was buried on 3 November 1617 'a poore man'. On 4 June 1624 his widow baptized a base son Richard. Smeeth is near Wye, and the Lord of the Manor was the Earl of Winchelsea. Anne, Countess of Winchelsea was not being malicious as Maureen Duffy suggests[23] – she was on her home territory, and if, as it seems, this was also the home territory of the Johnsons, she knew very well what she was talking about, and Aphra Behn was indeed daughter to a barber of Canterbury, formerly of Wye. The manorial records of Wye (which include Smeeth)[24] do not give any further information.

Elizabeth Denham's brother George was baptized at Smeeth on 22 August 1620. Another brother, Edward, was baptized there on 17 July 1623. Elizabeth herself was baptized at Faversham on 28 February 1612/13, where her sister Lucy was baptized on 13 August 1615.[25] Her father, Francis Denham, shown on his Marriage Licence as 'gentleman of Mersham' married Dorothy Thurston of Faversham at Preston next Faversham on 3 May 1611.[26] The description 'gentleman' would have been supplied by Francis himself. A surer guide to social standing is how a family is regarded by others, and recognized gentry families were described as such when entries were made in the Parish records. Nowhere in the Parish records above was this description applied to the Johnsons, Denhams, or Thurstons of the period. All the evidence from Marriage Licences and wills[27] is that they were 'trade' including a line of Thurston barbers. In the 1580s George Denham, father of Francis, was described in the Parish Registers of Milstead[28] as a gentleman – it would seem the family had fallen down the social scale. Nevertheless *Alumni Oxonienses*[29] and *Alumni Cantabrigienses*[30] show that Elizabeth's brother George was at University, and became a doctor at Stamford, Lincolnshire. Although the Denhams do not appear in the *Heralds' Visitation of Kent 1619–21*[31], George Denham does appear in *Lincolnshire Pedigrees*.[32] He entered and signed his pedigree of four generations in the Heralds' Visitation of

Lincolnshire in 1666. For some reason, he post-dated the marriage of his parents to 1617, and pre-dated his own birth to 1618, thus eliminating his sister Elizabeth. His will[33] makes no mention of her or her family. It seems strange that the sister to such a man should make her mark on her Marriage Allegation, although there were still 'educated' families where literacy was thought unnecessary for women. Perhaps her unwillingness to sign her name was in deference to her husband – it seems to have been a shotgun wedding to a man apparently from a lower social class than herself. Or perhaps it was a temporary incapacity – she may have hurt her hand. But whatever the state of Aphra Behn's own branch of the family (and her mother's employment as a wet-nurse does not suggest it was flourishing) there seems no doubt she could legitimately claim, on her mother's side at least, to be a gentlewoman of a good family. Although apparently contradictory, both contemporary statements about her were true.

Innholders were required to obtain a licence from the Justices of the Peace. Had Bartholomew Johnson been an innholder, his name should have appeared with other licensees in the Canterbury Quarter Sessions records. It did not, but there was another entry. In 1654 Bartholomew Johnson was appointed Overseer of the Poor for St Margaret's, a crowded parish in the centre of Canterbury.[34] In 1653 Francis Denham's widow Dorothy, described as of St Margaret's, married at Thanington.[35] The Register of the adjoining parish of St Alphege shows the burial of George, son of Bartholomew Johnson at St Margaret's in 1656.[36] The Parish Register of St Margaret's survives only from 1653, and there were no Bishop's Transcripts from 1640–60, so the baptism of Aphra's young brother is lost. The appointment of her father as Overseer is interesting in view of Aphra Behn's opinion of these officials expressed in 'The Black Lady'. She calls them 'the wolves of the parish' and 'the vermin of the parish who eat the bread from 'em'.[37] Both Duffy and Goreau suggest a Catholic influence in Aphra Behn's upbringing, possibly through a Catholic parent.[38] Her father's appointment confirms the Protestantism of the family.

One argument against Aphra Behn being daughter to a barber is that she was too accomplished, particularly in foreign languages. Maureen

Duffy says: 'Where she had originally learned French I don't know.'[39] None of her biographers seem aware that the Canterbury of Aphra Behn's period was full of French-speaking Huguenot refugees, and nearby Sandwich had a large Dutch Congregation which had fled from the Low Countries.[40] She would have had ample opportunity to learn both languages from native speakers. Barber's shops were noted for their music. Canterbury was the hub of East Kent, and on the route between London and the Continent. Her girlhood would have been cosmopolitan, not an isolated rural idyll.

Her mother's employment as nurse to Sir Thomas Culpepper would have been a great influence on her life. Sir Thomas was orphaned when he was five, and the relationship between nurse and young charge was obviously close, as they maintained contact long after her duties were done. In company with their mother, the two Johnson girls would have spent their early years with the Culpepper children. It is obvious from his *Adversaria* that Sir Thomas had a high opinion of Aphra's poetic abilities. 'One of the Fair Sex' says 'From infancy she wrote the prettiest softest engaging verses in the world.'[41] Finding such a child in their midst, the Culpeppers may well have encouraged her, and when she grew older introduced her to those circles where she was able to put her talents to use.

The relatively lowly status of her family makes the visit to Surinam and later her use by Charles II as a spy in Holland seem inexplicable, until they are looked at in the context of the times. The same combination of names, Sir Thomas Culpepper, Lord Willoughby (whose daughter married Heneage Finch, Earl of Winchelsea) and William Scot (son of Thomas Scot, the Parliamentary 'Spymaster-General') crop up several times in connection with her. These three were connected in 1659 when an attempt to restore Charles II was planned, but was betrayed to Thomas Scot, apparently by Lady Willoughby. Lord Willoughby was in Holland, Sir Thomas Culpepper (a closely watched known Royalist) in Kent.[42] Communication was obviously difficult. A traveller from abroad calling at a barber's shop in Canterbury would arouse no suspicion, neither would the fact that the barber's young daughter visited Sir Thomas Culpepper – she had been doing so all her life. Could Aphra Johnson have been used as a courier? 'One of the Fair Sex' writes 'For tho' considerable trusts were reposed in her, yet they were of that import, that I must not presume here to insert them.'[43] Her 1681 play *The Roundheads* dealt with the 1659 affair, showing considerable knowledge of events and the people involved. The fact that she had previous experience could well have prompted Sir Thomas Culpepper to recommend her to Charles II for the spying mission to Holland. Sir Thomas knew that she spoke Dutch, and of her marriage to a man with connections in that area, and of her previous affair with William Scot. In her financial distress in Holland she wrote[44] of a Sir Thomas connected with her mother, not often in town, and the one man she could trust. Maureen Duffy identifies him as Sir Thomas Gower of Stittenham and spins a complicated web with him as the centre of Aphra Behn's relations and connections and as a possible lover of her mother.[45] The description fits Sir Thomas Culpepper perfectly, and seems a much simpler explanation.

If the Johnsons had been involved in the 1659 plot, they would have known of the intrigues and betrayals going on behind the scenes, particularly where the Willoughbys were concerned. It has been assumed that 'her father's relation to Lord Willoughby' described by 'One of the Fair Sex'[46] as leading to his Surinam appointment, was a blood one, but the words do not necessarily mean that – indeed it seems most unlikely. The appointment in the early 1660s could have been a reward for services rendered during the troubled times so recently ended. Or it could mean that the Johnsons knew more than Lord Willoughby cared to have revealed, and he wanted them as far away as possible. No shipping records survive which might throw light on their journey there, but it does seem that the family left Canterbury then. Bartholomew Johnson does not appear on the Hearth Tax returns for 1664.[47] The St Margaret section of the 1662 returns[48] has been eaten by vermin.

On her return from Surinam, Aphra Johnson married a Mr Behn. According to 'One of the Fair Sex' he was 'an eminent merchant of this city though of Dutch extraction.'[49] The name is actually 'Deutsch' not Dutch.[50] Maureen Duffy put forward several possible candidates, culled from London Parish Registers. She favoured one who died at the time of the Plague.[51] There is no evidence that any of them had any connection with Aphra Johnson, nevertheless the biographical notes to Aphra Behn's

Love-Letters Between a Nobleman and his Sister[52] state 'On her return to England, she married a City merchant, who died in the Great Plague, leaving her virtually penniless.' Like Duffy, Goreau also favoured the theory that Aphra Johnson's was an arranged marriage to a much older man.[53] In fact, no record of the marriage has been found, and there is no known evidence about the fate of Mr Behn. That he was elderly, that he died in the Plague, or even that he pre-deceased his wife is purely conjectural.

Four words in Sir Thomas Culpepper's *Adversaria* comments on the husbands of the Johnson girls have been ignored by biographers, presumably because they were defeated by his writing. They are 'their names were Franck'.[54] Aphra Behn's sister did not marry an English Captain Wright, but both girls married foreigners of the same nationality, presumably with some connection between them. Murray's English Dictionary of 1681[55] says 'In Germany or Holland most of the Hosts speak a certain Franck.'

In the June 1962 number of *N&Q* H. A. Hargreaves draws attention to an item in the Calendar of State Papers Colonial.[56] This concerns the seizure of a ship from Hamburg, the *King David*, on 12 May 1655 at Barbados. Depositions from those on board were made by the Commander Erick Wrede and Johan Behn. The *King David* is mentioned as being seized twice more. On 6 July 1661 Oge Albert of Druntheim Norway, master of the *King David*, swears his ship is Norwegian but others still go about to trouble him.[57] In April 1665 it was seized again, and described as of Dronten Norway, with a Dutch master named Ock Alberts, who owned a sixteenth. The ship was principally Danish.[58] At that time the Schleswig-Holstein area of Germany was adminstered by Denmark. Pronounced the German way, Captain Write sounds very much like Captain Wrede. The man who 'before the war in her husband's time had been in love with her in England'[59] and with whom Aphra Behn made contact on her mission to Holland was called Albert. That three names associated with Aphra Behn should be connected with the same ship, and one which sailed in West Indian waters, seems more than a coincidence, and suggests this was the ship on which the bereaved Johnson family returned from Surinam, and that the girls married Captain Wrede and Johan Behn. If this were so, it raises the possibility that Mr Behn was a slave trader. It also suggests a spur-of-the-moment rather than an arranged marriage, and since seafaring was a strenuous and dangerous occupation, a younger and fitter Mr Behn than has been supposed. It could also indicate a possibly unsatisfactory marriage which may have broken up on the Continent. This may have been the occasion when a convent was contemplated for her. That she did not remarry may not have been entirely from choice. There are no known surviving records in Denmark, Germany, or Holland which might have provided the answers.

NOTES

This chapter was first published in *Notes and Queries*, September 1990.

1 I wish to thank Dr Carole Rawcliffe and Dr David Hayton of the History of Parliament Trust and Dr W. R. Owens of the Open University for their help in writing this paper.

2 Ed. Maureen Duffy (London, 1986).

3 British Library c 57 k.24.

4 British Library ac 2691 d/11.

5 British Library, Harley MS 7595, 25.

6 The Colonell was Sir Thomas Culpepper himself.

7 British Library, Harley MS 7595, 25.

8 *The Athenaeum* No. 2967, 6 Sep. 1884.

9 A. Purvis, 'Mrs Aphra Behn', *The Amateur Historian* (1953/4), 261.

10 Oxford, 1980.

11 *Reconstructing Aphra*, 17.

12 Ibid., 18.

13 Ibid., 13.

14 London, 1977.

15 *The Passionate Shepherdess*, 18–22.

16 East Kent Marriage Index 1538–1753. This is a card index of all marriages in East Kent during this period, prepared from the parish Registers and Bishop's Transcripts at Canterbury Cathedral Library and Kent Archives Office at Maidstone. It is at present in my possession.

17 *The Passionate Shepherdess*, 22.

18 Canterbury Cathedral Library a/c 4, 273.

19 Canterbury Cathedral Library a/c 4, 277.

20 Canterbury Cathedral Library a/c 4, 282.

21 Canterbury Cathedral Library: Uncatalogued, boxed by year.

22 Kent Archives Office, Smeeth Parish Register (from 1662 only) p4b.

Canterbury Cathedral Library, Smeeth Bishop's Transcripts (from 1570 with gaps) cc 380.

23 *The Passionate Shepherdess*, 18.

24 Now held by Wye College.

25 Canterbury Cathedral Library, Faversham Bishop's Transcripts cc 146–9.

26 Canterbury Cathedral Library, Preston next Faversham Bishop's Transcripts ac 318, cc 319.

27 None of Aphra Behn's immediate family left a will.

28 Kent Archives Office, Milstead Parish Register tr 1197.

29 p. 438.

30 p. 44.

31 Harleian Society, vol. 42.

32 Harleian Society, vol. 55, 1198.

33 Prerogative Court of Canterbury 15 February 1700/1.

34 Canterbury Cathedral Library j/q/453i.

35 East Kent Marriage Index.

36 Canterbury Cathedral Library u3/8/1/2.

37 *Reconstructing Aphra*, 82.

38 *The Passionate Shepherdess*, 92–3; *Reconstructing Aphra*, 13.

39 *The Passionate Shepherdess*, 121.

40 F. W. Jessup, *A History of Kent* (London, 1974), 84–5.

41 British Library c.57 k.24.

42 Alan Everitt, *The Community of Kent and the Great Rebellion 1640–1660* (Leicester, 1966), 302–5; *Reconstructing Aphra*, 20–1.

43 British Library c.57 k.24.

44 Public Record Office sp29/172 No. 14.

45 *The Passionate Shepherdess*, 51–7, 63, 81.

46 British Library c.57 k.24.

47 Kent Archives Office q/rth.

48 Public Record Offic e179/129/712.

49 British Library c.57 k.24.

50 Private information supplied by Public Record Offices in Holland and Germany.

51 *The Passionate Shepherdess*, 48–50.

52 Introduction by Maureen Duffy (London, 1987).

53 *Reconstructing Aphra*, 85–6.

54 British Library c.57 k.24.

55 At Canterbury Cathedral Library.

56 Series ix Addenda 1574–1674, 94.

57 Public Record Office SP29, vol. 39, item 22. During hostilities between England and Holland, Dutch ships detained in British waters often claimed to be Norwegian.

58 Public Record Office SP29, vol. 153, item 97.

59 'One of the Fair Sex', British Library C.57 K.24.

Index